without vodka

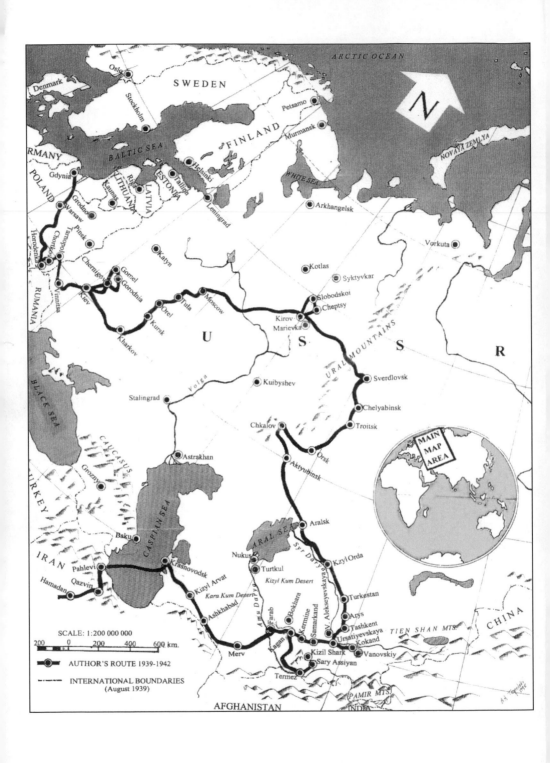

without vodka
adventures in wartime russia

Aleksander Topolski

Illustrations by
Aleksander Topolski

STEERFORTH PRESS
SOUTH ROYALTON, VERMONT

This edition first published by McArthur & Company, 2000.

Copyright © 2001 Aleksander Topolski

Steerforth Press edition copyright © 2001

For information about permission to
reproduce selections from this book, write to
Steerforth Press, P.O. Box 70, South Royalton, Vermont 05068

LIBRARY OF CONGRESS CATALOGING-IN-PUBLICATION DATA
Topolski, Aleksander, 1923–
    Without Vodka : adventures in wartime Russia / Aleksander
Topolski.
        p.   cm.
    Originally published: Without vodka: wartime adventures in
    Russia. Ottawa : UP Press, 1999.
    ISBN 1-58642-012-7 (pbk. : alk paper)
    1. Topolski, Aleksander, 1923–   2. World War, 1939–1945—
    Prisoners and prisons, Russian. 3. Prisoners of war—Soviet
    Union—Biography. 4. Prisoners of war—Poland—Biography.
    5. Poland. Armia—Biography. 6. World War, 1939–1945—
    Underground movements—Poland. 7. World War, 1939–1945—
    Personal narratives, Polish. I. Title.

    d805.s65 t675 2001
    940.54'7247'092—dc21
                                                    00-049285

Manufactured in the United States of America

On the cover: Topolski (crouching, left) in spring, 1939, with fellow
cadets Wieslaw Sobiech, Kazimierz Blyszczuk, Roman Ewy, Zdzislaw
Starzynski, Janusz Konopka (standing behind), and Eugeniusz
Kirszbaum (crouching right).

FIRST U.S. EDITION

To those who didn't make it

Acknowledgments

A special thanks to all the people (too many to list here) who have encouraged and helped me to get these memoirs onto paper to share with you. A few who deserve special mention are Kate Adams, Jennifer Balfour, Michael Becker, Katharine and Marcel Biolley, Denise Bukowski, Kristin Camp, Antoni Czulowski, Carole and Klaus Decker, Doug Fisher, Barbara and Dwight Fulford, John Hatfield, Catherine Joyce, Chip Fleischer, Edith and Brian Land, Ernie Mahoney, Meg Masters, Kim McArthur, Stanislaw Nowodworski, Martha Prince, Alexa Pritchard, Jeremy Rawlings, Glenna and Peter Roberts, Galina Smirnoff, Romcio Szymanski and Gerry Wagschal. And of course my children, Rory, Greg, and Alexa, who became more curious about it as they grew up. I am also grateful for the help I received from the Polish Institute and Sikorski Museum in London.

I want to thank my wife, Joan Eddis—my coach, goad, advisor, critic, unparalleled editor and tough adversary in semantic battles into the wee hours. Without Joan there wouldn't be *Without Vodka*.

TABLE OF CONTENTS

NKVD Corrective Labour Colony No. 7 Krasnykh Komandirov Street (formerly Degtiarevskaya Street), Kiev

1. Main gate, personnel office, and first drafting office
2. Prison and printing shop
3. Pipe extrusion and nickel plating
4. Prison for juveniles
5. Administration
6. Sawmill
7. Prison barracks
8. Hospital
9. Guards and kennels
10. Theatre and library (klub)
11. Furniture factory
12. Power plant
13. Paint shop and drying kilns
14. Bedstead assembling
15. Drafting office
16. Foundry
17. Metal workshops
18. Dining shed and kitchen
19. Lukianovka prison
20. Special prison

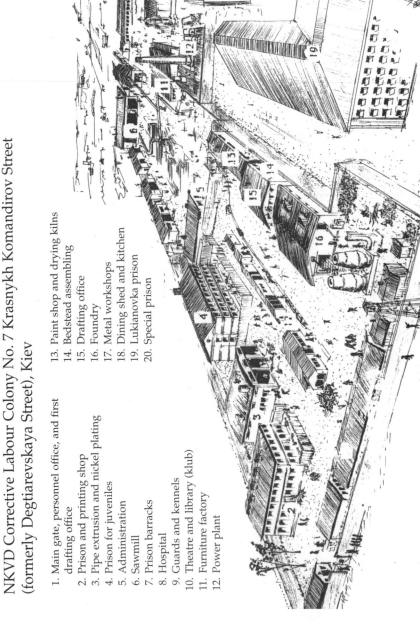

Без водки не разберёшь.

(Without vodka you can't figure it out.)

> – A Soviet soldier on a train from Krasnovodsk
> quoting an old Russian saying

Preface

This book is about three years of my life during the Second World War. In September 1939, when the war started, I was sixteen. I had been looking forward to that war, hoping that it would be an interesting episode in my life. It was—only the episode turned into a saga with all the ingredients of a "great adventure."

Countless times at dinner parties I have regaled my friends with humorous tales of shenanigans in prison and odd happenings in my life. But as my children grew older, I realized they had seldom been around to hear my stories. So I decided to set my memories down for them and their children before I'm dead, and it is all forgotten.

I began this as my own story, but as it unfolded it became more. In microcosm, this is the story of millions from the eastern half of Europe. People tried different ways to survive. God was with some of us, and somehow we lived to tell the tale—our own and that of others who didn't make it.

What I may have failed to convey in this book is the feeling of hunger that for three years was the *basso continuo* of my existence. Not the kind of hunger most of us feel when dinner is late or you go without food for a day or two. The hunger I am talking about is gnawing, incessant, pathological. It was the result of being underfed to the point of starvation for years. With the course of time, thinking about food became an obsession. We talked about it, and our nights were filled with dreams of it. To make the reader aware of this, I wanted to write "I AM HUNGRY" at the top of every page. That abiding hunger did not go away until long after I went back to three square meals a day and could fill my stomach at will. But it is futile to describe it to a person who has never starved.

All suffered in the Soviet Union, not just the prisoners. Our guards were conscripts with little education who had no choice of what job they had to do. They felt privileged when called to do their service with NKVD troops, although in the northern labour camps their privileges were only a slightly larger bread ration than that of prisoners and an occasional sliver of pork fat. They say that thirty million or more Soviet citizens lost their lives during the Second World War. Nobody knows the exact number. Even thirty million is more than twice the population of Canada at that time.

I apologize if I have offended any one group or nationality. In fact, I've probably offended everyone in this book, including my fellow Poles. But I have recorded the parade of humanity as I saw and heard it.

Remember, reader, this is memoir not history. It is the story of one boy's life during the opening years of World War II, and I've relied mostly on my memory. Some of my facts and dates I have checked with others who were there and with primary sources from the archives of the Sikorski Museum in London. Of the few of my former prison mates who are still alive, Romcio Szymanski has the most reliable and unbiased memory. Others seem to recall only the horrors, as if replaying a nightmare and trying to find some

Topolski, 18, in Samarkand, early 1942

A self-portrait drawn in 1942; I am standing in front of
a Soviet Army tent in Katta Alekseyevskayac.

scapegoat to blame for it all. One of my companions has coped with
those hard times by blotting out all memory of them. How can I
remember so much and in such detail? I don't know. I often wonder
that myself. However, Hanka Kowarzyk Moy, who also went through
those tough times in the USSR, said to me, "How could you forget?"

I am in my seventies as I write, but I experienced all this with the
outlook of a teenager. I have tried to tell the story as I lived it, based
on what I might have written in a diary if I'd kept one then. I hope
that I have managed to capture the hopeful, confident approach that I
had then and to reflect the faith in God that carried me through it all.

Chapter 1
ENTER REDS

A whisper rippled along our string of marchers: "Look right." On the ridge of a gentle slope I saw the silhouette of a Soviet soldier standing still. His black outline, topped by the soft gathered spike of a cloth budy-onovka *hat, was clearly visible against the dark blue sky. So was the long bayonet at the end of his rifle. He was no more than fifty yards from us. With our faces turned towards him we kept marching forward. He remained motionless as if mesmerized by the sight of the long line of people passing him in an orderly file. Then several soldiers emerged from the lower ground beyond him. They ran in our direction but didn't come any closer than the first soldier.*

Rifle shots and cries of "Postoi!" Stop! rang out together. We lunged forward. Our guide fired one shot from his revolver at the soldiers and quickly blended with the other scattering runners. The Soviets kept firing. Irka, who was running in front of me, fell face down. So did her brothers. Somebody running on my right followed suit. I was next. A moment later when I lifted my head, I could not see anybody running or standing—only the Soviets coming at us and still firing. A soldier stopped a few yards from me. I saw him aiming his rifle. He fired and a bullet hit the ground near my face, raising a small plume of snow. He kept his stance, still aiming at me. I was moving my head, shielding it with my little gas-mask bag, and trying to make it a less easy target. Four more shots and four more plumes of snow around my head. He stopped firing when he finished the clip. By then they were all over us.

♦   ♦   ♦

In mid-summer 1939 everything seemed to go my way. I had just returned to my home in Horodenka from a trip to Warsaw and to Gdynia on the Baltic Sea as a guest of the Polish Navy. With two of my friends I had won the first prize in the all-Poland Boy Scouts' competition for our model of the destroyer *Blyskawica*. By rights, my father should have shared in the prize because of all the help he gave us. The Navy, a gracious and generous host, treated us three winners as future ship designers. Apart from many happy memories, I brought back with me as souvenirs the special permits issued by the Admiralty to visit the naval base in Oksywie, the brand new destroyer *Blyskawica* and even a submarine. I never suspected that holding on to these souvenirs would cause me so much trouble in the months to come.

After my return I hardly had any time to gloat and boast about my exploits on the shores of the Baltic—in two days I left for the Boy Scout camp in the eastern Carpathian Mountains. But striving for proficiency badges and singing around the campfire had lost the attraction they once held for me. At sixteen I thought myself too old for all that. Instead I thought about the new tennis court at our high school, about my new, long white linen trousers, and my older friends who were passing their vacation time at the municipal swimming pool in the company of young women, dancing inept tangos with them in the evenings on the pavilion terrace and afterwards walking them home. Within a week I found some feeble excuse to leave the camp, and I returned to Horodenka.

Every day that August the newspapers and the radio brought foreboding news about Germany's latest demands and threats. Hitler felt confident that he could walk unopposed into Poland as he did into the Rhineland, Austria, Lithuania and Czechoslovakia. Our politicians spread false optimism, forecasting a quick victory over the Germans by the Polish-French-British coalition. The Polish people, on the whole, felt intensely patriotic and upbeat. Any form of acquiescence or compromise was out of the question. Men were not unduly worried. They thought of war as inevitable and dangerous but still an interesting interlude. Some were looking forward to it as an escape from the dreary life of daily chores, a nagging wife or an insufferable boss.

Our water carrier Mendel, an elderly Jew, said he was going to volunteer for the army. When the other water carriers (there was a whole guild of them in Horodenka) asked him if he was not afraid to go to war, he said, *"Oy-vey, war schmor*. I go to war, kill a few people and return home."

"And if they kill you?"

"Kill me? Why should they? What for? What have I done?"

For our family friend Mr. Krzyzanowski war was to be his salvation. He was so much in debt that it nearly drove him crazy. I still remember his furrowed brow at our card table when he would seek reassurance or at least a nod from his whist partners. "Say, director," he would ask my father, who had been the principal of a teacher's college, "there's bound to be war. There's no other way. Am I not right?"

After all, in Poland it was an axiom that each generation goes to war twice. (Our victorious war against the Bolsheviks had ended only nineteen years before.) Worry was left to mothers, wives, sisters and daughters. It was their job to fend for elders and the little ones while their men were denting their sabres on enemy armour. But meanwhile we youngsters in Horodenka were enjoying what proved to be our last carefree summer. The skies were blue, and the hot August sun tanned our bodies to the coveted chestnut brown. Our only worry was that something would go awry, and we would miss having a war. And then things began to happen.

"It's for your son."

I recognized the voice of the sergeant who worked in the local Draft Board office across the street. He must have been talking through the open bedroom window to one of my parents.

"Will you sign for it, please? Thank you."

I heard his army boots crunching gravel along the path as he marched back to the garden gate. The latch clicked and he was gone.

That morning I had been reading in bed before breakfast. But now I sprang out of bed and pushed open the door to my parents' bedroom, letting through a gust of the morning breeze. The muslin window curtains billowed in like the sails of a ship scudding into the room. Only my mother was there. She was standing near the open window with one hand clasping the top of her housecoat. In the other hand she held a small sheet of paper. A printed form with a diagonal red stripe.

Seeing me, she tried to hide it behind her back. Then her arm dropped down in a helpless gesture. The paper floated to the carpet. She stood still and stared at me.

"Holy Mother of God! They are taking my child!"

She made a small step forward and stretched her arms as if she wanted to embrace me. I picked up the intriguing paper from the floor and drew back from the range of her pleading arms. Signs of affection embarrassed me. Besides, I did not like being called a child. I glanced at the paper. Below the lines of fine print was my name and in bold type "Call-up to Active Duty. Group C." It was a surprise. I felt honoured. I was only sixteen.

I got dressed in no time. When I went back to my parents' bedroom, mother was still standing at the window motionless, only her lips were moving in inaudible prayer.

"I've got to go, Mum. You know. I've got to report at the Draft Board office."

She said nothing but kept staring at me and nodding her head. I came closer, and as I kissed her on both cheeks, I tasted the salty tears which trickled along the crow's feet around her eyes.

It was Thursday, the 24th of August, 1939, when I received my call-up papers. So did the other high-school students who had completed at least the first half of the military training course which normally started in the first year of the lyceum (equivalent of grade eleven). By some quirk the grade eleven class in 1938 had only eight male students, and so we boys from grade ten had been taken to make up the number needed for the course. Because I entered the high school a year earlier than normal, I had completed that half of the military course at sixteen instead of the usual eighteen.

Inside the Draft Board office, Sergeant Gruber greeted me with a short, "You are too early." For a moment I was scared—I thought he was referring to my age. But I was relieved to see that he was pointing at the clock which showed ten to nine. The office opened at nine. A few of my friends appeared. We were all sent to the local depot of Strzelec, a state-sponsored paramilitary organization, to get our uniforms and rifles. I could not find a uniform small enough to fit me.

4

While I waited for one to be altered for me, I wore my khaki Boy Scout shirt, the long, dark blue trousers from my high-school uniform, a forage cap and a wide army belt.

My first two days "on active duty" I spent riding furiously on my bike all over town delivering messages from the Draft Board to other offices and to individuals—including a love letter in a mauve envelope from Lieutenant Beloshiyev to his fiancée. On the third day, I was detached to the air-spotters unit, which formed part of our countrywide air observation system. Then on the 28th of August I was transferred to a border guards unit near Serafince village beside the Polish-Romanian border, just six kilometres from my home.

Our post was a white one-story house ringed by tall poplars, which stood out like a green island in the midst of rolling fields still golden with the stubble of harvested wheat. Despite the heat, the post's commandant, Senior Guard Mazur, sat in his office completely buttoned up. He got up when I reported to him and looked me over well, as if bemused by his new charge's childish appearance. Finding nothing else to compliment me on, he said, "You have a fine sounding surname. Now take your things to the big room behind the kitchen. You'll be sleeping there on the floor with the other draftees. Report for duty at 20:00 hours in this office—four hours at the telephone and four hours outside plane spotting."

"Plane spotting at night?"

"Yep. The buggers fly at night too. Dismissed!"

Sleeping on the floor was not too bad because the pine floor was scrubbed with lye every few days. However, the stench of human bodies in our sleeping quarters was so thick that, in Mazur's words, "You could suspend an axe in mid-air."

Our duties were undemanding and tedious. To keep us on our toes we had to send practice reports marked "Dummy" four times a day. Most of the draftees were from Polish farms in the nearby villages and were terrified of the telephone, never having used one before.

When off duty, I'd often ride my bike home for a meal, a change of clothes or just to get a good night's sleep in my own bed. It was after one of these nights at home when, on the morning of September 1st, I heard our national anthem being played on the radio before the eight o'clock news. That was unusual, and my heart pounded as I listened to the anthem. Then the speaker announced the President of Poland, Ignacy Moscicki. After a few clicks and squeaks came the voice of our leader.

"In the early hours of today, the eternal foe of the Polish Republic forced its way through our borders, a fact I state in the face of God and history. I declare Poland in the state of war." Then he listed the cities which had been bombed and proceeded with patriotic exhortations. I did not listen to the end. I leapt from my bed, ran to the kitchen and spun Pyotrusia, our kitchen maid, around. That wasn't easy for she was a strapping lass.

"Pyotrusia! The war has started! Yippee! No more school! We go to war!"

She thought it was one of my pranks.

"Don't say things like that. You may say it in an evil hour and cause it to happen."

She crossed herself. I told her I was not joking. I had heard it on the radio. When she realized that I was telling the truth, she opened wide her blue eyes and began to cry. Her strong jaw trembled as she tried to suppress sobs, while she continued to prepare breakfast. Then she said, "My brother!" and I remembered that she told us he had received his call-up papers the day before. Within minutes the entire house was awake. Mother came running in and embraced Pyotrusia. They both stood there crying and hugging each other. From the far room across the corridor my sisters, still in bed, were shouting, "What happened?! What's going on?!"

Father put the brouhaha to good use. He got dressed without attracting anybody's attention, skipped his morning coffee, and when Mother went looking for him on the front porch, she just managed to catch a glimpse of him as he was turning the corner at the end of the street carrying his fishing rods and tackle box.

For weeks we had expected the war to start any day. But it jolted everybody when it came, even though the general mobilization had been announced the day before. Throngs of called-up reservists, almost all of them Ukrainians, were already arriving from the neighbouring villages. I saw them being led first to the schoolyard. There they were seated at trestle tables laden with loaves of fresh bread, bottles of beer and coils of steaming fat sausages with garlic and marjoram, a gift from the wealthy, fat butcher Ludwik Tomkiewicz, who was also our mayor. After they ate their fill, it was time to go to the railway station. They would form in columns eight abreast, arm in arm, taking the entire width of the street so that nobody could pass them. This was to show their contempt for the lesser breed, the civilians. And they sang in harmony as they marched, making up new—and irreverent—lyrics that showed scant respect for military life.

It seemed that with the outbreak of war, a lot of men likely to be called up, and even some of those who were infirm or too old for the army, adopted a semblance of military bearing. With their heads high and chests puffed up, they would strut briskly, confidence beaming from their clean-shaven faces. Women were less affected by martial feelings. My mother busied herself with traditional preparations taught to her by her mother and grandmother. She began buying in bulk and storing flour, sugar, tea, salt and jars of lard. And in the darkness of the night, she and my father buried in the back garden some of our silverware and other valuables wrapped in grease-soaked linen.

Twice a day, at nine o'clock in the morning and in the evening, people would gather around their radios to listen to the news. Those who did not have a radio would go to neighbours who did. Mr. Ciolek, the tailor who lived next door, and his subtenant Mr. Piorewicz came every evening just before nine and sat in front of our Telefunken radio set, gazing at the green tuning light which glared back at them like the eye of a basilisk.

One by one Polish radio stations were knocked out by German bombs, and after two weeks all of them except the subsidiary Warsaw Two radio station went off the air. What news we did get was anything but good. The Polish Army was being cut apart by the steel of the German panzer division tanks. The German Luftwaffe ruled the sky, bombing and strafing towns, railway stations, military and nonmilitary targets, and the civilian population, which took to the road by the hundreds of thousands trying to escape the Nazis. That was well nigh impossible because the German armies were invading Pol-and simultaneously from the north, west and south.

Great Britain and France declared war on Germany, but it was a token gesture and did nothing to relieve German pressure on Poland. The unusually hot and sunny September favoured the advance of the Germans. We prayed for the fall rains that would have turned our dirt roads into mire and stemmed the onrush of the German mecha-nized divisions. Alas, the rains came too late.

When several of my high-school friends and I received our first army pay, we decided to celebrate it together at Spiegel's restaurant. For the first time I put on my army tunic, altered at last by the tailor to fit my boyish frame. I was so proud of it I wouldn't think of taking it off although it was a scorchingly hot day. We slouched at the central table and pushed our chairs away from it, so we could stretch our legs and show off our heavy army boots. We offered each other cig-arettes. Each one of us had bought a different brand. The owner himself came to serve us. Some ordered vodka, some beer. I opted for Gdanska Zlotowka (Danzig Goldwater), a liqueur with tiny flecks of gold foil floating in it. Maciek Konopka, who was a bit older than the rest of us, proposed visiting Stefa, one of the town's three pros-titutes. But most of us felt uneasy about his idea. We got out of it by saying that it was too early in the day even to ponder such matters, which bloom better under cover of darkness and discretion.

The speed of the German invaders was unbelievable. Refugees from western and central Poland started appearing in Horodenka. Rum-ours abounded about water wells poisoned by "fifth column" sabo-teurs, about poisonous chocolates and candies dropped by German planes, and about regiments of Polish-speaking German soldiers dressed in Polish uniforms. The refugees were talking about total disarray and the near collapse of the Polish Army. We did not want to believe them. But then my Aunt Jania arrived from Modlin in central Poland with her two small children after a nightmarish jour-ney on bombed trains. She was followed by more of my mother's relatives, including my Uncle Tadeusz with his wife and small daughter. Their stories confirmed our worst fears. The war was already lost.

This was brought home to us twice in mid-September when droning German squadrons flew high overhead and bombed Horodenka. This caused panic among the townsfolk but little damage. One batch of bombs fell in fish-breeding ponds. Most of the others exploded in gardens and orchards, leaving puny holes that looked to me more like pits dug to store potatoes for winter.

But much worse was to follow. On the 17th of September, a guard who had just finished his border patrol came to see our commandant. He said the Romanian border guards told him that the Soviets had declared war on Poland. We were all stunned by this news. Nobody had ever admitted such a possibility, although the improbable Ribbentrop-Molotov friendship pact between the Nazis and Soviets signed only a few weeks before made every Pole feel uneasy. The news was confirmed a few hours later on the radio.

That day the one-way traffic on the road leading to Romania was heavy with a procession of trucks, cars, buses, artillery pieces, horse-drawn carts, ambulances and even fire engines. The soldiers and civilians on them were grey-faced, exhausted after two and half weeks of retreating under bombs. They were leaving their homeland for some other country where—they were told—their army would be recreated to fight the Germans and come back victorious. How long that would take nobody knew. Perhaps it was just as well they didn't.

In the afternoon a rather old-fashioned plane flew by. A biplane. Its engine sounded like a slow motorcycle. As it was passing our border post, it let out a burst of fire from its machine gun. The bullets hit the ground near the main entrance. The plane flew away, but then it made a circle and started coming back straight at us. I started running toward the open field to be as far as possible from the house. I ran fast, stumbling and falling on the flat ground covered with wheat stubble. There wasn't a ditch in sight where I could take cover. I could hear the plane coming closer, and I felt as helpless as a rabbit being pursued by a hawk. I hit the dirt and when I looked up, the plane, which was flying very low, took such a sharp turn I could see the goggled face of the machine-gunner. The plane looked like the RB Soviet reconnaissance plane that I had seen on aircraft identification charts at the air-spotters unit. As it made another turn I noticed the red stars painted on its wings. There was no more guessing. It *was* a Soviet plane. I picked myself up and returned to our post feeling rather sheepish. But it seemed that nobody had noticed my panicky dash for escape.

Later that afternoon, Commandant Mazur gathered all his subordinates in his office. He told us that he and the other border guards were going to Romania in half an hour, after they had bid farewell to their families. The rest of us could either follow them or go home. Then he turned to me: "You go home. At least for the time being. You are young and the Bolsheviks may leave you alone. If things turn bad, you know the border and you can cross it any time."

Before I left, I saw the guards return and squeeze into a two-horse cart, their rifles upright between their knees, their belongings crammed around them. For the last time, they kissed their wives and patted the heads of their children. "Don't worry. Wait for us. We'll be back before the storks return."

I biked home to find my father and uncles playing cards. Father was a bit annoyed that they were not paying proper attention to the game but discussing the day's events instead. They said the Soviet army was already on the far shore of the wide Dniester River less than twenty kilometres away. But the retreating Polish troops had blown up the only bridge in the region, so the Russians were not expected to enter Horodenka before morning.

My Uncle Tadeusz, although a judge and a sensible, intelligent man, had yielded to years of Soviet propaganda. "You'll see for yourself what communism did for Russia," he declared. "Their standard of living surpasses that of Switzerland or America. There are no prisons in the Soviet Union because they've eliminated crime. And there's no unemployment. As for food, Russia was never short of it. In 1915, we all saw the mountains of flour, bacon, sugar and tea that came after the tsarist armies."

My father was not impressed. "Relax, Tadeusz. Stop waving your arms about. We can see your cards. You'll be the first unemployed when they come here. With crime eliminated, there'll be no job for you."

Next morning I left the house quietly while my family and my relatives were still asleep. The sound of engines and feeble cheers led me to the centre of town. There were only a few people in the streets. The stores were closed and the windows shuttered. Some peasants, hoping for loot, carried empty gunny sacks over their shoulders. About a hundred men stood on the sidewalks along the street through the main square. Many were members of the newly formed Communist militia, still in civilian clothes but with red armbands. The militia, or properly the People's Militia, was the name for the new policemen, the civil force of the communist state. Their job was to maintain public order and to serve the NKVD, the Soviet secret police. Our old police force was being disbanded. Its members were arrested, and the word "policeman" became synonymous with "enemy of the socialist system and torturer of the working classes."

Those in the streets welcoming the Red Army were waving their arms, cheering, throwing flowers and blowing kisses at the Soviet tanks as they rolled by. The tanks were small by today's standards, but they seemed huge to me then. Their crews in black leather helmets looked sullen and were not responding to the cheers of the onlookers. A red banner was stretched across the street with the inscription, *"Khay zhive Chervena Armia!"* the Ukrainian equivalent of "Long live the Red Army!" I noticed somebody had made a mistake by writing *khay* instead of *nay*. But I learned much later it was no mistake. The word *khay* was standard usage in the Soviet Ukraine. The "spontaneous" banner had been made in the Soviet Union and brought by the invading troops.

Gradually the crowd on the main square grew bigger as more and more people left their houses and came to gawk at the Soviets. After the tanks came columns of trucks packed with soldiers standing up. Then came heavy artillery with guns being pulled by tractors. They lumbered by at the pace of a turtle. The next column of trucks created quite a stir among the villagers, who were now coming in droves to see the "Russkies." Inside each of the canvas-covered trucks were two horses. The peasants were wondering why the horses were being driven instead of ridden. Then, seeing that the nags were in such poor shape, unkempt and with their ribs showing, they concluded that by driving them in trucks you could save on fodder. The cavalry, which appeared later near our house, had better-looking mounts. The old-timers noticed immediately that their cavalry sabres were from tsarist times, but the double-headed imperial eagles had been filed off the brass hilts.

In the afternoon, a few trucks and a bus loaded with Polish airmen and soldiers, who didn't know that Horodenka was already in Soviet hands, tried to drive through the town to the Romanian border. They got trapped by the Soviet tanks and taken prisoners. The Soviets locked them up in the girls' primary school near our house, which they quickly converted into a prison.

The behaviour of the Soviet troops astonished the people of Horodenka. There was no stealing, no raping. Even swearing was rare. The soldiers insisted on paying for everything they took and never haggled about the price when they were buying something. And buy they did. By declaring the value of the ruble to be on par with the zloty, the Soviets made their soldiers wealthy overnight. In Russia they had plenty of rubles, but there was precious little to buy in the state-run stores and the prices on their so-called free market were exorbitant. But here the prices seemed to them ridiculously low and the sight of stores loaded with merchandise unheard-of in Russia made them giddy. They were buying everything. With the exception of our tobacco and cigarettes, which they thought too weak for their taste, I cannot think of one thing they wouldn't buy.

They would enter any house they fancied, seat themselves at the kitchen or living room table and stay there just looking around, peeking into other rooms, smoking incessantly and trying to engage their hosts in primitive small talk across the language barrier. They would never admit to being ignorant of anything. Any attempt to explain something to them would by quashed by a vigorous, "*My znaem, my znaem.*" We know, we know. When caught looking with incomprehension or noticeable interest at some object they would smile condescendingly and say, "There's plenty of that stuff in the Soviet

Union." That was difficult to reconcile with their insatiable demand for watches, razors, flashlights, fountain pens, cigarette lighters, penknives and haberdashery.

People living near the boys' school, which the Soviet troops had commandeered for barracks, were quick to notice that the soldiers had no underwear. They wore their army trousers and tunics next to their skin. Other things about them also struck us as odd. They washed themselves without soap, lived on hot water, bread and thick soup, and rolled their cigarettes in pieces of newspaper instead of cigarette paper.

Our stores stayed open, but the shelves in them were emptying fast. Now food was getting scarce. Butter and lard had disappeared, and we ate our bread with thin slices of beef fat instead. We sweetened our weak tea with saccharin and washed ourselves with grey soap which Father cooked up from tallow and ashes. The older generation took it in stride. They had lived through it before. What was new to all of us was the quantity of Communist newspapers, propaganda books and posters showered on the public at little or no cost to the consumer. And now only Soviet films were being shown at the cinemas.

We couldn't get over the shock of Poland's defeat. It was beyond our comprehension that a country could collapse in less than a month. We laid the blame for it on our government, our politicians, our generals. The feeling of shame burned deep inside us. Only German conquests yet to come were to show that our debacle was not unique. Within a year the German armies were to roll over Denmark without a shot being fired. Norway showed only a token resistance. Then the combined forces of Belgium, Holland, France and Great Britain were to be swept away by a blitzkrieg that lasted only forty days. In less than three weeks, the Soviet Union would lose to the Germans an area four times larger than Poland did in 1939.

Our defeat spurred the small Polish community in Horodenka to tighten its bonds. Of the 17,000 inhabitants in our town less than 10 percent were ethnic Poles. The rest were Ukrainians and Jews. From the first day of the Soviet occupation small groups sprouted up to help other Poles in need. The airmen and soldiers imprisoned in the girls' school were going hungry. The Soviets would not or could not provide any food for them. Within a day, the wives, the sisters and the daughters of Polish families scrounged food from their larders and gardens, pooled their resources and set up rudimentary field kitchens in our garden. Soon unidentifiable soup was perking in the copper cauldrons and slices of bread were stacked on blankets spread on the ground. But it took hours of haggling and pleading before the guards would agree to distribute these among the prisoners. Meanwhile, young boys barely over ten years old brought baskets and handcarts full of apples and tomatoes and were pitching them to the prisoners standing at open windows. Chased by the guards, the youngsters would retreat behind the fences only to reappear in a few minutes and resume their charitable bombardment. Some of the apples were thrown back by the prisoners with messages scribbled on scraps of paper inside them. The messages were addressed to families and friends living all over Poland. Not one of them was ignored, and some people were assigned the task of finding a way to deliver them.

With the defeat of Poland, my army career had ended, and I had to go back to school. The subjects of science, maths and languages remained unchanged for the time being. Other subjects had to wait for new politically correct programs and handbooks. Trying to carry on with our lives as before, we laughed at the uncouth Ivans and their attempts to graft their "communist paradise" on our soil. Then the news of arrests and disappearances of harmless individuals began to strike home.

One day our geography teacher, Jan Jurkow, did not show up for his morning lecture. During the first recess the corridor was abuzz with news about him. In the middle of the night Jurkow was taken from his home by the NKVD, the Soviet secret police, assisted by the local militia who told his wife and nine-year-old daughter not to worry as he would be returned home in an hour. This was the last time they saw him. He was arrested for being the editor of the local biweekly newspaper *Horodenka News* and was destined to survive the war but never return home.

More arrests followed. Eventually they became a daily occurrence. We could see no pattern in the selection of people taken from their homes in the middle of the night—lawyers, teachers, factory workers, small farmers with half an acre of land and one mangy cow or two goats, young people and ninety-year-old pensioners. They were mainly Poles but with a sprinkling of Ukrainians and Jews. People disappearing from our midst, however, had not necessarily been arrested and imprisoned by the Soviets. Some of them had escaped to Romania or to the German-occupied part of Poland where they thought they might be safer.

Those who felt vulnerable (and that included my father) started wrapping up clothing and food in a bundle each evening in order to be ready in case they heard a quiet knock on the door during the night and the order *"Otkroitie dveri!"* Open the door! The dog collar of Soviet rule was being replaced by a noose of terror. And it was getting tighter and tighter.

For centuries Poles kept alive a tradition of forming clandestine organizations to fight whoever occupied our land. We had a lot of practice at it. There was no Polish state from the late 1700s until 1918. During those years our land was divided among Germans, Russians and Austrians. And now the resolve to organize a resistance group sprang to the minds of thousands of Poles who were watching their country overrun by Germans and Soviets. We were born with conspiracy in our blood.

So I was not surprised when, barely two weeks after the Soviets entered Horodenka, my friend Boguslaw Nowohonski asked me to come to a secret meeting at his home. He was only one year older than me but far more mature. There were only five of us besides him and we were told to come after dusk at irregular intervals. I was the last one to arrive. On two small tables were two chessboards with chessmen arranged as if in mid-game. "That's in case somebody comes and asks what we are doing here. We play chess." Nowohonski told us that we were to form a cell in an already existing secret underground army. For the time being he would not tell us the name of that organization. Each cell had five members, and only one of them would know the name of a member from another group. And we wouldn't know which of us was the chosen one. Our tasks would come from above. Until then, we would simply observe and report anything that might be of interest to our superiors. Then he lit two candles in front of a small bronze crucifix and asked us to place the tip of our hands on it and swear that we would never divulge to any non-member the secrets of our organization.

Meanwhile the local militia was trying to outdo the NKVD in their attempts to eradicate the "counter-revolutionary element" in Horodenka. They compiled lists of people who had been active in such pre-war "reactionary" organizations as the Red Cross, Voluntary Fire Brigade, Boy Scouts, and Sokol Gymnast Association. All of them were considered suspect, and one by one they were being arrested. Houses were searched for no apparent reason. Passersby were stopped and searched. At times innocent persons walking along a street and talking to each other would be pounced upon by militiamen or the secret police agents, separated, and then asked, "What were you discussing?" If their answers did not tally, they would be arrested, and they could expect unpleasant and lengthy interrogations. When I was with my friends in a public place and our conversation was likely to slide into a dicey topic, we would agree beforehand on a subject (usually football or bridge) that would satisfy an inquisitive gumshoe.

The wartime atmosphere and press of relatives loosened our home routine. Also Pyotrusia had left us, believing she'd find better work and pay under the new regime. (She didn't.) Casual help-yourself and grab-what-you-can replaced formal sit-down dinners and suppers. Nobody asked me to explain when I came home late or missed a day at school. I began spending more time in the company of girls from our high school.

Two witty and spunky sisters, Dzidka and Krysia Rutkowski, became close friends of mine. Their father, our reeve, had been arrested by the Soviets. When they were turned out of the reeve's official residence, they tossed a box of Polish passport blanks onto a pile of rubbish. Later, Krysia, the younger and prettier sister, carried them out under the noses of the militia guards. She also brought out the official rubber stamps buried in the bottom of a flower pot.

They moved with their mother into a large but dingy room offered by a friend, yet they carried on as charming and gracious hosts to many visitors including me. We played auction bridge on suitcases stacked between their two beds and danced to gramophone records on a small patch of floor between two tall wardrobes. Their mother was now supplying members of the underground with passports. Krysia presented me with one too, "just in case."

Day by day I got more enmeshed in the risky business of helping those who believed that their place was in the ranks of the Polish Army in France. I was meeting them at the railway station, taking them from there to safe houses through back alleys and garden paths, and delivering messages and parcels.

At the same time, unbeknownst to me, my sister Maria was doing the same things for another group which was in the business of smuggling volunteers across the border. Maria has always been the outgoing and athletic one with more concern for others than herself. She was to go on to be a doctor. My father took some risks too. One moonless and rainy night he opened the back door of the town hall with a skeleton key and, helped by two Boy Scouts, carried out from the storage room our troop's standard, tents and camping equipment without waking a sleeping militiaman. They had to make several trips to carry out all that heavy gear and tuck it away under the garret rafters of our old high-school building so that it wouldn't fall into the hands of the militia.

Two of those who took the oath of secrecy with me at Nowohonski's house called on me one evening. We talked for a while about nothing in particular. They kept cracking jokes, but their joviality seemed to me a bit overdone. They were smoking incessantly. Before long they let the cat out of the bag: they were going across the border to Romania that night. They couldn't contact Nowohonski, who was out of town, and so they asked me to break this news to him.

Next morning, when they didn't show up at school, everybody guessed what had happened. I decided that I was going to follow them to Romania very soon.

* * *

In October, the Soviets and the Germans reached an agreement about repatriating people who had escaped from the Germans occupying central and western Poland and found themselves in the territories annexed by the Soviet Union. My aunts and uncles started trickling back to where they came from. News about the departure of my uncles, aunts and cousins reached the local militia, and in no time, a red-haired creature with a star on his cloth cap banged at our front door. As soon as we let him in he started going from room to room, looking around. He carried a rifle slung under his arm the way hunters carry their shotguns. He wasn't used to carrying one and it kept banging against furniture and doors. His gibberish, which purported to be Russian, was a mixture of Yiddish, Polish and Ukrainian, garnished with a few Russian words. But his message was clear. We had too much free space in our house and father's study would be requisitioned for two Soviet officers.

The Soviets always billeted their men at least two to a room, not to save on space but as a way of tightening security. Roommates could see to it that neither one became friendly with people of un-proven loyalty.

Our two new tenants were a pleasant surprise: a colonel and a major. Both were polite, well mannered, quiet, and almost timid. They tried to make as little trouble for us as possible. They asked Pyotrusia —who had come back to us by then—not to bring them hot water for their morning wash and shaving. Cold water was good enough for them. And they were aghast in the morning when they found their shoes shined by her.

For a long time they would not accept mother's invitation to have tea with us in the living room. When they finally said "Yes" they brought with them a cup of crushed sugarloaf and a small packet of tea from Georgia. They stayed for twenty minutes or so. The conversation was limited to repeating *spasibo* (thank you) and, "What do you call that in Russian? In Polish?" while pointing at different objects. But as their visits became more frequent everybody became increasingly adventurous and talkative. In the course of time the Russians lost their initial shyness and started dropping in on their own for *chashku chayu* (a cup of tea).

Of the two officers, the colonel was more affable. He had some smatterings of German, which we understood, and called Maria *"mein Kaetzchen"* (my kitten). Once he brought a box of pastries from Bohrer's café. One day while listening to Maria playing the piano, he came closer and pointed out the notes of some chord that she continued to hit wrong. He even corrected the position of her hand. Asked if he could play piano, he smiled broadly and with one finger picked out the Russian equivalent of "Chopsticks." Then in a nice baritone he sang a little tune. It was a children's song about a puffed-up birdie, a siskin (*chizhik* in Russian). He sang it again and again until Maria learned the tune and the words by heart. We started calling the colonel Chizhik, and he liked that.

His roommate, the major, was a withdrawn character who seldom smiled. We could tell by the way he kept looking at my older sister Henia that he was smitten by her. But he was tongue-tied around her. To make up for his conversational shortcomings, he would read aloud to her long political articles from the Russian newspapers *Pravda* and *Izvestia* and from books by Lenin and Stalin. Henia—whose heart was already taken by another—not only put up with it, she even created the impression of being interested in what he read.

One evening, Chizhik came for tea without his pal, the major. He was in an excellent mood that evening, cracking jokes and paying compliments to my mother and sisters. He asked Maria and Mother to play the piano. Maria went through her short repertoire, good-naturedly laughing at her own mistakes. Mother followed her with bits and pieces of Czerny and Schumann, then ventured into Tchaikovsky's "Months" and "Troika." As usual she stumbled at the fast tempo of the finale of "Troika." She smiled and glanced at Chizhik. Turning her hands over, she looked at her spread fingers as if she was blaming them for letting her down. She got up and with a sweeping gesture invited Chizhik to take her place at the piano. A roguish grin broke out on his face as he accepted her challenge. We expected a joke. With a flourish he swept up the tails of an imaginary dress coat and sat down to play.

He took up the "Troika" where mother had left it, gliding with ease through the fast notes of the jingling sleigh bells. He went through another piece of Tchaikovsky's music that Mother had played that evening and then, while improvising with his left hand, leafed with his right through a stack of sheet music, pulling out those he was going to play. I don't know how long he performed, but the glasses of tea brought in by Pyotrusia grew cold.

Chizhik finished his impromptu concert with a mighty chord. He stretched, leaned himself back and rested his head on his hands which he clasped at the back of his neck. His eyes wandered from a gold-framed seascape by Wygrzywalski that hung on our wall to a small aquarelle by Kossak. He then gazed for a while at the credenza adorned with Bohemian crystal and at some family silver arranged on the shelves of the large cupboard. He closed his eyes and sighed. "My God! We used to live like this."

Then he jumped to his feet in a military fashion, went to the door to the corridor, opened it and without turning around said, "*Spokoinoi nochi!*" Good night!

After the unscheduled piano recital, Chizhik's visits became rare. He would drop in only for a few minutes and as often as not decline the offer of a cup of tea. It is hard to believe that we never learned the surnames or even the first names of our Soviet officer tenants. But they never told us their names and we knew better than to ask.

There were rumours among the members of the clandestine resistance that members of our secret organization in Horodenka, including me, were being targeted for arrest. Deep at heart I believed that I was too young to be a serious suspect on the files of the militia or the NKVD. But I was scared. I went to Lusia Klonowska, a friend of my sister Maria, who was said to know much about the situation in Horodenka. "All these stories," she said, "are pure gossip. Nobody knows anything for sure. And people tend to exaggerate. But if you feel that you are in danger, well then, cross the border. A lot of your friends are there so you won't be alone."

When I returned home from Lusia's, I found the house full of strangers—five men and a woman. "They are from Lwow," explained Maria, "and they are going to France via Romania. Somebody directed them to our house."

"I'll go with them."

"You'll what?!"

I just nodded and went into the dining room where my parents chatted with some of the unexpected visitors. Father and Mother were relieved to see me. They had not seen me for three days. They looked at my flushed face but remained silent as if expecting me to say something.

"I'm going with them!" I blurted out, turning to look at the strangers. "Tonight, tomorrow or whenever they go!"

At the beginning my parents wouldn't even talk about it. But I kept trying to persuade them to let me go. I gave them dozens of reasons why I could not stay in Horodenka and why I should go to Romania. Mother wanted to say something, but I wouldn't let her interrupt my torrent of arguments. Father sat with his head down, turning his signet ring around his finger. When I stopped my tirade for a moment, one of the visitors, a tall, dark man with a big nose and horn-rimmed glasses, who was a bit older than the others, turned to my parents.

"We probably could arrange for him to continue his high-school studies in France. Professor Kot, now a minister with the Polish Government in Paris, is our personal friend."

That was a breakthrough and I sensed victory—though limited. High school, my foot! I thought. The moment I'm there, nobody's going to stop me from joining the army.

Next day, Monday, December 11, 1939, was a busy one. Morning mass, confession and communion. A visit to a photographer, so my mother would have a recent picture of her boy. Selecting photographs and souvenirs to take with me. Scratching out and changing the date of birth in the passport Krysia gave me. I wanted to make myself one year older. To volunteer for the army one had to be at least seventeen.

I was itching to tell some of my friends that I was leaving, but no one more than Krysia. In the evening I ran to her place. I never realized how fond I was of her until the day of parting. I was out of breath when I got there. Her mother and her sister were outside in the shed chopping wood for the stove.

"Krysia's in. We'll join you in a moment."

She was standing at the window. She turned around as she heard me coming in. I saw her silhouette against the salmon-coloured sky of the sunset.

I said, "Krystyna!" It sounded more dramatic than the diminutive Krysia. "I am leaving tomorrow for Romania. From there on to France to join the army." I hoped it sounded as good to her as, "My regiment leaves at dawn."

With a mighty hug and a kiss she pre-empted my timid attempt to embrace her. We went into a prolonged clinch. With almost imperceptible steps I steered her in the direction of the part of the floor screened by the two tall wardrobes. Once there she pushed me away a little and began undoing the buttons of her blouse. I thought of an old oil painting of a romantic farewell scene that I often looked at in my grandmother's house. In it, a young woman was offering her rosy breasts for kissing to her swain who was about to depart for war. Krysia was giving me the same kind of send-off, one I wouldn't have dared to dream about.

We both spoke the last goodbye at the same time. Afterwards I realized that the scene in that old oil painting was not an artist's romantic vision but a living tradition.

Chapter 2

TIME TO GO

It was time to go. The double doors between the dining room and our parents' bedroom were wide open. We all milled around these two rooms, my family and our unexpected guests—six strangers who rang our doorbell two days before and asked for shelter while they waited for a guide to smuggle them across the border to Romania. It was an unusual plea, but we were living in unusual times. My parents had said "Yes" even though it was risky. Taking risks had become a way of life in Soviet-occupied Poland.

Of the six who had found temporary harbour in our house, I remember five. Tadzio Siuta, thirtyish, a tall, dark, bespectacled fellow with a big nose, was the one who told my parents he could get me into high school in Paris. As the oldest he seemed to be the leader of the group. He was the fiancé of the twenty-five-year-old, dark-haired beauty, Irka Lempicka, the only woman with them. Tadzio was also a close friend of Irka's two brothers—her slightly younger brother Zynio, who looked very much like her, and her half-brother Roman, twenty-eight, who did not. The three men had been together as students and then lecturers at the University of Lwow, their hometown. Their two other companions, also from Lwow, were Godlewski, a young pianist with wavy blond hair, and his friend, whose name I forget.

Now the guests were ready to leave. They had agreed to take me with them. Some mysterious person was supposed to come and take us to where we were to meet the guide.

I had talked my parents into letting me go. It was sheer blackmail. "Sooner or later the Soviets will arrest me. If you don't let me go now, I'll run away anyway, without proper clothes, without money, without your blessings." They sighed and then said yes. I had given them no choice.

Mother mixed her invocations and blessings with earthy advice. She lifted her eyes to the ceiling, placed her hand on my head and made the sign of a cross on my forehead with the thumb. Then she sighed again.

"Put on Maria's overcoat. It's warmer than yours. Also her sweater. May Our Lady of Lezajsk protect you! Did you remember to take a second pair of warm socks?"

"Yes, Mother."

"Holy Mother forgive us for letting this child go! Here! Tie up Granny's gold chain around your waist. Now don't lose it."

Then it was Father's turn. He put one hand on my shoulder. With the other he lifted my chin and looked into my eyes.

"Go in the name of God. Do your duty to your country as your forefathers did. Be honest. Think of us, my son. My only son. The last of the Topolskis."

His voice broke. Then for the first time in my life I saw my father crying. With trembling hands he unbuttoned his black coat, took his gold watch from his waistcoat pocket and pressed it into my hand. My sister Maria handed him a handkerchief.

The door from the kitchen slowly opened a little bit. In the gap we saw a red face with an even redder nose underlined by a grey handlebar moustache. The eyes of the intruder darted left and right sizing up the people in the room. Then the diminutive figure of our neighbour, the parish organist, crept in. He looked around with a knowing grin and without a word pointed at the clock.

Well I'll be damned! How could this be? How could this timid church organist, this little man, who bleated out the responses from the choir for the priest during high mass, be a secret underground agent? Him a link to the guide who would take us across the border?! Wasn't this the very tippler who irked Father Sobejko by tuning his throat on Sunday mornings at Spiegel's greasy dive?

We filed out in silence through the back door. For two months now we had had the Soviet colonel "Chizhik" and the major billeted in our house. They still kept mainly to themselves in father's study and only used the front door. Luckily, they never thought it strange that a dozen people lived in the other three rooms. Apparently, by

Soviet standards, it was perfectly normal. Still, we didn't want them to hear us going out. It was better that they didn't see half a dozen people carrying rucksacks and leaving the house after dark.

The weather was ideal for us. Through the heavy, wet snow I looked at the dimly lit windows and the yellowish halos of the street lights. It was like seeing them through the lace curtains of our dining room. The snow melting on my forehead and eyelashes ran down my face and my glasses. Wiping them did not help as my woollen mitts and scarf were covered with droplets of water.

The organist stopped briefly in front of his tiny one-room house. The house door was ajar. He looked around, checking for strangers, then whistled twice. The door opened wide and about ten men came out one by one to join our group. Following the organist we trotted along the slushy sidewalks. We didn't go far. After a quarter of an hour our leader turned around and steered his mute charges through the gate of a seldom used cemetery.

As soon as we passed through the cemetery gate I noticed that we were not the first ones there. I could see the tracks of people who came before us. The thin layer of wet snow had melted under their shoes leaving black footprints pressed into the whiteness.

One could not ask for a more conspiratorial setting. Laden with snow, supplicant tree branches bowed down over the tombstones and wooden crosses. The snow was easing and black clouds, hemmed with the light of the moon, raced through the indigo sky. Small groups of people scattered throughout the cemetery moved cautiously towards each other, hoping for a sign or a voice of recognition. Only the occasional reddish glow of a hard-drawn-on cigarette would reveal a grotesque human mask in a black cluster of men huddling together.

The organist led us to a large grave in the centre of the cemetery. One of the two men sitting on the ornamental railing around the raised slab lifted his hand and waved us closer. The organist stopped in front of him and, without a word, pointed with his thumb over his shoulder at our group standing behind him. The man sitting on the railing stretched his neck and moved his head as if counting us. Then he nodded and gave him a creditable imitation of a salute. The organist turned around and quickly trotted away back towards the cemetery gate. Soon we were joined by other groups, all in all about fifty people. Too many, I thought.

The man who greeted us climbed over the tomb's railing and mounted the raised slab. He was wearing a short coat with a leather belt, a peaked cap and riding boots. He introduced himself as our guide, speaking in a quiet but clear voice. There was no need to worry, he told us. He had taken many parties like ours across the border. The route was not strenuous, just a few kilometres, he explained. The last stretch before the border was an open field. At the end of it we would come to a ravine with steep slopes. The border was at the bottom of the ravine. From there a short walk would bring us to Schitt, a small Romanian hamlet.

"The friendly Romanian border guards might be even more friendly if you offer them a *pourboire*. Don't worry about the Soviets. You won't see them. Besides, I can smell a *tsap* [a ram—derogatory slang for a Russian] a mile away. We'll be going in a single file. When we pass the mill in the valley and the few huts around it, ignore the yapping dogs. We pay their owners well to keep them chained. No talking and no smoking. Everything clear? Let's go!"

We left the cemetery not through the gate at the front but through a gap in the crumbling stone wall at the back end. We had to jump down a couple of feet on the far side of the wall. The ground there dropped away onto the slope of a valley. People with heavy rucksacks (one man was carrying a large suitcase) found the jump onto the snow-covered slope hard. Not me. I carried all my belongings in a small canvas army gas-mask bag. But when I leaped down I found myself face to face with my mother and my sister Maria who had somehow managed to get to that point before we did. There was no time for a reprise of the farewell scene. At least I didn't want one. I just waved my hand and quickly slid into the line forming anew. We walked down a diagonal path towards the two wooden beams laid across the black ribbon of the stream at the bottom of the valley. When we were passing Hryniewiecki's mill, somebody from the far slope of the valley shone a powerful flashlight on us. That didn't seem to bother our guide. I was walking just behind him at the head of our group. Soon we reached the treeless, gently rolling ground that stretched for the last two kilometres before the frontier. By then the wind had chased away the last clouds and the snow-covered fields were lit by the waxing moon. Visibility was perfect, and one could see a man a mile away. Our guide kept scanning the horizon. He seemed to be less confident now, often changing pace and stopping for a second to get a better view of the fields around us. At such moments his hand would slide into the side pocket of his coat, probably feeling his revolver. That made me think that the head of our snaking column would be the first to run into any border guards or a trap set up by them. I crouched down, pretending that I was tying my shoelace, and let the marchers pass me. Then I rejoined the line as the second or the third from the end. If we ran into Soviets, I reasoned, being at the rear would give me a better chance to escape. We kept moving on in total silence except for the loud "slap slap" of the leather coat of the man in front of me against his boots.

Suddenly a whisper rippled along our string of marchers: "Look right." On the ridge of a gentle slope I saw the silhouette of a Soviet soldier standing still. His black outline, topped by the soft gathered spike of a cloth *budyonovka* hat, was clearly visible against the dark blue sky. So was the long bayonet at the end of his rifle. He was no more than fifty yards from us. With our faces turned towards him we kept marching forward. He remained motionless as if mesmerized by the sight of the long line of people passing him in an orderly file. Then several soldiers emerged from the lower ground beyond him. They ran in our direction but didn't come any closer than the first soldier.

Rifle shots and cries of *"Postoi!"* Stop! rang out together. We lunged forward. Our guide fired one shot from his revolver at the soldiers and quickly blended with other scattering runners. The Soviets kept firing. Irka, who was running in front of me, fell face down. So did her brothers. Somebody running on my right followed suit. I was next. A moment later when I lifted my head I could not see anybody running or standing—only the Soviets coming at us and still firing. A soldier stopped a few yards from me. I saw him aiming his rifle at me. He fired and a bullet hit the ground near my face, raising a small plume of snow. He kept his stance, still aiming at me. I was moving my head, shielding it with my little gas-mask bag, and trying to make it a less easy target. Four more shots and four more plumes of snow around my head. He stopped firing when he finished the clip. By then they were all over us.

"Keep your face down and spread your arms!" they yelled in Russian, swearing and blaspheming terribly. The one who missed me five times hit my shoulder with the butt of his rifle. I was too frightened to feel the pain. Somebody fired a rocket. Within minutes another Soviet patrol, led by a sergeant on horseback, arrived with a machine gun. They frisked us one by one, then ordered us to get up and form in twos. They had captured eight of our party, none of us hurt. The rest escaped.

Suddenly the sergeant pointed at something in the distance with the birch switch he was using as a riding crop and began shouting orders. The rifle bolts of the soldiers clicked again. We saw the dark figure of a man walking towards us with his hands up. He was coming from the direction where the Romanian border was supposed to be. He stopped when ordered, and two soldiers went forward to search him. When they brought him closer we saw that it was the tall, dark Tadzio Siuta, the man who had persuaded my parents to let me go and said he'd look out for me. He came back from the Romanian side when he realized that his fiancée, Irka, did not make it. He joined our group of captives.

The soldiers, their rifles with bayonets at the ready, surrounded our group. Their mounted sergeant looked around and turned to us. Then for the first time I heard the standard warning that I was to hear over and over again for a long time. "A step to the left, a step to the right counts as an escape. The convoy will make use of their weapons without warning." With his hand he pointed out some place beyond the dark horizon and added *"Davai poshli!"* Get going!

In less than an hour we realized that we were being led to a solitary building standing in an open field. One soldier carried a flashlight. It was rather unusual—a flat wooden box a bit larger than a telephone directory with a couple of glass, rechargeable, wet batteries inside it. The lens for the small light bulb and the switch were on the front of the box. The whole contraption hung from the neck of the carrier on a narrow strap. Dry cell batteries were still unknown in the Soviet Union. As we came closer to the building, I recognized it as the very house near Serafince where I stayed with the Polish Border Guards detachment. A few minutes after we entered it we were searched. I thought it a meticulous search at the time, but I knew little then about searches. Compared to later ones by trained NKVD prison guards that was just a routine frisk. They took away all my documents, among them my "corrected" passport and the souvenirs from my trip to Gdynia: the permits to visit the naval establishments and the warships. On the list of things taken from me were my father's gold watch and grandmother's gold chain—112 centimetres long, declared the soldier who conducted the search and measured it—both described as made of "yellow metal." They all disappeared into a small, canvas bag tied with a string. I was asked to sign a search record. Then the soldier took me to the front room and handed me over to an officer who was sitting behind a desk. This was the same desk at which I had spent many hours on night duty answering telephone calls, taking messages and transmitting air-spotters' reports. Nothing had changed in the room except the gold-framed portrait on the wall behind the desk. Instead of the somewhat obtuse face and bald pate of Polish Marshal Rydz-Smigly, the gold frame was now filled with the swarthy countenance of the son of the drunken Georgian cobbler Vissarion Djugashvili— Iosif Dzhugashvili, alias Stalin.

The officer, a man about thirty years old, pointed with his left hand at the chair facing him and asked me to sit down. His right hand wielded a pen poised to strike at the pale sheet of paper spread on the desk in front of him. My first interrogation had started.

"Your surname?

"Given name and patronymic?

"Year born?"

"1923." I had given my real name. Now I gave my real year of birth, hoping for leniency because of my youth. The vaunted NKVD never seemed to notice then or later that I had altered the birth date on my passport to 1922.

His questions were in Russian. He spoke no Polish. I spoke no Russian. But I did speak Ukrainian, a third Slavic language similar to both, which he could understand a bit. By mixing these three languages we were plodding through his questions and my answers. The officer's task was a bit easier because he had already interrogated Irka and was familiar with some details of the clandestine meeting at the cemetery and our march to the frontier. His manner of questioning was neither threatening nor polite. It was business-like and correct. Only once, when I said that during the last three months a lot of people I knew had fled to Romania, did he react. He clicked his tongue against his front teeth and sucked in his breath between tensed lips.

"It's bad. Just because we have some initial difficulties with the supply and distribution and you find that sugar and butter have disappeared from the shops, you think it a major disaster and thoughtlessly you run abroad."

Before the search and interrogations, the guards briefly left us alone in one room. The three Lempickis, Tadzio and I agreed to say that we had never met before. We didn't want to betray our escape contacts, in my case, the organist next door. I had a few minutes left to invent a story about meeting, in Horodenka, an imaginary student older than me, a refugee from western Poland who talked me into escaping to Romania. The physical appearance of this insidious character was to be that of my sister Maria's former boyfriend, Zbyszek, but I invented the surname Laszczak.

I don't think the officer swallowed my version of the unsuccessful escape. But he said nothing. He just kept covering page after page with ornate Cyrillic characters, taking down everything I told him. When, at the end of the story, I said that the scoundrel Laszczak had escaped to Romania, the interrogator turned to me.

"He didn't. We've caught them all."

It was now my turn to doubt whether he was telling the truth. Then he read aloud in Russian what he had written down in Cyrillic characters. I understood very little of it.

"Sign it!"

I did.

He opened the door to the corridor and summoned the guard. A short soldier dressed in a sheepskin coat entered the room, saluted the officer, then turned to me.

"Follow me down!"

The wall clock was showing quarter to midnight—Moscow time. By the central European time which we Poles still observed in private life it was only quarter to ten.

"Down" was a cellar. Just an ordinary cellar with damp stone walls, a narrow horizontal window with newly installed heavy iron bars, a kerosene lamp hanging from a hook hammered into a crack between the stones of the wall and a bucket to serve as a toilet. Upstairs, the interrogation went fast and soon all nine of us bedded down on the straw-covered dirt floor.

We woke up to find three more prisoners in our cellar. They had been brought in during the night when we were asleep. We barely had time to say good morning to them when the guards took us outside to an outhouse. We formed a line with "urgent cases" at the front. Nobody had used the bucket in the cellar because of modesty. Back in the cellar, a man who was caught with us on the frontier introduced himself, giving his name as Soltys. Over forty years old, he was of medium height, wore breeches and riding boots and walked with a slight limp. With an air of benevolent authority he told us to accept the reality and discard our inhibitions.

"When you have to, use the bucket for what it was intended. Forget that there are other people around. You'll get used to it very soon. The guards will take you to the outhouse two or three times per day but for some that's not often enough. Take it from me. I know what I am talking about. I've been in all kind of circumstances and conditions and I lived through two wars before this one started."

For a while everybody was silent. Then Roman, the older Lempicki brother, asked, "Mr. Soltys, how soon do you think they'll release us?"

Soltys made a face, but said nothing.

For breakfast we had a thick slice of bread and a mug of slightly sweetened ersatz coffee made of roasted acorns. After that everybody started talking about the night before. Tadzio Siuta said that we were caught almost at the edge of the deep ravine. From there it was no more than 200 metres down the steep slope to the frontier. That's why I did not see anybody running or standing in front of me when I lifted my head from the ground. Of the group that had stayed at our house along with the Lempickis and Tadzio, two got through to Romania: the pianist Godlewski and his friend. Besides Soltys there were three others who were caught. Zbyszek Wieckowski, a high-school student from Chodorow, was two years older than me, a husky fellow, tall and blond. Another captive was Oborski, a grey-faced man of nondescript age who had worked in a post office in Horodenka and was suffering from tuberculosis. I cannot remember a thing about the ninth person caught with us.

The three latecomers who joined us in the cellar during the night were Polish too. All of them middle-aged, well spoken and well dressed. They were trying to cheer themselves up, slapping each other on the back and joking, though their jokes were private. They claimed to be printers—at least that's what they told their interrogators they were—and laughingly addressed each other as *"tipograf"* (Russian for printer).

I was not too worried. I was sure that after a couple of days we'd all be released. And what a story I'd have to tell my friends! Being shot at and then taken prisoner. Interrogated at night and then locked up in a cellar with barred windows. An instant hero. Others in the cellar shared my optimism. One of the *tipografy* spoke authoritatively about the penal codes of different countries. All of them, he said, called for a fine or maximum of fourteen days in prison for illegally crossing a border. To us fourteen days seemed a severe punishment and a very long sentence. We hoped that the Soviets would show us clemency and release us after a day or two. Only Soltys seemed not to share our optimism. When we found out he spoke fluent Russian, we wondered if he knew more about the Soviet justice system than we did.

I wanted my parents to know what had happened to me and my new friends and to pass the bad news on to the Lempickis' parents in Lwow. Their father was a renowned professor at Lwow University and surely he would have some contacts who could pull strings and rescue us from this mess we had got ourselves into. Tadzio found a piece of paper in his pocket and one of the *tipografy* had the stub of a pencil. I scribbled a note with our news and waited for an opportunity to pass it to somebody from outside who would take it to my parents. The opportunity came sooner than I expected. At noon we were all taken upstairs to the soldiers' dining room. There they gave each of us a shallow, tin bowl of soup made of carrots and potatoes. The tin soup plates and the spoons were covered with congealed fat. Irka, myself and a few others found it disgusting, and we would not eat despite Soltys's admonitions. "Eat! You don't know how long it may be till we get the next meal."

Afterwards, when we were standing outside in line for the outhouse, I saw a village woman chopping firewood in front of the kitchen just a few steps away from us. When our guard was looking the other way I ran quickly to her and pressed my note into her hand. As I did so I asked her to deliver it to the janitor of the high school in Horodenka who would know who it was for. At that moment the guard saw me talking to her and yelled at me to get back into line.

The note never arrived. Maybe the woman was too scared to pass along something in writing or perhaps she handed it over to the guard. But two days later she went to the janitor and told him about my note. He thought that she had been sent by the militia to find out how much he knew about the border-crossing business. In any case he didn't believe her story and did nothing about it. He had already been informed by reliable people that I'd been seen in good health across the border in Cernauti, Romania.

The day ended with another plate of soup. When the guard brought in a kerosene lamp it was already dark outside although it was only about four o'clock. He said "Good night," then locked and bolted the door from outside. The fact that nobody was called upstairs for an additional interrogation was interpreted as a good sign.

"They got all the information they wanted. There is nothing more to ask for so they are just waiting for a word from some higher-up to let us go."

Another day and another night passed and still nothing happened. We found the guards and the officer who conducted the roll call in the mornings utterly uncommunicative. They would answer our questions with a curt, "Don't know." Or, "You'll be informed in due course." They wouldn't even answer such simple questions as, "What's the time, please?" or, "Is it snowing outside?"

That bothered me. My optimism began to wane. Why would anybody be so gruff and ignore friendly remarks or innocuous questions of polite and intelligent people like us? I recalled reading in novels and historical works written by authors who had managed to get out of the "proletarian paradise" about the horrors which befell people in Soviet prisons during the Revolution and afterwards. Fear started creeping into my mind. I began imagining the worst possible fate for us all. But then the reassuring voices of those who believed we would be set free any time now would quell my anxiety, and I would regain my buoyancy.

We talked to kill the time. But I talked more than anybody else. In fact, I babbled so much that months later Soltys admitted he had been ready to strangle me.

On the fourth day before noon the guard opened the door, looked around and said, "*Sobiraites' s veshchami!*" We were baffled. It sounded like an important command but we didn't understand what he wanted. The guard looked nonplussed by our inaction. He said it again, this time a bit louder. "*Sobiraites' s veshchami!*" We were looking at each other equally puzzled. Then Soltys nodded and answered the guard. "*Khorosho.*" Okay. Turning to us he said "Get ready with all your things. That's what he says."

The guard remained standing in the open door gaping at Irka as she turned around, and, facing the wall, began tucking her flannel blouse inside her ski-pants and then, in front of an imaginary mirror on the wall, combing her short raven hair. The guard kept staring at Irka and repeating, "*Davaite! Davaite!*" Get going! Get going! But it was obvious that he was hurrying not her but us.

All three *tipografy* had smiles on their faces and resumed their backslapping with double the vigour. Roman Lempicki, also sporting a big grin, kept nudging his younger brother and repeating, "You've lost the bet. You've lost the bet. You'll have to pay!" It seemed that they felt free already and that we were going home.

Outside, a convoy was waiting for us—five or six soldiers forming a circle. We were steered into the middle of it. The soldiers carried rifles with fixed bayonets. One of them lugged a Degtiarov machine gun, another held onto a mean-looking German shepherd dog. The happy chatter of those who moments ago were arranging rendezvous in Lwow suddenly ceased. I noticed Tadzio and Soltys exchanging quick glances and little nods. The soldiers did not look like a homecoming escort, and there was no sign of the bags and rucksacks taken from us before we were locked in the cellar. A moment later the convoy *komandir* (commander) came out onto the porch. His long overcoat, like all Soviet army overcoats, had no hem at the bottom. They believed it let the drops of rain or melting snow drip off faster and so kept the coattails from getting soggy. The straps for a Nagant revolver, for a map case and for a bulging, large, leather case, which looked like a saddlebag, criss-crossed his chest. One of the prisoners asked him where we were going. The *komandir* looked at him with disdain.

"Too much knowledge is no good for you. We are the only ones to ask questions. Your duty is to give answers."

He surveyed our group for a few moments and then intoned the warning already familiar to us. "A step to the left, a step to the right, counts as an escape. The convoy will make use of their weapons without warning. March!"

It was a sunny day, and there was a keen frost in the air. The ground was covered with a couple of centimetres of snow. We walked at a brisk pace. At the gate, instead of turning left to Serafince village, the convoy turned to the right, the direction of the Romanian border. I could not understand it. Unlike the others, who had only seen these surroundings in the middle of the night, I knew the area. When I said to my companions that we were being led towards Romania, they thought it nonsense and told me to shut up.

Suddenly we left the road, crossed the ditch and began to march across the wide open field heading for a copse on the horizon. We marched in silence broken only by the occasional whine or yelp of the German shepherd held back on a leash too short.

I had terrible premonitions. The worst stories about Bolshevik murders and executions flooded my brain. It was clear to me that the clump of trees was to be the place of our deaths. That's why they carried the machine gun and did not take our belongings. In vain I looked at the faces of Tadzio and Zynio for a sign of reassurance. But they seemed to have the same fears. I began to pray fervently. I kept repeating all of the few prayers I had learned in my life.

We reached the edge of the copse. The *komandir* yelled: *"Postoi!"* Stop!

"That's it," I said to myself.

The *komandir* took off his map case. He looked at his map for a while then lit a cigarette and spoke.

"Ten minute smoke break for those who have something to smoke. Those who are pressed may relieve themselves. Anyway, it's not very far to the place where we're going. Another hour or so."

The place where we were going was Stecowa, another frontier post. It became clear to us later that they took us across the fields because it was a short cut and because there would be less chance of us being seen by villagers and passersby. In Stecowa, they locked us up in a tool shed. It was long, narrow and dark. We sat on the bare floor with our backs against the whitewashed wall. There was no heating but the warmth of our bodies kept the shed bearable. We had no idea what was going to happen to us next. In the evening a soldier brought in a large kettle of boiling water, some enamel mugs and our rations of black bread, as well as a plateful of crushed sugarloaf. Everybody agreed that the Soviet sugar from the bluish-white conical loaf was much sweeter than the sugar we were used to. When Soltys saw that some of us were ready to drop the tiny sugar ration in a mug filled with hot water, he advised us to take our hot drink with sugar in the Russian way, called drinking "on a nibble." He explained that sipping the hot liquid while pressing a tiny piece of sugar with your tongue against the roof of your mouth would make the water seem much sweeter than if we dissolved it in our mugs.

Before noon the next day five more people were shoved into our shed. Three of them were young doctors from Cracow. Two of them introduced themselves as Jan Weissglass and Marys Epstein. The third doctor was a woman, Lila, but I cannot recall her surname. The other two fellows brought in with them were local peasants. They looked frightened. I recognized one of them as an air spotter who served with me at Serafince. His name was Kielec. The three doctors were caught by the Soviets while trying to cross the border to Romania. Somehow they had contacted Kielec who lived in Stecowa. For a few dollars he agreed to show them the way to Romania and walked them to a spot from where they could see the border. He had asked to be paid in dollars because in all serious deals peasants in eastern Poland used American greenbacks. The value of land was always calculated in dollars. No wonder. In the twenty-odd years since 1916, people in Horodenka had seen six occupying powers come and go and seven currencies (Poland had changed its currency twice). As each new currency came in, the old one became worthless. For them a dollar was a dollar.

Although they were left almost at the border, the doctors lost their bearings and ran into a Soviet patrol. Hoping for more lenient treatment by their captors, they led the patrol to Kielec's house. Kielec was arrested together with an innocent friend of his who just happened to be at his house when the patrol arrived.

The next day they marched us to the Sniatyn railway station some fifteen kilometres away. At the station we were herded into a waiting train. One car was reserved for the fourteen of us and our guards. It was an ordinary third-class carriage with hard benches. The heat was on too high and the windows were shut tight. We were all thirsty, but we had to wait several hours until our train stopped in Stanislawow and the guards fetched a bucket of water for us. One of them came running back from the station: "Comrades! They're selling French rolls!"

Hearing that, some of the guards rushed to the station buffet and returned with dozens of ordinary white bread rolls cradled in their upturned coattails. Soon from the part of the car occupied by our guards came the sounds of vigorous chomping and lip smacking. For them white rolls were luxury eating, and they were gorging themselves, biting off half of a big roll at a time and then, with grubby fingers, stuffing in the bits sticking out of their mouths. One of the soldiers, in an unexpected act of chivalry, presented Irka and Lila with a roll each. They accepted them gladly.

Five days had already passed since we'd been caught. The bread ration and the occasional bowl of thin soup were tasting better and better every day. Nobody minded any longer that loaves of bread were cut into rations on a dirty bench or that we had to slurp our soup from unwashed bowls.

The next afternoon our train dragged itself onto the sidings of the Czortkow railway station. We were only eighty kilometres from my home in Horodenka, but the train had taken the long way around instead of the short pre-war route, now closed, through the bulge of Romania which came between the two towns. Army trucks took us from the station to a walled compound in the town. As we rolled in through a heavily guarded gate, somebody from our group recognized it as the former Polish army barracks. The trucks stopped in front of a large, single-story building. Moments later we entered a dimly lit entrance hall leaving behind us Irka, Lila and our escort.

There were half a dozen unarmed soldiers standing in the entrance hall. One, dressed in an open sheepskin coat, sat at a wobbly table. He seemed to be in charge of the others. With the open palm of his hand he motioned us back to the wall beside the entrance door. Then he spread on the table a list of the new arrivals and ran his finger under our last names as he sounded them out one by one. After he heard a man respond with his first name and patronymic, he would point him out with a nod, and then tilt his head to a guard who would take the prisoner to the other end of the hall and search him. It went fast. While I waited for my turn I had time to look around the hall. There were two heavy doors on each of the longer walls of the rectangular hall and one on the shorter wall opposite the entrance door. All doors had heavy locks, a spy hole with a swing-aside flap and a foot-square hatch door at face level. The buzz and hum coming through the locked cell doors sounded like a giant beehive.

The search over, they took away my glasses. "Not permitted."

One of the guards came towards me. "You Topolski? This way."

He steered me to the far end of the hall opposite the entrance door. With a large key he opened the lock of the cell door and flung it wide open. A wave of warm, fetid air rushed towards me. The guard pushed me forward. "Get in!"

Chapter 3
A JOLLY SLAMMER

One hundred and fifty unshaven faces greeted me. Beards galore. Beards three days old and three months old. White, grey, blond, red, brown and black. Smooth, wispy and curly. The variety of beards was matched by the variety of faces. Being short-sighted, I not so much saw as felt everybody's eyes peering at me. From around a large stove at the far end of the cell a few raised arms beckoned me over.

"Hey, Miss! C'mon over here! This way!"

I was wearing my sister's coat with a lamb fur collar and a white knitted balaclava. That, with my short stature and smooth, beardless cheeks fooled them. They took me for a girl.

The floor of the cell was covered with wide, knee-high wooden platforms of various sizes which were separated from each other by narrow aisles. The straw piled on top of these platforms was held down by burlap nailed along the edges. Accumulated filth, sweat, spittle, spilled food and mud made the burlap stiff and shiny. Near the windows were two barrels filled to the brim with excrement and urine. Exuding stench like two sulphuric craters, they served as toilets for a hundred and fifty men. I covered my face with the sweater Maria had given me. It still held the scent of "Je Reviens" and the smell of home, and that lasted for a while. I found out later on that a stench, however vile, is one of the easiest things to get used to. In a few hours or even minutes you stop noticing it.

The cell I found myself in was the largest of the five in the building. Of the people I arrived with, four were with me in that cell—the enigmatic old-hand Soltys, the consumptive postal clerk Oborski and the two studious Lempicki brothers, Roman and Zynio. The rest were put in smaller cells around the entrance hall.

There were two groups in our cell, "us" and the "Romanians." "Us" were Poles, Jews and Ukrainians, all former citizens of Poland.

In the Romanian group there were a few real Romanians. The rest were Ukrainians who had been living in the Bukovina area of Romania and, hearing the incessant Soviet radio propaganda, decided to escape from Romania to the Soviet workers' paradise where "sausages hang on fences for the picking and wells are filled with beer."

Some of them fled alone, some with wives and children, and some even with parents and grandparents. A few were deserters from the army. However, as soon as they crossed the border they were arrested and treated no better, and sometimes worse, than those of us trying to escape from what was now the Soviet Union. These "Bukovinians" were charged with crossing the border illegally and, as often as not, accused of being spies. They were bewildered at the treatment received from the people they believed would be their saviours.

"It's all a big mistake," they consoled themselves. "Tomorrow or maybe a few days later this will change." Tall, handsome, strong, dark-haired men, they were terrified of even the lowest-ranking Soviet official. They would grovel when they had to make some trivial request. They always seemed to be more hungry than we were and would betray or denounce their best friend for a chunk of bread. At least thirty of them had the surname Sokholatiuk and some of these had the same Christian names and patronymics as well. This created a lot of confusion at roll call.

In charge of our cell was a trusty appointed by the Soviets to keep order and distribute food. His first name was Aron. A stocky, red-headed deserter from the Romanian Air Force, he still wore its grey-blue uniform and peaked cap. He pretended to take his cell duties seriously. When the cauldron with soup was brought into the cell, Aron would grab the broom and, wielding it like a rifle, perform the Romanian army ceremonial drill ending it with a theatrical "Present arms!" in front of the cauldron. With his chin up and his nostrils dilated, he would inhale the steaming contents and exclaim in Romanian, "The soup's here! Long live Romania!"

The food was terrible but by that time we didn't mind. We were hungry. We just wanted more of it. On my first day in the cell, Aron himself scooped the best bits from the cauldron for my bowlful. But when the other Bukovinians complained loudly that "the son of an exploiter of the working classes is getting preferential treatment" he didn't dare do it again.

He was a born clown. When a guard came in to make an announcement, Aron would place himself behind him and ape all his gestures. If the news was good, Aron's mouth would stretch into a silent smile from ear to ear. If bad, he would hang his head down and with his sleeve wipe invisible tears from a tragic face. He could be crude and vulgar—and dangerous too. He would invent some fanciful stories and tell them with a straight face. One evening, seeing that one of the Sokholatiuks was asleep, he woke him up and said in a confidential stage whisper, which was loud enough for everybody to hear, "You've had it, brother. There's no sense denying it any longer. They have undeniable proof that you are the former Romanian Minister of Foreign Affairs." The startled man jumped up and, crossing himself, began denying the terrible accusation.

"I never was the Romanian, Romanian . . ."—he found it too difficult to repeat Minister of Foreign Affairs—"whatever you call him, that Romanian prick!"

Aron enjoyed being the centre of attention. Sometimes as he looked through the sweaty window at the army tractors parked in the courtyard he would say, "Now, seriously. That's what I came here for! To be a tractorist. Soon I'll be sitting on a tractor ploughing the good Soviet soil for twenty-five hours each day."

It was no secret that he was often called outside by the prison officials to report on what his cellmates said about the communist system and whether some of them had accidentally betrayed their real identity.

Roman and Zynio Lempicki were just as shaken by our new surroundings as I was. Zynio, the younger brother, an aesthete who had studied the history of art at Lwow University, confronted our dismal reality with equanimity and a dry sense of humour, mocking the pretensions and fears of others. Like many artists, he seemed to feel that reality was whatever the individual chose to see. And Zynio usually chose to ignore the ugly world we'd landed in and enjoy the world of his imagination. Before the war he took pride in dressing and living well to express his artistic flair—and one-upmanship.

But now Zynio was resigned to making do with whatever came his way, even joking about it. He seemed to take everything in stride.

His older, half-brother Roman's reaction was the opposite. He had continued the classical studies tradition of his family at the same university and also taught there. Perhaps he believed his classical name dictated his destiny. He seemed to have taken up Latin as a shield against the problems of everyday life and lived in a world of declensions and conjugations where the scholar was not called upon to show initiative or make decisions. Roman looked on prison rules in the same way. To succeed in prison, as in Latin, the individual had first to memorize the rules and then to conform to them without question. It was unthinkable to change them.

Apart from Latin grammar, Roman had two other passions. One was movies, especially Westerns. The other was eating halva and washing it down with glasses of hot lemon tea. After our capture Roman was terrified of everybody and everything around him, especially of men in uniform who, in his view, had unlimited power over us. They could set us free or kill us. More than that. They could give us an extra bowl of soup. He sat as if propping up the wall with his back but he slouched sideways. Though under thirty, he had already developed the noticeable stoop of an academic and philologist. His whole body seemed amorphous and disorganized. Only the line linking the tip of his jutting chin and his prominent nose with the edge of the peak of his cloth cap was straight. He kept moving his head left and right trying to locate with his myopic eyes the source of every noise in the room. As soon as he saw a soldier entering our cell, Roman's body would stiffen. He would press his arms dutifully against the sides of his thighs and utter an admonishing shush to those who kept yakking. Even in the absence of any authority, when chatting with friends his gaze would be fixed on the entrance door lest an omnipotent Ivan slip into the room without being noticed. He hardly ever moved from his place unless sorely pressed to relieve himself and even that usually took place in the middle of the night.

His behaviour did not pass unobserved by the guards and one evening after roll call a sergeant pointed at Roman with the stub of a pencil and said loudly, "There is but one model prisoner in this cell and at the appropriate time we will take his exemplary conduct into consideration."

Roman beamed, oblivious to the contemptuous looks of his cell-mates.

For a few days I kept feeling some itching around my waist. I knew what it was, but I would not admit to myself that I had lice. Lice was something that poor, uneducated people had. It was something shameful. In the elementary school I had heard of boys being sent home and told not to come back until they got rid of the blight. My uncles used to mention lice when talking about being off soldiering in the trenches during the Great War. That was history. But lice on me? That was unthinkable.

Nevertheless, in the evenings more and more men would take off their shirts and underwear and hunt for lice. Those who didn't were looked askance at by the hunters who believed that only a common effort could slow down the lice invasion. I joined the hunters.

I had far more lice than I suspected. They looked revolting—grey, crab-like creatures with long abdomens that trailed behind them, as they crawled fast into the folds of the cloth seams. The larger ones had tiny black dots in the form of a cross on top of their bodies. Most of them were bloated with human blood. One had to look hard to find their eggs, shiny strings of tiny, transparent nits glued to the fabric. These were body lice (known to us as cloth lice), carriers of typhus. The head lice were smaller and almost black. Some men were also infested with crab lice embedded in the skin in the pubic area and, in neglected cases, even in eyebrows. Beginners would try to kill a louse by rolling it between their fingers, a long and not very effective execution. Later on we learned the right technique—squeezing it between the thumb and forefinger nails. Some Bukovinians, for whom lice had been lifelong companions, would crack the catch with their teeth. Soltys, whose secret past endowed him with practical experience in such matters, recommended placing a handkerchief or a clean piece of cloth on one's chest.

"They'll be drawn to it like magic and in ten minutes you'll have fifty of them squirming under your handkerchief."

It didn't work for me. However, searching for and killing lice became an obsession.

The cell was home to a number of interesting characters. One, a young but completely bald man, bore a strong resemblance to a Buddhist monk. He liked to sit on his hunkers regaling us with stories about his life in Warsaw. His name was Kubacki. There was no doubt he thought himself a true representative of Warsaw "high life," which he pronounced "heeg leef." He was not boasting or putting on airs. He genuinely believed himself to have been a fortunate fellow in pre-war days, having managed to get a good education and a good-paying job. The good restaurants and the Sluzewiec horse racetrack were within his reach. To him, Poland and especially its centre, Warsaw, were fine places to live in and he was proud of being Polish. He considered the lost battles, the German and Russian occupations, and the present hard times only a temporary aberration. A born optimist, he asked a number of the lice hunters to meet him at the Billiard Room of the Café Club in Warsaw "when things get back to normal."

One day he was told to get ready and a few minutes later the guards came to take him away. He shook hands with everybody around and as he was leaving he turned in the doorway, waved once again and shouted his last words to us.

"Don't forget, guys! Café Club! I am usually there on Thursdays!"

But the largest audiences gathered around a middle-aged, rotund man named Silberman. From the very first day when he was brought to our cell in the Czortkow barracks he endeared himself to us by the disdain he showed towards our Soviet captors. When a guard saw him sitting on top of the round iron stove and ordered him to get down, Silberman answered in Polish, "Kiss my ass!" The guard was not sure what those words meant but suspected something bad by the ripple of laughter which went round the cell. He left the room but came back with a NKVD officer. Silberman was already down off the stove. The officer produced a notebook and asked him a string of questions:

"Surname? Name? Patronymic? Profession? Nationality?"

"Mister Silberman, David Ushorovich, optical engineer, Yid," was his reply. Then he added, "Don't attempt to write it down. It's too complicated for you."

The officer swallowed the dig but said, "Not Yid, but Hebrew." At that time in the Soviet Union, *zhid* (Yid) was an offensive word for a Jew.

"I know a Yid when I see one. Even in a mirror."

"Don't be too smart, Silberman. It's not good for you."

"How can I avoid it in these surroundings?"

"Silberman, why did you tell the guard to kiss your ass?"

"You must be joking, *komandir*. Me? Telling such a thing to the esteemed guard? I have a hundred witnesses here that I didn't say it. What I said was that in this packed cell I had to look for room for my ass. It's not my fault that the uncultured beast understands only Russian."

The *komandir* put the notebook back in his breast pocket and started a dignified retreat to the door. But he felt he had to do something to uphold his authority. He stopped, turned around and yelled at the top of his voice, "Quit yapping all of you. And if I catch anybody smoking here, he'll get ten days in the cooler!"

"Some *komandir*," Silberman sneered. "I could buy half a dozen like him for my one cufflink."

Silberman was no common man. His clothes, though rumpled, were of excellent quality. His hat was from Habig, a well-known Viennese hatter, his shoes from Hiszpanski. He told us that he had started his commercial career as a leaseholder of several lakes in central Poland. He tried fish farming. It went well. He invested in real estate. That went well too. Then import and export. Money was flowing in. He travelled all over the world.

Gambling was his vice. He knew every casino in central Europe, he told us. He ate in the best restaurants and stayed in well-known hotels. A couple of fellows who knew the casino in Sopot tried to trap him by asking about the value and colours of the chips there. He knew it all.

From the stories he told us emerged his other weakness. It was Zuza, his spendthrift mistress. When he talked about her he waxed lyrical and sentimental. It was like listening to a modernized version of Solomon's *Song of Songs*.

"She's golden-haired—most of the time. Her legs are like those of a finely crafted piano. Her waist is so tiny and hips so broad that a kitten could perch comfortably on her hip. When I take her to a jeweller's store you can't tell whether it's the diamonds or her eyes shining. My, she likes that! And the boobies she has! And a tummy like a satin cushion. And below that, the sweetest little honey pot that ever was."

He lowered his head and grew silent. Then, his head still down, he looked up and blinked several times as if he just woke up. He raised his eyebrows and turned to us.

"You know, three of my apartment houses in Jaroslaw were sunk into that sweet little honey pot."

Days went by and we were still living under the illusion that the next day would bring us freedom. We were getting worried because some men also accused of attempting to cross the border illegally had already been here longer than fourteen days, which we thought was the maximum penalty for that offence.

Some were called out for interrogation, always after midnight, and would come back after several hours of grilling being none the wiser about their immediate future. Interrogators followed the same routine. "Tell us all about yourself and the true reasons why you decided to cross the frontier. We know it all, but we want to hear it from you. We deal leniently with those who feel contrite and admit their guilt of their own volition. We are patient but if you won't come forward with the true story we have means to extract it from you. We give you time to think it over. You'll be called back."

But a few of those who came back from an interrogation kept silent and would not say what had happened.

The guards were working twelve-hour shifts changing at the morning and the evening roll call. They would enter our cell for roll call yelling at the top of their voices. "Up! Up! All of you! Stand up on the platform in two rows! Silence!"

Then the guard commandant read aloud our surnames from the list which he kept in a hardcover holder, making a pause after each name to hear us answer in turn with our Christian name and patronymic. We were quick to notice that the Christian names and patronymics were marked on his list only by initials. A new game started in which some of us would answer him with most outlandish names and patronymics. Much to our amusement, the guard commandant, unfamiliar with foreign names, would accept them as genuine, as long as they began with the same letter as the initials on his list. Thus I, Boguslaw Aleksandrovich, once answered Barbados Argentinovich, and Tadeusz Ludwikovich sang out Te Deum Laudamus in a solemn, churchy voice. This was acknowledged by the commandant with a nod and a crisp, *"Pravil'no."* Correct.

A new arrival in our cell was Gryz, a sixteen-year-old from the Polish province of Silesia. He was mature for his age and proud of his trade as a builder of clay-tiled stoves, following his family tradition. He escaped from a small Silesian town, Mikolow, after his father was arrested by the Gestapo and then sent to a concentration camp for organizing Polish voters twenty years earlier during the plebiscite of 1920, when people in Silesia were asked to vote whether they wanted to be part of Germany or Poland. Young Gryz did not wait for his turn and fled to the Soviets who promptly put him in prison. He was bitter about their treatment of him and at times revenged himself on them in an amusing way.

After roll call, two guards counted the prisoners as they stood in double rows on the platforms. One of the guards started the count moving along sideways from one end to the other, shuffling his felt winter boots while counting aloud, "Two, four, six, eight, ten. . . " The other guard double-checked by starting his count from the other end. Gryz would stand at one end of the back row and when the guard who had counted him had moved to the middle of the row, Gryz would scramble on all fours underneath the platform and rejoin the row at the far end. Upon finishing the count the guards would face each other, one looking terrified, the other astonished, and exclaim, "The devil take it! One has given us the slip!"

"No! There's one extra!"

"Let's start from the beginning!"

One afternoon the door opened and a bunch of children spilled into our cell like potatoes from a split bag. There were twenty or maybe thirty of them, all between eight and eleven years old. These boys jumped from platform to platform stepping on people lying down or anything else in their path and settled themselves in the Bukovinian corner near the window. They kicked and spat on those men who were slow in making room for them. Any attempt to restrain them or to curb their wild behaviour would bring shrieks of, "Little ones are being beaten!" Then a guard would stick his head in through the half-open door and admonish those men who had only been trying to defend themselves.

"Leave the little urchins alone! Aren't you ashamed of bullying the little buggers?!"

We soon found out the little buggers were Ukrainian children from the Bukovina area of Romania who, in following the example of their fathers and older brothers, had crossed the border into the USSR two months before. They were all from the same village and the same school. They wore black felt hats and long trousers that looked a bit like the dress of Hutterite or Mennonite children. The Soviets did not know what to do with them. They were too young for the institutions for juvenile delinquents, so they put them in prison. By the time we met them they were already seasoned jailbirds. They were crafty, stole food and other things from their fellow prisoners, and spewed nonstop obscenities in their newly acquired Russian. When they got extra rations of bread that were too much for them to gobble then and there, they would tear the loaf into small pieces, and toss them into the air, laughing to see grown-up Bukovinians jump like dogs trying to catch them. These children had already been shunted around from one prison to another, from Kiev to Kharkov to Odessa. Nobody wanted them, yet nobody had the power or the courage to release them or send them back to Romania. They vanished one day just as unexpectedly as they came. Nobody had told them where they were being taken, and we never learned anything more about their fate.

A couple of days before Christmas I was called for my first interrogation. It must have been around four or five o'clock in the morning. A soldier escorted me through the deserted, snow-covered streets. During the ten-minute walk he kept clicking the safety catch of his rifle, a common practice intended to unnerve prisoners and soften them up for the interrogation. However, I didn't know that then, and I was frightened by it. But I would never give him any satisfaction by showing my feelings. He took me to the modern barracks in which the elite troops of the Polish Frontier Defence Corps used to be stationed. Now they were occupied by the Soviet state police, the feared NKVD.

My escort took me through a couple of check points to an office on the second floor and left me in front of a desk behind which sat a thickset man in uniform who eyed me with unfeigned disinterest. He was resting his clean-shaven chin on his clasped hands, his elbows on the arms of his chair. He pulled out my file from the stack of files on his desk and as he leafed through it, he stopped to examine briefly my souvenirs—the permits to visit Polish Navy sites. Then he went back to the first page and, without raising his head, spoke for the first time.

"Topolski Boguslaw Aleksandrovich, tell me all about yourself and about your intended flight to Romania."

He dipped his pen in an inkwell and began writing down everything I told him, checking it against my previous statement. Sometimes he nodded. At times he would interrupt me.

"Say that name again?"

It took us a long time to get to the end of my story.

He cranked the handle of an ancient field telephone, lifted the receiver and said something in Russian. Then in an offhanded way he asked me, "What are you talking about with others in the cell? What are others saying about life under Soviet rule?"

I gushed out the stories about Silberman's gambling, and Kubacki's "high life" billiards sessions and other harmless bits and pieces of conversations I had overheard. He barely bothered to listen to them and with a sweeping gesture dismissed my tales.

"Is nobody complaining?"

"No. Not really. People are worried about food and other things being hard to buy in stores but that's understandable. After all, we've been through a war."

"You're lying, youngster. Didn't you hear Michiel complaining about the sugar mill being dismantled and shipped to Russia? You were there when he said it. Listen! I can help you. In no time I can get you out from that stinking hole and send you back home to your family. But not if you don't co-operate and you lie to me!"

This shook me. An old roué in our cell, Michiel, did say that, and I was there. But I was saved from having to answer right away because the side door in the office opened and a boy of my age in an army uniform brought a glass of tea on a tray and placed it in front of my interrogator. He stirred the sugar in the glass, and, lifting the glass with the handle of the spoon sticking out from between his index and middle finger, began sipping the hot liquid.

Suddenly he leaned forward and almost shouted.

"Tell me the names of the officers who were dispatching you to Romania!"

"Nobody was dispatching me. It was that scoundrel Laszczak who talked me into it."

"You lie. The same as you lied about Michiel."

"I didn't know that things Michiel said were important."

"Don't play stupid!"

He was, or pretended to be, angry. The uniformed teenager who brought tea stood near the window listening impassively to what was being said. The interrogator finished his tea, looked at him and nodded. The youngster nodded back. There was a moment of silence, then the interrogator turned to me.

"Topolski Boguslaw Aleksandrovich. Tell me all about yourself and how come you wanted to escape to Romania."

"From the very beginning?"

"That's how stories are told. Get going and then don't omit anything."

He kept writing down with undiminished vigour everything I was saying, as if he never heard it before. I was getting tired and sleepy but kept on talking. Through the clear glass of the upper half of the window—the bottom half of it was painted over with white paint—I could see that the sky had begun to redden and the still unseen sun began to cast a golden rim around the long patches of purple clouds. A flypast of mute crows and the long wail of a factory siren announced the daybreak.

A sudden sharp pain in my left hand cut into my droning. It took me a second to realize that the interrogator had hit me hard across my fingers with a long, unsharpened pencil. I could not believe that a rap with a thin pencil could be so painful.

"Quit looking out the window! Concentrate on your story! You've forgotten to mention Oborski. Put your hands back on the desk and continue!"

I told him that I didn't know Oborski's name until after the arrest so I couldn't mention him at the beginning of the story.

"Nonsense! Go on!"

He was getting angry, but his voice was quiet and measured. And as he kept writing with his right hand, the pencil that he held in his left kept swinging menacingly. He would hit me again and again with it whenever he thought that I was "twisting the story." It seems ridiculous to complain about being hit with a pencil when others were beaten with the leg of a broken chair or an iron rod. But the anticipation of a rap was worse than the physical pain. Even so, at the end of the interrogation the fingers of my left hand were badly swollen.

A man appeared at the side door and beckoned my interrogator, who went out of the room with him, leaving me alone with the teenage soldier.

"What is going to happen to me?"

He quickly glanced at the closed side door and then said quietly, "Don't worry. You'll be sent to a correctional labour colony for a few years. There will be many others of your age."

That was bad news, but I consoled myself by thinking that the boy was either trying to scare me or did not know what he was talking about.

My interrogator returned with another officer. Back at the desk he quickly read aloud what he had set down and asked me to sign it. Though I could not understand even half of what he had read out in Russian, I signed. Then he pressed a button on his desk. A soldier came in and was ordered to take me back to my cell.

The alarm clock that stood on the table in the entrance hall said nine o'clock when the escort handed me over to the turnkey—well past our morning teatime. The turnkey produced a loaf of bread from a wicker basket covered with burlap, cut off half of it and gave it to me. This was double the daily ration. I hid it under my coat and entered our cell. There, Roman and Zynio Lempicki, the old hand Soltys and others surrounded me in a tight circle.

"How was it? What did they ask you? What did you tell them?"

There were no revelations for them in my story except the part about being hit with a pencil. When I showed them my swollen fingers, they shook their heads in disbelief. They had all been through the interrogations already. Theirs seemed to follow a similar pattern to mine with one exception—not one of them was physically abused, not in the slightest. As I talked about my interrogator, the Lempicki brothers, as well as the consumptive postal clerk Oborski, recognized him as the same one they had and judging by remarks he made to them, he had also been questioning their sister Irka and her fiancé Tadzio. Roman Lempicki had found out his name and rank. When he was signing the report of what he'd said, Roman managed to decipher our interrogator's signature at the bottom of the statement. It was Kolopayev, Major of the Black Sea Fleet.

As December dragged on, the Polish prisoners began talking about arranging some kind of Christmas Eve celebration. For years the Roman Catholic Church has insisted that Easter is the principal religious holiday of the year. But the Polish people attach far greater importance to the observance of Christmas, especially the traditional family Christmas Eve meal, *Wigilia* (the vigil), when we follow a ritual of embracing and kissing on both cheeks. In Polish we call this a kiss from a double-barreled gun. This follows the communal breaking and sharing of thin wafers like those used during mass for holy communion. The origins of *Wigilia* go back to the solstice rites of pre-Christian times. These celebrations have always had strong nationalistic overtones. Even the Christmas carols have patriotic overtones. And in nativity plays, Polish kings and heroes of yore mingle freely on stage with Herod's entourage, while Polish shepherds clad in colourful, regional peasant dress try hard not to pinch the bottoms of the comely angels standing in front of them in their diaphanous gowns.

There was no danger of that this year. But for most of us even an imitation of the Christmas Eve meal was important, and so we agreed to observe the obligatory fasting from dawn to dusk, to forgo our noon soup and to save our daily bread ration for the evening supper of bread and water.

Everything went well. Instead of delicate white wafers we broke crusts of black bread together, while wishing each other an early release and the next Christmas at home with our families in a free Poland. Homesickness and reluctance to rile up our guards kept our caroling down to humming and crooning. We were just finishing our feast with "marzipan cake," improvised from a soft chunk of bread sprinkled with that day's half-teaspoon ration of sugar saved from morning tea, when the door was flung wide open and a platoon of soldiers marched in. They started a search. And what a search! Clouds of dust filled the room as soldiers began ripping off the burlap from our sleeping decks and turning over the layers of flattened straw underneath it. The whole place looked as if hit by a dust storm. The searchers were crawling under the platforms, checking every ledge and cornice high up the walls, peeking inside the stove and inspecting floorboards for any sign of looseness. Every piece of clothing was meticulously inspected while we stark-naked prisoners were being herded from one corner of the room to another.

We did not know whether the search was ordered to disrupt our counter-revolutionary religious celebration or because some stool pigeon reported conspiratorial conversations among the Poles. Whoever ordered it got slim pickings for his effort—a pocket mirror, a nail file and two six-inch spikes. The searchers looked upon these spikes as dangerous weapons and went to great lengths trying to find the man who hid them in the straw. We knew it was Kubacki, the "high life" buff, who had pried these spikes from the wall and stashed them away under his spot. But he was gone and two Bukovinians were now sleeping in his place. They, yelling at the top of their voices, accused each other of hiding the spikes. The cheeky gambler Silberman added to the confusion by mischievously backing up first one, then the other, shouting, "Yeah! Yeah! I saw him burying these swords in the straw! No! Not him. The other one. No! I am wrong. That one! They all stink alike."

The guards took both of them outside for further questioning but soon brought them back without laying any charges. The Bukovinians scowled at Silberman who wagged his finger at them.

"You can fool Tovarish Komandir but not M-i-s-t-e-r Silberman! You idiotescu, stupidescu, peasantulu, Rumunescu!"

He hated them and the other Bukovinians there for their eagerness to denounce and betray each other.

Our first real shock came one morning a few days after Christmas when the guards dragged in a man who had been taken for interrogation during the night. They hauled him in with his feet trailing behind him. We couldn't see his face because his head was bouncing off his chest as they pulled him along the narrow passage between the platforms and threw him face down on his place. He was unconscious but kept moaning. Then we saw that the shirt on his back was covered with congealed blood and welded to his back. There were bloody stains on his trousers. The guards withdrew without a word. That morning for once there was no need for them to open the door and bawl out, "Enough of this noise! Quit yakking!" There was an unusual hush in the room. We all talked in whispers.

I don't know if I ever knew the name of that middle-aged man they dragged in. He had never mixed with anybody but always kept to himself. A nondescript character. He was still unconscious or asleep at noon when the soup came. Even in the evening he did not react when bread was being distributed. Aron, the trusty, placed his ration on the burlap close to his face. At night he managed to hobble to the barrel to relieve himself. Next morning he sat up. His face was full of bruises. He slowly chewed bits of bread which he first dunked in hot water. We could see that eating was painful for him. He would not talk to us. Before noon the guards took him from our cell for good.

The two waist-high barrels that served as our latrine stood beside the window. They had a plank across the top for squatting and they had to be emptied every day. It was not a pleasant job. They were heavy and as often as not were overflowing with urine and excrement. Two staves, on opposite sides of the barrel, were longer and stuck up above the others: They had holes cut in them near the top. A stout wooden shaft would be pushed through these holes. It took two strong men to lift the barrel and, with the pole on their shoulders, carry it some hundred yards beyond the barracks to the edge of a deep ravine to empty it down the steep slope. There were some perks attached to this lowly task. It let the carriers have the joy of being in the open air for a while and gave them a chance to cadge a puff or two from a cigarette smoked by the soldier who escorted them. The Bukovinians had usurped the right to carry out and empty the stinking barrels.

There were two young men in our cell, both Polish, whose confinement here was perhaps even more wearisome than for the rest of us, because Czortkow was their hometown. Though pleasant and polite, they were not outgoing types. They kept to themselves and we learned little about them. Whenever the guard looked for shit-barrel carriers, the two would hide behind other prisoners as if afraid that the guard would select them for the slopping out. But one day they were doing it in such an ostentatious way that it caught the eye of the Bukovinians, whose inferiority complex was stirred by the sight of two Poles who put themselves above that kind of work. The Bukovinians complained to the guard on duty that day. His name was Kaplan. He already had a reputation among us as a loudmouth and a boor.

"Is that so?" sneered Kaplan. "Well, well. Come, come, you two gentlemen with the lily-white hands. Put your coats on and take the shit out. Right now!"

The two began getting dressed slowly and reluctantly to the accompaniment of snide remarks by the delighted Bukovinians and urgings of the equally amused guard. They heaved the barrel up clumsily, nearly spilling its reeking contents and carried it out with an air of hurt dignity. They were followed by two Bukovinians with the second barrel.

A few minutes later we heard some commotion and shouts coming from outside and we saw a few soldiers running through the courtyard. In less than half an hour the two Bukovinians brought back both empty barrels. There was no sign of the gentlemen shit carriers. Obviously forbidden to tell us what had happened, the two Bukovinians kept mum. But in the evening, cajoled and bribed with a piece of bread by the trusty Aron, they spilled the beans. Huddled together in a corner they told him in low voices the story of the Poles' disappearance. At one point in their story Aron couldn't contain himself any longer. His sudden loud guffaw made us all jump. Aron found the story too funny to keep to himself. Wiping away tears of laughter, he came over and told us that when the two Poles carrying the barrel reached the edge of the ravine, they swung the barrel back and forth with "A one and a two" but before "three" they flung the contents backwards onto the escort soldier behind them and vanished down the brown ice glissade. The soldier had lunged forward to stop them but slipped on the fresh excrement and fell, dropping his rifle. By the time he retrieved it and got up, the two had indeed given him the slip.

After that there was a lot of merriment among us non-Romanians at being banned from slopping-out duties. Michiel needled the Bukovinians by saying loudly, "When you are born a shit carrier, you stay a shit carrier for life, whether in Romania, Poland or the Soviet Union."

A few days later the impudent gambler Silberman volunteered to carry out the barrels. The guard glared at him and said something uncomplimentary about Silberman's legitimacy and the alleged profession of his mother. Silberman acknowledged the remarks with a benevolent smile and, spreading his arms in an exaggerated helpless gesture, added "I just thought—"

Chapter 4

ONE STAR SING SING

The sixth of January, 1940. Epiphany. In Poland, we call it the Day of the Three Kings (the Three Wise Men). But for Ukrainians, whether of the Greek Catholic or Greek Orthodox religion, who still go by the Julian Calendar, it is Christmas Eve. But there were to be no celebrations that evening. Not even covert ones. As soon as it started getting dark outside, we were told to pack up and get ready to go.

Army trucks with tailgates down were waiting for us in the courtyard. They loaded us on the open trucks five at a time. The first five were ordered to sit down on the truck's floor with their backs against the wall of the driver's cabin, their knees up and their legs open. The next five sat down between the legs of the first row, their backs pressing against the chests of the men sitting behind them. The next row of five was seated the same way, and so on, all in all thirty or thirty-five prisoners to a truck. In the gap between the last row and the closed tailgate stood two armed soldiers, facing us. We prisoners were nailed down by the weight of men sitting in front of us. The last row aboard was facing the gun barrels of the two guards. There was not much time to speculate about our destination. After a short ride the trucks stopped in the courtyard of the main prison in Czortkow.

It was a new, modern prison. High concrete walls surrounded the building. There was a watchtower in every corner. We were taken straight into a wide underground corridor for roll call. There we found some of the men we were first shut up with but separated from for nearly a month. It was a brief encounter. We had a chance to talk and exchange the latest prison gossip, and soon realized that none of us had any idea what was in store for us. Then we were taken off in small groups to different cells for a meticulous search. The windowless underground cell I was taken to was gloomy, lit by a solitary, dim yellow light bulb.

The prison staff who conducted the search were a forbidding-looking lot. They were recent recruits from the local population. Although they could have spoken to us in Ukrainian, Polish or Yiddish, they insisted on speaking broken Russian to flaunt their new importance. Afraid of catching lice, over their uniforms they wore womens housecoats in flowery patterns of rose, lemon and other dainty shades. I did not find it funny but macabre and scary, like seeing a hangman masquerading as a clown.

The guards took away all our clothes, leaving us only our shoes, and steered us into the shower room. Hot water gushed from shower heads mounted high along one wall. It was a pleasure to get the grime off our skins although the smidgen of soap handed to each of us was no bigger than a sugar cube. After the shower, we were issued prison garb—long underpants, a torn shirt, coarse linen trousers and a loose smock made from unbleached linen with a red stamp on the front: "*Wiezienie w Wisniczu. Skladnica No. 1*," Polish for "Wisnicz prison. Warehouse No. 1." Wisnicz was a large pre-war prison near Cracow. Along with the clothes each man was given an aluminum spoon and a shiny aluminum bowl with Wronki (the name of a prison near Poznan) stamped into the metal.

A prison official checked a list and read aloud the names of the Lempicki brothers, the two doctors Weissglass and Epstein, their unhappy guide Kielec, as well as his friend, and me. He ordered a guard to take the seven of us to Cell Number 42. That was on the third floor, and we walked up through the brightly lit flights of stairs. Access from the staircase to each floor was blocked by a grating made of shiny steel bars extending from wall to wall and floor to ceiling. In its centre was a heavy sliding door with awesome locks and latches. On the third floor the guard handed us over to a fat turnkey. On each story, a gallery like a long balcony ran along the four walls around an open well, which allowed guards to see the galleries on the floors above and below them. On the wall side of the gallery were the cell doors, made of solid wood reinforced with metal plates. Each cell door had a number painted on it and a "judas," a spy hole covered with a metal flap. On the open side overlooking the well, the gallery had a continuous steel railing. Looking around I was dumfounded by the sight of it all. While we were cloppity-clopping along the gallery, being herded by the beer-bellied turnkey, Doctor Weissglass, who was walking in front of me, turned his head around and whispered, "Sing Sing." I nodded with a half smile. A certain amount of pride crept into my heart. I was in a real prison.

The turnkey opened the door, and we saw a small man standing in the middle of the cell. Instead of a prison uniform he wore a shabby and shiny brown suit. He had short legs. His face was wrinkled like a shrivelled apple. Bat-like ears stuck out from his head, which he held tilted to one side. He stood with his hands in his trouser pockets, scratching the calf of his leg with the shoe on his other foot. He was not so much looking at us directly as studying and appraising us, the newcomers to his cell. He was the only one in the cell, and after the turnkey slammed the door he said to us politely, "Good evening, gentlemen. My name is Misior and I am in charge of this cell—Cell Number 42."

It was our turn to introduce ourselves, which we did with the utmost formality, shaking hands and bowing our heads. I noticed that his hands were tiny, almost childlike. He listened to our introductions attentively and asked us a couple of times to repeat a name to make sure he got it right.

I looked around the cell. I never expected anything like it, although I knew that it was a modern prison built in the thirties. The parquet floor was shiny and the walls painted white. The two horizontal windows with heavy bars were too high to look out of and anyway they had wooden screens tilting out and up from the sills so inmates could see only a rectangle of sky. A cast-iron radiator, albeit only lukewarm, gave an illusion of heating. But the most surprising thing was a gleaming white, flushing toilet tucked away in the corner. Thin mattresses were rolled up, stacked against the walls and covered with coarse grey blankets. Hanging in the centre of the blank wall, printed in Russian, and mounted on sturdy cardboard were "The Rules of Internal Order in NKVD Prisons." This was to be our Russian language primer. The rules listed the duties and privileges of prisoners. However, rule number one made all the others irrelevant. It said, "Prisoners must fulfill every demand of the prison staff."

We bombarded Misior with questions about conditions and life in prison, and he fielded them competently as only an old lag could. He freely admitted that he was a professional thief now awaiting his trial for stealing a few boxes of soap. For him, prison was a second home—he had done a fair number of stretches before the war. He benefited from being on good terms with the few prison guards who had managed to keep their jobs from the pre-war days. For us he was a gold mine of useful information and of many tricks that helped to make prison life bearable.

One of the first things we learned about him was that he attached great importance to dreams. He said he often dreamed about a fist fight with his brother who, he told us, was to be the main witness for the prosecution in his soap-stealing case. At least in his dreams, he always clobbered him. He referred to his brother as a whoreson, and then would add, "I shouldn't be saying that because our late mother was a decent woman. But a whoreson he is."

Misior often would be called outside for, as he put it, "further questioning about my case." At that time I saw nothing unusual in it and accepted it as a perfectly legitimate reason for his frequent absences from our cell. But in hindsight I see he was a stool pigeon whose job was to report on our conversations and on anything else that could be of interest to our investigators.

The cleanliness and orderliness of our new prison was matched by its strict discipline. These were holdovers from pre-war Polish times. Food, unfortunately, was no longer the same. We listened in disbelief to Misior's tales about prison meals in pre-war days: beef goulash, kasha, pea soup and unlimited amounts of bread. And we shook our heads when he told us prisoners had rioted over that diet — they found it monotonous.

We were slowly starving. This was our second month of imprisonment, and every day we were getting hungrier and hungrier. For breakfast it was lukewarm, black ersatz coffee. Nothing more. Noon was the big meal of the day. First we got a bowlful of soup made of a few wedges of mangel (a type of beet normally used as cattle fodder) boiled in salted water or a so-called "potato" soup named after the sediment from overboiled potatoes that settled to the bottom of the warm water. The second course was about a spoonful of boiled millet or mashed potatoes scraped into the rim of our bowls with a wooden spatula. In the evening we would get our daily ration of bread: 550 grams—just over a pound. The bread seemed to be a mixture of wheat, corn, oats, bran or whatever else was available. It was light grey in colour. A vaguely sweet, warm, straw-coloured brew, referred to as tea, completed the daily menu. It took real willpower to save even a small piece of bread crust to eat with my morning "coffee."

Besides starving we were suffering from cold. Winter that year was one of the harshest in memory. The temperature in the cell was barely above the freezing point. Our summer prison garb—linen jackets and trousers—was not enough to keep us from shivering day and night.

The day started with the sound of latches sliding, keys being turned in the locks, and the opening and slamming of doors along the corridor. Then the turnkey would come into our cell. Each of the turnkeys had his own way of waking us up. The new ones with stars, hammers and sickles pinned all over their civilian jackets and trousers would shout sharply in Russian "Reveille!" The pre-war ones who had retained their jobs said simply "Get up" or "Good morning" in Polish or Ukrainian, and the beer-belly fatso barked in German in his low bass voice "Auf!" (Up!) Then we had to roll up our thin mattresses and blankets and stack them up against the wall. Under prison rules, they remained there for the rest of the day. We could stand or walk or sit, but we were forbidden to stretch out on the floor. We were allowed to talk, but not too loud. And that's what we did all day long and well into the night.

One new guard, a swaggering young Jewish fellow, was the most abusive of them all, swearing at us in crude Russian. When a prison officer visited our cell the ever *comme-il-faut* Zynio Lempicki took him at his word when he asked if we had any complaints. Pointing at the surly guard, who just happened to be on duty at that time, he complained in pidgin Russian about the guard's coarse language. I suspect that the officer understood only the swear words

Lempicki repeated, plus "Soviet Union" and "uncultured"—the word which fans the flames of the inferiority complex smouldering in the heart of every Russian. The officer was taken aback. A prisoner, a foreigner accusing the Soviet Union of doing something uncultured?

"Very well," he said, "We'll look into it." And we never saw that abusive guard again.

I think it was Doctor Weissglass who did most of the talking. He was interested not only in urology, his specialty, but also in many other subjects which were indispensable to people who wanted to be considered members of the intelligentsia. Doctor Weissglass was well read and *au courant* with the latest events in arts and science. He loved to talk about Cracow, the historic city in which he grew up and worked. He was proud of being a graduate of the famous medieval Jagiellonian University in Cracow and of having studied under a foremost surgeon in pre-war Europe, Professor Adam Gruca, who in later years also taught my sister Maria. With equal enthusiasm he talked of the venerable medieval buildings and walls and gates of Cracow, and of little cozy cafés, of the scholastic world and its luminaries and of the shady characters from the city's underworld. Street people had often been his clients at the emergency ward of the Holy Spirit Hospital during his internship there.

Short and ginger-haired, Weissglass was not only a good storyteller, he was always ready with witty remarks—sometimes cutting. He had a well-developed sense of humour tinged with cynicism and couldn't resist getting off a good riposte even if it deflated somebody else's ego. But we welcomed being able to enjoy a laugh, even if it was at the expense of one of us.

Weissglass's stories about Cracow became even more interesting after Doctor Epstein, a gynecologist who was also born and educated there, took exception to some of Weissglass's anecdotes. A big man with a spherical head and black hair, Marys Epstein seemed twice as large as Weissglass—in all dimensions. He was less erudite than Weissglass, but he spoke English (he had spent some time living in London) and German. And he vied with Weissglass for recognition as the true connoisseur of Cracow's lifestyle.

As well as being an anglophile, Doctor Epstein was an aficionado of German lieder and Wagner operas. Often constipated, he would spend a lot of time sitting on the toilet seat. It was then we would be treated to his singing verse after verse of long German ballads like "Nach Frankreich zogen zwei Grenadiere" or "Wer reitet so spaet durch Nacht und Wind?" followed by a creditable rendition of arias from *Lohengrin* and *Parsifal*. As he sang the prolix "In a faraway country where the Alps glooow, stands a castle known as the Monsalvaaaat!" the strain caused by his affliction would help him hit high notes.

Epstein's down-to-earth talks on pregnancy and childbirth were listened to with keen interest by the entire cell. They gave me more insight into the complexity of the female anatomical labyrinth and its working than any lectures I attended or handbooks I read before or after. For Kielec, the sturdy farmer from Stecowa, most of it was a revelation, even though he had been married for many years and was a father.

I also did my share of talking, perhaps too much for some people's liking. I was always ready to discuss and question both doctors' stories. At the beginning they treated me with condescension like a precocious upstart. That softened a bit when they started discovering that I could add to Weissglass's list of titles for volumes in the saga of *Les Thibault* and supply a missing line in one of the Heine ballads sung by Epstein. But he then put me down again, saying that my German was very bad and my German accent was atrocious. I enjoyed showing off my knowledge of geography, but they drew the line at Kanchenjunga and Popocatepetl, flatly accusing me of making up unpronounceable names. On that, Misior the thief sided with the two doctors.

Roman, the obedient philologist, sometimes corrected the doctors' Latin, pointing out grammatical mistakes they were making in their medical terminology. They just laughed it off.

"It's good enough for us. If you find it difficult to understand, that's how it should be. Same as doctors' writing is for the pharmacist, not for common people."

One day a guard who was dishing out our midday meal dropped a glob of boiled millet on the floor. After he left, our eyes were glued to the yellow lump as firmly as the lump was glued to the floor. It was Doctor Epstein who made the first move. He crouched on the floor and began eating the gooey stuff, which he scraped off the floor with his spoon. As we were watching this, some with envy and some with disgust, Weissglass quipped, "Epstein, just wait till we get invited one day, when this war is over, to some elegant dinner in Cracow, dinner jacket, black tie and all. I swear I'll fling on the floor some of whatever we're eating there and say: 'It's for you, Doctor. Go ahead! I know you like eating off the floor.'"

The big man looked up at Weissglass with disdain. "You're just mad because I beat you to it." Which probably was true.

Meanwhile, the interrogations went on. As before, prisoners were taken from their cells in the middle of the night and brought back exhausted and bleary-eyed in the morning. The NKVD seemed to want to tire out the prisoners and to throw their biological systems out of kilter. Their resistance lowered by the lack of sleep, they would be easier to intimidate and to get to confess even to crimes they didn't commit.

Moreover, in those days, as I learned later, high officials in most Soviet ministries, and even lesser officials in the NKVD, all worked at night. It was because of Stalin. He liked to work at night and demanded an immediate response to his questions and orders. No official who might be called upon dared to be away from his desk when a telephone call came from the Kremlin for him, or for his boss who in turn might expect information from him for an answer. Whether there were any rooms for interrogating prisoners in the building we were in, I cannot say. But several times at night we heard men howling and screaming from pain. They could have been belaboured by a NKVD goon or a prison guard punishing them for some breach in the prison rules. The noises came from the basement floor of the prison but the walls around the central open well acted as a resonance box, which intensified the agonizing sounds. A couple of times it was the same man who was beaten. We recognized his yelling, which would start with a series of moans accompanied by the thud of blows. The rhythm of the beating was constant but the pitch of the victim's cries rose higher and higher, changing to short dog-like yelps and ending in a loud almost inhuman scream. Once we heard a woman being beaten or tortured, and her plaintive and muted whimpers and sobs affected us more than the men's loud yells. The following day everybody in our cell was subdued and hardly a word was spoken.

We never talked about these beatings although we all heard them. Misior's allusions to the "night games in the cellar" brought no response from us.

I don't know about the others, but I was scared and my nights were filled with silent, selfish prayers that it wouldn't be me who was taken downstairs for an interrogation. So one night when the cell door opened, and I heard my name half-whispered by the turnkey, my heart started to pound and my legs to shake. But instead of taking me to the basement, the guard took me outside to the courtyard and then into the waiting van for transporting prisoners. It was a frosty night, but I was so scared that I didn't feel the cold, though all I had on was my thin summer prison uniform. The ride was short, back to the NKVD barracks and offices where I had been questioned before. Moments later I was again facing my interrogator, the Major of the Black Sea Fleet, Kolopayev, who gave me a cursory look and said aloud to his teenage acolyte, "Here comes another poor innocent who was bamboozled into running away from the Soviet Union by some wily bastards who have miraculously vanished from the surface of the earth. But, somehow, the little angel found himself in a Soviet prison."

Then, turning to me he added, "Let me tell you this, you crafty little Pole. Under the Soviet rule of law, innocent people are not held in prison. You understand that? So as you are a prisoner, how can you claim to be innocent? You imbecile!

"Sit down! Hands on the table! And now, Topolski Boguslaw Aleksandrovich, tell me all about yourself. How come you wanted to escape from the Soviet Union? And what about this?!"

He waved the small sheaf of permits from the Polish Navy to visit the Oksywie naval base on the Baltic that they found on me at the time of my arrest—the very souvenirs I was so proud of and eager to take with me when I left home.

"What about these permits from the Admiralty?! What the hell were you doing at a naval base?! Whatever did you go into a submarine for? Your shifty answers betray your guilt. You are too stupid to outwit us. I know everything about it, but I want to hear it from you! Start with telling me the names of the Polish officers who were dispatching you to Romania."

As he was taking down my statement, his pen at times ran ahead of my story. Again he prompted me with occasional raps with the pencil across my fingers. After he finished a page he would place it on top of the other completed pages, meticulously aligning their edges. He eyed the growing file with pleasure, as if aware that his performance appraisal by his superiors depended on how much he wrote.

But that night Kolopayev was less interested in the details of my unsuccessful escape to Romania than in solving the mystery of my official permits to visit a destroyer and a submarine at the Polish naval base near Gdynia. These permits bore the heading "Ministry of the Armed Forces, Navy Department" and equally imposing signatures and stamps at the bottom of each sheet. Kolopayev kept looking at them and then at me and shaking his head. He could not reconcile them with the figure of the slight sixteen-year-old who sat in front of him and who looked more like a twelve-year-old to boot.

"What the devil would you be doing inside a submarine?"

My honest explanation that it was a reward for winning a warship model-building competition was also beyond his grasp. In the end he removed the perplexing papers from my file and put them aside.

They brought me back to the prison before dawn. But this time nobody gave me an extra chunk of bread before I was taken back to our cell, Number 42.

Misior, the thief, listened with great interest to stories told by the two doctors and by the Lempicki brothers who also had a lot to say about their life at the university in Lwow. Their lifestyle baffled him.

"Why do you need a seven-room apartment if there's only four of you in your family? And why buy a car when you got the money to take a taxi any time? And all that Latin? You know what's that for? I'll tell you. It's a secret language for those phonies in cassocks from the Black International, for doctors and for people like you, so the other guys won't understand you when you want to gyp them. But that's fine with me. Gypsies got their lingo and we thieves got our cant. But, mind you, we don't make money like you do, just by speaking it. We gotta steal to make a living—or work, if we're too stupid for that."

Misior was neither angry nor jealous. He just wanted to give us a piece of his mind for our alleged vainglory which he thought plain bullshit. Now he stood with his back to the radiator and his hands clasped behind him. His eyes shifted from one face to another awaiting our response which took some time to come. It was the well-read Weissglass who took on himself the role of our spokesman.

"Mister Misior, you are absolutely right. What you've said is true. But we were born into this highfalutin mire. And our parents were. And even if we tried to wash it off ourselves, some of it would stick to us. It has sunk too deep into our skin to wash off. But there is nothing wrong with it. It's neither better nor worse than Gypsy lingo. It's just different."

Misior was visibly impressed with the urologist's reply and also pleased with himself for becoming a member of the Cell 42 Debating Society. He celebrated it with a smoke. It was a long routine. From the depth of his pockets he fished out a couple of cigarette stubs which the few friendly turnkeys (who remembered him from pre-war days) would, as if by accident, drop on the floor. Then he would dredge with his fingernails the lining of his pockets for strands of tobacco fallen from the stubs. Whatever he found there he would add to the tobacco retrieved from the stubs, pile it on a piece of paper and roll up a neat cigarette. Smoking was not forbidden in the cells but the guards were not permitted to give any cigarettes or matches to inmates. Lack of matches was no problem for Misior. He had a cig-arette lighter that required no fuel and no flint. It was like a string toy we played with as children. We used to thread a string about three feet long through two holes of a button, tie the ends together and loop the string around the middle fingers of the left and right hands with the button hanging down between them. With a few circular swings we wound up the string and then pulled our hands in and out to make the button spin first one way, then the other, faster and faster until it would hum. But in Misior's hands it was not a toy. It was a tool.

With deft fingers suggesting years of practice, he looped one end of the string over his big toe, freeing a hand to hold a matchbox packed with charred cotton cloth. A few twirls and pumps and the button was soon a blur. He tilted his toe to touch the spinning button to the cast-iron radiator. Sparks flew. Some fell onto the charred cotton cloth making it glow. He blew gently on it and with a few drags lit his cigarette. It was all done within seconds. The button had to be porcelain or mother-of-pearl, he explained, in order to make sparks.

He also told us about another way to light a cigarette. But that was possible only when a paramedic or a nurse visited the prison cells. One prisoner would ask for a small wad of cotton with a few drops of glycerine on it to relieve an imaginary feeling of roughness and burning in his nostril. Another would beg for a pinch of potassium permanganate so he could dissolve it in water to gargle for his sore throat. These two ingredients, when mixed and then squeezed hard with the heel of a shoe, would burst into flame. I saw it done later in another prison, and it worked just as he said it would.

It was also Misior who showed us that an aluminum bowl placed against the wall could be used as a primitive stethoscope. With the rim of the bowl tight to the wall surface and your ear pressed to the bottom of it, you could hear people speaking on the other side, though the sounds were muted and the words garbled.

We were getting used to the prison routine. But not the starvation diet. Food became the main topic of our conversations. Finding a morsel of disintegrating potato in one's soup was a great event and warranted congratulations and comments from everybody. Between meals we talked a great deal about the dishes we ate at home or in restaurants. And woe to him who interrupted Roman's description of a succulent roast duckling stuffed with apples and served with new potatoes in dill sauce, or Epstein's exploit of eating exotic concoctions in a Chinese restaurant in London.

"You must have been really hungry to eat that," remarked Misior. Epstein (who had a big belly to fill) and Roman complained of hunger more than the rest of us. We all thought it inconceivable that there could be a shortage of millet or potatoes. "Why wouldn't they give us more of them?" Epstein wondered. "After all, potatoes are used to feed pigs."

For something to do, Epstein and Weissglass gave each of us a thorough physical examination. When my turn came, the two doctors each tapped on my chest and back, and put their ears against my ribs to listen to my lungs. Both heard some rumblings they didn't like. They were concerned about my health in such a cold prison with so little food. I could see their long faces as they glanced at me and talked quietly to each other in long Latin phrases. However, they had reassuring words for me. "It could be serious. But don't worry. You'll be out of here soon. And with rest, good conditions, and lots of good food you'll get over it." To help cheer me up, the well-read Weisglass quoted a Jewish proverb that says whenever there is total darkness it can only get lighter. But what we didn't know was that we were still a long way from total darkness.

One day, one by one, we were taken downstairs to have our hair clipped because of head lice. For me it was like a tragedy. In those days well-groomed hair was just as important for young men as for young women. Like the others I still believed that I might be set free any day. I couldn't bear the thought of having to be seen by my friends with my head shorn so, especially by Krysia with her rosy breasts.

It was Monday, the 22nd of January, 1940. Another uneventful prison day was drawing to a close. The night shift of guards was on duty. We started unrolling our thin mattresses, getting ready for another night's sleep on ever-empty stomachs.

Just as we were lying down to the sighs and grunts of Kielec, who was trying to find enough room on the narrow mattress for his muscular and knotted body, a rifle shot rang out from the direction of the main gate. We all sat up as if on command. Before we could exclaim, "Did you hear that?!" or, "What was that?!" several more shots cracked through the frosty winter night followed by shouts and yells from inside and outside the prison.

We heard the guards running in the corridors, slamming doors, clanging bolts and squeaking the sliding iron gate at the end of the corridor. In the din that followed the first shot, the shouted commands were hard to understand, although we heard clearly the voice of one man bellowing in Russian, "Shoot from the watchtower!" That was followed by a short burst of machine-gun fire. We could also hear rifle shots coming from a distance and a few muffled booms of exploding hand grenades. By then prisoners in some cells had started banging at their doors. The two Lempicki brothers, usually so passive, surprised us by saying, "Let's try the door. Maybe it will give in," and began pushing it with their shoulders. The farmer Kielec stepped in and said, "If you want to do it, do it the right way." He told us to stand up and put arms around each other so as to make a tight bunch of bodies as far away from the door as possible. Then with short steps we were to increase the speed as we lunged forward and slammed into the door like a living ram. Kielec placed himself and Epstein, who was the bulkiest of our group, at the point of impact. We were so caught up in the excitement of the moment that nobody thought about what we would do if the door did indeed give in.

"Ready? Okay. Hold tight! Forward!"

Even in that tense situation Zynio, with his dry sense of humour, found something amusing or absurd because he grinned as we started running. Half a ton of human flesh and bones slammed into the door. Nothing happened. We broke neither the door nor the locks. But the constipated Epstein broke wind, which sent Zynio into paroxysms of laughter. This annoyed his earnest big brother Roman, who was so distraught by the whole business that he tried to hit him.

The rifle fire ceased. The guards outside stopped shouting. But we could still hear orders being given in a quiet voice. The prisoners stopped banging the doors. The screeching of the sliding gate at the end of the corridor sounded the jarring finale. Suddenly it was quiet. We strained to hear. But the silence was interrupted only by the sound of the measured steps of the turnkey pacing the corridor.

We talked in whispers almost until reveille. Everybody agreed that it was an attempt at a breakout—perhaps even a successful one.

In the morning, when the turnkey wheeled in the cauldron with acorn coffee, Misior, who knew him well, managed to winkle some news out of him. The night's pandemonium was not an attempt to break out. Just the opposite. It was an attempt to break in and free the prisoners. It had failed. Some of the attackers were caught and a lot of suspects arrested in town.

"Soup will be thin today," said the turnkey. That meant more prisoners to feed.

Chapter 5

IN TRANSIT

A few days after the attempted break-in a guard told me to get ready to go. Where? What for? He would not say. Misior was sure that I was going to be released because of my young age. He had also convinced himself that he would be freed any day now because even if convicted for stealing soap, his sentence could surely not be longer than the three months he had already spent in prison.

"Don't forget to visit me in my little house here," Misior invited me. "There is always something to eat and a snort of hooch for guests—unless that whoreson brother of mine drank it all already. The place is easy to find. About ten minutes walk beyond the station, Gliniana street, number three."

I was not released. They transferred me one floor down to a "single" cell, Number 38. When I got there, there were already two prisoners in it. Both were young, maybe a year or two older than me. One, a tall and handsome fellow, wore a short, bluish serge coat with a grey lamb fur collar and matching fur hat. His trousers were tucked into handmade, high, black leather boots. He carried his heavily bandaged left hand on a sling. A fledgling beard and moustache added a little solemnity to his youthful face. He looked like a portrait of a typical insurgent from our 1863 uprising against tsarist Russia as painted by Artur Grottger, a 19th-century Polish artist whose works glorified that fateful period of our history.

His name was Kozakiewicz. He came from a hamlet near a little town called Nowy Pohost on the former Polish-Latvian border. Today that area straddles the Lithuanian-Latvian border. The people living there were well known for their steadfastness, honesty, piety and unwavering patriotism. In many ways their lifestyle was akin to that of the early Pennsylvania Dutch. They tried to be self-sufficient, and they scorned machine-made goods, preferring those handmade by themselves or by others like them. And they worked hard on their farms, raising cattle and breeding big, strong draught horses which resembled Percherons but were also good for riding.

Kozakiewicz, though older and dwarfing me, always addressed me as "Sir." He had been captured in the Carpathian Mountains a thousand kilometres away from his hamlet when he was trying to cross the southern border into Hungary and so go on to France. When he had heard that a Polish army was being formed on French soil, he felt it was his duty to join it.

After his arrest, when he was being escorted to a frontier post, he tried to flee his captors and got shot by them. The bullet shattered the bones in his left hand and lodged inside it. They operated on him in the Czortkow prison infirmary, setting the shattered bones and removing the bullet. No anaesthetic.

He kept inviting me to visit him in his hamlet "when the war is over."

"Come and see me there, Sir. You'll see for yourself the God's country we live in. The forests, the lakes and rivers. It's beautiful all year round. You'll eat the best bread you ever tasted in your life, with fresh cream butter every day. For breakfast, milk still warm, straight from the morning milking. Sausages flavoured with marjoram. You ever had a ham from a wild boar cured in juniper smoke? And the pickled mushrooms and preserves our women make. Come! The larder is always full."

What impressed me most about him was the way he said his morning and evening prayers. Not for him the furtive mumblings lying down with his head covered with a blanket. He would go down on both knees, his body straight like a candle. Lifting his eyes to the small, barred window, he would make the sign of a cross with broad gestures and recite his prayers in a loud clear voice. During prayers he would repeat, "God, have pity on me, a sinner!" and beat his chest with a closed fist. It sounded like a big drum being thumped. His prayers were that of a free man who just happened to be locked up in a prison cell. He never asked God for anything but extolled Him and thanked Him for everything. Even the turnkey who opened our cell door would remain quiet until Kozakiewicz finished his prayers.

The other fellow in the cell was an unhappy teenager, bitter and weepy. Denounced by somebody to the NKVD as a member of an underground organization, he was arrested and accused of "counter-revolutionary activities." He really was not sure himself whether he did belong to one or not. He said that he just talked with some of his pals about the secret anti-Russian organizations to which their fathers and grandfathers had belonged, and they thought that they should start one too.

In a few days he was taken from our cell and a sturdy-looking guy stepped in, Staszek Mazur, a farm boy with a perpetual grin on his round face and—a welcome sight—healthy, red cheeks. An easy-going, cheerful fellow, he made friends with everybody in no time. A farm boy he might have been, but he felt equal to if not better than anybody in the entire world. He said that, thanks to his father, he already knew as much about farming as any greybeard in his village. He boasted that he was just as at ease with a plough horse as with a four-in-hand team when he drove a bridal couple to the church on their wedding day. This happened often because no one in the village could crack the whip louder than he could.

Staszek talked a lot about the village girls, especially one he hoped to marry but not before he was "Jesus's age"—thirty-three was considered by many the right time for a man to start a family. I don't remember his beloved's name or age but I do remember him saying that she had "tits like turnips and nipples so hard that you had to be careful not to get your eye gouged out."

The prison governor came to inspect our cell. It was the middle of the night and we didn't know who he was until afterwards when the turnkey rolled his eyes as he whispered his rank and office. The governor was less than five feet tall. He looked terrifying and hideous to me, like an evil Rumpelstiltskin. His long overcoat swept the floor, almost always hiding the toe tips of his highly polished black boots. His enormous, hooked nose separated two pitch-black eyes half-covered with heavy eyelids. His face was sallow and his eyes drilled through the person he was looking at. He called each prisoner in our cell by name without once looking at the list he held in his hands or consulting the turnkey. But he didn't say anything else. He just looked us over like a hangman appraising the weight of condemned men for his noose. By his accent and the name we knew he was from the Caucasus, either an Armenian or, like Stalin, a Georgian.

Then one day I received a parcel. It wasn't really a parcel, just a ball of butter, the size of a small cabbage. It was wrapped in a square linen serviette. There was no message attached to it and the turnkey who brought it was not allowed to say who sent it. But I recognized the napkin by its hem stitching. It was from my family—the first sign that they knew what had happened to me and where I was. I inspected the butter. It was hard, nearly frozen. I waited until dinnertime when the usual watery soup with a few grains of millet arrived. Then I added half a spoonful of butter to it. And I gave even less to Staszek. I felt that it was better to eat it that way instead of—as Staszek suggested—spreading the butter thickly on bread and making a feast of it. The soup with the small lump of butter in it tasted heavenly.

Early in February, I was moved to yet another cell. This time it was Cell Number 2 on the ground floor at the end of the corridor next to the prison kitchen. It seemed they wanted to have all the younger prisoners together. There were seven or eight of us in it, all under eighteen. Among them I recognized Gryz, the proud, young, tile-stove builder from Silesia, who played tricks on the guard in the large detention room in the old barracks. The others were new to me. Four of them were from Zaleszczyki, a town on the Romanian border. One of them named Tomkow, a high-school dropout, was accused of unspecified counter-revolutionary activities. Sooner than the rest of us, he realized that no defence or alibi would clear him from our captors' trumped-up charges and he adopted a rather unusual form of defence: massive self-accusations. He told us with glee how his interrogator, a young NKVD lieutenant, was sweating and running out of paper as he tried to keep up with Tomkow's inventiveness and write down all his confessions. Tomkow poured out incriminating stories about himself: hiding on the roof behind the chimney and pelting the entering Soviet troops with clay roof tiles; cutting power lines to plunge Zaleszczyki into total darkness; tearing down Soviet posters; splashing ink on Lenin's portrait on the front wall of city hall; and putting salt into sacks of sugar in the co-op store.

The interrogator was beside himself with joy at having found an exemplary "enemy of the people" who was not only confessing to all charges but eagerly adding such horrid crimes that the interrogator himself would have had a tough time trying to make them up. However, after a few weeks the dim and gullible lieutenant began viewing the ever-growing file of Tomkow's confessions with apprehension. Could someone really black out an entire town by snipping just a couple of wires? And surely this cunning *Lyakh* (a derogatory name for a Pole) must know that only an insane person could contemplate committing such a hideous outrage as splashing ink over the face of the Father of Revolution? What if his superiors took the accused's stories as a joke?

So at the next session he interrupted Tomkow's story (this time about crossing illegally to and fro over the Romanian frontier disguised as a nun).

"You lie!" the lieutenant yelled.

"Of course, I do!" cheerfully admitted Tomkow with a disarming smile on his face. "But now I realize the futility of trying to conceal the truth from a person of your astuteness and sagacity and I confess that everything that I have told you was a damned lie. You see, Citizen Lieutenant,"—prisoners were not allowed to use *tovarishch* (comrade), only *grazhdanin* (citizen)—"living under the capitalist system made such a liar out of me that I cannot tell whether I am lying or telling the truth."

The lieutenant paled at the thought that his laboriously built case was about to collapse through the machinations of that Polish reptile, Tomkow.

"Don't give me none of your lip, Tomkow! You are charged with anti-revolutionary activities and it would be better for you if you confess before we apply other means of extracting confessions from you!"

"Heaven forbid that I should try to keep something from you, Citizen Interrogator!" Tomkow then proceeded to spin yet another tale about how he misdirected a Soviet tank regiment that was passing through Zaleszczyki into a narrow cul-de-sac and how it took them two days to extricate themselves. But when he noticed the lieutenant scowl and stop writing in mid-sentence, he turned meek.

"That's the truth, Citizen Interrogator, but if you don't believe me I'll take it all back."

We wondered whether what he told us was true. But we wanted to believe it. It brought some humour into the dreariness of our prison days and it was refreshing to hear somebody making light of the Russkies so feared by most of us.

Three high-school students in our new cell were also from Zaleszczyki. All of them were accused of being counter-revolutionaries and were undergoing the usual routine at interrogations. One of them, Byczynski, was beyond redemption. His parents were "wealthy capitalists exploiting the working class." Their sin was to be the owners of a small hotel. Byczynski talked a lot about that hotel and about some important visitors who stayed there. Ministers of the government, generals, bishops, they all enjoyed the comfort, the hospitality and the food. His mother was the maître d'hotel and the chef. Zaleszczyki is located in what used to be part of southeastern Poland, the warmest part, where peaches, apricots, watermelons and even grapes grew in abundance. We made Byczynski describe again and again the dishes his mother used to prepare for the hotel guests: the czeczuga fish, pullet fried in fresh butter, baked potatoes stuffed with wild mushrooms, and cantaloupe filled with crushed ice and smuggled Romanian brandy.

Every day before our skimpy supper, all three of the students would "take a walk along the main corso in Zaleszczyki." Walking three abreast, they'd take eight steps forward, turn around at our cell's wall and take eight steps back to where they started. While they went back and forth like this again and again, they ran a commentary on everything they "saw" on their imaginary ramble.

"Hide your cigarette in your sleeve. Old Reiff [their math teacher] is walking on the other side of the street. Hello! Wanda!

[They would doff their school caps in Wanda's direction and smile.] See how she wiggles her bum? Now let's stop for a minute in front of the cinema and look at the posters. Not bad. Gharry Kuper and Loreta Yank. [For that's how we said Gary Cooper and Loretta Young in Polish.] Now, watch out. Quick! Cross the street before that old bore Gawlik gets a hold of us. Should we stop at the ice-cream kiosk?"

It went on and on like that for half an hour until they "reached the bridge" and turned around to start their promenade home. They were imaginative, and we all enjoyed their walks. But the mundane young stove builder, Gryz, who grew up in stodgy Silesia, was puzzled and bewildered by their daily pantomime. At last it became too much for him.

"I know and you know that you are not going anywhere and you don't see a soul. Why do you grown-up guys make fools of yourselves like this?"

"To preserve our sanity," shot back Byczynski.

It was in that cell that I suffered the worst toothache I ever had in my life. Before I was arrested I was being treated by our dentist, Dr. Karol Kaufman, who lived two doors from us. He had begun a root canal treatment on one of my molars before I left. And now in prison a cyst had formed on the end of the root. The root canal was blocked solid by Dr. Kaufman's temporary filling and the pus and gas forming there had no way to escape. Instead they kept pressing harder and harder on my nerve which was still all too alive. After a few days of agonizing pain, the pus pushed up around the root and the jaw bone. It made a plum-sized swelling on the edge of my gum. There was no dentist for us in the prison, only a paramedic who could do nothing. He did not even have an aspirin to offer me. All he said was that when my head swelled up like a balloon the pain would go. And he was right.

Years later I learned how my family located me in Czortkow Prison. One day out of the blue, they received a telegram from the Lempickis' mother who lived in Lwow. It said, "Our children in Czortkow. Lempicka." They had never met her.

My family immediately started figuring out how to get to Czortkow to visit me. My father, being the sole breadwinner, was unable to take time off. My older sister Henia was pregnant at that time and living with her husband in Obertyn, a small town a day's ride from Horodenka which was not on a railway line. And so it was my mother, accompanied by my sister Maria, who made many trips to Czortkow trying to see me or at least to deliver some food and warm clothing for me. Time and again they were turned away at the prison gate. After many tries, the prison officials agreed to accept just one kilogram of butter. Nothing else. My enraged mother paraded back and forth in front of the prison gate holding aloft my little shirt—I still wore the size for a twelve-year-old—and shouting at the guards and passersby, "Look at the size of prisoners the Soviets are keeping in their prison!"

My dear mother was never afraid to make her feelings known to anyone at any time. If she felt she was being dealt with unfairly, there was no way of stopping her from speaking out.

Later during the Nazi occupation of eastern Poland my family was living in and around Lwow. One day my mother, who was then about fifty, found herself caught in a roundup of civilians. Each street leading out of the Lwow town square was blocked off by the trucks of German soldiers. They were surrounding and closing in on the people they found there—a standard way of arresting Poles. There was no hearing or trial for such detainees any more than there was for Jews and Gypsies—being Polish was guilt enough in the eyes of the Nazis. Poles died by the hundreds of thousands, starved, beaten to death or gassed at Auschwitz and the other concentration camps. When my mother saw the ring of soldiers tightening and people being loaded onto trucks, she marched straight to the highest-ranking officer she could see and began berating him in her accented but passable German.

"*Das ist eine Schande!*" (This is a disgrace!) she fumed. "I have to get home! I am already late and those soldiers of yours won't let me through!"

He was taken aback by her outburst and waved to the soldiers to let her pass. He then saluted her, and she trotted home to safety.

My family also tried to obtain my release by bribing NKVD officials in Czortkow. They did not know then that NKVD officials at every level of the Soviet administration were terrified of being denounced by somebody for helping imprisoned "enemies of the people." As a rule they would refuse even to meet petitioners. However, the local militiamen would hint to the naive that they had ways and means to reach the top commissars who could drop the charges and release the prisoners "but it would cost a lot of money."

After the war my mother and my sister Maria told me that they both fell for that. For a pair of golden earrings with emeralds and a matching brooch, a local militiaman promised to arrange a meeting with the "top NKVD man." That took time. They had to make several trips to Czortkow from Horodenka, which was not easy. Each time they had to spend nearly a day travelling on the train and then look for a brave person who would let strangers stay in their house overnight. Hotels at that time were out of bounds to the general public. Finally, when Maria reached the office of some Soviet official—he refused to meet Maria and my mother together—he greeted her with a broad smile on his face.

"You're wasting your time by coming here, young woman. We released your little brother yesterday, and he is already at home resting and waiting for his mother and sister to come back and prepare a square meal for him. So stop worrying and hurry back!" Maria told me it was not a convincing performance. They did not expect to see me at home.

About the same time a guard came into our cell one day.

"Topolski. Follow me!"

He looked at the thin prison uniform draped around my skinny frame, made a wry face and turned to Byczynski, the hotel owner's son. "Lend him your fur jacket there. He'll be back in a moment." In the corridor the guard looked me over once again. "Rub your cheeks a little. Put some colour in them. Now go slowly to the end of the corridor. Don't look left or right. Look straight ahead and stop when you get to the far wall."

It seemed to me that in the middle of the corridor I saw out of the corner of my eye some people standing behind the grill of a doorway. Somebody was trying to see me without being seen. But nothing happened, and the guard took me back to my cell. I have never found an explanation for that strange incident.

There was not much time for trying to guess the reason and ponder over that mysterious corridor walk. The next morning, February 19 (the day before my seventeenth birthday), I was taken down to a large room in the cellar. All my friends from captivity were already there—those caught with me on the border and those who joined us later in Serafince and Stecowa on our way to Czortkow. It was a real pleasure to be together again. We greeted each other like long-lost friends. It felt as if we had known each other for years. I was very happy to see the Lempicki brothers and Tadzio Siuta—their sister's fiancé who had promised my father to look after me. A turnkey brought our own clothes from storage telling us to get into them and give back the prison uniforms. Doctor Epstein thought of smuggling the prison togs out under his own clothes. What a souvenir they would make! Especially the jacket with "Wisnicz Prison" stamped on it in red. But it was too risky. We hurried to exchange the latest news and gossip while we could. Actually there was no need to rush. What we did not know was that we were to spend two days together in that large transit cell. The main news was the details about the shooting and explosions we heard on the night of the 22nd of January. Roman and Zynio Lempicki had shared a cell for a while with two young men from Czortkow who were captured during that ill-fated attempt to storm the prison and learned first-hand some of what had happened that night.

These two attackers, who were caught and put in cells along with the Lempickis, were somewhat reluctant to divulge all the details about their role in what eventually became known as the Czortkow Uprising. Legends about it abounded during and after the war. The post-war Polish Communist government was loath even to admit that there was any anti-Soviet activity in the Polish lands occupied by the Russians. Not until 1992, after the fall of the Communist regime, did I get a full and reasonably accurate picture of it.

The story started with the ZWZ (*Zwiazek Walki Zbrojnej*, the Armed Struggle Union), the umbrella underground organization branching out from Warsaw at the end of 1939 into both sides of the German-Soviet line. The ZWZ was in its early stages and many local commanders acted on their own without asking or awaiting approval from ZWZ headquarters in Warsaw. The ZWZ chief in Czortkow developed a plan for freeing prisoners held by the Soviets in the local prison and in the army barracks, as well as those sick or wounded prisoners kept under guard in the local hospital. To say that the plan was imaginative and bold would be an understatement.

The day chosen for action was the 22nd of January, 1940, it being the seventy-seventh anniversary of the outbreak of the January Insurrection by Poles against tsarist Russia which, in 1863 too, was occupying eastern Poland. On the chosen night, ZWZ hoped to muster about eighty men at the Roman Catholic cemetery. They were to be divided into three groups. The first and the strongest task group was to attack the old army barracks (where I was first held in Czortkow) and free prisoners held there. The ZWZ intelligence had learned that the Soviet army unit stationed in the old barracks was to be moved in the middle of January to the Soviet-Finnish front where things were going badly for the Soviets in 1940. The insurgents expected to face only a small detachment of regular soldiers at the barracks and a few NKVD men guarding the prisoners. The second group's task was to break into the main prison (where we were) either by the main entrance or by scaling the high wall and then getting through the service entrances from the prison courtyard. The last and the smallest group was to "neutralize" the soldiers guarding the special ward for sick prisoners in the Czortkow hospital. Some nurses who were party to their conspiracy had stashed away warm clothes for fleeing patients. A dozen of the seriously ill were to be taken to safe places in private homes and nursed there until they recovered enough to have another go at crossing the border illegally.

But what was to be done with the other two hundred or more escaping prisoners? Few of them were local people. They had no knowledge of Czortkow and its surroundings nor could they speak Ukrainian, which was the main language of that area. To solve this problem the conspirators turned to the railwaymen, for most of the trains there were still being run by their pre-war Polish crews. On the night of the uprising the railwaymen had a train under steam at the station ready to take the escapees to the Romanian border which was only forty kilometres away. They had also secured the co-operation of all stationmasters, signalmen, switch men and shunters down the line right to the railway bridge over the Dniester River at Zaleszczyki. There the train would ram through the barbed wire and the barricade erected by the Soviets in the middle of the bridge to mark the boundary between Romania and the USSR. Once in Romania the freed prisoners would be cared for by the Polish organizations there and sent by official and not so official routes to the Polish Army recruiting centres in France and Syria. All three places of detention—the barracks, the prison and the hospital—were not far from the railway station and the waiting train. The freed prisoners would have to run north along the main streets then turn east to cross the bridge and south again to the station—all in all a little more than about a ten-minute walk.

So it seemed that everything was prepared and taken care of. Then Murphy's Law took over.

At the appointed hour, 9:00 P.M., only half of the expected task force showed up at the cemetery. Not that the other half got cold feet and chose to stay at home. The official Czortkow time—then the same as Moscow's—was two hours ahead of the pre-war Polish time stubbornly clung to by some Poles as a symbol of still belonging to the Western world. Those who came at nine o'clock Soviet time were mainly young, gung-ho, impatient individuals. They were poorly armed, some with pistols, some with sporting rifles or shotguns, a few with hand grenades and some with no weapons at all. The only machine gun in their possession was to remain in the cemetery to be fired sporadically in order to draw the Soviets' attention away from where the three groups were attacking. After waiting for half an hour, those who had arrived at the cemetery at 9:00 P.M. Russian time decided to start on their own rather than wait for another two hours for more men who might or might not show up.

The first group reached the main gate of the barracks without attracting anybody's attention. An unarmed high-school student, Czajkowski, jumped the guard and strangled him with his bare hands. The others rushed past him into the entrance hall and engaged the soldiers inside it in a wild free-for-all. The alarm went up and suddenly they were being surrounded by more and more soldiers running out from the barracks. Their intelligence had been wrong. The Soviet regiment had not left for the Finnish front but was still in the barracks. In the melee several guards were wounded. Most of the attackers turned around and escaped, leaving behind them half a dozen of their colleagues who were either wounded or overpowered and captured by the guards, among them Czajkowski. Not one of the prisoners was freed.

Things went as badly for the second group tackling the main prison where I was. These insurgents could not even break through the main gate. Rifle shots were exchanged and a few hand grenades tossed. The attackers also failed to scale the walls. In the end they were forced back by machine-gun fire from the watchtowers.

However, at the hospital the third group did better. The few guards there were quickly overpowered, gagged and bound. The sick prisoners were let out without any bloodshed. They were taken to hideaways in town where they stayed until fully recovered. What happened to them afterwards I don't know.

As soon as they got the message about the failure of the plan, the railwaymen cancelled all the arrangements for prisoner evacuation and passed the message down the line. So good was the spirit of conspiracy and secrecy among them that the NKVD and their local hirelings never learned about the existence of the "Romanian Express."

Having exchanged what we knew about the uprising and other news, we sat around in the crowded transit cell waiting. All we knew was that we were about to be moved from Czortkow prison to somewhere else. But where? Probably another prison. We spent the time in endless speculation about our next destination. Tarnopol, a large city in that southeastern corner of Poland, was mentioned most often. The optimists were still hoping for release any day. After morning roll call on the third morning in the transit cell, we were told to get ready to leave. I decided to write a note to my family in case I got a chance to pass it to somebody outside the prison. Tadzio Siuta, my mentor, had a tiny piece of pencil lead and the resourceful old-timer Soltys gave me a piece of pink paper about the size of a candy wrapper. It was part of a pre-war blank railway ticket for "prisoners and accompanying escort." Holding the short piece of lead with my fingernails, I scribbled on the back of it.

Please convey to the following address. Horodenka, Ormianska St. 9 for Mr. A. Topolski that his son Boguslaw received the parcel. That he is sound and in good health and on 21st of Feb. 1940, he leaves Czortkow in a transport for an unknown destination, possibly for Tarnopol.

Please kindly transmit this news to the above address.

This I wrapped in a piece of stiff brown paper, the bottom of a Soviet cigarette packet found in the lavatory. I printed on it "Attention. Letter" and slid it in the wide cuff of the sleeve of my overcoat.

In less than a quarter of an hour we were being loaded onto the waiting, open trucks, where we sat packed in as before, pinning the man behind us. This time I was one of the last men on the truck and as a result I found myself sitting next to the guard, my face almost touching his knee. He was perched above me on the corner of the truck's box where the side panel met the tailgate. He steadied himself by holding the top of the side panel with his right hand. His left hand clasped the barrel of his rifle, which he planted firmly on the truck floor for balance.

The truck convoy moved fast along the streets of Czortkow. It was cold with blowing snow. The morning shift of factory workers was going to work. When they stopped to look at us we could see their eyes in the gap between the peaks of their cloth caps and the edges of their upturned coat collars, which they held fast with gloved hands. They would nod sadly as we passed them. I removed my note from the cuff of my sleeve and pressed it against my cheek with the palm of my hand. I made it look as if I was protecting my face from the freezing wind. I caught sight of two teenage girls dressed in high-school uniform coats. They were standing on the curb of the sidewalk looking at our truck. I flicked my wrapped note into the gap between the soldier's coat sleeve and the edge of the tailgate. For a second it hung in mid-air. I feared the updraft would blow it back into the truck. Then it floated down and landed on the ridge of snow between the street and the sidewalk curb. I thought that, before our truck turned into a side street, I glimpsed one of the girls stoop and pick up the note. In a few minutes we reached the railway station.

What happened to my note written on that pink piece of paper? Some unknown person delivered it the very next day to our house in Horodenka. Nobody saw him or her. My family found my note on the kitchen table along with a short letter. It is more than forty kilometres from Czortkow to Horodenka and at that time there was no bus service between the two towns, and almost nobody had a car. Even private phones were rare outside the big cities. One could go by a train as my mother did, but it was a circuitous trip that would take most of the day. Translated into English, the letter that accompanied my note says:

Czortkow. 21.2.40

Dear Madam!

Walking along a street I found this note which I am sending to the address written on it. I found it wrapped in thin cardboard with "Attention. Letter" inscribed on it.

Probably, you will recognize your son's handwriting. I would like to add that our sons being driven in Soviet trucks were dropping cards with requests to notify their parents etc. Therefore I hurry with this news to calm and console you, Madam, at least in part, though I am a total stranger, but I also have a son.

H.P.

It's still a mystery to us how anyone could travel there so quickly. My note was addressed to my father. But the stranger's letter was addressed to my mother. That and the reference to "our sons" suggest it was written by a woman whose son was also in prison. The spelling, grammar and handwriting are those of a well-educated person.

So it was apparently not the high-school girls who picked up my note from the snow-covered street. I have never learned the identity of the woman who found it and wrote the accompanying letter. My sister Maria guarded and saved my note and the letter through the turbulent and dangerous years of the Soviet and German occupations, and they are now in my possession.

As soon as we reached the railway station, the guards started loading us on to a long train of boxcars. A burly NKVD sergeant shouted out our names from a list and pointed at the yawning doors of the boxcar we had to clamber into. There were forty prisoners to a car. Although of Polish make, these cars had recently had their interiors altered to make them fit for transporting people—at least, fit by Soviet standards. All they did was increase the floor area by rigging up a sort of raised deck to make room for more people to lie down, put in a primitive wood stove fashioned out of an old oil drum, and cut a hole in the floor to serve as a toilet. After the parquet floors, flushing toilets, mattresses and blankets of Czortkow prison, the boxcars we were being shoved into looked dismal indeed. Cold and dark, they had a layer of frozen mud on the floor.

With the exception of the three *tipografs*, all the men from our group captured at the border and those who joined us later in Serafince and Stecowa were now among the full complement of forty prisoners in our car.

It was devilishly cold in our boxcar and the sight of a heap of coal on the floor next to the cold stove just added to our frustration. With no wood and no matches we had no way to kindle a fire. But one man was more determined than the rest of us to do something about it. And no wonder. He was the last one ordered by the guard to climb into our car. Even his name was not yet on the list of prisoners. He had been taken from his home only a few hours before. The soldiers who arrested him were in such a hurry that they wouldn't even let him put his coat and hat on. He was dressed only in a tight army jacket, trousers and shoes. He shivered all the time. With his white, frozen fingers he was probing every board on the wooden deck until he found one with a long crack in it. With his bare hands he tried to pry it from the deck. Two Bukovinians, who saw what he was trying to do, came to help. They pulled and pulled one side of the cracked board until their hands were purple. Finally, the wood gave way and they tore off a long slat from the board. By then they were sweating. The rest was easier. They splintered the slat by stomping on it and then, by hitting the sticks of wood against the edge of the stove, smashed them into smithereens. By the time the guards brought in our bread rations and a bucket of water, the coat-less latecomer had built an elaborate wood and coal pyramid inside the stove. The guard, cajoled and beseeched by the entire car, deigned to leave us an almost empty box of matches. After a few unsuccessful tries which brought our hearts to our mouths, the flames caught on and our Prometheus in the tight army jacket took the best place in front of the stove. No one disputed his right to it.

One good thing about such makeshift stoves of thin metal is that they get red-hot in no time. Soon it was so warm inside the car that those sitting close to the stove took their coats off. A few strong-willed men who hadn't immediately gobbled up their entire bread ration were now toasting pieces of it on top of the stove. The car smelled like a bakery. Heavenly scent.

The square hole in the floor, our toilet, was much in demand and the uniformly grey cone was growing fast on the rails below. "It really looks as if a giant shat there," remarked the ever-constipated Doctor Epstein with admiration.

During my visit to that popular spot, I somehow dropped my white, knitted wool hat on the floor. It fell into a lagoon of urine. I felt I couldn't pick it up. It seemed too revolting. Besides, I still had my school cap. The man who kindled the fire saw me leaving my sodden hat on the floor. He touched my shoulder:

"If you don't want it, I'll take it."

"Go ahead. It's yours."

"Thank you." Prometheus wrung out the dripping hat which by then had changed from white to canary yellow. He stretched it with his hands and held it for a while over the hot stove to warm it up before easing it over his head.

"You have to dry it on your head, otherwise it'll shrink," he explained.

The train left Czortkow during the night. Soltys, who was nesting on the upper deck near the barred narrow window, looked outside at the starry sky and said, "It'll be Tarnopol all right. We're heading north."

Tarnopol greeted us with bright sunshine and 30°C below zero. Our train stopped a couple of hundred metres away from the station. We crowded around the two small windows, taking turns to peek outside. An asthmatic locomotive levitating on a cushion of steam kept shunting the headless snakes of railway cars. We waved and shouted to the muffled up figures of railwaymen walking by and puffing out plumes of steam with each breath. They did not respond and steered away from our train as if avoiding contamination. But it was the sight of two or three wider railway tracks matching the Soviet gauge that we found foreboding.

Soon enough we were treated to the spectacle of a Soviet train passing through the station. We were flabbergasted by the sight of the mammoth engine rolling in slowly and a woman driver who was leaning out from the driver's cabin. She was looking ahead at the clump of semaphores, screening her eyes with her mitt. As the engine was passing our car, she pulled the whistle cord and two mighty blasts shook the station.

The engine trailed behind it an equally imposing cortège of huge cisterns and boxcars, all of them painted mustard yellow. After the train passed the station we looked at each other with disbelief and gasped "Wow!" But young Gryz, the stove builder from Silesia, muttered, "It's propaganda." Kielec, the farmer–cum–aircraft spotter from Serafince, looked awed by this display of Soviet might. He scratched the stubble on his chin. "I'd be scared to find that in my bed." Later it clicked for us that he meant not the train but the woman engine driver.

We spent all night and the morning of the next day waiting for any kind of food, but to no avail. However, more coal was brought in, so at least we did not freeze. In the afternoon the doors to our boxcar were rolled open and a gust of freezing air rushed in together with the yells of several armed guards facing the open door of our car. They were standing on the snow-covered ground below so that all we could see was their heads and shoulders.

"Hurry up! Get out with your belongings!"

Other squads of guards were standing not far from each boxcar's door. The cars had no steps and the floors of the cars were high above the ground. To get down we had to slide backwards on our bellies over the rim of the boxcar doorway, lower ourselves until we were hanging down suspended on our elbows and then drop. Some of us did it well. Others lost their balance on landing and fell on the packed snow. The guards found it amusing and laughed loudly. Then a guard would take the prisoner a few metres away from the group.

"Get undressed!"

The body search started. We had to strip stark naked, take off our shoes and socks and put all our clothes in a heap in front of us. The day was sunny with almost no wind but it felt at least 30° C below zero. In spite of the cold, the search went on in a routine and unhurried manner.

"Turn around! Bend down! Squat! Raise your arms! Let's see the sole of your left foot! Other foot!" The guard looked up my nostrils then inside my ears. He was astonished that after two months in prison I still had a small silver pendant around my neck with the Virgin Mary on it. He called his *komandir*.

"Look at that *bozhenik* (god thing) on his neck. How did he manage to hold on to that? What'll I do with it?"

The *komandir* took the pendant between his thumb and index finger to look at it, holding it away from himself like some kind of venomous insect. Then he rolled it into a ball inside his palm and threw it away as far as he could over the railway tracks.

"That's it. There's no need for any protocol."

The search continued. Inside my shoes. Inside the band of my cap. Each item was examined carefully and each seam in my clothing probed with fingers.

It was getting colder and colder. When you have clothes on, you can do a few things to warm yourself up. You can pull the collar up over your chin or pull your hands inside coat sleeves. Rub your cheeks with your gloves. Or kick one shoe against the other. There isn't much, though, that you can do to warm yourself when you are standing naked in subzero cold.

The same search was going on all along the train. When the guard finished with me, I put on my stiff and icy togs. The guard ordered me to join the bunch of men already searched. Some of them were still trying to button themselves up with numb fingers. One of them pointed at something behind me. I turned around and for the first time I noticed that about a hundred metres from us there was a bridge over the railway tracks. The railing was crowded with women, men and children, watching the scene unfold along the tracks below them. Some of them waved to us. Others shouted to us, but we were too far away to catch their words. A couple of women lifted small children high up to let them catch the last glimpse of their fathers or brothers. More and more people coming from both ends of the bridge were joining the crowd of onlookers. The sounds of their voices gradually merged into an ominous hum. Our guards kept casting nervous glances at the growing crowd above them. Amidst the sea of faces I could make out the figure of a bareheaded priest. Clad in a black cassock, he held his hands up in a gesture of silent benediction.

Chapter 6

ORIENT EXPRESS

Suddenly the cries on the bridge became even louder. As we looked at the people, we heard behind us the clunking sounds of a train being shunted in on the track parallel to ours. A long line of boxcars with the brakes screeching and doors wide open came to a halt right in front of us.

The mustard-coloured boxcars were three times the size we were used to and the train was on the wide-gauge Soviet track. As soon as the train stopped, the guards started merging batches of prisoners into larger groups. They read our names from long lists and ticked them off with pencils held clumsily in their mitts. More NKVD soldiers arrived, some with fierce-looking German shepherd dogs on leashes. Thirty or so men from another car were added to our group.

The convoy commander caught everybody's attention by blowing a whistle. He stood on a baggage trolley beside the first car of the train. Dressed in a sheepskin coat, he wore felt overboots on his wide-spread feet. A Nagant revolver, leather map case and a kind of saddlebag—the usual *komandir's* paraphernalia—were dangling from his belt. A tall, fur hat at a jaunty angle over his smiling red face completed the picture of comfort and self-satisfaction. He raised his hand and bellowed the command, *"Po konyam!"* (To horse!) like a cavalry officer. His troops understood and, turning to us, responded with loud yells of, "Crawl into the car!"

That was it. I felt a slight twinge in my heart and glanced at the faces of men around me. They looked unruffled. Too unruffled to be really so. Zynio Lempicki, the art historian who seldom betrayed his feelings, stood next to me. When our eyes met, he closed his eyelids and tilted his head with a hint of a shrug. The corners of his usually sardonic lips curved up in a resigned smile. He picked up his bundle and started walking in the direction of the wide open maw of the fifty-ton boxcar. Others followed him. The guards stepped up their shouting. "Get in! Faster! Hop in!"

Easier said than done. Jumping down from a boxcar is not that difficult but to jump up from the ground onto this high boxcar floor was well nigh impossible. At the time, the *komandir's* "To horse!" sounded facetious to most of us. Now some took it as a useful hint. They bent over and clasped their hands as a stable groom would, making a step for others to mount the boxcar. Once up and in, the men above pulled in those left below. It was weird, almost as if the condemned were helping each other to scale the executioner's scaffold.

Inside there was the usual scramble for the best places—away from the toilet hole and as close as possible to the iron stove, and if there was no more room around the stove, a place on the upper deck, which was cleaner and warmer than the car's floor. The guards closed the huge sliding doors with a bang. There was no coal or kindling of any kind around the stove. Tiny, high, corner windows with heavy bars let in little light, so we were sitting in semidarkness. Someone said, "Hush! Listen!"

We could hear the sound of a song coming from the direction of the bridge over the tracks. The hundreds of people who stood on it were singing an old, solemn hymn, "O God, who for centuries covered Poland with a shining mantle of might and glory." Then the prisoners in one of the cars joined in. And then in another car, and yet another. Within seconds we added our voices to that unplanned oratorio. We sang our hearts out. In the pauses between verses we could hear the hysterical screams of women on the bridge.

The guards went berserk. Their orders to stop singing were ignored. They swore, blasphemed and shouted dire threats. In sheer desperation, they banged on the walls of boxcars with their rifle butts. Nothing would stop us. The singing died only with the last line of the hymn, "We beseech You, return to us our fatherland and our freedom." Many of us had tears flowing down our cheeks. Only the Bukovinians made no sound. They just stared blankly at us with their mouths open.

This was our second day without food. To all our requests and pleas for bread and water the guards would simply answer, "If you didn't get any, it means you'll get some." It would take us a long time to get used to this Mad-Hatter's-tea-party logic. We started banging and kicking the boxcar walls and shouting in unison, "We want bread! We want water!" Prisoners in other cars joined in. The crowd on the bridge responded with cries of "Red hangmen!" The situation got so tense that more NKVD troops arrived. They came with machine guns and dogs. The shouting stopped when the convoy *komandir* announced that the bread rations would soon be issued. But our escort felt uneasy about the mutinous mood of the prisoners and the possibility of an attempt at a mass escape. Instead of having a few prisoners from each car carry bread and buckets of water, the guards were doing it themselves, one car at a time. They also brought sacks of coal and kindling for the stoves.

Most of the prisoners gobbled the half-frozen bread ration, but nobody could eat faster than the poor Bukovinians who'd been starving all their lives. They just wolfed it, and when they swallowed the last bit, they would say *"Gata!"* (Done!) accompanied by a loud belch.

Some men would not eat their bread until they toasted it on the stove. We all knew that toasted bread tasted better and seemed to be more satisfying, but it took a strong will to wait for the fire to be kindled and to delay eating for half an hour or so.

One of the prisoners, a fellow who had once been in the Polish cavalry, lost his balance when the train jerked upon starting up. He tore into an old man who had chuckled.

"I am not laughing at you, my dear sir," said the greybeard. "In fact I was laughing at myself and my fate because often the highest form of despair is laughter. You see, sir, I was arrested and banished to Siberia by the tsar after taking part in the demonstrations against losing our voting rights in 1905. Then in the 1920 war, the invading Bolshies grabbed me in my village and shipped me off beyond the Urals and released me only after the Brest peace treaty a year later. And now it seems that I am again on my way to Siberia for the third time in my life. It's funny, isn't it?"

The old man fell silent. And only then we realized that without anybody noticing it our train had already left the station and was now gathering speed, wending its way in the direction pointed out by the shadows of telegraph poles cast by the setting sun.

We woke up in the middle of the night when the train stopped at a station. We could hear a railwayman's whistle and voices outside. Somebody ran along the top of our boxcar's roof.

"What's that? Where are we?"

"Pod-wolo-czyska," said Soltys slowly with his face glued to the small window. There was no open reaction to this five-syllable word. For some it was just a name of a place but the majority of us knew that Podwoloczyska was the last Polish town on the former Polish-Soviet border. Suddenly I had a lump in my throat, for Podwoloczyska was the full stop at the end of the Polish chapter of my life. What was beyond it was *terra incognita*. For twenty years the Soviets had kept their frontiers sealed lest spies, tainted news or subversive ideas from the "capitalist encirclement" attempt to penetrate the "paradise of the proletariat." Though officially the Soviets had made occupied Eastern Poland an integral part of the USSR, they kept the old frontier just as hard to cross as before. The frontier guards were still there, so was the triple barbed-wire fence and a wide strip of finely raked soil on which they could see the footprints of anyone who dared cross it.

Our train hissed its way into the red Shangri La. Neither imprisonment nor hunger had diminished my curiosity. At night there wasn't much to see there. The train kept stopping at small, dimly lit stations only to be promptly winked away by lanterns carried by the dark figures of railwaymen.

At daybreak, sitting at the small window high in the corner, I saw miles and miles of snow-covered, flat land and the occasional anemic imitation of a forest, then glimpses of little hamlets with houses stooping from age, many of them with thatched roofs. Some of the large barns and storage buildings were new and built of brick and concrete blocks. Around them were hibernating tractors half-buried in the snowdrifts. The small, open, flatbed ZIM trucks, all a

95

dusty military green and all the same size, were a common sight in towns and on the main roads, but most people seemed to be going by horse-drawn sleigh. Their horses were skinny and had ribs showing. This prompted our cavalryman to say, "People who keep their horses in such a deplorable state cannot be happy themselves."

On the second or third day of our journey through the Soviet Ukraine we got a treat. In addition to our daily ration of bread, they gave each of us a piece of *treska*, dried cod. There wasn't much of it—the portion was about the size of a pocketknife. It was glazed with salt and as hard as a piece of wood. We had to gnaw at it like a dog with a bone. Nevertheless we found it a delicacy. But the salt on it made us very thirsty and the guards refused to bring any more water than the usual couple of buckets.

We had no clue where they were taking us, but wherever it was supposed to be we were going there at a snail's pace. There was some commotion in the morning at the Zhmerinka station after we had spent a night on the sidings there. We could hear the voices of the guards running around cursing and swearing. The loudest of them was the baritone of the escort *komandir* letting off strings of invectives couched in obscene language of astonishing inventiveness. We were baffled by all these noises and a few days passed before prisoners from another boxcar told us what had happened that morning.

In one of the boxcars were two Polish prisoners who had happened to live in Zhmerinka before the Soviet rule and so knew the town well. They decided to escape. In the darkness of the night they managed to pry loose two floorboards and slipped out without attracting anybody's attention. During morning roll call, the guards found two prisoners missing and a thorough search revealed the loose boards. The escort combed the area around the station but found nothing. The panic-stricken *komandir*, who already saw himself doing a minimum of ten years of hard labour in Siberia for negligence, ordered the arrest of two innocent simpletons who just happened to be working nearby clearing the tracks of snow. They replaced the two escapees "To make up the number." The convoy *komandir* threatened them with dire consequences if they made any fuss about it. "At the end of the trip we'll sort all that out," he consoled them.

But he was not there when the time came to sort it out. During the roll call at our destination, where a new escort had taken over, the names of the two escapees were read out but nobody answered. The two "replacements" stood there mute and bewildered. The new *komandir* was quick to figure it out, at least to his satisfaction.

"So you two little birdies, you Trotskyite spies, you've caught yourselves in your own snare, I see. You gave false names to your interrogators and now you have forgotten them, you scum! We'll teach you to sing a different song!"

When the two started protesting their innocence, he looked at them with contempt and told them to leave their feeble excuses for the prosecutor who knew better than he did what to do with scoundrels like them.

Our next stop was Vinnitsa, a town of about 50,000 and a railway junction. Here we were put on another train and into a *stolypinka*, a railway car especially designed for the transport of prisoners. It was named after its originator, Stolypin, Minister of Internal Affairs in the tsarist government at the turn of the century. From the outside, it looked like any other passenger railway car but for the heavily barred windows. Inside it had a corridor running on one side for the whole length of the car. On the other side were cages about the size of the usual compartments in a passenger train. The cages were separated from each other by solid hardwood walls and from the corridor by a grill of heavy steel bars crisscrossed diagonally. The door was also a steel grill and had a hatch in it about a foot square for passing in food rations and water. At one end of the corridor was a squat-down toilet with no door, at the other end a cubicle for guards and a small "cooler"—a punishment cell. On the floor of each cage were two built-in benches. Above them, at chin level, were two wide shelves with hinged extension leaves. When swung into place, these would close the gap between shelves and form a mezzanine floor. Just over a foot below the ceiling, two narrow luggage shelves ran along the partition walls. The cage was lit by the light coming from the corridor and from a tiny window above the mezzanine.

We noticed that once we crossed the former Polish-Soviet border, the guards became more relaxed and talkative. They were no longer on "foreign soil." Here they felt more at home and more confident. At the big Vinnitsa station, they asked us if we had any money because they could buy tobacco for us here. Somebody in our compartment handed over a ten-ruble note to one of the guards. Our compartment soon changed into a smoking den as everybody lit cigarettes rolled from a packet of Okhotnichiy (Hunters') tobacco. It was the largest packet of tobacco I had ever seen, and it was accompanied by an equally large booklet of cigarette papers.

The *stolypinka* was heated (and, as we were to find out, overheated) by cast-iron, steam radiators. All the woodwork was oak and was heavily varnished to a deep brown. Indeed the whole car had an air of pre-revolution quality and solidity. A compartment, or "cage" as we called it, was designed to hold five prisoners. There were eleven of us in ours. "Don't complain," said one of the guards. "Sometimes we squeeze in twenty or more. So consider yourself lucky." There was only this one *stolypinka* in our train, the rest were the usual boxcars. In our cage, four men were on the benches at floor level: two Ukrainians from the Bukovina area of Romania, Gryz (the young stove builder from Silesia), and the cavalryman. Lying side by side on the mezzanine were the two Lempicki brothers, Tadzio, Doctor Weissglass and me. Above us, Soltys and the consumptive Oborski stretched themselves out on the narrow shelves near the ceiling. Soltys, who didn't feel too well, lay face up, his clasped hands resting on his chest. "Gentlemen," he said, "this is a good place to die. I hope I succeed in rendering my soul to God without making a nuisance of myself." Then he crossed himself.

"Amen!" said Tadzio, who disliked any kind of theatrics. "But while you are in full possession of your faculties, would you kindly bequeath your posthumous ration of bread to me?"

Soltys demurred, knowing very well that Tadzio's irreverent remark was less a joke than a scolding of his pessimism. We all joined Tadzio in making light of Soltys's forebodings. Only Doctor Weissglass remained quiet. We spent our time lying down. Twice a day the guards would take us, three at a time, to the toilet. That was not often enough for some, and they had to plead with the guards for additional visits. This and our constant requests for more drinking water

—the heat in our *stolypinka* was drying us out—made our guard grumble. "What strange people! All they do is drink water and go to the can!"

We talked with our friends and prison mates in the neighbouring compartments to our left and right. Irka and Lila (the doctor captured with Epstein and Weissglass) and half a dozen other women were in the third or fourth cage from ours. We saw them when they were passing our cage while being led along the corridor to the toilet and back, and we could exchange a few words as they passed. They all seemed to be in good spirits and always had some encouraging words for us. We also relayed verbal messages to them from cage to cage. It felt like the "telephone" game we used to play as giggling children garbling messages. But here it worked for simple things. One of these relayed messages was for me. It came from a stranger, a woman named Bronka Stachowicz. She said in an oblique way that a couple of times when crossing the border to Romania or coming back from there she had used our house in Horodenka as her hideaway. She got caught only two weeks ago. She said my parents were okay, and called my sister Maria a "brave young woman." She asked me to stay close to the bars next morning so we could see and identify each other.

The following day as they were going to the toilet, one of Bronka's two companions in front of her "twisted" an ankle as planned. When she fell to the floor, Bronka was able to stop at our cage and exchange a few words with me. She was over thirty and stocky, with short cropped hair. When she saw me she exclaimed with feigned disappointment, "Is that really you?! I was expecting to see a young man and what do I get? A pale little bugger! Still I am pleased to meet you. Keep your beardless chin up. Don't worry. All this stuff won't last. Nothing ever does!" The guard tried to interrupt her and get her to move along. She told him to shut up but soon had to give in and resume her unhurried amble to the toilet.

Weeks later, Bronka escaped from a prison train somewhere in central Russia and made her way back to occupied Poland. There she carried on with conspiratorial work only to be caught again. Sentenced to death, she survived in prisons until the amnesty for

Poles was declared. Soon she was busy organizing women's units in the Polish Army in the USSR. She told me her story herself when I visited her three and a half years after we first met in that *stolypinka* car. It was in her tent strewn with maps and ornate leather cushions in Al Mughar in Palestine. By then she was Commanding Officer of the crack 317th Polish Transport Com-pany operated entirely by women. Their exploits on the Italian front were yet to come.

Nearly a week had passed on the train since we had been given a hot meal or even a mug of hot water. Six hundred grams of moist, dark bread and a heaping teaspoon of sugar were our daily ration. There was never enough drinking water, mainly because the guards did not relish toting bucketsful from the faraway pumps in subzero temperatures. A couple of times a guard brought us pieces of bread wrapped in a kerchief. "Gift from the women in the other compartment," he said, shaking his head with disbelief. Thinking that they were making heroic sacrifices, we tried to send the bread back to them, but they persuaded us to accept it, saying that for some of them 600 grams was really too much. It seemed that the women were putting up with short rations and physical discomfort better than we were.

Doctor Weissglass kept his eye on the fading Soltys. All of us were getting weaker and weaker on this diet but Soltys was in the worst shape. Once, during a chat with a bored but kind guard, Weissglass told him that, as a doctor, he did not think we got enough food, and we could not go on like this much longer.

"Nothing wrong with your food," said the guard. "You can live on it until you die."

"I know that. But aren't you responsible to your superiors for our lives? What happens if one of us does die?"

The guard looked puzzled. He scratched his head and swept aside the forelock from his forehead on which a furrow had now appeared. He had to think it over. Nobody had ever asked him such a question before. Blinking his limpid blue eyes, he pondered a bit longer.

"Well, we'll cross him off the list."

It was a straight answer. But hardly reassuring.

Weissglass had some messages for Epstein who was in the neighbouring cage and for Lila who was in the women's cage. The three doctors were trying to co-ordinate their stories for possible further investigations but didn't want them blabbed along by our cage-to-cage "telephone." Now young Gryz, who was sleeping on the floor, had discovered gaps at the bottom of the partition walls. Thus it was possible to pass pieces of paper from compartment to compartment. He became our "postman" and with the help of neighbours was passing messages written on the flimsy cigarette paper. A Bukovinian who watched this clandestine mail business said that he was going to denounce Weissglass unless he gave him half of his bread ration. Weissglass beat down the price of silence to one-third of his ration. Then the moment the Bukovinian had gobbled up his ill-gotten gain, Weissglass told him that he was now an accomplice to the crime and so better be quiet and forget any more thoughts about blackmailing.

One of the less pleasant guards was making a real nuisance of himself by taking his duties more seriously than was necessary. He was always rushing us when we were in the toilet and was bringing us less drinking water than the others. He was short and squat with a shaven head, flat face and an upturned nose with large nostrils.

"Where did they dig up a creature like him?" somebody wondered aloud.

"That," said the cavalryman, "is what you get when two tractors mate."

One day Offspring-of-two-tractors thought he saw the cavalryman receiving a piece of paper with a note written on it from somebody in the next compartment. This time it was not a note but a pinch of tobacco, although he wouldn't believe it.

"Where is that note?! Give it to me! I saw it!" Getting nothing but a vacuous stare from the cavalryman made him even angrier. "Answer, you scum, when a Soviet soldier asks you a question!"

The cavalryman, who was sitting on the bench, shifted his weight slowly to one side, lifted his haunch a little and let out a loud fart, echoed by a salvo of laughter from the neighbouring cages.

Offspring-of-two-tractors was livid. If his rifle with fixed bayonet had been shorter and he could have turned it on the cavalryman from the narrow corridor, the enraged guard would have shot the cavalryman then and there. In the end he received five days in the cooler on half-ration. Of these he served only two because on the third day of his sentence our train stopped at Chernigov, the capital of the northernmost region of the Ukrainian Soviet Socialist Republic, and we were ordered to get out.

Chapter 7

DUNGEONS AND DRAGONS

The guards herded us onto an open platform not far from the Chernigov station building. It was sunny and cold. Very cold. The snow on the ground sparkled and tiny glittering needles of ice whirled in the air. Irka Lempicka stood with other women not far from us. She made a few steps in our direction. Stopped by a guard, she called to her younger brother.

"Zynio, I feel like I have just arrived in Zakopane!"

I wondered why she said that. Zakopane was a fashionable Polish ski resort for those who could afford it. It was and still is famous for its beauty, being framed by a horseshoe of sky-reaching peaks of the Tatra Mountains. And here there wasn't a hillock in sight. The only thing that could link these two was the keen frost burning our cheeks. Maybe she said it just to avert his thoughts from our cold reality.

The yells of "Get going! Get going!" by our escort drowned his reply. As we were leaving the railway station more rifle-toting soldiers surrounded our group. Flanked by them on both sides, we marched down the middle of the street through Chernigov. We were a sorry sight. Some of the prisoners had only summer clothes. Some were wearing sneakers. Those who were weak kept falling down only to be jerked up by the guards and prodded along with hefty kicks. Soltys hobbled along, stumbling a few times but keeping pace. When they saw us coming, people in the streets would scuttle into doorways or side streets. Those who stayed on the sidewalk would turn their heads away. Though it must have been a common sight for them, they knew that it was wise not to see or be seen.

The marching column stopped when we reached a large building that looked like a church. We could see only the upper part of it because a high stone wall with a barbed-wire fence on top of it blocked our view. When we got through the arched gate we found ourselves in a quadrangle paved with cobblestones. On one side of it stood a church with a stubby tower without a spire. Two- or three-story greyish-blue stone buildings formed the other sides and almost all the windows in the buildings were heavily barred and boarded halfway up. Well, once upon a time it could have been a church, or more likely a monastery, but now it was a forbidding-looking prison.

Pretty soon the entire complement from our cage in the *stolypinka* plus two newcomers were shoved into a dank, windowless cell. The narrow cell had a concrete floor, concrete walls and a high concrete ceiling with a lone, bare light bulb hanging from it. The only piece of furniture was a cylindrical cast-iron bucket with a hinged lid which served as a toilet. The turnkey told us that we were in quarantine and were to stay here for ten days.

The two new prisoners were lawyers from Prague, "Littman and Brohl" as they introduced themselves. They said they were Czechoslovaks, a clear indication that they were Jewish. Non-Jewish citizens of Czechoslovakia invariably referred to themselves either as Czechs or Slovaks. The lawyers' first language was German, although they could also speak Czech and Yiddish. Both of them were in their late forties. Their well-cut overcoats with shawl-style fur collars, Homburg hats and shoes with galoshes had an air of elegance befitting successful *"advocaty,"* as they called themselves. They had escaped to Poland when their native Prague was overtaken by the Nazis, but a few months later they had to flee the Nazis again when Hitler's troops invaded Poland in 1939. For a few months they lived in Soviet-occupied Eastern Poland until their arrest on unspecified charges by the militia only two weeks ago. Then they were put on the train, which brought them to Chernigov.

Perplexed and scared, they still retained their dignity and good manners. They were polite, almost deferential when talking to fellow prisoners. In no time my mentor Tadzio became Herr Doktor Siuta; both Lempickis—Herren Dozenten (docent); Soltys and his fellow cavalryman—Herren Kommandanten; Oborski—Herr Postmeister; and even I was Herr Student. For some reason they addressed Doctor Weissglass simply as Doktor.

Roman Lempicki, the timid Latin scholar, found a fellow soul in Littman. Once upon a time they had both started learning English, and now they were competing to see which of them could remember more English words. The game was simple but long lasting. One of them would say "flooor." After a long pause during which they were scanning their memories, the other would counter with "dooor." Deuce. This was followed by a short period of mutual congratulations, and then they both would lapse into silence. The game went on and on, sometimes well past our "bedtime." Once Roman nudged the sleeping lawyer and pronounced triumphantly "spooon." The startled Littman conceded, "Ja! Goot! Shpooon. For drink zoop. Goot night." Vantage, Roman.

Littman and Brohl were searched by the militia after their arrest. They were allowed to keep some personal items and Littman still had his pocket watch on him. It was a shiny silver, or perhaps nickel-plated, watch of modern design. When we told him that they would take it away from him at the next search, he showed it at suppertime to the turnkey and asked "Mister Tovarish" if he would be interested in buying it.

When the Mister Tovarish saw the proffered watch, his eyes lit up like the lights on Red Square on the first of May. He said, "Yes, yes. Of course," and promised to come back later on with money.

He did, when everybody was asleep. As the guards were not allowed to enter a cell alone at night, he just opened the hatch in the door, making only enough noise to wake us up. He beckoned Littman to come to the hatch. The wordless transaction went smoothly. Littman handed over his gleaming watch. The turnkey, licking his thumb each time, dealt out five-ruble banknotes from a stack that he held in his left hand. He kept looking over his shoulders and then studying Littman's face, waiting for an approving nod, which came at forty rubles. Both of them thought they'd made a killing.

The quarantine cell was dismal. We kept warm by huddling together whether sitting or lying on the damp concrete floor. But, after a week on the train diet of stale bread and water, the food seemed heavenly. Our daily bread ration remained the same in weight but tasted much better. The bakery was probably in the prison or very close to it because the bread arrived moist and still warm. Each ration had been scrupulously weighed and small bits of bread, some no more than half an inch square, were attached with wooden pins to the main portion in order to make up the regulation 600 grams. Twice a day we were getting watery soup. The occasional fish broth—fish bones and a sludge of some overboiled, coarse fish settling in the heavily salted water—was a real treat. A glob of boiled barley at noon and a brew from roasted chicory and dried berries with a teaspoonful of sugar in the evening completed the daily menu.

After ten days in quarantine we were moved across the courtyard to the main building of the Chernigov prison complex. The routine search followed. After so many searches, I thought, what on earth are they hoping to find? To my surprise they found several twenty-dollar gold coins sewn into the cloth-covered buttons of Tadzio's winter coat. The guards were fascinated by their find.

"Look at that! American gold dollars!"

There were no repercussions, just one more written record of a search, this time listing "coins of yellow metal."

Our new cell was a cavernous cellar, a real dungeon, with a vaulted stone ceiling and two or three barred windows up near the ceiling, which meant they were just above the ground level on the outside. For sleeping there were iron bedsteads with bare wooden planks—no bedding, just two beds, each for five men to lie across. Primitive perhaps, but better than the wet concrete floor of the quarantine cell, although here, too, drops of condensation kept falling from the vaulted ceiling onto the stone floor. Two evil-smelling cast-iron slop buckets stood like sentinels on either side of the heavy wooden door.

While we were making ourselves at home, more and more prisoners kept filing in. Half of these were Ukrainians from the Bukovina area of Romania. By the time the search ended there were about seventy men in our cell.

Next day they took us to the bath. Two *banshchiki* (bath attendants) took our clothes for disinfecting. They put them inside a huge steam boiler—big enough to walk into—to kill lice. The *banshchiki* were the first Russian prisoners we met. We tried to talk to them but they parried all our questions by putting their index fingers to their lips and shaking their heads. They were forbidden to talk to us. We spent a long time showering. There was plenty of hot water but the matchbook-sized slices of grey marble-like soap wouldn't lather. When we finished our much appreciated washing and returned to the changing room, we found that there weren't any towels to dry ourselves and that all our clothes had already been taken back to our cell. The guard opened wide the door leading to the outside and, pointing at the opened door on the far side of the courtyard, said "Run!" The men in front felt the full blast of icy wind and tried to back off but were pushed forward by those behind them. Littman, seeing that his efforts to push back with all his might were futile, cried, "We'll die of pneumonia! But what the hell. You die but once!" and sprang forward like a middle-aged gazelle. I followed him. It didn't feel that cold although it must have been at least 30°C below. After the scalding shower our skin was still hot. In a cloud of steam rising from our bodies, our naked bunch galloped through the snowdrifts into the open door and down to our cell. Nobody died. Nobody got pneumonia.

With so many people in one cell, our social life flourished. Two new arrivals had their own stories to tell. Both of them were accused of being couriers between the underground organizations in occupied Poland and the Polish government in exile. Captured in the Chornahora Mountains, one told us he was a ski instructor, the other a gamekeeper for some absent landowner. Their descriptions of the trails, mountain passes, meals and maidservants in the inns and hotels on both sides of the border rang truer than their alleged professions. Like Soltys and the cavalryman, they wore riding boots and breeches. When chatting, all four of them had the habit of standing with one leg on the floor and placing the other foot on the edge of the bedstead with their crossed forearms resting on the bent knee. Then they would sway back and forwards, stopping occasionally to rub off with a coat sleeve a speck of dirt from their boots.

In his stories, Soltys more or less admitted that he had been one of the bodyguards to the late Marshal Pilsudski, the virtual dictator of Poland from 1926 until his death in 1935. He said that in the last months of his life, Pilsudski became paranoid and shot one of his own bodyguards whom he mistook for a would-be assassin.

The routine prison life was often interrupted by unexpected events such as a nurse's visit. The moment she entered our cell everybody developed some kind of illness. She listened patiently to a hundred symptoms described in pidgin Russian by prisoners of five nationalities and then conscientiously dispensed from her portable mini-pharmacy aspirin, eye drops, Vaseline, iodine and a grey powder made from burnt and crushed animal bones (the common Russian remedy for acid indigestion or an upset stomach).

Once in a while the prison librarian brought in a basketful of books. Two or three were in Ukrainian, the rest in Russian. We'd pounce on them, or at least, we readers did. I guess that out of seventy men in the cell no more than half a dozen were interested in the books. We knew that Soltys spoke good Russian and was clearly an educated man, but he preferred to spend his time with his cavalry friends. I don't ever recall seeing him with a book. The variety of titles was truly amazing. Some, such as *A Short History of the Great Communist Party*, were to be expected. And there were books on Lenin and Stalin, as well as topical propaganda novels. But we also found some poetry and party-approved classics. Like some of the others, I knew the Ukrainian alphabet from pre-war times, so learning the Russian letters, most of which are the same, wasn't that difficult.

Once I could sound out a Russian word I sometimes was able to recognize it or at least find an approximate meaning from similar sounding words in Ukrainian, Polish, French or German. We pooled our thin Russian vocabularies and helped each other out when we could. Sometimes we asked a turnkey what a word meant. But more often it was the context that gave us a clue to the meaning of an unknown word. We enjoyed the books we read. It was like solving puzzles. It beat reading and rereading "The Rules of the Internal Order in the Prisons of the NKVD" displayed in every cell, which was all we had before the librarian's visit.

The real treasure for me was a book that dealt with air forces of different countries and had plenty of photographs and drawings of their diverse war planes. We were surprised at the detailed drawings of the British Bristol Blenheim bomber and the photographs of the French Devoitine, Bloch and Morane fighter planes.

"What an intelligence service the Soviets have!" marvelled Soltys and his riding-boot-clad companions. Years later I found out that these "scoops" were mere reproductions from weeklies freely available in the West such as the *Illustrated London News* and *l'illustration*. Apart from a few hazy photos of some vintage planes and of Stalin viewing a flypast of the Red Air Force, there was nothing in the book about Soviet planes.

It was in Chernigov prison that we were confronted for the first time with the rather unusual exigencies of Soviet censorship. The names and photographs of former communist leaders who had fallen into disgrace or were "eliminated" during Stalin's purges had their images blacked out or cut out from the pages of every published book. Thousands of people must have been working on these excisions. Some of them must have seriously contemplated suicide when they discovered that by cutting out the name of that renegade Trotsky they would mutilate the face of the Sun of Humanity, Stalin, on the back of the same page.

One day the Chernigov prison governor visited us. He asked a number of prisoners the usual questions: "Your age? Profession? Under what paragraph charged? Married?" and so on. He parried skillfully all questions about our future, court proceedings, the right to correspondence and what was going on in the free world. As we were cut off completely from the outside world—no letters, no newspapers, no radio—we attached great importance to every remark uttered by prison staff. When somebody complained about the quality of food, the prison governor said casually, "Well, you know how it is. Up and down. One day you get dry bread. Next day you may get French pastries."

That casual remark became the subject of many heated discussions and interpretations. One of the cavalrymen convinced himself that it meant the French government, as host of the Polish Government-in-Exile, had made representations to the Soviet authorities on our behalf and was going to send food to the USSR for the Polish prisoners.

Before the governor left our cell the Lempicki brothers and Tadzio Siuta pointed at me, and asked if under the Soviet penal system, the adolescent prisoners were entitled to special food rations. He thought for a while, said "Yes" and then added, "We'll take it into account." Sure enough the next day after everybody received their daily 600 grams of bread, the turnkey looked at a piece of paper with a name on it.

"Which of you is Topolski?"

"Me!"

"Here's your bread ration." He handed me a chunk of bread much smaller than the others. No more than 450 grams.

I raised Cain and didn't stop until the Corridor Supervisor came and explained what happened.

"Yesterday you asked Prison Governor Tovarish for the special ration for underage prisoners. These rations include butter, eggs, meat and cod liver oil. You are entitled to these, but we cannot give you something we don't have. However, we did cut your bread ration down to the prescribed 450 grams for the underaged. You understand?"

I had to wait another day to have my name struck off the "list of those eligible for special rations."

A few days later, I broke out in an itchy rash all over my thighs, chest and abdomen. I told the guard that I wanted to see a doctor.

"What's wrong with you?"

"I have this rash and it itches like hell!"

"Okay. I'll report it to the doctor."

Nothing happened. In the evening I called the guard again.

"I reported sick this morning with this terrible itching rash and the doctor didn't come!"

"If he didn't, that means he will come."

We always found that quirky Soviet logic very annoying. I spent half of the night scratching myself, but then I fell asleep and when I woke up in the morning the rash and the itching was gone. Both doctors, Epstein and Weissglass, thought that it was caused by the slightly putrid fish that was used for making our fish broth the day before.

However, two days later a guard told me to leave all my things in the cell and took me one floor up and along a winding corridor. At the end of the corridor he opened the door leading to a small cell and said "Get in!" I took one step forward and backed up immediately. Inside the cell in the dim light of a ceiling light bulb, I saw two naked black men sitting on the floor. The guard pushed me forward.

"Get in! Don't worry. It's the cell for those with scabies."

"But I don't have any scabies!"

"Get in! I am not a doctor. If you don't have scabies then you'll soon get them here. Take off all your clothes and smear yourself with *vilkinsonka*."

The two naked "black" men turned out to be two prisoners covered with the dark brown gritty ointment known as *vilkinsonka* (Wilkinson ointment), the Russian treatment for scabies. There was a large jar full of it standing on the window ledge. Both of my cellmates were Poles who—hoping for leniency—were trying to pass themselves off as Ukrainians and had adopted very Ukrainian-sounding names. They were born and had spent all their lives in western Poland, where no Ukrainians live, and their attempts to speak their fanciful Ukrainian were so funny that they themselves would stop in the middle of a sentence and burst out laughing. I found them cheerful and good companions. They talked a lot but said very little about their past. Being in the scabies' cell had some perks for us: no morning and evening roll calls. The guards, afraid of contamination, would just peek through the spy hole to make sure we were still there. And, as the cell was at the end of the corridor, we were often given an extra helping of whatever was left in the cauldron before it was returned to the prison kitchen.

I applied *vilkinsonka* religiously as a preventive measure and avoided catching scabies. After a few days I was taken to the bath for a good scrub and then returned "healed" to my cell.

In spite of the dripping ceiling, overcrowding and half-starvation we kept our spirits up. Joke-tellers were always in great demand and the cavalry squad held sway in that field. Because our dungeon was far away from other cells, we also got away with singing. The guards had nothing against it as long as it wasn't too loud. The Ukrainians took advantage of it and sang to their hearts content all day long. Harmonizing was part of their heritage. They crooned lengthy *dumki* folk songs in which sadness and gaiety mingled freely.

A popular game in which almost everybody in the cell took part was known either as *salonowiec* ("The Dandy")—named probably to mock the game's lack of finesse—or "bum whacking," which was more descriptive of that uncouth entertainment. An umpire chosen by common consent—usually an older or frail man whom no one wanted to hit—would sit on a bench or the edge of a bed and select the first "Dandy," otherwise called the "whackee." This victim would bend over and place his head on the knees of the seated umpire who cradled the victim's head while covering the man's eyes. That way he could not peek at the players/whackers who were standing in a semicircle a couple of steps behind him. When one of these players slapped his bottom hard, the whackee would quickly turn around and scan the faces and the stances of the men standing behind him to try to guess who hit him. If he didn't name the right one, the game continued with the same whackee. If he did, the guy who hit him had to take his place. The whackers sometimes hit lightly, sometimes they really whammed one, making it difficult to guess whether the feeble smack did indeed come from the delicate hand of the *advocat* from Prague or the breadloaf-sized paw of Ziola, a hotel porter from Zaleszczyki.

The game was crude and painful at times but played in a friendly spirit, with plenty of laughter. The Bukovinians were almost addicted to this game, but it seemed that they never fully grasped the idea of it. As the game progressed, people would get tired of it and, rubbing their sore rumps, would start drifting away until only two players were left—both Bukovinians—who continued to slam and thump each other with glee.

A real surprise to us was an announcement that we would be allowed to buy cigarettes, tooth powder and onions from the prison store. Those who didn't have the money would be allowed five rubles credit. The prices of these items were nominal, and the amount of the merchandise limited, so that everybody received one hundred cigarettes, a large box of tooth powder and three or four onions depending on their size. The cigarettes came from Winniki near Lwow where there was a large tobacco processing plant before the war. They were nicely packaged, but the guards found these cigarettes too weak and turned up their noses at them. "They may be all right for delicate Polish gentlemen, but we hardy Russkies need something stronger."

The tooth powder, which came in crude, plain cardboard boxes, was of no use at all. We had no toothbrushes. It had a strong mint flavour, but after a few tentative tries we found it inedible. The onions were a great success, but we ate ours up within a day or two.

After a couple of weeks in Chernigov, we started being called out by the NKVD officials for further interrogations. Again prisoners were taken from their cells in the middle of night and returned before dawn looking drawn, sullen and at times badly beaten. From the stories of those who did talk about what they had undergone, we found that some of the threats were so repetitive that they must have come from a kind of interrogator's handbook. When yelling and beating a prisoner failed to draw out the required answer, the NKVD man would ostentatiously load his revolver and then order the prisoner to face a wall or an open window. Then he would click the safety catch.

"You have thirty seconds to confess your hideous crimes. If you don't, I'll pull the trigger."

Thirty seconds gone, he would add, "A bullet costs three kopeks. But you're not worth it. Guard! Take this stinking shit back to his cell!"

There were also women interrogators. One of them was known to tell the prisoners, "Well, so you don't want to co-operate and admit your guilt. For that kind of man we have labour camps in the land of white bears. You'll rot there."

Then all of a sudden, she would lift her skirt up to her navel. Like many Russians then, she wore no underwear.

"You see this?! You'll never see it again in your life!"

Some of the prisoners taken for interrogation never came back. Among them was Soltys. A guard took his belongings from our cell.

It was useless asking him what had happened to Soltys. To all our questions the guard replied, "Don't know" or, "He was, and now he's gone." Maybe the Russians discovered who he really was and so had other plans for him.

We lost track of Soltys after that. The name Soltys was probably a pseudonym, and not knowing his real name, we had no way of learning later on through other prisoners or pre-war friends about what became of him. We found his disappearance unsettling.

Most of the prisoners did come back unscathed. Tadzio's education, however, got him into hot water during one of his interrogations. In our cell, Tadzio had established his authority in so many fields that even the Bukovinians, who had their own debating society in the far corner of the dungeon, would come to him for arbitration or a verdict.

"Mister professor, is Khotim the northernmost district of Romanian? Was Maria Teresa the wife or the mother of Franz Josef [longtime Emperor of the Austrian-Hungarian Empire]? Can the tax collector take a shoemaker's tools for unpaid taxes?"

Whatever Tadzio said was final.

During his interrogation, his new interrogator, an ill-bred and dim character, had asked him, "What's your education?" Words like university, docent and lecturer were meaningless to this rube, who finally rephrased his question.

"How many years did you complete?"

Tadzio totalled up his four years in primary school, eight in high school and four at the university and said, "Sixteen." That flabbergasted his interrogator.

"C'mon, stop joking. There's no school that takes sixteen years to complete. What am I supposed to put in the space marked education?"

"Write: higher than Stalin's."

That blasphemous remark earned Tadzio the serious threat of a new charge and trial but it ended with two days in a punishment cell, which he took lightly. Tadzio was made of the same clay as Socrates and Diogenes. He probably didn't even notice that he was in a punishment cell. He was hungry like all of us but he never talked about it. Roman and Zynio told me that before the war he wore the same suit every day and had to be reminded to go for a meal. In 1944, I visited Tadzio in the port of Bari in Italy, where he was working in the editorial office of the *Polish Army Daily*. I found him at a typewriter in a dingy room. The floor, the window ledges and the table were covered with books and papers. He wore a rumpled battledress without any badges on it. It had been two years since we'd seen each other. He recognized me and smiled a welcome in my direction when he saw me entering the room but did not stop writing. When he did stop, it was to check something in a huge dictionary. Then he smiled again and said, "Help yourself!" pointing to a loaf of stale bread with a knife stuck in it and an open bottle of rosso wine half hidden by the pile of papers on his desk.

I knew that my "date" with the NKVD could come at any time. And I was very scared. Mainly of beating. There seemed to be no pattern to the investigators' behaviour. Some people accused of counter-revolution and espionage were treated well. Others, like some of the half-literate Bukovinians who fled from Romania seeking social justice and a better life in the Soviet Union, were beaten and tortured time and again. So when they called out "Topolski, come for an investigation!" I tried to make a brave and nonchalant exit from the cell, but I was trembling with fear.

It was one of the rare daytime hearings. A Black Maria, known in Russia as a Black Crow, was waiting in the prison courtyard. Its idling motor was sputtering and spewing out clouds of white smoke from the exhaust pipe. It was twice as long as the average passenger car and higher, like a big panel truck with windows at the back. Two armed soldiers escorted me to the open rear door. I saw that the entire car body was built from armoured plates. The open door led to a narrow corridor with three cubicles on each side. The cubicles were small with a shelf-like seat, just wide and deep enough to squeeze in a prisoner in sitting position with his back against the wall. An iron door extended down from the ceiling to the lap of the sitting prisoner and its hinged flap swung down to cover his thighs and also serve as a seat for the guard. The whole contraption looked like six upright sarcophagi flanking the armoured car's corridor.

It was difficult to accept that all this was constructed just to transport prisoners from the prison to NKVD offices in the centre of town where the interrogations took place—a five-minute ride. Gossip had it that a few years before on the same route a group of prisoners were freed by their henchmen as they were being driven in a truck. After that, the NKVD wanted to make sure such a calamity would not happen again.

While I sat entombed in icy steel, waiting for the other prisoners to be loaded, I spent my time alternating my prayers with thinking of answers to questions my new interrogator might ask me.

The NKVD headquarters was in a three-story building with a yellow stucco facade. Two open staircases led from the main entrance hall to the upper floors. An intricate net of ropes filled the stairwell between the two staircases. It looked like a huge spider web. This was to stop any desperate prisoners from jumping to their death, preferring to smash their skulls on the marble floor below than undergo another session of interrogations combined with torture.

My fears increased when, after a few preliminary questions, my new interrogator called in a short dark-haired man in civilian clothes and pointed at me.

"He's yours. Bring him back here when you finish with him."

It sounded ominous. I followed the man through a dark corridor into a brightly lit room. I sighed with relief when I saw a tripod with a large camera mounted on top. The man in civvies was a photographer whose job was taking mug shots of the prisoners.

Then the investigator asked me to tell him the whole story of my unsuccessful attempt to cross the Romanian border. As he listened to my story he took down everything I said. From time to time he turned the pages of my earlier depositions, hoping to find some discrepancies between them and my latest version. I was truly amazed to see my interrogator setting down my story on the back side of thick wallpaper cut to the size of standard writing paper. He wrote with a straight pen, dipping it in an inkwell filled with purple ink. As I was to find out, the use of wallpaper for writing was quite common. Something must 've gone wrong with the Soviet industry Five Year Plan and the dearth of writing paper was offset by an overproduction of garish wallpaper.

I noticed that the family photos I took with me were still on file but my passport with the faked date of birth and the permits to visit the Polish naval base near Gdynia were gone. I didn't know what to make of it. It bothered me. The NKVD was not in the habit of losing pieces of evidence, and if these were removed from my file there must have been a reason for it.

I had the impression that the interrogator considered the investigations of my case completed. Most of his questions were perfunctory, and at times he yawned. My morning fears of a tough session faded. My faith in the power of prayer grew stronger.

Towards the end of March 1940 all the Romanians and the Ukrainians who came from Romania were told, "Get ready to go with your belongings." Everybody in the cell had his own idea about what that order might mean, but the Romanians themselves came to the conclusion that it had something to do with a petition they had sent to the NKVD authorities. In it they said that those who believed in communism and sought a better life in the Soviet Union should be given thicker soup than those who were trying to escape from it. That was the reason, they said, why the two groups were being separated. When the time came for them to go, they filed out from the cell with smiles on their faces and with their hearts full of hope for soup so thick that a spoon would stand up in it. We marvelled at their naïveté.

Chapter 8

DOING TIME

There was plenty of room in our cell after the Romanians were gone, but it became much colder. Their thirty or forty bodies gave off a lot of heat. As long as the cell was full, the outside stone walls stayed damp and droplets of water would fall down from the ceiling. Now the walls were covered with white frost and tiny icicles decorated the vault. Again we started huddling together and sleeping as close as possible to each other in order to keep warm.

But we didn't have to stay long in that icy dungeon cell. In a few weeks they called us to pack up and get ready. We were leaving for an unknown destination. At the railway station, I got separated from my friends and found myself in a boxcar together with Kielec, the farmer from Stecowa denounced by Weissglass and Epstein as the guide who helped them to cross the border. His friend, who was arrested just for being at Kielec's home when the NKVD came, was also in the same boxcar. The rest of the prisoners were strangers to me. Most of them were Jews who had escaped to the USSR from German-occupied lands.

There were few prison cars on that train, perhaps just two or three. The guards didn't have a car for themselves. They occupied the upper platform on one side of our car, and there they stacked the unwrapped loaves of bread and boxes of food for the trip. Before nightfall, in addition to the usual ration of bread, each of us received a handful of small smoked fish. They were about half the size of a sardine. They had some seasoning on them that tasted so bad that some prisoners wouldn't eat them. Instead they used them as missiles, tossing them at each other in the dark like a bunch of school kids. I ate mine.

Kielec and his friend had a feast. They were sleeping under the platform on which the bread supplies were stacked. During the night they enlarged the gap between two boards just wide enough to tear out pieces of bread from the loaves stacked above and gorged themselves through the night. In the morning the guards did not notice that a few loaves were missing.

Our train first went south to Nezhin then turned east to Konotop and finally north to Gorodnya where we were told to get out. It was not a long trip, about 150 kilometres, but it took two days to cover the distance. We were now just inside the northern border of the Ukraine, not far from Belarus. Gorodnya is near the town of Chernobyl, which half a century later was to become infamous for its nuclear reactor meltdown.

From Gorodnya station on the edge of town we trudged along a slushy dirt road to Gorodnya prison, which was six kilometres away in the middle of nowhere. A thaw had left puddles on the road, and now water was sloshing inside my laced leather boots. The guards were in a foul mood because the column of prisoners marching up the middle of the narrow road left little room for them on either side, and often they would slide into a ditch filled with melting snow. The flatulent innards of the prisoners, who had gobbled their bread rations just before they left the train, made things worse for the escort on the leeward of the column. The guards spat and referred to us as "farting cattle returning from pasture to the barn."

By the time we got to the prison it was already dark. The prison had no electricity so the obligatory search was done by the light of kerosene and carbide lamps. One of the searchers got suspicious of the thickness of the soles of the boots worn by Zynio Lempicki, who had taken such pride in his clothes. The Soviets had never seen boots with such ultra-thick leather soles. The searcher started prying apart layers of leather with a chisel and hammer. He found nothing, but kept at it until he had ruined an excellent pair of boots.

The search was going on in the long corridor on the ground floor. I saw most of my friends there and managed to exchange a few words with them. After the forbidding stone dungeons of Chernigov, the heavy timbers supporting the ceiling, the wooden floors, stairs and doors looked almost cozy. This prison was bound to be warmer and drier. And it was—a bit.

Our new cell was on the second floor. There were five of us from the old group: Tadzio Siuta, Roman and Zynio Lempicki, Doctor Weissglass, and me, plus five others whom we had never seen before. Like us they were Polish, and four of them were charged with trying to cross the border illegally. The fifth one was a big Jewish man, a saloon keeper from Horodenka. His name was Spiegel. I knew his establishment. That saloon was where we boys went with our first army pay, and I ordered a yellow liqueur with golden flakes in it. What Spiegel was accused of we never learned. He was a bit hazy on this subject. Though arrested more than three months ago his face was still red and fleshy. He sported a black moustache and thick bushy eyebrows. But he had lost a lot of weight and his trousers kept sliding down. He must have had an imposing belly because later on when I saw him under a shower he had a fold of skin hanging down like an apron.

Spiegel had been taken from his home by local militia and then handed over to the NKVD. His description of his arrest, when he was given but a few minutes to pack up and say goodbye to his young wife and three-year-old son, was painful. The little tyke was screaming his head off, somehow sensing that his father was being taken away.

It must have been Spiegel's story that led Tadzio to talk about the life and writings of Ovid. On a couple of cigarette papers Tadzio wrote for me in Latin an excerpt from Ovid's heart-rending description of parting with his wife on the night of his expulsion from Rome to the barbarous lands of Dacia north of the Danube's delta on the Black Sea. It begins with, "When I [think] of the scene of that saddest night . . ."

Another of my new cellmates in Gorodnya was a class-conscious character named Butiov. White-haired and pushing sixty, he was cynical but with a good sense of dry humour. He referred to himself as a "proletarian," but his work as a waiter in an aristocratic club in Lwow had turned him into a snob.

A simple and naive nineteen-year-old boy named Budulak, who slept next to Butiov, was not impressed with his tales of class and quality.

"Mister Butiov, you talk all the time about elegance and style and yet you fart all day round like a cabbage-gobbling peasant! Tfui!"

"Hold your horses, young man! I don't fart. I break wind. And you must admit I do it in style. My fart is clear and crisp. It's like the clang of a bell. Not like the sneaky hissing of a snake slithering in the grass. Maybe one day you'll overcome the inhibitions of your low class origins and you'll learn to break wind in a manner befitting a man who knows his worth."

On the other side of Butiov slept a certain Strachocki. I remember well the wine red of his alcoholic face. He slept with his cloth cap on. A taxi driver from Stryj, a town in southeastern Poland, he made his living not so much from taxi fares as from smuggling watches and flints for cigarette lighters in from Czechoslovakia and Hungary. He made no bones about it. His stories were highlighted by descriptions of his cleverness in dodging customs and the long binges that followed his successful forays. Strachocki was short, wiry and sinewy—the kind of guy I'd give a wide berth to in a bar.

The last of the new acquaintances in our cell was a beanpole of a man, an ex-soldier, Sapper Sacha. He must have been well over six feet tall and the flaming red beard down to his midriff set off his sky-blue eyes. After completing his compulsory military service, Sacha, like many others, opted to stay on in the engineers corps. He was proud of being a professional soldier and talked in a clear and interesting way about sappers' work, which ranged from bridge building and mine detecting to digging trenches and constructing field latrines. Soon we found out that the red-bearded Sacha had other talents.

At one time or another, every one of us tried to mould some simple things like a pair of dice or marbles from kneaded bread moistened with saliva. Some people were better at it than others, but Sacha proved to be a highly skilled artisan, if not an artist. One had to have a real surge of creativity to sacrifice one-third of his daily bread ration in order to make a ring, dice or some other knick-knack. Obviously Sacha thought it worthwhile, and he was constantly using part of his bread to make tiny ashtrays, cigarette holders and even a pipe.

Before shaping an object, it took long hours of chewing the bread and a lot of saliva to get the proper consistency. Sacha would spend a day and a half on chewing and kneading. Then he would add to the paste the soot that he had collected by holding a plate over the burning kerosene lamp. After a couple of hours of more kneading, the black Plasticine-like material would be sculpted to its final shape and left to dry for a few days. After that it was hard as rock. Finally, with a small shard of glass the surface would be polished to a fine black gloss. The finished product was so strong and hard that a pipe made in that fashion was not only good for smoking tobacco but its stem would not get soft even after being held for hours between the teeth of the smoker.

Sacha volunteered to make a set of chessmen if we all agreed to chip in a chunk of bread each. The reply was a unanimous "Yes!" and so for days the sapper was chewing and kneading while fashioning exquisite chessmen.

We all played chess for a few weeks on a chessboard drawn on the bottom of the drawer of the night table. Tadzio and the innkeeper Spiegel were the best players. The red-faced smuggler Strachocki and the farting waiter Butiov played checkers. Budulak, the naive young man, never went beyond the simple "Four sheep and a wolf" game on the checkerboard. One day the governor of Gorodnya prison spotted our chessmen during a visit in our cell and liked them so much that he confiscated them. In vain we protested, pointing out that the Rules of Internal Order allowed prisoners to play chess.

"*Da*! (Yes!) You may play chess, but it is forbidden to manufacture them." He promised us a set of "real" chessmen, but we never got them.

At the next visit by the portable prison tuck shop, we were allowed to buy—apart from cigarettes and tooth powder (no onions this time)—plenty of wooden matches. As I gazed at the matchbox, an idea came to me. Now it was my turn to display some creativity. The matchboxes were made of thin, veneer-like wood with a paper label on top.

The bottoms of the matchbox drawers were smooth pieces of uniform size. From these I decided to make a pack of cards for playing bridge. I got moral support from everybody in the cell, even though Strachocki's card playing was limited to blackjack—which Butiov insisted upon calling *chemin de fer*—and the callow, blond youngster Budulak had mastered only the rules of "war," a child's game barely a step above snap.

I was given a free hand in the design and manufacture of the playing cards. Tobacco steeped in our hot evening brew made a rusty-brown ink for painting hearts and diamonds. The kerosene lamp soot mixed with sugar and hot water was as black as any India ink for spades and clubs. Sharpened spent matches served as my disposable drawing pens. It was tedious and time-consuming work, but I enjoyed every minute of it. All of my matchbox-sized cards had the corner markings the same as regular bridge cards but I replaced the pictures of kings, queens and jacks with crowns, fans and swords. The rest of the cards had just a large number painted in the centre. The cards worked well although they were awkward to shuffle.

We played on Sapper Sacha's bed, the only one in a blind spot where the guard peeking through the spy hole could not see us. We played auction bridge, the most popular version of that game in Poland in those days. Without a doubt, the brilliant Tadzio was the best bridge player in our cell. We were often exasperated by his habit of laying down his cards after a finesse or two and declaring, "Two over!"—or however many it was—"And that's assuming that you two play faultlessly. Any objections?"

At first we doubted him and would demand he play out the hand from his exposed cards. But time and again he proved to be right —sometimes winning even more tricks than he claimed he would— so we gave up challenging him.

Doctor Weissglass and Zynio were close at his heels, but Roman and I were nowhere near their level of playing.

The red-bearded Corporal Sacha made some half-hearted attempts at learning bridge, but the others in the cell were not interested or, more likely, found it too complicated.

We soon settled down to the routine of prison life. Reveille was early. We assumed that it was at six in the morning—assumed because we never knew the time. The guards would not tell us. It was considered secret. So was the date and the day of the week.

Our morning toilet was simple. A cupful of cold water was enough to wash hands and face. Some did not bother even with that. No one was able to shave—of course I still had no need to. There was a cast-iron bucket in the cell for peeing. However, a shrill whistle in the corridor meant, "Get ready for the latrine."

The latrine itself was of an interesting design. It was a squat-down eight-holer with evenly spaced openings on a ten-foot-square platform built of wood. The platform was calf-high and up the centre of it a cast-iron pipe, at least a metre in diameter, ran from the top floor to a cesspool in the basement. A space wide enough to walk around was left between the edges of the platform and the whitewashed walls. The central pipe had side openings to collect waste from the sloping floor under the platform. Similar latrines were on the floors below and above ours. Once we heard women talking in the latrine on the upper floor. The Lempickis and Weissglass recognized the voices of Irka and Lila. Now we knew that they were in the same prison.

We were let in eight at a time. The guard who let us in would lock the door to the corridor and come back after ten minutes to take us back to the cell. On my first trip I scribbled, with a small piece of a pencil lead, "Topolski from Horodenka" in Polish on the whitewashed wall, at the eye level of a squatting person.

In Soviet prisons we realized how hard it was for our families to get news of us. We still had no right to send or receive letters. We also wanted to keep track of the friends we'd made in prison and get news of them after we'd been separated. So we wrote our names when and where we could. In transit, when discipline was more lax, such as at the military barracks in Czortkow, we had seen names or initials and dates scratched into wood or paint. Later in Gomel transit prison, I saw a whole wall was covered with names and dates. Among them I found one I recognized—the name of a man from Horodenka, the father of a girl in our high school. His first name (which I no longer remember) was followed by his last, Lat, and the number seven. Sometimes we would write our names—with soot or whatever we had—on the bottom of the plate that made the rounds with each cell's ration of sugar pieces. The plate was never washed and once in a while we would spot a name on it, maybe with a hometown or a cell number—another way to leave one's mark. And so I felt the urge to leave my mark on the wall.

The guard who took us back to our cell returned after a couple of minutes and beckoned me to follow him to the latrine. He pointed at the wall with my message written on it and said, "Read and translate." I did. Then he asked, "Who is Topolski?"

"Me," I replied, expecting the worst.

He took pity on me and, instead of sending me to a punishment cell, gave me a long lecture on prison discipline. He wiped out my minuscule graffito with a wet cloth and checked the walls again and even under the lip of the platform, for more messages before taking me back to the cell.

That guard was a stickler for prison rules, but he was never mean or abusive. Often in the middle of the night he would enter the cell and turn the face of a sleeping prisoner in the direction of the burning kerosene lamp. According to prison rules, all prisoners were supposed to sleep facing the source of light in the cell and keep their arms on top of the blanket. That last rule was too difficult to enforce. Before locking the door after the night roll call he would recite the standard order: "Cleanliness and silence will be observed in the cell and no clothing will be hung on the foot of the bedstead in such a way as to obstruct our view of the prisoner on it. Good night."

When on duty, the guards wore sneakers so they could glide silently along the corridor. But they could not catch us unaware because the sound of unlocking the clunky double locks on the doors always gave us enough time to hide our homemade needles, threads, pencils and playing cards.

There were four regular guards or turnkeys who worked in shifts. We were more than astonished when we found that two of them were women, both of them in their late twenties. They took guard duties in their stride and seemed to have no problems in maintaining order and discipline among their charges. One of them was dark haired and dumpy. More than that, her figure was bursting out of her tight uniform and according to Weissglass, she was a living copy of the Heidelberg Venus. Hearing that, Spiegel, who was eyeing her, turned quickly to Weissglass.

"What did you say? Venus Heidelberg? Was she Jewish?"

Weissglass's denial did not diminish Spiegel's interest in the "Dumpling" as he called her. Nor was he interested in Weissglass's explanation that the Heidelberg Venus was a prehistoric clay figurine of a grotesquely buxom cave woman, probably a fertility fetish, unearthed by archeologists near Heidelberg. Like all guards on night duty, Dumpling had to bang the iron bars in the cell windows with a wooden mallet in order to check if they had been filed through by would-be escapees, and if they were still firmly embedded in their frame. The wooden mallet had a long handle, but not long enough for the short-legged Dumpling to reach the barred window. To bang the bars she had to climb the bed next to Spiegel's. When confronted with her derrière, Spiegel's face would turn even redder, his nostrils would dilate and we could hear him panting heavily.

The other woman guard was a flat-chested, mousy blonde. Quiet, with an expressionless face, she was given the unkind nickname of "Vtoraya blyad" (The Second Whore).

We never learned their names or if they were married or had children. They would neither answer any such questions nor ask any. In this respect male guards were a bit more open. But the names Dumpling and Second Whore cropped up often in our daily conversation. After all, they were the only women we had seen for a long time.

The taxi driver Strachocki, when queried once which one of them he would prefer in bed, remained silent for a long time mulling over the question. Then, probably realizing that there wasn't even the remotest chance of it ever happening, he let his patriotic feelings override his sex musings and declared: "Neither! I'd rather hammer my cock into a wall and use it as a peg for hanging my hat on than screw any of these Soviet whores."

Every couple of weeks or so we prisoners and our cell would be thoroughly searched by a group of guards. On such occasions some of the guards would take us to the corridor for an individual search while the others would go over the cell with a fine-tooth comb. It happened once that two searches were conducted within a very short period of time. But the second search was rather unusual. As we were waiting in the corridor, we thought that it was taking a long time for the guards to search the cell. Butiov peeked through the spy hole to see what was going on there and then quickly made room for others to look inside. The cell, as always during a search, was in shambles. A guard was sitting on one of the beds. In front of him, stretched flat on the blanket, was a green flannel shirt which belonged to Zynio. The shirt had a long zipper in front. With his mouth half open, the guard kept pulling the zipper up and down. He had obviously never seen a zipper before. Nor had the other guards. Fascinated by that "Amerikansky" invention, they crowded around the bed, turning their heads left and right to follow the zipper with their eyes as if watching a game of tennis being played on a miniature grass tennis court.

At the end of the search the guards took with them some pieces of our clothing including a shirt, a pullover and a pair of socks, but promised to return them the day after the morrow. We were puzzled by it, but the guards would not say why they were doing it.

The next day was the First of May, a national holiday in the USSR. Only then did it dawn on us that all the garments taken from us by the guards were red in colour. But we were still in the dark as to why.

We got the full explanation of that unusual happening months later from a prisoner who told us that some years ago on the First of May the inmates of one prison made some makeshift banners out of red scarves and sweaters. They tied them to broomsticks and stuck them out of the barred windows to let outsiders know that some true communists were being held locked inside a Soviet prison. In order to prevent a repeat of such a provocative display, all togs of red colour were taken from the cells before the First of May and returned after the May Day celebrations were over. This explanation tallied. Our red clothes had indeed been returned the following day.

Tadzio taught me the Greek alphabet. He wrote a good hand in Greek even though his handwriting in Polish was barely decipherable. His stories about his stay in Italy before the war were always interesting. He thought little of Mussolini. "He speaks and writes too much and does not read enough." (Besides being a dictator, Mussolini was also a journalist.) More out of boredom than curiosity, we asked Tadzio to tell us the history of Bulgaria, Paraguay and other outlandish countries. He always obliged and seemed to have in his head an inexhaustible supply of names, facts and dates sprinkled with anecdotes to rekindle our waning interest. Strachocki was overheard mumbling to himself about Tadzio, "Sure he talks a lot, but who can check if what he says is true?"

Then one day the prison librarian lugged in his basket filled with a hodgepodge of books. As we crowded around this bonanza, Weissglass fished out a folio book with a brown, hard cover and opened it to read the title. A triumphant smile lit up his face. The book was one of ten volumes of the *History of the 19th Century* by the French historians Lavisse and Rambeau. Except for Tadzio himself, not one of us had ever heard of Lavisse and Rambeau.

The cry went up: "Don't give it to Tadzio! Now we have him!" It was all good natured, but we did arrange an "exam" for him. The urologist Dr. Weissglass, dressed in a professorial gown fashioned from a blanket, would leaf through the book and ask in a solemn voice, "Docent Siuta, tell this assembled board the story of the conquest of San Domingo." Tadzio would rattle off names and dates and places. Most of them were in the book, but he also told us about others that weren't. Soon we gave up. Tadzio knew it all and more.

One day we were taken to the showers. A most welcome event. The last shower we had was in Chernigov, over two months before. There were two bath attendants, both Ukrainians. Because of the guards, they were afraid of talking freely to us. Still we learned that our prison here in Gorodnya was a former monastery. The younger Ukrainian managed to tell us that he was a local man arrested for stealing hay from a kolkhoz, a collective farm, to feed his cow. Somebody asked him, "What did they give you for that?"

"Two years."

"TWO YEARS!?"

"Yes. Two years. The judge, a woman, was lenient. I was lucky."

We didn't know what to make out of it. If someone gets two years for stealing hay then what do you get for an attempt to escape from the Soviet Union? Maybe the guy was a notorious thief? Maybe he lied to us? But why would he?

The optimists among us clung to the illusion that our already long stay in prison was caused by some administrative mess, and one day they would open the gates and send us home. The pessimists kept their thoughts to themselves. I was neither an optimist nor a pessimist. My mood kept changing from day to day, from hour to hour. Luckily for me, I never analyzed my situation. I was busy most of the time—talking, listening, reading and rereading, sketching and scribbling on any available scrap of paper. At night, instead of brooding about our grim reality, I daydreamed, making detailed plans for my future voyages and studies and for enjoying life with the friends I'd left behind. When things were really bad I would seek refuge in silent prayer.

My prayers, though mute, were heartfelt. Apart from repeating the few I knew, I talked to my very personal God and even more to the Virgin Mary who, according to Polish traditional beliefs, has more time and patience to listen to our praises, entreaties and supplications than God himself.

The spring came. Now that it was warm, everybody looked forward to the daily ten-minute exercise walk in the prison courtyard. The yard at the back of the Gorodnya prison building was about half the length of a football field but narrow, not wider than twenty yards. As we circled it in a single file—hands clasped behind our backs, no looking sideways, no talking—the guard who brought us from the cell would stand in the centre of the courtyard pivoting on his heels like a trainer exercising horses in a circus ring. Twelve-foot stone walls crowned with barbed wire surrounded the yard on three sides, the prison building itself formed the fourth. From the two watchtowers at the corners of the yard, two more armed guards supervised our exercise.

We could not see the fields and the meadows stretching beyond the prison walls, but we could smell them. The fragrance of the new grass and the wild flowers wafted into our cell with the gentle warm spring breeze. The sweetest aroma I could remember. When a guard brought into our cell a broom made of young birch twigs which still had green leaves on them, we gazed at it and sniffed it, burying our faces in the green bouquet. We marvelled at the design of leaves, their saw-like edges and their delicate veins, as if we had never seen them before. Just as being cut off from the outside world had heightened our appreciation for nature, so the months of hunger had sharpened our ability to smell food. We could smell fresh bread even before it was unloaded in front of the prison gate from the van that brought it from a bakery in town.

From the windows in our cell we could only look upwards. All we could see was a patch of sky. Once a day around noon we could see a big airplane flying northwards. Its slow, ponderous flight was accompanied by the vibrating hum of its engines. It reminded me of the lowest note our organist in Horodenka could get out of the church organ. In prison one notices and remembers inconsequential happenings like a twig broom or the sound of a plane because they break the daily monotony and offer a link to the world outside.

One day the classical scholar Roman suggested we make a Ouija board. It was an instant, though qualified, success. We drew the circle of letters and figures on the back of our chessboard and then drew an arrow on the bottom of a saucer. We were ready for the first seance. Four of us, Roman and his younger brother Zynio, Sapper Sacha and myself, put our fingertips on the upside-down saucer while Roman invoked the spirit of Aniela, one of his aunts who had died a few months before. The rest of the cell declined our invitation to participate. They pretended not to be interested but followed our ritual and would perk up and look over when an unusual answer came up. Somehow, at first without realizing it myself, I became the *spiritus movens*, the moving spirit, in more than one way. The first few questions, asked by Roman in a solemn, if not lugubrious voice, were predictable: "When will we get out? Who's going to win the war?"

The saucer would glide in all directions and then stop abruptly, like a hockey player braking to avoid a body check along the boards. The saucer with its arrow moved faster and faster. From letters, we formed words, from words phrases. Pythia, the Delphic Oracle, would have stood in awe at the ambiguity of the answers drawn out from the spirit of Roman's late Aunt Aniela. After a while the spirit of Aniela got tired, the words and sentences became blurred and Roman, who was an old hand at these matters, had to invoke another spirit. It was some journalist or politician from Lwow, his hometown. We peppered the poor ghost with questions on the future of Europe. To inspire the responses, I had to prod my imagination to work harder. When the spirit's answers and messages started foretelling the creation of a Polish-Hungarian Union, of a Kingdom of Bavaria and of a Free Port of Hamburg, some people said "Wow!" some "Fancy that!" The two skeptics, Tadzio and Weissglass, moved closer to the Ouija board.

At that time, just for a few days, we had another prisoner in our cell. He was a Romanian. He asked us to ask the spirit what was going on in Romania at that time. I knew that Carol the Second was the King of Romania and that in the Romanian language a road was *strada*. The Latin *gravis* (hard, difficult) must have a linguistic cousin in that language, I thought. With some fanciful suffixes of my own, the Ouija board's answer read, "*Strada Carolu gravula.*" (The road for [King] Carol is difficult.) That produced more "Ahs!" from the audience and a "You're telling me!" nod from the dejected Romanian.

Next was the Horodenka innkeeper Spiegel, who wanted to know where his three-year-old son was. He gave a sigh of relief when we read the answer "Beim Schwieger." "With your brother-in-law" in my garbled German, which purported to be Yiddish. I was pleased with myself. It wasn't because I managed to hoodwink the others, but because the Ouija board was able to lift some of Spiegel's anxieties about the fate of his family. But what pleased me most was that my invented Yiddish was good enough to fool the grown-ups.

Still skeptical, Tadzio wanted to know whether Count Ciano (at that time Italy's foreign minister) ever washed his black shirt, the symbolic dress that earned the fascists their nickname. That flippant question deserved a flippant answer. My Italian was zero, but I remembered that Tadzio, when he talked about his work in Italy, often used the mild Italian oath *"Accidenti!"* meaning roughly "Good heavens!" or even "Damn it!" When the letters of the answer started forming "a-c-c-i-d," Tadzio smiled at us knowingly and said, "There's no Italian word starting with these letters." But when he saw the rest of the letters he exclaimed, "Yes! Yes! There is! *Accidenti!* Go to hell!" He paused and then he laughed. "Serves me right!"

By then the spirits were tired. So was I. We now had enough subject matter to keep us talking for the next few days. They never suspected me of being the "spirit," and I didn't let the cat out of the bag, at least not until well after the war. And we never held another seance.

Directly above us there was a cell for teenage boys. All day long they were screaming and swearing. They banged the floor with the bedsteads. They broke windows to make it easier to talk and yell to the juvenile delinquent girls who were in a cell next to theirs. Judging by their voices most of them were still children.

The Gorodnya prison governor, referred to as *nachal'nik* (a word that can mean chief, leader or head), paid us an occasional visit. Always neatly dressed in his well-cut uniform, he enjoyed talking to "Westerners" (as we were often called by the locals), especially to the professors, the doctors and other educated people who were so different from his usual crop of hooligans and petty thieves. He was an intelligent man, and in his conversations with us, he avoided asking questions that would either show his ignorance or embarrass the prisoners. Judging by his swarthy complexion, black hair and aquiline nose, we guessed he was of Armenian or Georgian extraction. When he talked one could get a glimpse of a gold tooth under his Chaplinesque moustache.

One day in June when the hot weather set in, he came dressed in a summer uniform. It was immaculate, white and well ironed. Even his high boots were of white canvas. Only his collar was cherry-red. He came by to be admired. He often glanced at his shiny new wristwatch, and several times he pulled out a white handkerchief just to touch his nose, not to blow it. He was in a good mood, talkative, almost affable. He advised the lanky Sapper Sacha on how to style his long, red beard. Tadzio and Doctor Weissglass asked him why he wouldn't transfer me to the cell for the underage prisoners where the food was supposed to be better. At that very moment an infernal racket came from the cell above us. The youngsters there raised a frightful din, shouting, swearing and banging the floor and the door. The *nachal'nik* looked up at the ceiling and smiled, "They would kill him up there. He is better off here."

One of the worst things about Soviet prisons was that we were completely cut off from life beyond. There were no more prisoners arriving from outside. Those who did join us were from other cells or prisons, and they were just as much in the dark as we were. We had no clue what was going on out there. Who was winning the war? England and France? Or Germany? What was the outcome of the Soviet-Finnish war? When would we be allowed to write to our families? How soon would our court cases come up? To all our questions the prison staff had only one answer: "I don't know." Secrecy and lies were a way of life for the NKVD. They knew that keeping a prisoner in the dark and thus a prey to uncertainty could make him lose heart.

But we had a premonition of some big changes in the offing. We heard people walking along the corridor at unusual hours. Guards would come into our cell with a list of names asking, "Who here has a name starting with the letter G [or some other letter]?" This was the usual way of asking for a prisoner. The guards were warned not to read out a name in case the names and the cell numbers got mixed up on the list. If they did, then the inmates could learn the names of prisoners whose existence the NKVD wanted to keep secret. For instance, in order to extract a confession, a prisoner might be told by the investigator that the friend he was arrested with had already co-operated with authorities, confessed, recanted and been set free. But if the name of his friend were to be accidentally read from the prisoner list it would give away the interrogator's ploy.

So prisoners with names starting with, say, the letter G, would shout out their names—"Grynszpan! Gawlik! Grzybowski!"—and the guard would check the names on his list until he heard one which matched. Only then would he check the prisoner's first name and patronymic and, if satisfied, recite the oft-repeated "Pack up your belongings and get ready to go."

The first man to leave our cell was the tall, red-bearded Sapper Sacha. He felt sad about being separated from his new friends, but he put on a brave face when he shook hands with us. Two days later while exercising in the prison courtyard somebody from our group noticed a perfectly formed little pyramid on a low ledge of the prison wall. He was able to pick it up. Made of kneaded bread it had rounded edges and was no larger than a thumbnail. On each of the four sides of the pyramid was neatly engraved the figure "7." The workmanship was exquisite.

When we returned to the cell nobody talked about it. We all knew that it was Sacha's work and that the figure "7" meant that his sentence was seven years.

After that everything began moving faster. One by one we were called outside "with belongings" and when my turn came a few days later only the taxi driver Strachocki was left in our cell. I wound up in a new cell on the third floor that was already filled with Polish prisoners. The company there was less intellectual than in the previous cell but included a number of interesting characters. One of them was a brother of the aircraft designer Misztal. I remember him because he had one blue eye and one brown. Then there was a professional pickpocket whose name—probably assumed, anyway—escapes me.

His cellmates told me about an impressive feat that he had performed a few weeks before. Like us, they played cards, not bridge but simple games like skat or blackjack. They had made their cards from pages torn out from the library books.

Cards, of course, were forbidden. The guards knew there were cards in that cell—they caught glimpses of them through the peep hole. But by the time they unlocked the door, the game and the cards would evaporate. Yet, each time, almost as soon as they locked the cell door behind them, the gamblers would be at it again. One day, frustrated, the guards mounted a minute search of the cell and every inmate. They still could not find any cards. That baffled them. A deck of cards is not like a needle or a tiny piece of pencil lead, and they were experienced guards who knew every cranny and crevice where cons could hide their forbidden treasures.

I don't think they ever figured out that the answer lay in the skill of the pickpocket. According to prison rules, as soon as we heard the clinking of the lock and the bolt being drawn, we all had to stand up in a semicircle in front of the door. The light-fingered genius, holding the pack of cards tucked in the remnant of a sock, stood closest to the door and with a flick of his wrist dropped the deck inside the large side pocket of the overcoat of an entering guard. When the guards were leaving the cell at the end of their fruitless search, he fished it out from the guard's pocket. Not one of cons in the cell saw how he did it. All they saw was him tapping the shoulder of the leaving guard and asking him some trivial question. The guard turned around and that was enough for the magician to do the trick.

Then there was a talkative prisoner, a Jewish baker from Cracow, named—of all things—Beigel (which means bagel). His mood kept changing from hour to hour and he felt he had to keep everybody posted about how he felt. He had left his wife and his little son in Cracow and he talked about them a lot—too much, some felt. Once as we were falling asleep, he went droning on about being kept in prison though innocent. Talking away more or less to himself he declared that we should take a different approach to our captors.

"All this crap! I am innocent! Why did they lock us up? Those legal deliberations, political arguments. It leads us nowhere. Now, what we must do is organize compassion and sympathy, appeal to their feelings. Let them realize that we are human beings, just like them. Then they will listen, take pity on our fate and do something about it."

None of us took him up on it, which annoyed him.

"Okay, you cowards! I'll start it myself right now!" He ran to the door and started hammering at it. In a minute or two the hatch in the door was flung open and the night guard pushed his sleepy face in. He looked at Beigel who was standing in front of the door clad only in his undershirt. It was already June and the nights were hot.

"What do you want?!"

By this time we were all wide awake, curious to see what would happen. Beigel made a few dainty steps towards the door and smiled at the guard. A torrent of words cascaded from his grinning mouth. Unfortunately, Beigel's pidgin Russian was so bad that the guard could not make any sense of his tirade. Beigel pressed on, mixing Polish, Yiddish, Ukrainian and Russian words, anything to get his story across. When talking about his little son, instead of saying *rebyonok* (a child), he called him *zherebyonok* (a colt).

The guard kept peering at the half-naked Beigel, who was now prancing about playing charades trying to make himself better understood. He was showing how small his son was and demonstrating how he still ran around on all fours. The large, bovine face of the guard showed no glimmer of understanding. But when he heard Beigel saying that every night before going to bed he kissed a colt and the colt kissed him good night, that was too much for the guard.

"Go and fuck yourself, you queer beast!" he said and slammed the hatch door.

I spent only four or five days in that cell before I was told once again, "Get ready with all your belongings." A guard took me down to the ground-floor corridor. Everybody from our group from Horodenka plus some who joined us within days in the border-post cellar in Serafince and the tool shed in Stecowa were already there. Some of them I had not seen for seven months. The guards allowed us to mix freely in the corridor. The two doctors, the big gynecologist Epstein and the witty urologist Weissglass, were obviously pleased to see and talk to each other, but it didn't stop them from immediately throwing a few good-natured barbs back and forth related to their medical specialties. Roman and Zynio were talking with their sister Irka, who looked as beautiful as ever in spite of seven months of dingy cells and starvation diet. Tadzio Siuta, her fiancé, joined them. It was not part of Tadzio's character to display his feelings, certainly not in a hallway crowded with prisoners. It seemed to me that Irka was more concerned with the health and well-being of her "baby" brother Zynio than about Tadzio. Lila, the third doctor, also looked healthy and well groomed. The women rode out the many deprivations better than we men did. Lila told Weissglass that a month or two after their arrest she thought she might be pregnant because she stopped menstruating, but soon learned that this was common among underfed women in prison.

We had a premonition that it was not going to be just another move to another prison but something more important. Indeed, the personable prison governor clad in his white uniform appeared, followed by a soldier carrying an armful of files. They passed us without so much as a good morning and went into an office behind a glazed wall next to the main entrance. We could see them through the glass as they arranged files on a table. The main door leading to the front courtyard was open, and we could also see our escort, a few soldiers sitting on the ground in the shade with their backs to the whitewashed wall and holding their rifles upright between their knees. The peaks of their army hats were pushed well back on their heads to let out the heat. Although it was morning, the hot July sun was already baking the courtyard. We kept milling around the corridor talking to one another and comparing impressions of our sojourn here in Gorodnya.

Until then I had buried any memory of the number scratched after the name of that Horodenka father—"Lat 7." And in spite of the story of the bath attendant who got two years for stealing hay for his cow and the ominous portent of Sacha's little pyramid with the sevens carved all over it, we kept deceiving ourselves with visions of an instant release and going home. After all, hadn't we already suffered enough for our peccadilloes?

Our musings were interrupted by an order barked by a guard.

"Epstein and Siuta! Leave your things on the floor and go to the office. Lempicki and Lempicki, you'll be next!"

It didn't take long. In less than a minute Epstein was out. His face was chalk-white. His eyes wandered blankly from one person to another without focusing until they met Weissglass's.

"FIVE years!" And then he added, "Of corrective labour camps."

Tadzio came out next. He just said casually "Five." The rest kept going in and emerging with "Five. Five. Five . . ." The same for Irka and Lila. The last two were Weissglass and me. We went inside the office together. The white-uniformed *nachal'nik* looked at me. Then he opened the file and silently started reading a note attached to the first page. Weissglass, who stood behind me, leaned over my shoulder and tried to read it upside down. "You know," he said, " it looks like . . ."

At this very moment the *nachal'nik* covered the note with his hand and yelled at Weissglass in German. "Shut your trap!" Then he turned to me. "You'll go free. Back to your family." He smiled and dismissed me with a wave. As I was leaving the office I heard him droning what sounded like a formula, ending with ". . . five years of the corrective labour camps. Sign here." That was for Weissglass.

I don't remember much of what happened afterwards, probably because I was feeling sick at the time. Everybody was telling me, "Your worries are over. In no time you'll be back at home." But even that didn't lift my spirits. Somehow their words sounded hollow.

Chapter 9
BAD TO WORSE

We marched in blazing heat to the railway station along a dirt road flanked by tall weeds, the same road we'd trudged along in the slush that March or April night four months earlier when we arrived in Gorodnya. At the station we had to wait. A passenger train was standing there, but it wasn't ours. Travellers were hopping on and off it going to the station buffet. A neatly dressed young woman stood on the platform. She carried a thermos flask on a leather strap over her shoulder. We gazed at her as if she were a film star about to board the Orient Express. Nobody dared to look at us, thirty or forty filthy and smelly criminals clad in weird, winter clothes despite the devilish heat of a day that sent rivulets of sweat carving white lines on our grimy faces. I cannot remember a thing about our 100-kilometre train ride to Gomel, a Belarus town of 150,000 inhabitants. I suppose I slept.

The cobbled courtyard of Gomel prison was L-shaped, and it was packed solid with prisoners. This was one of the largest transit prisons in the USSR but was so overcrowded that the throngs of new arrivals were kept for days in its courtyards waiting for space inside the two brick prison buildings. That we did not mind. We enjoyed the clean, fresh summer air and felt freer by not having to look at the blue sky above through iron bars. But we wondered what had happened to Irka and Lila. Somewhere between Gorodnya and Gomel, they had gotten separated from us.

While we sat on the ground, two young boys, probably not more than fourteen, approached us, looking curiously at our foreign clothes. They spoke Russian. We told them that we were Polish, and that seemed to satisfy their curiosity. One of them held a newspaper in his hand, and when we asked whether we could have a look at, it he tossed it to us saying, "There's nothing interesting in it. Keep it."

Like most of the Soviet newspapers it had only four pages, and three of these were full of long stories about the fulfilled and over-fulfilled quotas of production in the kolkhozes and factories, new targets for production and lengthy speeches by party officials. But on the last page a small space titled "Beyond Borders" dealt with foreign news. We were puzzled by a communiqué from "the French Government in Vichy." Vichy? What is the French Government doing in Vichy? We could not understand some of the Russian words. An elderly Russian who heard us arguing about their meaning offered to help. Soon he realized that we had been cut off from the outside world for a long time. The news he gave us on that July day in 1940 was shattering. The Soviets had defeated Finland and created a new Karelo-Finnish Soviet Republic. Lithuania, Latvia and Estonia were now under Soviet rule and so was a part of Romania. Germany had defeated and occupied Norway, Denmark, Holland and Belgium. France had fallen. Only the south of it was unoccupied by the Germans but it was ruled by a pro-German French government from Vichy. Italy had lined up with the Germans, grabbed bits of France, occupied British colonies in East Africa and was now threatening the Suez Canal. The French Navy had battled the British Navy, and England was preparing for a German invasion while the Soviets and Germany kept issuing declarations of their mutual and ever-lasting friendship. For us it was a cataclysm. Everything we believed in lay in ruins. Hope that the West would come to our rescue was gone. A five-year sentence now meant five years.

This news was difficult to accept. The war was no longer a polit-ical and military chess game. No more of "They go here; we go there. They take this, and we take that." Now it looked as if a churl, ignor-ing the rules of the game, had swept away all our chessmen from the board with his sleeve, leaving us with a solitary King George to play the end-game alone. Epstein, the anglophile, tried to console not so much us as himself. "Remember, England loses every battle with the exception of the last one." But the pragmatic Weissglass saw it differ-ently. "There's no sense deluding ourselves. We lived to see the end of an era. Forget your allegiances and adapt yourself to the new world if you want to survive."

We spent the whole day and the night in the crowded courtyard. As soon as one gang of prisoners left the compound, another one would come in through the main gate. Because of the overcrowding, meals were served at unusual times. We could not tell whether the soup at midnight was a belated supper or an early breakfast. What's more, there were not enough bowls to go round, and we had to slurp the soup in a hurry, standing up while the others waited for the never-washed bowls.

The guards came and segregated us before taking us to the different cells in the main building. It happened so fast that we hardly had time to shake hands and say goodbye to each other. Roman and Zynio asked me to go see their parents in Lwow. They really believed that I'd be set free, just as the prison *nachal'nik* in Gorodnya said. Both doctors, the Horodenka saloon owner Spiegel and I were taken inside the large prison building and pushed into a cell on the ground floor. Literally pushed in, because when the turnkey opened the door, we saw in front of us a huge cell paved with the near-naked bodies of prisoners. Maybe two hundred, maybe three. We had to step on the sweaty bodies lying on the floor and walk forward in the direction shown by the stretched hands of the inmates. "Walk fast!" they yelled. "Don't hesitate! Don't stay standing on somebody, looking for a place to make your next step. Just walk!"

The spot they pointed us to was beside a large cast-iron slop barrel. The immediate area around the barrel was smelly and the floor was damp from spilled urine. An unwritten law scrupulously observed in camps and prisons was that the last man in had to take the place nearest to the evil-smelling barrel and remain there until a new prisoner was brought in and took over his place. With each new arrival he would move further and further away from it.

For the first time since our arrest we were sharing a cell with Soviet citizens: Russians, Ukrainians and Byelorussians (the name we used then for people from what is now known as Belarus). We could not tell these three groups apart because almost all of them spoke Russian. Only a few of the non-Russians knew or spoke their native language. They looked at us with curiosity and asked a few questions but found our self-taught Russian difficult to understand.

On the whole, the Russian prisoners left us alone as much as anyone could in a cell packed with men whose sweating bodies were pressed tight one against the other. You had to rest your head on the back or thighs of the man lying next to you and intertwine your legs with your neighbour's. The steamy heat in the cell was hotter than the hottest sauna. Spiegel came down with a severe bout of asthma. He looked as he was going to die then and there. It took a lot of persuasion and pleading with the inmates to let him move close to the door. He lay there on his belly with his open mouth pressed against the narrow chink between the bottom of the door and the threshold, sucking in the air from the corridor. Every half an hour or so the turnkey would open the door for a few minutes and let the slightly cooler air from the corridor flow into the cell.

The turnkeys kept bringing buckets of water, but trying to quench the thirst of a couple of hundred men was Sisyphean labour. The guards also had to supervise the distribution of food, take groups of prisoners to the latrine and back, and let visiting officials in and out. They worked hard.

By this time I was feeling ill. I was feverish, my head was aching and I lost my appetite. Epstein and Weissglass checked me all over. "You are really sick," they said, but were not sure what was wrong with me.

Every so often a white-coated doctor or a paramedic would enter our cell looking for a particular prisoner. He would give him a cursory examination, checking his pulse, eyes and genitals and pronounce him fit, which meant that the man had to pick up his things and leave the cell right away to join a shipment of prisoners leaving for labour camps in Siberia.

During one of the doctor's visits, Weissglass and Epstein asked him to take a look at me. They told him in Latin that they themselves were doctors and suspected that I was suffering from typhoid fever. The young doctor spread his arms in a helpless gesture. There was no more room in the prison hospital, he said, and conditions in it were no better than in the cells.

I spent another day and night in semiconsciousness, adding my fever heat to that of the cell. When I woke up the following morning, my fever and the headache were gone, but so were Weissglass, Epstein and Spiegel. In spite of the crowd around me, I felt very much alone.

Beginning in the early morning of that day, more and more people were pushed into our cell. Eventually it got so tight that the turnkey ordered the prisoners in one half of the cell to stand up jam-packed, so the other half could lie down head to foot. We would take turns every two hours. It was unbearably hot. All we got to drink were a few gulps of water from time to time, and yet our bodies were drenched, as the sweat kept trickling down us like a tepid shower. The slop barrel was overflowing. We were gasping for air. The opening of the doors for a few minutes every half hour gave only a short respite from the stifling heat. As soon as the guard closed the door the inmates would begin again their plangent cries. "Chiefkin! Open the door for we are going to perish!"

Late that evening the guards took me out of the cell by myself and rushed me through the corridors. For some reason they were particularly rough and impatient that night, yelling and swearing and shoving me quickly through the crowded courtyard. At the main gate they pushed me into a Black Crow. I was the only prisoner in it. After a short ride the door opened and I found myself again at the Gomel railway station. It was all *"Davai! Davai! Pobystrei!"* Get going! Get going! Hurry up! And in no time I was shoved inside a cage of a *stolypinka* railway car for prisoners. I didn't see any other prisoners being loaded onto the train. It must have been on or about the 20th of July, 1940, because the daily paper that we read a few days earlier reported Marshal Pétain becoming the Chief of the French Government in Vichy. There were also Tass communiqués about the "joy" with which the Lithuanians, Latvians and Estonians voted "spontaneously" for the inclusion of their countries into the USSR.

The *stolypinka* cage was full. Most of its occupants were middle-aged and late-middle-aged men who wore uniforms of the pre-war Polish police. As I stood in the narrow passage between the two benches of our cage they looked me over.

"Student?"

"Student."

"What for?"

"Border crossing."

"To Hungary?"

"No. Romania."

"Going where?"

"Don't know."

"Hmm."

But they weren't really interested in me. They didn't even ask my name or where I came from. They looked old and tired. I noticed that the narrow upper luggage shelf was unoccupied. I stepped on the edge of the bench, pulled myself up onto the upper bunk and from there onto the luggage shelf. The oldest of them, a grey-bearded man with bushy eyebrows, followed my quick climb with a nostalgic eye. "How easy it is for you, youngster. Just hop from one shelf to another and then, like a sparrow, perch on a narrow ledge."

Later on as I lay stretched on my shelf, I struck up a conversation with the man below me. He told me all of them were policemen and the grey-bearded oldie who had remarked on my agility was—here he lowered his voice—the retired police colonel Pauli (or some similar sounding name) from Lwow. They were captured in 1939 in eastern Poland by the invading Soviet army, he said, and since then had been kept in a prisoner-of-war camp in Ostashkov in western Russia. During the last few weeks several thousand Polish policemen and border guards were being evacuated from Ostashkov. They didn't know where to. All they knew was that they were heading south. He wondered why the NKVD had put me in their car. Never before had they ever had a fellow prisoner who was not either a policeman or a border guard.

I travelled with that group of policemen for another day, and when we reached Kiev the following night I was taken off the train just as quickly and mysteriously as I was put on it.

For years we Poles wondered what happened to those policemen from Ostashkov and other camps. It took over half a century to get the full answer. The bodies of 5,000 Polish officers had been unearthed by the Germans in Katyn Forest in 1943 under the eyes of a commission of forensic experts sent in by the International Red

Cross. The commission found that they were murdered in 1940 when they were prisoners in Soviet hands. But there were at least 10,000 more unaccounted for—Polish military, police, border guards and public administration officials who vanished without a trace while in Communist captivity. Stalin denied any responsibility and blamed the Nazis for shooting all of these Polish prisoners of war and burying them in the Katyn Forest. During the war the Western democracies accepted the official explanation from their Soviet allies and stuck to it despite the overwhelming evidence against it. The postwar Nuremberg War Crimes Tribunal dropped the charges against the Germans for the Katyn Forest slaughter but did not pursue the matter any further. Nor did the Polish Communist government.

It was the Russian Premier, Yeltsin, who dispatched a special envoy to Warsaw in 1992 bearing the original decree of the Supreme Soviet of 1940—he found it hidden in Gorbachev's private archives —approving the execution of 25,000 Polish prisoners who were considered politically beyond rehabilitation: army officers, policemen, border guards and selected public administration officials. The decree was signed by every member of the Supreme Soviet including such "peace-loving" individuals as Stalin, Khrushchev, Molotov and Mikoyan. The bodies of the policemen were recently exhumed from mass graves near Kharkov, 500 kilometres east of Kiev. Like those murdered by the Soviets in Katyn, the prisoners were shot with a single bullet in the back of the head. Also like them, their hands were tied with a piece of cord looped around their wrists and neck in such a way that if a prisoner struggled to get free he would strangle himself. A few women, shot the same way, were found alongside them in the mass graves.

I have no doubt that those policemen I shared the *stolypinka* with were being carried to their death in one of those mass graves.

As far as I could tell, I was the only prisoner taken off the train in Kiev. It must have been well past midnight. Again, the guards wasted no time. I was whisked into another of those empty Black Crows with no side windows. When the truck stopped, a guard opened its back door and then steered me through a narrow corridor into a large, brightly lit room. Three sides of it were lined with what looked like a wainscotting made of heavy wood panelling about as high as a man. The fourth side was blank except for the iron grill door we came in through. Along that blank wall, a motley crowd of prisoners was squatting on the floor or standing up leaning against it. The guard who had brought me in ordered me to join them. In the middle of the foyer, a dozen or so NKVD soldiers stood well apart from each other. A soldier would beckon one of the prisoners from the waiting group to come close to him for a personal search. I had already experienced several thorough searches in prison but this one beat them all. While we sat and waited our turn, we watched as each prisoner had to strip naked and put all his belongings on the floor on one side of his searcher. Then the searcher would check the soles of the prisoner's feet for anything that might be glued or taped to them, look between the toes and then under his armpits, inside his ears, nostrils, mouth and under his tongue. Next the guard would order him to squat and bend over, while the guard probed the prisoner's rectum with his finger. No rubber gloves, not even a bowl of water and soap were deemed necessary for this task.

Then the searcher would take a piece of clothing from the heap on one side and examine it meticulously before dropping it on the floor on the other side. Each seam was checked inch by inch. The lining of a hat, jacket or coat was ripped partly off to allow the searcher's hand to grope for anything hidden behind it.

I now saw why the heavy wood panelling was there. Each panel was in fact the door of a shallow, narrow cubicle smaller than a telephone booth. As soon as the guards finished searching a prisoner they would lock him up in one of these tiny windowless closets, which were like upright coffins built into the thick walls. This was to deny searched prisoners any contact with others before they were taken to the cells.

As I watched that search I grew frightened. Hidden in the high cuffs of my winter coat was the pack of cards that I had made from matchbox bottoms in Gorodnya. Possession of playing cards was a serious offence, and these searchers looked like a tough and unforgiving lot. I was scared of being sent to the cooler on a half-ration of bread and water. Silently I prayed to God to help me. My turn to be searched came. When the body search was over and I stood by naked, the soldier started fingering pieces of my clothing. At one point he turned around for a few seconds to say something to another searcher behind him. That was long enough for me to pick up my coat with the accursed cards and drop it on top of the second heap with those togs already searched. It worked. The soldier didn't notice anything.

It was still night when I was let out of the "upright coffin" and escorted through many floors and seemingly unending corridors to a large cell. When I entered it, about a dozen inmates opened their eyes, lifted their heads up and peered at me as if expecting me to say something. It was too early for "Good morning." What else could I say? And in what language? I just stood there, and the men who raised their heads when I entered looked at me for a bit longer, scratching their arms and chests at the same time, and then, one by one, put their heads down and closed their eyes. I clambered onto one of the free iron beds and fell asleep.

A shrill whistle woke me up in the morning. In the lineup to the slop bucket somebody standing behind me asked in Polish, "Where are you from?" I turned around and saw a boy of my age dressed in a tatty high-school uniform, same as I was wearing.

"I am from Horodenka and you?"

He was from some small town in the same southeastern corner of Poland. We struck up a rather one-sided conversation. Many people have told me that I speak fast and too much, but in this fellow I met my match and more. Dobek was his surname. Because it was short and easy to pronounce, people called him just that. Nobody bothered to find out what his first name was. He spoke so fast you would think that he was leaving in five minutes and in the meantime he had to tell you everything he knew. He looked gaunt like most of us only more so. Unlike the rest of us, however, his skin was a peculiar deep grey hue. His ears were big, out of proportion to his egg-shaped head, almost transparent and sticking out like those of a bat. His Russian was lamentable, but that didn't stop him from talking to our Russian cellmates all day long.

I learned from him that we were in the famous, if not notorious, Lukianovka Prison, then over 150 years old. Apparently the prison's plan was based on the shape of the letter "E," the initial of its founder, Ekaterina II (Catherine the Great), tsarina of Russia. One side of it, the "Special Block" for the dangerous political prisoners, was built during Soviet times. At times Lukianovka held 15,000 inmates. The prison had the reputation of being the most bedbug-ridden in the USSR. And indeed it was. Millions of acrid smelling bedbugs lived in the crevices and cracks of the plastered walls, in the joints of the scanty furniture and even in the seams of the iron bedsteads. For food they never lacked a steady supply of prisoners' blood. I watched them crawl one after the other across the ceiling and free-fall down as soon as they sensed the heat of the body of a prisoner asleep below. I was lucky. There must have been something in my blood they didn't like, and so I suffered fewer bites than the others. But when eating bread, the occasional crackling sound between my teeth accompanied by a bitter taste and blood-tainted saliva reminded me of their omnipresence. The guards used to laugh about them. "Don't blame us. These bedbugs are of tsarist stock. The original capitalist bloodsuckers!"

Dobek knew a lot about the other prisoners in our cell. One of them, a young Russian, spent most of his time lying on his back and looking at the ceiling. He had been recalled for a retrial in Kiev after spending over a year in the Far North labour camps. Dobek befriended him and got from him stories about life in those camps. The Russian spoke of labour camps run by the inmates, hardened criminals. The guards used to toss the bread over the fence, he said, because they were too scared to come inside. Prisoners fought among themselves for their daily bread rations. Those who were too weak to fight starved to death. The guards' only task was to see that nobody escaped. But that was easy. In the desolate Arctic tundra there was no place to escape to. Some tried. There were many stories about those who failed, but I had not heard of a single successful escape. One of the ways of escape "recommended" by the hardened criminals was *troyachkom*, a threesome escape. For this, two prisoners who decided to escape would seek a third, preferably a dim-witted fellow, then bamboozle him with tales of caches of food hidden in the taiga wilderness, about friends they had in native villages, and about the infallibility of their scheme. Eventually they would persuade him to join them. Before the escape, the trio would try to save or steal some bread, enough for two or three days of marching. When the last chunk of bread was gone they would kill their naive companion. Eating his flesh would keep them going for another few days. It was convenient to have the future roast walking by itself even if for only a few days.

Cannibalism was a recurring theme in the stories told by Russian prisoners. Some of the stories went back to the famines during tsarist times, but most of them referred to more recent ones. The famines of the early twenties and thirties were created deliberately by the Communist Party in order to eliminate the small farmers and force the starving peasants to join kolkhozes, the collective state farms.

Dobek pointed out to me a haggard-looking man about fifty, sitting on the edge of a bed. He swayed and rocked back and forth, his lips moving in a continuous, soundless monologue. "That man," Dobek whispered, "ate his own daughter. He told us himself about it. It happened during a famine ten years ago. The NKVD troops confiscated all the food in his village. There was nothing to eat. His family decided to kill one child, so the others might survive. He killed one of his daughters, quartered her body and kept it preserved in salt in a barrel. They lived on it for a while. But the neighbours denounced them. He got sentenced to death, then it was changed to life imprisonment. Now he prays all the time, begging God's forgiveness. You'll hear the whole story from him. He tells it to everybody whether they want to listen or not."

Among my remaining cellmates were Russian soldiers who had taken part in the invasion of Finland, which began in 1939 a few days before my arrest. The Finns, while vastly outnumbered, had put up a courageous and ingenious fight. The Soviets suffered enormous losses to capture a piece of Finland, and Stalin accused the Red Army of not showing enough zeal. The disgraced Soviet soldiers who fought in that war disappeared into forced labour camps in Siberia. In the same way, that war itself disappeared from the Soviet history books and as late as the nineties there was no mention of it in *The Great Soviet Encyclopedia*.

Inside the grim Lukianovka Prison, the July heat was becoming oppressive. A daily ten-minute walk in the exercise yard brought no relief. The exercise yard was small, perhaps about half the size of a tennis court. It was just a flat roof at the bottom of a light well several storys deep. It was depressing. We'd have skipped that "exercise" if we didn't have hopes of seeing something interesting when passing through the long corridors and stairs on our way to the "chimney," as we called the exercise yard.

Then one afternoon I heard yet another, "Get ready with all your belongings."

"Where now?" I thought. "Is there no end to it?" But this time it was different. A guard took me almost to the main entrance but instead of going out, from there we went upstairs along a carpeted corridor lined not with cells but with interrogators' offices. They were easily recognizable from the outside because the doors were covered with leather quilting. To muffle the cries of tortured prisoners, I thought, and a shiver of fear ran down my spine. The guard stopped at one of the leather-quilted doors and carefully checked the number of the room. He pressed the button of the doorbell, opened the door and motioned to me to enter.

The office I entered was not big, but it had a high ceiling and wood-panelled walls. The heavily barred window was half open but all I could see through it was a nearby brick wall. Behind a large, heavy desk slouched an NKVD officer in an upholstered chair. I didn't see his rank because his dark green tunic was unbuttoned from top to bottom and his collar was turned away from me. His black hair was cropped short, like that of Stalin. He glanced at me as I entered and without saying a word gestured at me to sit down on a wooden stool in front of his desk. He looked between thirty and forty years old but his face and his clean-shaven double chin were flabby. I could see droplets of sweat on the chest hair protruding from the edge of his not-too-clean undershirt. He leaned a bit to one side, grabbed the spine of my file between his thumb and middle finger and pulled it in front of him. By now my file was as thick as Webster's unabridged dictionary. When he opened it I saw again the mysterious piece of paper pinned to the front page. "My God,"

I thought, "maybe this is my release document and he is going to read it to me now." But he removed that note from my file and put it aside. Now on top of the file was a two-page form typewritten on yellowish paper.

My heart was pounding, my knees were shaking and my hands were sweating. I waited for him to say something. He lifted his double chin, ran his hand over his hair and looked over my head at the wall behind me.

"Surname?"

"Topolski."

"Name and patronymic?"

"Boguslaw Aleksandrovich."

"Year of birth?"

"1923."

"Correct. Your case has been heard in Moscow." And then in a bored, slow voice he started reading aloud the text of the yellowish form: "The Special Council in Moscow has examined your case and according to paragraph eighty, section sixteen of the Ukrainian Soviet Republic penal code has found you guilty of an attempt to cross the border illegally with disloyal intentions and sentences you to five years of imprisonment in the corrective labour camps of the Soviet Union."

He turned the paper around towards me and pointing with his finger to the dotted line at the bottom of the page, said "Sign." By that time I had stopped shaking and felt rather composed. Looking straight at him I asked, "What will happen if I don't sign?" He shrugged his shoulders.

"Nothing. You'll sit in prison anyway."

"I have one more question. What happens to me after I complete my sentence?"

This he must have found amusing because he smiled before he answered. "If you survive that, we'll give you some more."

So that was that. And already the guard was waiting at the open door to take me down.

I took the verdict and the sentence calmly. After the two-year sentence for the boy who stole hay for his cow, the five years for the

Jews who fled from the Nazis into the Soviet Union and the seven years for Sapper Sacha for being a corporal in the Polish army, my five-year sentence came as no surprise. But I never believed that I would remain a prisoner for five years. Unlike the pragmatic Weissglass, I did not feel that we had "lived to see the end of an era." I rejected the idea that in order to survive I should "forget my allegiances and adapt myself to the new system." On the contrary, I refused to accept what Weissglass saw as the new reality. Despite all that was going on around me, I held fast to my conviction that this was but a temporary reversal of fortune in my life. Somehow I was able to dismiss the hideous present from my thoughts. Instead of dwelling on my sordid surroundings, in my mind's eye I lived in an idealized past and a romantic future. If I hadn't, I doubt if I would have survived.

In a way I felt proud that my case was dealt with in Moscow by the Troika, a special court of three men for dealing with political cases. This, I thought, set me above the thieves, cheats and thugs. At that time, I didn't know that in the Soviet Union it was better to be accused of murder than of telling a political joke.

The guard escorting me out stopped near the main entrance on the ground floor and kept looking left and right for somebody who was supposed to be waiting for us. While we were waiting, he told me not to worry about my sentence. In fact, I should consider myself damned lucky. "You are not being sent to the white bears [meaning the Far North labour camps] but to a corrective labour colony in Kiev for underage prisoners, just a short walk from here." His remark helped me to keep my spirits up.

We were waiting for an escort to take me there. My guard was getting restless. He took me down to the basement corridor where the punishment cells were and opened the door to one of them.

"Step in and wait here while I look for your escort."

I waited a long time. One thing you soon learn about in prison is waiting. The cell was a small, windowless cubicle about the size of a toilet stall only longer. It had concrete walls and a concrete floor that sloped towards a trough running along the cell door. The only light came from one small bulb, which gave off little more than a dim glow.

Hours passed and nothing happened. I curled up on the damp and smelly floor and fell asleep. In the morning I heard the steps and voices of the day guards. The morning roll call was proceeding with doors being banged and orders being shouted. But nobody opened the door of my cell. Evidently it was listed as unoccupied. But when I heard the clatter of water buckets and smelled the savour of fresh bread, I started pounding at the iron door. The guard ignored it. When I turned to yelling, he opened the door and yelled back at me, "Quiet! Once they put you in the cooler, stay in it and shut up, you scum!" He swung at me with his bunch of keys and slammed the door.

It was late afternoon when the door hatch opened, and I saw the face of the same soldier who had brought me there the day before. He was surprised to see me still in the cell. "The devil take it! You still here?!" He took me upstairs and talked to the corridor superintendent. They both found it hilarious that by some oversight I had spent one day in a cooler without food and water.

Finally my escort came, leading with him the bat-eared babbler Dobek and two frail and bewildered looking Romanian teenagers. Dobek got a three-year sentence. So did the Romanians. At least we thought so. They spoke no Russian or Ukrainian. Dobek was engaging the two teenagers in a one-sided conversation, but his newly acquired Romanian was limited to, "*Ci faci ci? Vaca, lingura, pua.*" (What are you doing? Cow, spoon, prick.) They acknowledged this with smiles as wan as their complexions.

Chapter 10
CORRECTIVE LABOUR COLONY No. 7

The escort took us out through the main prison gate into a quiet street named Krasnykh Komandirov (Red Komandirs Street)—Degtiarovskaya Street to old-timers. We turned right and for a couple of hundred metres followed along the high brick wall of the prison complex before stopping in front of another doorway. Above it was a sign: Corrective Labour Colony NKVD No. 7. Our escort rang the bell, the hatch opened and the gatekeeper scrutinized us for some time before opening a narrow door in the iron-clad gate to let us in one by one.

We were now in a small courtyard. Opposite the gate we came through was another gate leading to the penal colony area. The gatekeeper phoned for somebody to take us in. He was moving and talking slowly with an air of dignity to match his self-importance on the job. He stopped in front of me and, pointing with his finger at the band of my peaked high-school cap, said with a smirk, "I see the silver eagle has flown away!" He was referring to the Polish national emblem. I told him we didn't wear silver eagles on our school caps but a badge with a burning torch. He nodded. "Ah! The flame of enlightenment." Then he proceeded to tell me a long story of how, during a severe winter when he was serving as a border guard on the Soviet-Polish frontier, he had pitied Polish guards. They were shivering with cold in their thin, dark blue coats adorned by a multitude of silver eagles, he said. They envied his sheepskin coat. One of them asked him for a match to light a cigarette. He tossed him a box of matches, but the poor Pole tossed it right back to him because he was scared to keep a box of matches with the Soviet star on it. I didn't tell him that only a few weeks before I had read exactly the same story in a novel, *How the Steel Was Tempered*, by the Russian writer Nikolai Ostrovsky.

A man with black curly hair came to take us inside the corrective labour colony compound. He said he was a counsellor and was to be addressed by his first name and patronymic, the standard way of addressing a person of higher standing or older than you who is not your intimate friend. So he became Avram Davidovich to us.

It was late afternoon as we were entering what looked like a factory compound. The sinking sun was just about to touch the roof of a long shed and everything was bathed in an orangey light. All over the place there were teenagers and grown-ups walking and standing in pairs or groups. A bunch of youngsters perched on a mound of rusty pipes. They shrieked and laughed and swore. One of them was strumming a little tune on his guitar. It sounded familiar and soon I recognized a raunchy old Russian song that my nanny Tanya used to sing to me when my mother was out of earshot. I hadn't heard it for years.

"Tell me why, old man, you've no hair on your head?"
"As a young man I took many wenches to bed."

The sound of that familiar ditty cheered me up a bit. Some of the youngsters came running up to us and followed along while peppering us with questions. "Who are you? Where do you come from? What's that uniform you're wearing?" They were intrigued by our high-school uniforms. When we told them that we were Polish, they said they already had some Poles here. There wasn't much time to talk because our counsellor Avram Davidovich steered us through the thickening crowd of the curious to the back entrance of a three-story brick building and into a huge shower room. There were only four of us prisoners, but a bath attendant was there to regulate the flow and the temperature of water, issue soap and disinfect our clothes in a huge steam boiler.

While we were showering, a young man came in to wash and have his clothes disinfected. He sang under the shower and seemed friendly and cheerful. He had good reason to be. He had just completed his two-year sentence and was about to be released the following day. Although a Russian, he had lived in Kiev all his life. He told us that he had his appendix removed in the prison hospital and pointed at a long, red line down his belly. The scar had many twists and turns. It looked like a map of the Nile River.

Although it was well past suppertime, a man brought from the kitchen four bowls of thick barley soup with scraps of meat in it. It was the best meal I had had since the day of my capture eight months before.

From the shower area we were taken into the quarantine wing. I got separated from Dobek and the two Romanians and put into a cell already full of juvenile Russians. They looked at me curiously and asked a few questions, but could not understand my answers because of my quaint half-Ukrainian, half-Russian self-taught pidgin.

Those in the cell spent most of their time playing cards. They played blackjack and some other card games unknown to me. They gambled for food, clothing, cigarettes and money. When not gambling they talked about their experiences in other prisons—in spite of their youth they were seasoned convicts.

In the evenings they would huddle together on the iron beds and listen to the *romanist*, a storyteller. That was a common feature of prisons and camps in Russia. A fellow with the gift for memorizing novels, who could tell them in installments night after night, was held in great esteem by his cellmates. Using all the tricks and techniques of storytelling including breaking off the daily installment at the most exciting place, he kept his audience in thrall and was rewarded by an extra bowl of soup or a cigarette. The listeners never got tired of it and didn't mind hearing the same tale time and again.

I listened too, and every day I understood more. The stories were from pre-revolutionary times. They were full of bandits, Gypsies, rich men, beautiful women, duels and ghosts. A typical beginning was, "At midnight in the former town of St. Petersburg, a man dressed in a black cloak, wearing a black hat and dark glasses, emerged from the shadows of the bridge across the Neva River." That was enough to hush the entire cell. Jack London's tales of the Klondike gold rush and Dumas's *The Count of Monte Cristo*, as well as the stories of the American detective Nat Pinkerton, until then unknown to me, were the favourites.

When they were not listening to stories or playing cards, their main entertainment was masturbation in which they displayed an amazing ingenuity in their methods and variations. They enjoyed doing it individually, mutually or in groups. They never tired of it. Buggery, though often mentioned, was not in evidence. I was to learn later on that it was considered the domain of Georgians, Uzbeks and Armenians. In Russia the name *Armyashka* (little Armenian) was a synonym for a homosexual. The derogatory term *pederast* was reserved for passive homosexuals. They were held in contempt and constantly vilified, while the active ones were seen as normal, "real" men and no stigma was attached to their proclivities.

One day I complained about the unjust sharing of our food, which was brought into our quarantine cell in buckets by the guards and left for us to dole out and share among ourselves. My complaint annoyed the young thieves. Their leader, a tall, strong semi-idiot, threw a bowlful of soup in my face and, joined by the others in the cell, began to pummel me. What amazed them was that I fought back. They were not used to that. As I was to observe later, the outcome of a fight between two young *zhuliki* (criminals or thieves) was decided even before the fight started. After an exchange of verbal abuses and increasingly threatening gestures accompanied by colourful and inventive cursing, one of the contestants, feeling that he had no chance to win, would assume a submissive pose and cover his head with his hands. Then, while the other guy was belabouring him, the victim would whine and beg for mercy. "That's enough! Enough, Kolya! Have pity on me! How long can you keep torturing me? I swear I'll never do it again! Enough!" He would never even think of fighting back, but would yell and moan until his opponent got tired of beating him up.

The gang that attacked me fought crudely. They just kept flailing their arms, hitting blindly. Despite my only minimal knowledge of boxing and self-defence, I scored a few hits. In the end, of course, I got badly beaten but not before I cut the lip of one of them. When the fight stopped, the fellow touched his lip with his finger and, seeing blood on it, growled, "I see. In capitalist Poland they started teaching you early how to draw blood from the working class."

I didn't want to provoke another fight, so I kept mum. They said they were going to kill me one day, but for the time being they left me alone and went back to their card playing. There's no fun in beating up somebody who fights back. In spite of their warnings not to do so, I complained to the guard. When he saw my swollen face covered with blood smudges he called somebody in the corridor. He asked who hit me. While I was pointing out those who did it, the *zhuliki* pretended to be so engrossed in listening to a hastily arranged storytelling session that they didn't hear or even notice either the guard's questions or my answers. Soon a half dozen youths came into the cell. They were laughing and joking as they began to batter those who beat me up before dragging them across the corridor and into the punishment cells. They beat them without mercy, hitting and kicking them until they tired of it. Not one of the *zhuliki* tried to defend himself. Then the thumpers locked them up in the cooler, returning whenever they were in the mood for another session of punching and kicking. Those *zhuliki* who were left in my cell became sickeningly obliging and obsequious. "Give the soup to our Polish friend first." From them I learned that the trusties who were meting out punishment to the *zhuliki* were young prisoners known as the "activists." They helped to keep in check the unruly juvenile criminals who in turn detested them and called them *suki* (bitches).

In the quarantine cell, we were visited by all sorts of officials. The man who met us at the prison gate and took us to the showers, Avram Davidovich, came daily. One day the top boss came in. His name was Kretov. He was big and strong and he seemed to be a cheerful person. He asked everybody where they came from and cracked a lot of jokes. But, as we learned later on, he was a real brute. Some boys were sent to the prison hospital with ruptured internal organs after being punched and kicked by him. He narrowly escaped death one day when some of the *zhuliki* dropped an iron ingot from the roof of a workshop just as he was passing underneath. They missed him by only a fraction of an inch. He never found out who the culprits were.

Then came a white-haired, lean, old man who was the leader of the prison band, which was a part of the Cultural and Educational

Section. He asked if anyone played a musical instrument. All the *zhuliki* declared that they played guitar. That was just wishful thinking, but it tallied with their ideal of a ruthless but romantic bandit. I said that I had taken piano lessons. He was pleased to hear that, adding that he himself was a pianist and he promised that he would arrange piano lessons for me, but nothing ever came out of it. I saw him later at some prison concert. Frail and frightened, he sat hunched at the piano accompanying a group of "activists" who were shrieking a medley of propaganda songs extolling "Our Beloved Sun, Stalin." He played with closed eyes, probably dreaming of Glinka and Tchaikovsky.

Another visitor to us in quarantine was the prison doctor, who was accompanied by a pert nurse. They gave us inoculations against all kinds of diseases. The young bandits were terrified of injections. They gladly and proudly suffered real tortures while being tattooed by their cellmates, who ripped their skin with sharpened nails, but now they were trembling at the sight of a syringe. They pleaded with the doctor, tears streaming from their eyes, not to stick the needle in their arms. To no avail, of course.

I asked the doctor if he could get me glasses. I'd done without ever since mine were confiscated in Czortkow Prison. Being short-sighted, I could read without them just by holding a book closer. But I wanted to see farther than that. I remembered my prescription and told it to the doctor. I figured, however, it'd be like the piano lessons and didn't really expect anything to come of it. Within two weeks, though, a serviceable pair of glasses arrived and the world became clear to me again.

When the *zhuliki* noticed that I could draw, they soon enlisted me as a tattoo designer. Later, I learned the whole procedure of tattooing and became reasonably good at it. On the whole the designs of tattoos were quite conventional: a heart pierced with an arrow or a dagger, a rose or the very popular combination of a cross, anchor and heart, symbolizing faith, hope and love. Later, in other prisons and camps, I encountered some unusual tattoos. The most bizarre was of two copulating rabbits tattooed on a prisoner's forehead. By frowning and moving the skin on his forehead up and down the two rabbits came to life and appeared to be doing exactly what they were meant to do. An inmate in Gomel Prison asked for a sailing ship to be tattooed on his back. The tattoo artist, with the connivance of the entire cell, tattooed on him a huge erect penis instead. There was no mirror of any size in the cell so the poor guy could not see this work of art. He had to rely on his cellmates glowing descriptions of it. As soon as he saw a newcomer enter their cell he would turn around, pull down his trousers, lift his shirt up to his neck and expose his bare back with the tattoo on it, then ask him, "How do you like my sailing ship?" The newcomer soon noticed scores of eyes winking at him. He would quickly catch on. "Splendid! Splendid! What a craft! It would make many a mermaid unfurl her sheets! Heave ho!"

Some simpletons had a crude drawing of Lenin's head tattooed on their chests, convinced that with it they could never be put to death by a firing squad. After all, who would dare to shoot at the image of the Redeemer of the Proletariat? They really believed it. I was never tempted to have a tattoo myself—despite the urgings of my clients—and left prison unmarked.

Next in line of our official visitors were the *vospitateli*, a term loosely translated as educators or counsellors. They were free men who lived outside the prison. Avram Davidovich was one. This title was applied to individuals whose official job was to indoctrinate us with the proper communist ideas, explain current affairs, look after our needs, act as monitors, and watch for any signs of negative attitudes toward the Soviet system, all the while quietly organizing a network of stool pigeons.

All of the *vospitateli* counsellors were Jewish. As a matter of fact nearly the entire administration of the corrective labour colony was staffed by Jews. They also held all the better jobs where no hard physical work was needed. Some of them had Russified their surnames and first names, but they could not change the names of their fathers, so patronymics like Shloimovich or Chaimovich gave away their origins. On a Soviet identity card or passport the word *Jewish* indicated not the bearer's religion—all religions being banned—but his nationality. After the revolution, the Communist Party tried to eradicate the historical Russian anti-Semitism—but failed. Anti-Semitism broke out again after Stalin's death, affecting even those who had Russified their names and no longer observed Jewish rites or high holidays. Many lost their jobs. But in my day, the Jews held the majority of high positions in the Party and in the state administration.

Each of the counsellors had about a hundred inmates to look after. It was hard work and badly paid, but it was a stepping stone to the coveted membership in the Communist Party and to all the privileges that came with it. You could always tell a Party member by the quality of his clothes. My counsellor Avram Davidovich was shabbily dressed—obviously not a Party member. And Yakov, his colleague, wore a black overcoat always buttoned up, probably to hide the sorry state of his garments underneath.

There were also some unofficial visitors—the young inmates who were already working in the prison factory. They would find a toehold on the narrow plinth, grab the heavy iron bars of our window and hoist themselves up to peer inside our quarantine cell. They were coming to barter clothes, to sell cigarettes or just to satisfy their curiosity.

Avram Davidovich brought some books for us from the prison library. Among them I found short stories by Pushkin. I started reading them and loved them, especially "The Queen of Spades" and "The Duel." The simplicity of Pushkin's language made it easy for me to read, and there were only a few words that I did not understand. The *zhuliki* regarded my reading with suspicion. "What a strange creature! Can't speak Russian yet reads books faster than any of us can. A sly fox. Foreigner."

Our quarantine cell was slowly emptying. First, two *zhuliki* were taken to hospital. One of them, watched by his fascinated cronies, swallowed an aluminum spoon. It wasn't easy. He kept gagging and nearly choked himself while trying. But he did it. As soon as he got it down, his pals started hammering and kicking the door.

"Guard! Guard! He's swallowed a spoon. It's true! May I turn into an old whore if I am lying! Bring the doctor!"

They took him to the hospital. I never saw him again. Another *zhulik* wanted to join his pal in the hospital. He took scrapings from the lead of an indelible pencil and put them under his eyelids. The whites of his eyes turned deep purple. It looked terrible. They took him to the hospital too, but released him after they washed his eyeballs. I think both of them did it just to impress their friends.

The counsellors started bringing foremen of the different workshops to our quarantine cell. The foremen wanted to pick out the boys who would work for them. It was a bit like a slave market. Their criteria for selection were traditional, going back to tsarist times. Preference was given to "the stupid, the strong and those who couldn't read the clock." Boys who met these requirements went to work in the foundry. It was hard work carrying molten iron in ladle-like buckets from the furnace to the forms. No one lasted there for long. Heat, fumes and terrible burns—accidental or caused by feuding prisoners—took their toll. There were many other workshops, all of them unhealthy, as I learned later. In the metal polishing workshop, by the end of the shift, all the workers were completely covered with some green paste that was used on the rotating brushes for cleaning the metal pipes before anodizing them.

Conditions were just as bad in the prison painting department. After work there the boys had to wash from head to toe with turpentine. Those who were tired or lazy would go for days if not weeks encrusted in dry paint. Metal cutting and forming as well as the pipe-extruding workshops were also dangerous. Only the wood furniture department with its wood-drying kilns, wood shavings and isinglass glue smelled inviting, but it was the domain of grown-up prisoners and no youngster stood a chance of getting a job there.

It began to look as if my counsellor Avram Davidovich didn't want to place such a small, foreign boy in any of these places but couldn't make up his mind what to do with me. Then one day he saw me sketching and doodling on scraps of paper. As he watched, he tugged at his chin and rubbed his badly shaven cheeks.

"Ty mozhesh chertit'?"

I understood the first two words "Ty mozhesh." Can you . . . I told him I didn't know the word "chertit'." He took the pencil from my hand and scrawled on a piece of paper something that could pass for an original Miro.

"Now you know?" I didn't. But I nodded my head quickly. He smiled and said he would arrange a job for me in the technical department where they were preparing plans and designs for the new types of beds and other furniture. I would be given the job of a tracer-draftsman. He was as good as his word. It was a godsend.

Now out of the quarantine cell, I got a better look at our labour colony. It occupied about ten acres of land, enclosed by a red brick wall four metres high covered with lichen and ivy and topped with barbed wire. There were watchtowers at every corner. Within the perimeter walls, it was divided into two compounds. In the first compound was the bedstead factory and two three-story brick buildings housing prisoners.

I was now in one of these three-story buildings along with about three hundred underage prisoners. Their ages ranged between twelve and eighteen. Each building had its own separate courtyard surrounded by a wooden fence two metres high. A gate, manned by a guard, cut off the workshop area. Just inside the perimeter wall was a strip of land three metres wide. It was raked daily and checked for footprints. This zone was forbidden to everybody and anyone seen on it would be shot without warning by the guards manning the watchtowers.

A high wooden fence separated the bedstead factory from the second compound, which housed the furniture manufacturing plant. It also had a sawmill, workshops and its own power plant. There were also half a dozen one-story wooden dormitories for the prisoners, including one for women. In one corner of the sprawling site were the offices for the free workers who came daily from the outside.

The Technical Section was in the two-story building I'd seen that first day off the small courtyard tucked in between the inner and outer gates of the main entrance. I had to ring the bell to summon the guard who would let me through the inner gate into the courtyard. Then I'd climb a few stone steps onto a covered porch and from there up to the second floor where the drafting office was. Next to the drafting office was a small room for the chief of the Technical

Section. The remaining rooms on that floor and the ground floor were occupied by the plump and sweater-clad female staff of the personnel and records office. The building was old and neglected. The rooms and corridors were lit by bare light bulbs dangling from the ceiling. The wooden floors stank of creosote. All the windows had heavy iron bars, and ours looked out onto the backyard of the prison kitchen.

Yet compared with the institutional dreariness of our dormitories, eateries and workshops, I found that building pleasant, almost cozy. In the corridor and in the office, the beige wallpaper, darkened with age and dampness, had a pattern of roses the colour of clay tile. The white-painted wooden doors had the same door handles as we used to have at home, and on the wooden windowsills stood flower pots with straggly plants. But it was the free people around that made all the difference. Myself and an old, grizzled man named Bashko were the only prisoners working in the building.

The Technical Section had a staff of eight people led by its dark-blue-suited chief Boris Ivanovich, a Party member, and, as I soon learned, a professionally incompetent man with the title of engineer but little education to justify it. A white shirt, cufflinks, a heavily scented handkerchief, a wristwatch and the sound-muffling leather padding on his office doors were the insignia of his position and power. He was always well groomed with a neatly trimmed, toothbrush moustache and wavy black hair. Polite, with an elementary sense of humour and often humming a little tune, he kept a wider than necessary distance between himself and his subordinates. I was yet to discover some of the less pleasant traits of his character.

When I reported to work at his office he had the grace to receive his new, unasked-for apprentice civilly, almost affably, because he knew that my counsellor's idea of placing me in the Technical Section must have been approved at a much higher level. He and the staff of the drafting room seemed to accept me as an equal, not a prisoner. But his demeanour might have had something to do with a recent political development. In 1940, a special ukase (edict) on "tightening work discipline" was proclaimed by the Supreme Soviet. It called for lengthy prison sentences even for such "crimes" as being late for work three times. The real reason behind that ukase soon became obvious. The enormous projects in the Far North—such as new railway lines, new coal mines at Vorkuta, new ports and the increased demand for Soviet gold and timber in the West called for more manpower. As there was nothing more economical than forced labour, the prisons were soon filled with those who "broke the work discipline." The prisoners had a saying about this. The population of the Soviet Union, they joked, was divided into three groups: those who have been in prison, those who are in prison and those who will be in prison. And my still-free workmates felt vulnerable.

Chapter 11

CELLMATES

When my quarantine ended I was ushered into Cell Number 6. The two-room cell already held about twenty boys my own age. With one exception all of them were "Westerners" as the Russian prisoners used to call Europeans who came from outside the Soviet Union. We Poles earned ourselves another sobriquet, *Psheki*, on account of our sibilant language full of "sh" and "ch" sounds. In my room there were Poles, Romanians, two Austrians, one Czech, and one Finn plus one Russian who was a stool pigeon. He was a planted informer, but otherwise a likeable fellow. His first name was Shura.

We were only beginning to learn the complexities and varieties of the diminutives of Russian names. Shura was a diminutive of Aleksandr (Russian for Alexander), but to our amazement so were Sasha, Sashka, Sashenka, Shurka and Sania. All these nicknames could also apply to Aleksandra, the feminine form of Aleksandr. The polite form of address would be to use the first name Aleksandr and add to it the patronymic derived from his father's first name. Shura's father's first name also happened to be Aleksandr and his surname Aleksandrov (quite a common one). To add to our confusion, surnames came first. Thus, formally, Shura should have been addressed as Aleksandrov Aleksandr Aleksandrovich. It took a while to get used to it. It's no wonder that for a long time, for the sake of simplicity and clarity, we Westerners referred to him simply as "that Russian prick."

Filek Birnbaum, a seventeen-year-old Polish Jew from Sniatyn near my hometown of Horodenka, was in charge of our cell. Lean and tall, with slightly bulging eyes, he looked—and was—mature for his age. He and a dour teenager, Grzybowski, had been there longer than the rest of us. They were still awaiting their trial and were not sure what were they accused of. Their interrogators had never laid any specific charges against them. But they had no doubt that they were arrested for being from the "socially dangerous element"—Grzybowski's father was a sergeant in the Polish Frontier Defence Corps in charge of a post on the former Polish-Soviet border and Filek Birnbaum's dad was a wealthy merchant in Sniatyn.

When Birnbaum and Grzybowski were brought into the labour colony, they were the first prisoners there from outside the Soviet Union. All prisoners as well as the officials were curious about the people from the putrid West and the quality of their clothes. They knew that it would be improvident to ask such questions as, "What was the daily wage of a manual worker in Poland?" or, "How much does a pair of shoes cost?" The political officers and any stool pigeon would regard such questions as a symptom of an unhealthy interest in the capitalist system.

But curiosity was stronger than the stigma of independent thinking, and Soviet citizens did ask us questions even when the answers they got shook the foundations of their beliefs. "You really want us to believe that there was no food rationing in Poland? That you could listen to foreign radio? Even the Moscow radio? That your family could own a car? A telephone? Or visit another country? Well, come off it! How can you expect us to believe that? That's going too far."

When asked by the Russians inmates, "What were you doing for a living before you were arrested?" most of the prisoners from the capitalist countries tried to belittle their pre-war status and pass themselves off as members of the working class. But one prisoner from our group, Pachura, when asked what he had been doing in Poland before his arrest had stunned the Russians by replying, "I was a bouncer in a brothel." Officially only seventeen but with a scraggly beard and the neck and shoulders of a mature street fighter that suggested he was well over twenty, Pachura also admitted to hawking dubious wares on the streets of Cracow, stealing and pimping. This news spread as a fast as a virus throughout the factory and from that time onward, he was held in great esteem.

Pachura's frequent references to the brothel made his short, squat friend Morajda contemplate what he would do when free in his beloved Polish hometown of Przemsyl. Sitting on his bed,

Morajda would muse, sotto voce, to himself: "First I'll go to church. Then to a brothel. No! First to a brothel and then to a church. But perhaps that's not right. After all, I should go to church first before going awhoring. But then in church I'll be thinking all the time about going to the brothel. What do you say, Pachura? What should I do?"

Filek Birnbaum had been under the wing of a group of Jewish adult prisoners who were working in the bedstead-assembly shop. This was a good place to work. The low norms of production in that workshop had been set in cahoots with the *normirovshchik* (official who establishes the norms), the *naryadchik* (output calculator) and the accounting office. As a result every worker there was a "Stakhanovite," a title awarded to those whose output soared well beyond the norm for the job. The Stakhanovite Movement took its name from a miner named Stakhanov. One day, "inspired by his love of Stalin and the teachings of the Communist Party," he exceeded his daily quota by eight and half times. That started the Stakhanovite Movement in the Soviet Union. Almost every kind of work was allocated norms and people were exhorted to follow Stakhanov's example. Those workers who more than fulfilled their norms were not only paid extra but given access to special stores with better food and clothing, and sometimes even moved into better apartments. But when their productivity started slipping, they would lose all their perks. Wherever too many workers became Stakhanovites, the norms were raised. Then everyone had to work much harder just to reach the required minimum of 100 percent. The capitalist exploitation of the working class paled beside that devilish scheme designed by the Communist Party in order to extract from workers the maximum of labour for a minimum of wages.

After the downfall of Communism, a young reporter from a Moscow newspaper wrote about his encounter in the early seventies with the decrepit and alcoholic Stakhanov, who lived in a luxurious apartment in Moscow. The besotted idol of the working classes freely admitted that the whole story of his superhuman productivity was a scam designed by the Party. He said he had enjoyed the adulation accorded to him, the books, the portraits and the monuments, but added, "Don't blame me for anything. I'm just a figurehead."

And so in the bedstead-assembly workshop Filek became a hero of socialist labour, a Stakhanovite, with his name and the figure of 250 percent inscribed on the Board of Honour. He was earning good money, which he could spend in the prisoners' tuck shop (when there was something to buy) and ate his meals in the special canteen for Stakhanovites.

One name on the Board of Honour, however, was blackened out about a month after it first appeared. It belonged to a juvenile whose work technique was far ahead of his work ethic. His job was to cut lengths of angle iron used for the sides of the bed frames on which the bedsprings or palliasses rested. For each length he had to step back and forth several times to clamp the iron in place, set the cutter blade, pull the power lever at the other end and finally unclamp and unload it. He was quick to realize that if the length of the rail he cut was shorter by a mere few inches, he could do the whole operation without changing his stance or making steps left or right. All he had to do was stretch his right hand a bit further.

All of a sudden the juvenile metal cutter's productivity soared to 200 percent. His pay more than doubled. Extra bonuses rolled in. He ate in the Stakhanovite dining room. And soon he was declared a Hero of Socialist Labour.

Weeks later the first batches of our hero's shortened frame sides reached the bed-assembly shop. Before long the shop foreman went to see the plant manager with the startling news that some of the newly finished beds were too short for regular mattresses, while others were shaped like trapezoids instead of rectangles.

The young Hero of Socialist Labour was reduced to the rank of a saboteur and an Enemy of the People. But in the yard, the rusting pyramid of mini-bed frames stood as a lasting monument to their creator's fleeting fame.

One day after work I saw Filek sitting on his bed reading a letter from home. On his lap with the letter was a photograph. Our cell leader's face was awash with tears. He kept peering at the photo. At that moment Shura, our Russian stool pigeon, came in. He too was stunned by the sight of Filek crying—Filek, a stalwart Stakhanovite and a no-nonsense fellow prisoner. It touched Shura's sentimental Slavonic soul. He tiptoed to Filek, and resting his grease-covered hand on Filek's shoulder asked with a voice full of sympathy, "Fila, what's the matter with you?"

Filek, his eyes still streaming with tears, stretched his hand with the photograph in Shura's direction. "Look! My mummy."

In the hand-tinted photograph, the middle-aged Mrs. Birnbaum sat in a high, wicker chair. At her side, on the stump of a Corinthian column was a basket filled with deep red paper roses. She looked straight ahead. Benevolence flickered over her stern face as she forced a feeble imitation of a smile. Her well-fed body had been squeezed into a purple silk dress, outlining every fold of her figure so that she looked liked a trussed mortadella sausage. Her pudgy bejewelled hands rested on her lap and a pearly butterfly perched on her ample bosom.

Shura held the photograph gingerly, cradling it in his grubby palm. As he squinted at it, you could almost hear his brain ticking as he tried to find just the right words to do justice to Filek's mother's beauty. His head was swaying in admiration as he blurted out, "Some whore! I'd fuck her any time!"

The living conditions in the colony were marked by erratic ups and downs. The only explanation I can offer is that this labour colony was perhaps a showpiece, a pearl of the Soviet Correctional Labour system and therefore received many important visitors. Before every visit by a high-ranking Party official, food would become better and plentiful, and such luxuries as cookies, fruit, candy and cigarettes would appear in the prison store. Most of the time, though, we lived on thin cabbage soup, a few spoonfuls of kasha, sweetish ersatz tea and 650 grams of dark bread per day.

Other supplies also came and went. Suddenly, for example, soap would appear and new clothing would be issued—at least for some inmates. But all that would disappear even faster as soon as the visitors were gone. For weeks we would be eating with aluminum spoons from dark blue enamel bowls and mugs. And then one day they would be replaced by coarse clay bowls and wooden spoons. What had happened to the enamel bowls and mugs? None of us knew and nobody dared ask.

In the early fall of 1940 the entire labour colony was being prepared for some important visit. I cannot remember who the "Distinguished Visitor" was. Come to think of it, we were never told his name or rank. Probably even Kretov's successor, Nachal'nik Shishkin, didn't know it. In the Soviet Union secrecy was the number one security measure.

The prison band rehearsed morning and evening every day. Their repertoire was limited to one tune, "*Smelo shagaite!*" ("March bravely!") All juvenile delinquents were trained for parade in which we had to perform some rudimentary gymnastics. Swing your arms. Turn your head left then right (very difficult for some to memorize). Make a little jump. More arm swinging. End it with clenched fist raised above the head (a perfect excuse to hit the fellow on your right). During the rehearsals the timing was atrocious and the performers less than indifferent.

On the day of the visit and the big show we were awakened at 4:00 A.M. (two hours earlier than usual), herded under the showers and issued with new trousers, tunics, gaudily coloured undershirts and sneakers. Prisoners with visible physical defects—the lame, amputees and ones with obvious skin blemishes—were kept out of sight, locked up in the punishment cells.

We were kept waiting long hours in the main courtyard until the Distiguished Visitor arrived with his entourage. The show went on as rehearsed. Arms swinging, heads turning, a little jump and the clenched fist raised above your head. All in perfect discord with the braying band. Still, the soup was thicker that day and those who had money could buy 100 grams of a sort of halva (made of sorghum and molasses) in the prison store.

The visit ended with a photo session of the Distinguished Visitor surrounded by the top brass of our correctional labour colony. The younger officials crowded around the visitor trying to get as close to him as possible. But the experienced men kept hiding their faces behind those eager fools who stood in front of them. Who knows? Maybe one day the Distinguished Visitor would be pronounced an enemy of the people and an American spy to boot? Then how would you explain to the political commissar your smiling face and your proximity to that Enemy of the People?

Indeed the photo sessions were not the only pitfalls for those trying to walk the tightrope of the Party line. The labour colony housed a theatre and an atelier where propaganda displays, stage sets and countless banners were manufactured. The artistic freedom of the designers was limited by the Political Propaganda Section, which passed on the directives received from Moscow regulating the size, colours and shape of the displays and banners. Even stricter were the rules controlling the texts and the precedence of slogans for each occasion.

A week or so before a national holiday all newspapers would carry a list of the approved slogans and the order in which they had to appear. Woe (plus a prison sentence) to him who changed a comma or missed an exclamation mark in the approved text or wrote "friendly" instead of "brotherly." The experienced artists set aside dicey slogans, especially those containing names of politicians and policies. They would postpone the painting until the dawn of the red-letter day to make sure that those personages and ideas did not fall into disgrace at the last moment. If a warning of a change came too late and the finished banners and placards did not reflect the latest political shift, heads would roll, starting from the big fish in the politburo to a miserable minnow in the workshop who stirred the paint in the pot for the sign writer.

After the photo session on that big day, the Distinguished Visitor vanished in the blue exhaust smoke of his departing ZIS limousine. Ninety percent of the new trousers and tunics vanished next day, bought and smuggled out by the free workers who came daily from outside to work in the workshops and offices. But we were reminded of the visit for weeks to come by the red banner with gold lettering high above the main entrance still proclaiming: "Thank you Comrade Stalin for our happy childhood!"

During the summer, tension was brewing between two rival *urka* groups living on the second and third story of our building. *Urka* was a slang word for a juvenile *zhulik* (criminal or thief). And an *urka* was dreaded in prisons and camps by everybody. To say that *urki* behaved like beasts is both an understatement and a slander against animals. They were oblivious to rules or restrictions. Their clan, protected by adult criminals, was almost immune to prosecution. All prisoners young and old, as well as the prison staff, were afraid of them. *Urki* would throw hot soup or water in the eyes of prison guards or attack them without provocation or warning with makeshift knives or shards of glass. Afterwards they accepted their punishment as something normal, be it a beating, hunger, the cold, waterlogged cooler or an additional sentence. Most of them were permanently on a punishment diet because they never showed up for work. But they got their own back by stealing food. They would take anything they fancied from anyone. And they would throttle or gouge out the eyes of anyone trying to thwart them by hanging on to their own belongings. Pity and compassion were unknown to them. They would beat an old man to death just for the fun of it, gang-rape a nurse and then slash her throat, or starve a defenceless cripple to death by stealing his food day after day. When they gambled at cards everyone was fearful because they were known to bet someone else's food ration, shirt, trousers or even finger or eye, which they had to deliver if they lost. I never saw them gouging out an eye or chopping off a finger of an inmate but old lags were full of stories about it. Later on in the camps in the North I was to witness even greater cruelties committed by *urki*.

Despite their youth, the *urki* had a kind of culture of their own. Some danced the *chechotka*, a combination of step and tap dancing accompanied by the rhythmical slapping of their thighs. They also sang long ballads. Although Russians swear magnificently, *urki* outdid them all. Their swearing was picturesque and evocative. They would curse a person to the umpteenth generation leaving no sexual perversion unexplored. Swearing for a couple of minutes without repeating the same word was not uncommon. How trite and dull is Anglo-Saxon swearing compared to theirs!

But in spite of their miserable life and the dreadful conditions in which they existed, *urki* and older *zhuliki* were staunch supporters of the Communist Party. Stalin was their beloved leader and their guiding light. They would gladly kill anybody who was an enemy of the Party. In their eyes, everybody in prison, unless he was a convicted bandit or thief, was a counter-revolutionary, a Trotskyite or a spy and had no right to live, let alone eat good Soviet bread.

Although the *urki* considered themselves true communists, their dream was to be free in a capitalist place such as Paris. There they would be able to rob and kill some wealthy person and live like kings, if only for a few days until caught. And afterwards? "Who cares! Let them kill us! It would be worth it!"

The *urki* shared the Russians' great craving for alcohol. They would drink anything even remotely connected with spirits. I saw some of them taken to hospital after drinking turpentine. They thought little of life and limb, even their own. And tomorrow never mattered.

There had been occasional stabbings, beatings and skirmishes among *urki* in the prison and between *urka* factions, but the real war erupted one night after the main entrance door was closed by the guards. There were no guards inside our building at night. A fight that started in one of the cells on the third floor spread to the corridors and staircases linking the two floors. Both sides were armed with knives, machetes and dreadful maces made of metal rods dipped several times in molten iron. The battle cries mixed with the screams and moans of the wounded.

On the ground floor we barricaded the door to our cell with stacked up iron beds and hoped that the warring *urki* and *zhuliki* would not declare a truce and turn their unspent fury against us, the hated foreigners.

The fight stopped at sunrise when the morning shift of guards opened the front door. They must have known what went on throughout the night because they arrived fully armed. Only after the barking of orders by the guards and the whining of the *urki* being led out to the transit cells had ceased did we dismantle our barricade and go out to survey the battlefield. On the corridor floors we could see small pools of coagulated blood and on the stairs lay a dead boy. His skull had been shattered by many blows of a mace. His brains were hanging from the edge of the landing like festoons of spaghetti.

The prison administration took quick action. The leaders of the gangs and their lieutenants were to be sent immediately to the camps in northern Siberia. For several days we could hear their howlings and moans in the transit cells at the main gate where they were held without food or water awaiting transport.

Reading let me escape the realities of prison life. On the upper floor of the *klub* (the social and cultural centre of the colony) there was a large library and reading room. There was also a smaller library in the building where our cells were—really just one of the cells filled with bookshelves, a desk and a wobbly chair for Malin, the librarian. He was also a prisoner but about forty years old, husky and strong enough to throw out those *zhuliki* who came in to borrow books printed on paper suitable for manufacturing playing cards. It may have been one of the reasons he got that job. An avid reader himself, he spent his days poring over books and did not like being disturbed by would-be customers. Most of the time he kept the door of his domain locked and bolted from inside. I had to knock at the door for a long time and ignore his growls of, "There's nobody in! Go away!" before he would relent and let me in. But he approved of the books I borrowed and we became friends. I read a lot and borrowed from the main library the Russian translations of Balzac's *La Comédie humaine*, *Illusions perdues*, and *Le Père Goriot*.

One day the woman running the main library called me in. Holding in her hand a list of the books I had borrowed, she said in a voice that both approved and disapproved, "You're reading good books. But you should take an interest in Soviet literature." She gave me a copy of *How the Steel Was Tempered*, a propaganda novel that was being pushed by the authorities. I had already read it—but I didn't tell her that. The book's author, Ostrovsky, had an almost pathological hatred of anything Polish.

Malin, however, produced a brand new edition of the Soviet equivalent of "Teach Yourself French" and suggested we have a go at it together. It was a handsome edition with its drawings, plans and photographs packed in a box-like cover. Although a Russian raised on the Cyrillic alphabet, Malin could read the Roman alphabet and had some smatterings of German. But he had a hard time trying to explain to me some of the Russian grammatical terms. Nevertheless, we plodded ahead—too slowly for me, too fast for Malin. The text was easy because it was so predictable. Instead of the usual *la plume de ma tante*, the first sentence was "Under the leadership of Comrade Thorez, the French proletariat fights against capitalism."

Our venture came to an abrupt stop when the stool pigeon Shura threatened to denounce Malin to the *politruk* (political commissar) Zelikov for secretly studying the French language in the dark corners of his library in a manner befitting only saboteurs and spies. Malin dropped our lessons like hot coals. He remained friendly with me, but somewhat aloof and the "Teach Yourself French" book disappeared from the library.

The see-saw changes in the labour colony never stopped. All of a sudden all adolescent prisoners were ordered to attend an evening school to continue their long-neglected education. Teachers were brought from outside and crates of books arrived. Some of the dormitories in the prisoner barracks were converted into classrooms.

The classes ran from 7:00 to 10:00 P.M. after our long day of hard work. What with additional checkups and counts, the evening roll call ended at midnight. Night shift workers were supposed to go to school in the morning. Few of them ever did. They hid and slept wherever they could—under the beds, in the washrooms and even in the workshops. And those who went to school slept during classes anyway.

The lectures I attended were interesting. The teachers were good and dedicated. I could understand almost everything that was said. I read well—better than most Russian boys in my class, but with a terrible Polish accent. The teacher of the Russian language seemed perplexed by my progress. "Why is it that you, Topolski, understand what we say and your pals from the West don't?" I couldn't tell him that most of my Polish friends had no desire to learn Russian. They considered it the language of peasants and oppressors. Nor did I mention my trying to learn French from that Russian "Teach Yourself French" handbook with Malin, the librarian, which had forced me to learn the two languages at the same time.

The subject of history was a surprise. What I had learned in high school as pre-history now became the "era of primeval communism." That was followed up by the history of Egypt, taught as a chronology of different slave uprisings against the Pharaohs. I also learned that the Spartacus mutiny was the foremost happening in Roman history.

The noble attempt to bring education to the criminal masses in our labour colony did not last long. Two months at most. It just petered out—to nobody's regret.

More consistent than the attempt at academic classes were the public lectures, variety shows, films and plays arranged by the Cultural and Educational Section. These were held on Sundays in the *klub's* theatre, and attendance was compulsory. The prisoners scorned the lectures on productivity and the communist work ethic. Instead they treated the event as a social gathering, changing the auditorium into a vast gambling den. The players and the kibitzers swore loudly, often confusing the lecturer with exhortations like, "Cover it with the ace, you asshole!"

Slightly more interesting were the propaganda talks by the Heroes of the Soviet Union. In one of them a bemedalled Soviet pilot explained how, in a skirmish near Khalchin-Gol in Mongolia, he scared a Japanese pilot into crashing just by flying close and shaking his fist at him. But his war story was spoiled by his wooden, monotonous recitation that made boys around me yawn.

The film show repertoire was limited to half a dozen movies. But the Russians didn't mind watching the same films again and again. Among them were *Lenin in 1918*, *The Battleship Potemkin* and *Modern Times* with Charlie Chaplin, which seemed to be the only foreign film shown in those days in the Soviet Union. The Russians loved it, and many a youngster would adopt the Chaplinesque gait as his usual way of walking.

But the real treat for inmates was the occasional visit by theatre groups and variety shows, mainly because they brought with them live women, not just actresses but also female singers, dancers and musicians. Unlike the female workers in the factory or even the office workers from outside, these women on stage were flashily dressed, wearing heavy makeup and high heels. The *zhuliki*, who fought among themselves to get into the front rows, sat through the entire performance ogling the actresses. The young criminals couldn't have cared less about the plot of the piece or the words uttered by the players. They just sat there transfixed by the sight of the women, commenting loudly on every aspect of the female anatomy—albeit covered—of the artistes and on what they would do to them and how, if given a chance. Such remarks were appreciated by the rest of the audience, who would reward the most inventive quips by a short round of applause. Such an appreciative audience would make the ears and the necks of the actresses turn red. The blushing of their faces could not be seen under their heavy makeup.

Every play, with the exception of a period piece from the time of Peter the Great, had the same plot. It went more or less like this: In a factory, kolkhoz, ship or city council, a spy planted by a foreign power tries to sabotage productivity. A hard-working Party member uncovers this plot set up by the "capitalist encirclement." The spy is arrested. The workers promise to work harder in order to make up for the losses created by the enemies of the people and send a telegram to Dear Iosif Vissarionovich (Stalin) paying homage to his leadership and wisdom.

According to the theatrical conventions set up by the Cultural and Educational Department, the spy wore capitalist clothes—Homburg hat, spats, flashy tie and glasses. His makeup was what you'd expect for a sadistic strangler, made even more threatening by his twisted lips and throaty voice. The well-versed audience spotted him the moment he appeared on the stage, unlike the clods in the cast who took three long acts before unmasking the culprit.

The theatre was also used for staging a show trial when I was there. It took place one Sunday. On trial was a young hooligan. He was accused of robbing and assaulting his fellow prisoners, attacking the cashier of the prison store with a knife and throwing a bowlful of hot soup in the face of a counsellor. The accused, dressed in a filthy white sweater, sat between two guards in the front row of the auditorium. Every few minutes he would make an attempt to free himself and run away from his guards, but after a few steps they would catch him, wrestle him down and then plop him back into his seat. His friend sitting at the back of the theatre encouraged him and applauded his attempts to escape.

"Don't let the bitches break your spirit down! Once they do it you'll be just a piece of shit, not a *zhulik*!"

On the stage behind a long table covered with a red cloth sat the court. The prosecutor, a middle-aged man, was flanked by two women assessors. A white-haired, frail old man, counsel for the defence, sat at one end of the table. The court clerk, a bespectacled woman with a parrot face, occupied the other end. In front of her lay a volume of the penal code, writing paper and an inkwell with a pen stuck in it.

Without any preamble, the prosecutor recited the charges, modulating his voice like an actor. He would make frequent stops to peer at the accused as if to make sure that he understood what was being read to him. During these moments of silence the accused, imitating the prosecutor's voice and diction, would acknowledge that part of the charge with a loud "Fuck you!" and get a whack on the neck from the guard sitting next to him.

The indictment was followed by a long line of inmates—witnesses for the prosecution—including me. A few weeks before, the accused *zhulik* had nearly choked me to death as he wrenched two packets of cigarettes from me outside the prison store. As a witness I wasn't coherent. I was flustered by the crowd and the proceedings. The judge had difficulty understanding me and asked me if my testimony was in Russian or Ukrainian. That unsettled me further because I wasn't even sure myself. Finally the judge said "Two packets?" I nodded and he dismissed me. After summing up the charges, the judge called upon the Counsel for the Defence to take the floor.

The white-haired *advokat*, who kept leafing through the Penal Code with trembling fingers, got up to address the court, supposedly on his client's behalf.

"Ashamed as I am of having to defend this reptile unworthy of consuming good Soviet bread, nay, unworthy even of breathing the pure Soviet air, I must say that in one area the court has made a serious mistake in charging him according to paragraph 165 section two [or whatever the paragraph and section numbers were]. This paragraph refers to a common assault whereas my client committed a more serious armed attack on the clerk of the prison store. That kind of offence requires the application of paragraph 167 section one [or whatever] and calls for a penalty of five to seven years of imprisonment, not the three to five years called for by paragraph 165 section two applied by the prosecutor."

The prosecutor looked around at his assessors. They all nodded their heads in agreement and the prosecutor expressed thanks for the astute observations of the Counsel for the Defence, echoed by a loud "Fuck you!" from the accused.

After perfunctory deliberations the prosecutor pronounced the verdict. Five years in corrective labour camps in the Far North were to be added to the present five years being served by the accused. The verdict made no impression whatsoever on the sentenced hoodlum. As the court officials were leaving the stage, he made yet another attempt to escape. This time he managed to get nearly to the main exit before being caught by the frustrated guards.

Other than the visiting actresses, two women dominated the erotic yearnings of the inmates of the labour colony and divided them into two rival groups: the Maria Ivanovna fans and the Maria Petrovna fans. Both women were employed as nurse/hygienists and their duties ranged from checking cleanliness in the prison kitchens to inspecting prisoners' hair for lice. They wore white coats short enough to reveal their bare legs above the tops of their high boots. Even the sight of that small patch of uncovered skin was enough for some prisoners to sense a feeling of disquiet in the most masculine regions of their anatomy.

The fans of the strapping and cheerful Maria Petrovna outnumbered those of Maria Ivanovna. The tall, flaxen-haired Maria Petrovna had a permanent smile on her face and a figure like a sackful of pumpkins. Whether in the courtyard or a corridor, a crowd of young inmates would quickly surround her and besiege her with complaints and details about their imaginary ailments so they could ogle her longer. They would also try to cajole her into telling them for the umpteenth time the story of how she got wounded during her service with the Soviet troops in 1939 when they went to "liberate Ukrainian proletarians from the Polish yoke." The captive audience would listen impatiently to her lengthy preamble to the story, waiting for the description of a dramatic episode when a stray artillery shell exploded not far from the horse-drawn cart in which she was travelling and a piece of shrapnel hit her and imbedded itself in the inside of her thigh. But the grand finale of her story was yet to come.

At that point it was usually the short Zajtfeder, an ex-cabdriver, who would plant himself in front of her on his widespread bandy legs and speak for all of them. He had the gift of the gab. You could never tell whether he was serious or joking but he was very persuasive and Maria Petrovna had a weakness for him and his cheek.

"Maria Petrovna, that is an amazing story. It's a good thing that you survived that artillery barrage to tell us about it. I am sure you'll get a medal for your bravery one of these days. But would you be kind enough to show us where, exactly, you were hit by the shrapnel and show us the scar?"

"Come off it, Zajtfeder! I've showed it to you many times, you rascal!"

"Maybe you did, Maria Petrovna, but our memory is very bad and truly I cannot remember if it was your left or right thigh. Unless we see that scar again we'll have some doubts if it really did happen."

"Okay, children. But this is really the last time!"

And as she began to hitch up her white coat and the skirt under it, Zajtfeder would go down on one knee and bend to one side so much that his ear nearly touched the ground. Propping himself with his elbow, he tilted his head and kept peering upwards at the expanse of Maria Petrovna's fat white thighs as if expecting an ultimate revelation. From the side his contorted body looked like a three-dimensional ampersand.

But the miracle never happened. Although it was clear that Maria Petrovna enjoyed playing games, she also knew when to stop. After the double curtain of her skirt and coat came down she dismissed her enthralled audience with a curt, "That's enough, kids. And don't ask me to do it again." Her six-foot height and 200 pounds of flesh protected her from any rash attempt to touch her or from a crude remark by any of the undernourished weaklings in front of her.

But such was not the case with the second nurse, Maria Ivanovna, a slender, auburn-haired, quiet good-looker. A few months before I came to the labour colony, she was gang-raped by half a dozen teenage convicts whose cell she went to inspect alone. It is likely that the rape would have never been reported if it wasn't for the *urki* themselves who started bragging about it. The burly Kretov, *nachal'nik* of our labour colony, nearly beat to death the underage rapists when trying to get the truth out of them. But for reasons known only to herself, the demure victim tried to make light of it— or so the story went. "Some rape," she was said to have scoffed. "By the time I collected my thoughts about how to escape and whether to yell for help, it was all over." Afterwards, she and the other nurse, Maria Petrovna, kept on working as if nothing had happened.

As far as I know, during my stay in the colony neither of them ever missed supervising the biweekly showers for the inmates. Both of them would sit in the centre of the shower room on a low bench provided for changing and drying. They would look over us showering youths and make loud comments such as, "Don't skimp on soap and water, Smirnov. Make a good job of it. Your bottom and your heels are still black!" They laughed heartily as they exchanged their private jokes, which we couldn't hear. And they never passed up the chance to rumple the rusty stubble on the head of bowlegged Boris, an imbecile, whose abnormally large head was matched by his imposing baton in a state of seemingly perpetual erection.

For the shower we each got a little cube of soap about the size of an Oxo cube. There was no soap for washing our clothes. When we were in the showers our clothes were usually taken for steaming to disinfect them and kill the lice and nits, but they were not washed. In most other prisons and camps the guards would sometimes gather up our clothes and they would be laundered—after a fashion. But not in Kiev. I'd see the odd fellow keep on his underwear or a shirt to try to wash them under the shower. However, most of the cons who had a crumb of soap left after showering would save it for shaving. The workshops and even the dorms were filthy and so it was hard to keep clean. But I tried. There was a sink with a cold water tap at the end of our floor, and I used to rinse out my clothes under it when I could.

At that time I did not realize how lucky I was in not having to toil in any of the workshops among the *zhuliki*. As a rule they disliked "Westerners," and did everything they could to make our life miserable. In my case they were irked by the sight of me going to work in clean clothes to an office situated beyond the prison gate. They used to ridicule my unsullied hands.

"You call that a man's hand? Look here! These are the hands of the working class. Of honest workers!"

They'd show their grubby, unwashed hands and try to smear my face or my clean clothes. Not only in prison, but also everywhere in Russia, men would pride themselves in having their hands caked with dirt and grease.

Fights were commonplace in prison. In fact, there were always fights going on around us. During one melée in the yard an *urka* swung an iron bar at my face. It split my lip and broke off part of an upper tooth. Sometimes I got into fights that were nothing to do with me. We Poles were loyal to each other and would jump in to defend any other Pole under attack. This surprised and annoyed the *zhuliki*. "Look at that," they marvelled. "If we were like that, the whole world wouldn't stand a chance against us."

One of them called Shumsky, a broad-shouldered character with a perpetual snarl on his grimy face, developed a real hatred for me. He persuaded or bribed the youngest *urka*, twelve-year-old Andreyko, to hit me over the head from behind with an iron mace while we were lining up for our bread ration. Only the quick reaction of Filek Birnbaum, who was standing behind me and deflected the blow, saved my skull from being cracked.

And so the grumbling and complaining continued about the "fascist Polish spy getting a cushy job and preferential treatment." In order to pacify the "true working class," the counsellors would order me to do some menial work like washing the stairs or cleaning the toilets. This I didn't mind, because I would do the job in half the time allowed and spend the remaining time reading—which infuriated the complainers even more.

Chapter 12

BEAUTIFUL ZHENYA'S ENTOURAGE

At the Technical Section, boss Boris Ivanovich soon put me to work tracing pencil design drawings with India ink. They were technical drawings of the bedsteads with their ornamental headboards and footboards, forms for iron casting, construction details and shop drawings. Drafting was not a mystery to me. I had used the special pen and ink in high school for drawing maps and graphs. Here, the drafting instruments and the makeshift tracing paper were of poor quality, but I managed all right and was pleased to get approving glances from the seasoned draftsmen in the office. Soon I became a full-fledged tracer.

It was at that time and in that office that I met Nikolai Nikolayev, one of the few true friends in my life. Known to everybody as Nik, he was a designer/draftsman about forty years old, married (I believe) but childless. We didn't talk about such things. He was of medium height and his brown hair was streaked at the temples with the first hoar of middle age. Kindness, honesty and intelligence were written all over his lean face. Behind the thin, black frames of his glasses you could see the inquisitive eyes of a photographer, for photography was his passion and what he didn't know about it wasn't worth knowing. A 35mm FED camera—a Soviet copy of the German Leica—was his proudest possession. Films, printing paper, developer and fixer were almost impossible to buy, so he pondered well the light and the subject before clicking the shutter. As a result, each of his shots was a little gem of photographic art.

We hit it off from the first day. Like me, he was a compulsive reader, and he loved to talk about his favourite books, whether they were now banned or not. He brought me a weekly magazine called *Ogoniok* (Little Flame). He had no problems understanding my garbled Russian, but with great tact let me know that some of the words and idioms I had picked up in prison were less than acceptable among cultured people. Nik would comment on the skimpy news in *Komsomolskaya Pravda* about the war in North Africa where success on the battlefield kept swinging like a pendulum between the British and Axis forces. One day, after the Brits began retreating from Cyrenaica for the third time, he said, "I still hope that the English will thrash the Krauts and the Macaronis." That was a dangerous thing to say in the autumn of 1940 when Hitler and Stalin were still buddies, but Nik found it hard to smother his honest opinions.

As a university student Nik had joined the Communist Party in 1918 at the beginning of the Russian Revolution. For him, the Party and its ideology were the only answer then to the problems of the moribund tsarist regime. At the age of nineteen he was already in command of a platoon in the fledgling Red Army. There was one story about his days as a commander that has stuck in my mind. He enjoyed the irony in his tale but kept a solemn face even when we laughed at it and shook our heads in disbelief.

In a small provincial town during the great famine of 1920, he told us, he begged the warden of the local prison to "arrest" him and his soldiers, hoping to get at least a prisoner's food ration for himself and each of his men while they awaited a train that was due in two days.

"No dice," said the warden. "You must commit a crime first and then you can be duly arrested." Nik spent hours with his starvelings trying to think up a crime that would secure them prison accommodation and food for two days. The prison warden himself suggested that "threatening behaviour and verbal abuse of the prison warden" might do the trick. They had to go through a veritable *commedia dell'arte* of abuse and threats and the rigmarole of the arrest, all for a plate of watery nettle soup and a thin slice of corn bread twice a day. Later that day, however, the warden realized that feeding a platoon of soldiers even for one day had dwindled his food supplies to an alarming degree. He opened the door to the cell where Nik and his warriors were huddling.

"Your sentence has been reduced to one day. You are forgiven. Now get out! All of you!"

"Nothing doing. Take it easy *nachal'nichek* (little chief). Two days is two days!"

Both sides stubbornly stuck to their rights and only a rhetorical question asked by Nik's mean-faced subordinate—"Would *physical* abuse of the prison warden secure another day of incarceration?"—made the warden relent.

In the early thirties, Nik was asked to photograph a tractor. That photo was to accompany a newspaper article about the Five Year Plan for mechanizing Soviet agriculture. The photo was a piece of art—a gleaming new tractor, symbol of the merger of the two pillars of the Soviet State (industry and agriculture), photographed against the lyrical background of the Russian paysage. Unfortunately Nik, ever innocent and naive, failed to notice that a compendium of vernacular terms for reproductive organs and functions was chalked in large letters on the wooden fence behind the tractor. He was accused of sabotage and anti-Soviet propaganda. Only his record of lengthy membership in the Communist Party saved him from a prison sentence.

Nik's next faux pas was more serious. That happened in 1938 when the Civil War was raging in Spain. At first the Soviet Union helped the Republicans in their struggle against the monarchists led by Generalissimo Franco, who was supported by the fascist dictators of Italy and Germany. But as the Civil War dragged on, Stalin sniffed too much independent thinking among the Republican communists. They refused to be mere puppets of the Soviet politburo. He chopped off all help to them and ordered the Soviet units home. The Spanish Republic soon began to founder.

When the imminent collapse of Republican Spain was mentioned during a public lecture on the international situation given by a party propagandist, Nikolayev stood up and plainly asked, "If this is so, then why don't we send them more tanks and planes to fight the fascists?"

No one was supposed to ask such questions in the Soviet Union. Nikolayev was accused of criticizing the politburo. He lost his job and was kicked out of the Party. He became a marked man for the rest of his life.

Nik felt sorry for me. The more we talked and the longer we worked together, the more he came to believe that it was wrong to keep me in prison.

"But he did try to cross the border illegally, didn't he?" remarked our accountant, Peschanskiy, one of the two "non-technical" people in our office. It was one of the few comments he ever made.

"Yes. He did. But, as he says, in Poland crossing a border illegally was a minor offence like crossing a park after the official closing time."

Peschanskiy did not answer. He was a taciturn character about double my age, with wavy black hair and sharp features. He was always busy. As he sat hunched over an old desk, the fingers of his left hand moved the beads of an abacus with the speed of lightning while the sharp pencil in his right hand kept entering long columns of figures on his makeshift graph paper. He would signal the end of a page with a sigh of relief then check it once again on the abacus. If the figures tallied he'd put it in the "out" tray. However, a prolonged hiss told us that something had gone wrong with his calculations. He would start erasing the figures while whistling softly a nondescript tune in a minor key.

But there was one person who kept listening and memorizing everything that was said in the office. It was our girl Friday, Sara, the other non-technical. Of indeterminate age, she could have been twenty or forty. Summer or winter she wore the same faded pink cardigan. She got on everybody's nerves by continuously singing the only two lines she knew from a current popular song.

Sara was in charge of our scanty drafting supplies. She also updated files and helped make blueprints. But most of the time she just sat at her tiny desk with nothing to do. To kill time she kept making dots with coloured pencils on scraps of paper and would link them later on with straight lines. I cannot understand why it took me such a long time to figure out what her real job was—in spite of warning glances cast in my direction by others when my conversation veered towards forbidden subjects—for Sara's job was to report everything that went on and was said in our office.

I was still in the quarantine cell when Avram Davidovich brought some good news. He said that as the investigations of my case were over, and I had already received my sentence, I now had the right to send and receive letters. I immediately began to write home, but it was a long time before I was to receive a reply. I had had no news from my family for eight months. I had written my first letter as soon as my counsellor said I could. After a few days I wrote another. I gave these letters to the counsellor for mailing. That was the required procedure. Two weeks passed. Three. No reply. I wrote more letters. Some of them to my friends in Horodenka. Still no reply. The next two letters I wrote in Russian. Nothing. Perhaps my letters never left the office of our political commissar, Zelikov. Most of them were written in Polish and probably the censor could not understand them. Then again I was a Pole who tried to escape from the Soviet Union and now wrote letters not only to his family but also to other people. All that could have looked suspicious to Zelikov.

I decided on a ruse. Zelikov was a Jew. And the feeling of solidarity among the Jews was strong in Russia. So the next letter I wrote was to our Jewish neighbour in Horodenka, the dentist, whose son Maurycy was my classmate in high school. I addressed the letter to his father as Citizen Doctor Karol Kaufman. In less than a week Avram Davidovich galloped into our cell from Zelikov's office. "Topolski! Telegram for you!"

The telegram was open. It was in Ukrainian. It said: "All in good health. Letter mailed."

That was followed by a stream of letters. It was Doctor Kaufman who, with tears in his eyes, had delivered my letter to my sister Maria during one of her visits to Horodenka. My family had left Horodenka. They were living 350 kilometres away in a small village called Czyszki near Lwow. Their letters seemed cheerful. Everything was fine. I sent them a list of things I needed: warm trousers, long johns, mitts and a Richter drafting pen (that would impress people in the Technical Section!) and some other things.

Then a letter came from my older sister Henia who, without the knowledge of the rest of the family and without beating about the bush, described their plight. In the early spring of 1940 the NKVD began rounding up and deporting to Siberia or the steppes of Central Asia the "socially dangerous element" from Soviet-occupied Poland.

About that time an unexpected visitor came to see my family in the middle of the night. He was the aged Mr. Frischling whose son had been my father's pupil before the First World War and whose grandson Dov was in one class with me in our high school. Under the Soviets, Dov's father became the chief of the local militia unit. It was he who sent his old father, Mr. Frischling, with a message that our family was on the list of people to be arrested and deported the following day. They left Horodenka by train in the wee hours of the morning, taking with them a few suitcases and a large wicker basket full of clothes. It was kind of the Frischlings to warn them, but they rewarded themselves promptly for that good deed. No sooner had my family left Horodenka than the Frischlings and their friends helped themselves to everything they fancied in our house.

My family went first to Stanislawow where they had some friends, but after a few days they had to move to Lwow, a large cultural and economic centre and the hometown of the three Lempickis who were captured with me. My family was on the run and, quite understandably, nobody wanted to take the risk of harbouring them. In Lwow my mother's cousin, Professor Juliusz Kijas, was too scared even to let them in the door. It was also in Lwow that the wicker basket with their clothes got stolen. They were selling whatever they could, including my mother's gold wedding ring, to buy food. My sister Henia had a two-month-old baby son, Andrzej. Her husband, Woytek Gorka, a former landowner, was in a Soviet prison. Eventually the whole family found a relatively safe place in the small village of Czyszki near Lwow. All five of them lived in a tiny room with an adobe floor. Maria found a job in the village school teaching illiterate adults to read and write. She also made several trips back to Horodenka to retrieve any sellable things left in our house, which was still unoccupied. Father, who was then over sixty, earned a few rubles by digging peat in marshy land around the village for fuel for the nearby brickyard.

I felt bad for having sent the letter asking them to mail me things they couldn't get. I realized I was in a better situation than they were. In October when I received my first monthly salary of fifty rubles, I persuaded my office friend Nikolayev to send it to them. They got that money all right. But poor Nik got into trouble because of it. Sara denounced him for helping a prisoner to bypass the official channels of communications.

One morning in the spring of 1941, more than half a year since I had first met Nikolayev, he stopped me in the corridor as I was going to the toilet. He looked about as if checking if anybody was around and, while still gazing over my head at our office door behind me, said quickly "Boguslaw." He always called me by my first name. "I was called to Zelikov's office. It was an unpleasant meeting. It's not your fault. I can only blame myself and my stupidity. I have been told not to talk to you unless it's business. No more newspapers, no books, no *Ogoniok Weekly*. But we will remain friends. Watch out for Sara. God be with you." It was strange to hear "God be with you" from Nik, an avowed atheist living under a regime that outlawed religion.

In spite of the confidentiality requested by *politruk* Zelikov, the entire office soon sensed what had happened. The invisible barrier between me and Nik was conspicuous and our silence screamed out the new restrictions. Everybody was more polite, even deferential, to Sara, with the exception of the young designer Polubenik. Every morning he greeted her with an exaggerated effusiveness, a low bow and "Greetings, Comrade Sara" drawled with a mocking smile on his lips. Polubenik had come to the Technical Section straight from an Air Force unit where he completed his three years of national service. Rosy-faced, with a blond forelock that he constantly kept tossing back with a sweep of his hand, he gave the impression of a man without cares who took everything lightly. He talked a lot about girls and vodka, which earned him dirty looks from old Bashko. But he was a good designer and his creation of the "Slavonic Wardrobe" (a freestanding clothes cupboard with little windows high in its gable walls to let in light) was a great success. Invariably, at the end of the working week before leaving our drafting room, he would look Sara up and down and announce for everybody to hear, "I invite you, Comrade Sara, to the public baths tonight." His scoffing invitation had innuendos of a sexual put-down as well as suggesting her need for a good wash. She pretended not to hear.

When the news about the young boys murdered in the *urki*'s fight in my dormitory building reached the office, Polubenik was outraged. "Scandal! Scandal! The whole Soviet Union should know what's going on in this den of criminals!" Shortly after that, Sara went out, and when she came back she said that Boris Ivanovich, the boss, wanted to see him. Polubenik returned a different man, pale and silent. Gone forever were his uncouth but funny remarks and his off-colour adaptations of patriotic songs. He had now joined the cowed, glum majority of Soviet citizens.

The only other tracer in the office besides me was Zhenya Titova, a twenty-seven-year-old beauty with raven tresses. Though her wardrobe was limited, she was always well dressed and well groomed. Ever ready for a good laugh, she could tell a risqué joke without batting an eyelid. She was the darling of the office. Her table was next to mine. When drafting, she preferred to sit or kneel on an ordinary office chair instead of a high drafting stool. That was fine with me because at times I could peek at the cleavage revealed by the décolletage of her dress. I had no doubt that she must have noticed my furtive glances, but she also made it obvious that she didn't mind my interest in her Dianesque shapes.

Once she brought me a real treat, a handful of fresh strawberries, and, on another occasion, an apple. These were great gifts. In those days such delicacies were rare in Kiev. It was the first fruit I had eaten since my capture. When I received my first parcel from home, among other things in it there was a tiny tin of scented petroleum jelly. I gave it to Zhenya. She was elated with it. She would open the lid and with closed eyes sniff the jar as if it contained Chanel or Guerlain.

She was married but she told us precious little about her husband. We did know that they had no children and lived at the other end of the city. To get to work she had to walk a couple of kilometres, take a tram and then change to a trolley bus.

Her good looks did not escape the attention of our chief, Boris Ivanovich. He spent a lot of time at her drafting table checking her work and asking her to design new forms and production charts. Then he would call her to his office to discuss changes and corrections. One day after coming back from his office she burst into tears.

She put her head down on her table, burying it between her arms. Her shoulders kept jerking as she sobbed quietly. Nobody in the office asked her what happened. Nobody tried to console her. After a few days the same thing happened again. And then again.

Finally late one afternoon as we were ready to call it a day, Zhenya was summoned to the plant manager's office. We lingered awhile, awaiting her return. It didn't take long. She came back with her head held high.

"They've fired me for incompetence. That's what they said. But I know that you know why: because I refused my favours—there is another word for it—to that snake. Well, we better say farewell now because you won't see me again. Now you, Nik," she turned her head to the shaken Nikolai, "don't do anything stupid, like protesting or intervening on my behalf. Your goodness has killed good sense in you. You won't help me and you'll put yourself again in a terrible mess. Stay out of it!" She gave him a peck on the cheek and went around the room to shake hands with the rest of us. Nik took out a handkerchief to wipe a tear off his spectacles while he followed her moves with his myopic, expressionless eyes. She went to pick up her things from her desk. When she finished she looked at me, shook her hair and said, "Keep on dreaming, youngster. That's what makes you strong." And she was gone.

Next morning, Boris Ivanovich came to the office in an excellent mood. Groomed to perfection, he was sporting a new tie. He sang his favourite tune, "The moon is hiding behind the cloud. Give me your hand, my dear," a bit louder than usual. As he went from desk to desk, he had something pleasant to say to each of us and passed around the expensive and hard to get Linkor cigarettes. We smiled in turn and said "Thank you" in the over-polite way a guest would to a hostess who served them stale sandwiches made with rancid butter. Within days Boris Ivanovich brought to the office Zhenya's replacement, a churlish simpleton named Hawryluk. As soon as the chief had disappeared into his office and Sara had left the drafting room on some errand, Hawryluk tried to break the ice, to introduce a spirit of camaraderie and to establish himself as one of us. He recounted in great detail what and how he did it with his last mistress before his arrest. There were no comments when he finished. Only the truly astonished Nikolai piped up.

"And why on earth would you do that?"

Silence fell over the room. We were just as embarrassed by Nikolai's innocence as by Hawryluk's vulgarity.

I do not remember the first name and the patronymic of the senior draftsman Popov. It was Zhenya who gave him the nickname Popik ("little Popov"). It stuck to him and everybody called him just that. He was about forty, quiet and circumspect. He had to be. He was a candidate for membership in the Communist Party and so had to watch his step. He shied away from office gossip and teatime chatter, and would leave the room whenever the talk could be construed as having political connotations. Any improvident remark by him could be reported by the ubiquitous informers to the *politruk* Zelikov, who in turn would notify personnel and the higher-ups in the Party. That would diminish if not nullify Popik's chances of joining that exclusive club. He was a good worker and knew his job. In fact he was the one who introduced me to the arcane details of technical drafting. Popik took his candidature to heart. He went to the evening classes on political education and even during lunchtime he would leaf through the pages of the Party catechism. Once in the office somebody reading a newspaper tossed a question to nobody in particular, "Say, what's opportunism?" Before anybody could clear his throat or say a word, Popik closed his eyes and recited by heart as if reading from *The Great Soviet Encyclopedia*:

"A conciliatory stance, resigning from one's principles in order to achieve an immediate objective, like the tendency in the workers' movement of the Second International striving to adjust the workers' party to the structural conditions of a bourgeois society."

When he finished, Popik was beaming and looking around for an accolade, but all he got was, "Well, quite a mouthful" from old Bashko.

After a few weeks in the drafting office I couldn't help noticing some furtive deals that went on between the old prisoner Bashko and Popik. Without saying a word Bashko would slip into Popik's desk drawer a packet of something wrapped up in a newspaper. It was about as big as half a brick. In turn Popik would press into Bashko's hand a few ruble notes and put that mysterious package into his briefcase to take home. One day that mysterious package slipped from Popik's hand and unwrapped as it fell on the floor. Inside it was a chunk of bread, about half of a prisoner's daily ration. It happened at the end of the working day when everybody else was gone, and so I was the only one who saw it. Popik looked embarrassed when he picked the bread up from the floor. He turned his face away from me and, looking through the window at the courtyard below, mumbled something to the effect that not everything in the Soviet Union was as perfect as the propagandists and the newspapers would have us believe. I now understood the mystery of their stealthy exchanges. The daily bread ration for Popik's family was not enough and he was buying bread from Bashko, who needed money for cigarettes. That incident shook me. I knew that "not everything is perfect in the Soviet Union" but I never thought that it was so bad that free citizens would be buying bread from prisoners. (And this was in 1940, before the Soviets were at war with Germany.)

Old Bashko, the bread seller, who must have been over sixty, was a Ukrainian who spoke only Russian. In the Soviet Union there were millions like him. Officially the Soviet Government encouraged the national traits of different republics, their language and customs, although no distinctive flags were permitted. Generally speaking, it was the Russians who ruled the entire country. Deep at heart they believed themselves superior to those nationalities, and most of them considered the Soviet Union to be the continuation of the old Russian Empire and its colonies. For them a good Ukrainian was the one who might speak Ukrainian in the office but spoke only Russian at home.

Bashko knew a bit about prejudice himself. As a soldier during the First World War he had spent some time on Polish soil. He recited to me with glee every derogatory name and synonym for a Russian soldier to be found in the Polish language. We had a jolly good laugh together over them all.

Old Bashko, although of Ukrainian origin, thought of himself as a Russian not a *khokhol* (a derogatory name for a Ukrainian). A staunch adherent of the banned and officially non-existent Russian Orthodox

Church, he joined the atheist studies group in prison whose aim was to eradicate the last vestiges of religion—the opiate of the masses, according to Karl Marx. Bashko joined it because it gave him access to books on religious subjects that the general public were prohibited from reading. Often I saw Bashko in the reading room of the prison library poring over pages of the Holy Scriptures. He was fascinated by the Apocalypse and was convinced that the end of the world was at hand. "Aren't these the Iron Birds prophesied in it?" he mused one day looking up at the planes in the sky.

Bashko had only one tunic, which he wore over his threadbare trousers. It was a faded blue with a low mandarin collar with some remnants of embroidery on it. He wore it every day and washed it once a week. It was girded by a narrow leather belt hanging loose from his bony hips—bony because he was consumptive. His persistent hacking cough was interrupted occasionally by a low rumbling and gurgling noise followed by a bout of hawking to bring up phlegm from the depth of his throat. He spat it out with amazing accuracy into the knot hole in the floorboard next to his chair. His sonorous expectorations would have been a good enough reason to get rid of him, but Bashko was indispensable to the Technical Section. He was the office scribe. He wrote in such a beautiful hand that even a teacher of calligraphy would be envious. Bashko was industrious and filled reams of paper day after day. He was our living typewriter and copier. An order for twenty-five copies of a letter would not faze him at all. But he wrote at his own pace and no amount of urging could speed him up. You could just as well urge a clock to go faster. He had his own supplies of purple ink and paper which he squirrelled away in his padlocked desk drawers together with a collection of blotting papers, pens and nibs. He would never compose a letter: he would only copy a letter written by someone else. Even Boris Ivanovich could not talk him into making any small changes in a letter, such as changing the date or substituting a plural for a singular. Bashko would, so to speak, dig his unwashed heels into the creosoted floorboards and shake his shaven head in wordless refusal. He was certainly intelligent enough to write a letter or make some changes in an existing one, but by doing so, he would be making a decision and accepting responsibility for it.

Topolski's parents, Aleksander and Henryka (née Kijas), on June 14, 1914, about the time of their marriage.

Aleksander Topolski, 14, in school uniform, standing on his street in Horodenka (then in Poland, now in the Ukraine).

Topolski's mother, Henryka, with his older sisters Henia, 19 (left), and Maria, 16 (right), in Horodenka, 1936.

Topolski, 16, at Gdynia on the Baltic Sea during a boy scout trip in July, 1939.

Pre-war view from Topolski's home up cobblestoned Ormianska Street in Horodenka.

Topolski at the Polish naval base at Oksywie in Gdynia.
Behind the *Delfin*, the Polish destroyer *Blyskawica*
(Lightning) can be seen in the far distance.

Topolski (crouching, left) in spring, 1939, with fellow cadets
Wieslaw Sobiech, Kazimierz Blyszczuk, Roman Ewy,
Zdzislaw Starzynski, Janusz Konopka (standing),
and Eugeniusz Kirszbaum (crouching right).

Topolski (center) with school friends during weekend
maneuvers in Horodenka, early spring, 1939.

Horodenka high school cadet corps on Polish Independence Day,
November 11, 1938 (Topolski is in the front row, furthest right). Of these
26 young men, only five are known to have survived World War II.

Photo taken December 11 , 1939, on the morning of the day Topolski
left home and was captured by Soviet border guards.

Poles, who suffered severe hardships in the Soviet Union, line
up to register for the newly formed Polish Army.

Polish Army volunteers line up for soup in Totskoye, USSR (1941).

A typical scene of ex-prisoners and deportees getting their bread rations after finding and signing up for the Polish Army.

Polish military cemetery (First Signals Regiment) in Katta Alekseyevskaya, Uzbekistan, where Topolski served. Soldiers died of malnutrition and disease. Elsewhere, soldiers were shot for stealing food.

Topolski, 19, in his new army uniform with New Zealand hat
two days after his arrival in Iran in August or September,
1942, near the Caspian Sea port of Pahlevi (now Enzeli).

He wouldn't make the tiniest change unless the boss wrote out the complete revised version for him to keep for his files.

In our office there was only one fully qualified engineer with a university education. Known to us as Boris Vasilievich, his family name was Batalin. From the tsarist capital of Russia, St. Petersburg, he earned his degree at the venerable university in the city of Dorpat (known to Estonians as Tartu). He would often reminisce on his student life there and was proud of once being a member of a fraternity. Another source of his pride was a set of pre-revolution German-made Richter drafting instruments. His drafting board was at the far end of the room. When he was bent over it, his bald pate glowed like an ostrich egg against the background of his shiny black jacket and the black-bound books on the shelves behind him. When talking he would lift his head just a little, peering out from above his steel-rimmed specs. The top of his ill-fitting, yellowed dentures seemed to disappear under his moustache. Only the corners of his lower lip curled up or down to signal whether he was serious or just retelling one of his six smutty jokes.

From time to time we were called to a "production re-assessment meeting." These meetings were boring and annoying. Most of them were tacked onto the end of our working day when people were tired and tempers short. During one of these meetings, a well-known bore with a whining voice began once again to explain how he would increase productivity in the wood workshop.

But the others knew it wouldn't work. Insults flew back and forth. They swore at him and told him to shut up.

A burly foreman butted in. "Comrade Chairman! You can hear shits and fucks flying to and fro in the air like swallows before the rain. It's a very uncultured discussion. Aren't those sons of bitches aware of the women's presence in this room?!"

Broad-chested Lonya got up. "We don't give a fuck about discussion, Comrade Chairman. Give us the resolution. It's getting late. We haven't had our supper yet!"

She was joined by a chorus of female voices. "Yes! Yes! Give us the resolution! Let's vote and get it over with!"

Politruk Zelikov, who was watching the proceedings with disgust from the back of the room, turned to the armed guard standing beside him.

"What a bunch of scum! Open the door as soon as the voting is over."

The amount of propaganda directed by the state at its own citizens was unbelievable. All day long, starting at six o'clock in the morning, the loudspeakers (which we referred to as "the radio") in every room blared patriotic marches and songs, "inspirational" talks, and news about over-fulfilled production quotas in factories and kolkhozes. Everything was aimed at persuading the listeners that they lived in the best country in the world. Real radios (which could bring in forbidden foreign stations) were locked up in special rooms closed to all but politically reliable citizens, who tuned them only to Radio Moscow and its local subsidiaries. From these radio rooms the programs were relayed by the speakers (which had no on or off switches) installed in workplaces, institutions and apartments. Shaposhnik, a young man in his early twenties, had the job of tuning in the radio that fed our speakers. He was good at it. At night he would find for us good dance music: tangos, rhumbas and Gypsy tunes from neighbouring countries—probably from Germany or Hungary. We couldn't tell where they came from because he was careful never to let through even one word by a foreign announcer. However, he knew his music and didn't chop off the final bars. He must have been sitting at the radio with his hand on the volume control and his ears tuned to the musical measures, knowing well what could happen to a radio controller who slipped up and let through a foreign voice.

The daily papers were controlled in the same way. Skimpy, carefully selected and edited foreign news underlined the dire poverty, hunger and oppression of the working classes in capitalist countries. What's more, ubiquitous posters and banners repeated slogans praising the strength of the Party and the wisdom of Stalin. Those who grew up under the Soviet regime believed—or professed to believe —the propaganda. Here, unlike Western countries, the word *propaganda* had no pejorative connotations. On the contrary, working in *agitprop* (the Russian abbreviation for agitation and propaganda) was an indispensable step in the career of an aspiring Party member.

But the arrival of us foreigners into the labour colony planted seeds of doubt in the minds of the locals. The braver ones would tackle the omniscient counsellors.

"How come those Westerners, even those who were working as shepherds in villages, have clothes made of wool and boots of real leather, all better than ours?" Their counsellor's reply, though long and convoluted, failed to satisfy them. I also found that some Russians, after being pounded with too much propaganda, not only became cynical and mistrusted everything they were told, but believed that the opposite must be true.

On the corridor wall just outside our cell door was a large political map of the world in Mercator's projection, which flattens the globe and overly enlarges the northern and southern regions. I often thought that if Mercator had not invented his way of portraying the earth in the 16th century, the Soviet cartographers would have invented it, for it made the Soviet Union look twice as big as it really was. Its blood-red amorphous blob before me spread through eleven time zones and dwarfed countries like Germany, France and Great Britain. I spent a lot of time standing in front of this map following on it the vicissitudes of the British Army fighting the Italians and the Germans across North Africa. I also loved to trace with my finger my imaginary route to the Afghanistan border in quest of freedom and soon knew by heart the names of key cities along the railway lines to the south.

Then one day as I was doing my map gazing, I felt somebody was standing behind my back. I turned around and saw a boy younger than me, Plygan I think his name was, also looking at the map. When he saw my face he winked at me, looked around to check if anybody was within earshot, then whispered, "I know, I know. I know what you think. You don't have to tell me. I am sure in Poland you had maps where Poland stretched for half of the globe and the Soviet Union was little bigger than a wart. Those bastards always lie to us."

Chapter 13

ARMA VIRUMQUE CANO

"Of arms I sing and of the man"
  – first line of *Aeneid* by Virgil
  (Translation: James Rhoades, 1921)

In the late spring of 1941, letters received by me and my more trustworthy friends often hinted at the buildup of the German forces on the Soviet border. These letters were coming from Soviet-occupied eastern Poland (renamed Western Ukraine and Western Byelorussia by the Soviets) and from General Gouvernement, the name given by the Germans to the parts of western Poland that had not been incorporated into "Great Germany" (Hitler named it Grossdeutschland, not to be outdone by Great Britain). The coding of the news in these letters was naive, and it would take a real clod of a censor not to spot them. Besides, most of the political news was no news to us, as we now had access to the Soviet radio and press plus considerable experience in deciphering the official style of the Soviet news media. Such gems of cryptography from our families as, "Auntie Greta got clobbered by Adolph last month" (Greece was beaten by Germany in May) or, "Francine has sent some of the children to Uncle George" (France sent some of her troops to England) did little to increase our knowledge of the international situation. But my sister Maria and other writers congratulated themselves on outwitting the odious Communist censorship. A village boy in our group received a letter from his peasant father who wrote, "The old barrel, as you know, was rotten and fell to pieces, but the new one that we have now is not going to last much longer." Few people had confidence in the might of the Soviet Union.

On letters from Germany, the face of Hitler on postage stamps was blackened out by censor's ink and even the tiny swastika inside the wreath held by the German eagle was laboriously scratched out with a pin or the tip of a knife. At the same time, the Soviet radio and press were full of communiqués praising "the friendship and spirit of co-operation developing between two great nations in spite of the dirty machinations of the Western capitalistic states who try to spoil the existing cordial relationship between the Soviet Union and Germany."

Daily editions of *Pravda* and *Izvestia* were thumbtacked into a long display case on the wall that divided the courtyard of the dormitory building from that of the workshops. They were ignored by 99 percent of the inmates. The remaining one percent of us read them avidly, trying to glean important news by noticing omissions, a sudden change of adjectives, the emergence of new names or the change of page on which the articles appeared. The papers were read in total silence by men with impassive faces, shuffling their feet sideways without glancing left or right lest the reader's face betray his politically incorrect reactions to the news content and he be denounced to the Cultural and Educational Section.

But the signs of approaching war were multiplying and only well-trained Party stalwarts could ignore them. German Ambassador Count von Shulenburg was reassuring Stalin in Moscow about his führer's commitment to peace at the same time as family letters from both sides of the new Soviet-German border hinted at the massing of Nazi troops there and at frequent overflights by the Luftwaffe's reconnoitring planes. In one of the letters about that time, a brother of one of the boys in our cell wrote he'd seen "many Kraut planes on spying missions flying over our village in the direction of the military airfield newly constructed by the Russkies. But sooner or later with God's help we'll chase all those whoresons from our holy patrimony." In that sentence, only the word "God" was deleted by the censor. But then everybody knew that the chief censor was Marusia, a simple young woman with a round face and black hair. Although she was officially a polyglot, her knowledge of foreign languages was limited to the Latin alphabet and a few dozen German words. No wonder she always had a worried look on her pretty face.

When some thinking and bold prisoners tackled the prison's education officer about these rumours of a German invasion of the

USSR, he glanced at them incredulously, taken aback by their daring and naïveté. He thought for a while, then pushed his spectacles back, rubbed his eyes with the back of his hands and, looking straight ahead with his myopic, vapid eyes, mouthed the pat answer to any question for which a Party line explanation was not available, "All this is a dirty intrigue of the Roman pope."

But these hints, rumours and denials began to add up. As one of my Canadian friends, a government official named Joseph Hrazdira, used to say to me years later, "Nothing is certain unless officially denied." I sat down and wrote a letter to my family—one of those letters that start with, "Don't worry if you don't hear from me for a long time." It was good advice. They had to wait for four and half years for my next letter.

Sunday, June 22, 1941. A day of rest. On that morning, for some reason, we were not queuing up for breakfast at the serving hatch in our own drab eatery. Instead, we were heading for the Stakhanovite dining room in the *klub* where women waited on the tables. The guards lined us up in front of the gate into the furniture factory yard where the *klub* was. As we waited for the gate to open I heard the distant droning of plane engines. It startled me, for this was a familiar sound—the sound I had heard in September 1939 when the Germans bombed Horodenka. A current of fear ran through my body. But neither the guards nor the prisoners paid much attention to the noise. I looked at my friend Bastomski who, like myself, had already had an encounter with the Luftwaffe. He stood motionless, his neck craned, his head tilted away from the direction of the droning noise, which grew louder. He caught my eye and nodded. This was it.

When the silver specks appeared over the horizon in the cloudless blue sky, the prisoners and the guards lifted their heads to look at the unusually large number of planes, counting them with pointing fingers. There were forty-nine. All of them Junkers 88 bombers. But to the guards they were just planes. They soon lost interest in them and started herding us through the open gate. I followed the others and, with my eyes still glued to the planes, stumbled over the scraps of wood scattered all over the factory yard.

Suddenly a squadron of twelve bombers peeled off from the main formation, made a neat turn, and started descending in the direction of the 43rd Aircraft Factory where the beautiful Zhenya was now working, about two miles from the prison compound. As they flew over it, the flashes of exploding bombs, the loud rumbling noise, the fast rising plumes of black smoke and the trembling earth shattered the peace of that Sunday morning. The fear-stricken guards halted our column. They were at a loss for what to do except gaze at this classic bombing raid. The three other squadrons followed the path of the first, unloading their noisy cargo with utmost precision. The flashes of the explosions became more visible against the background of smoke that by then had blackened half the sky. Within fifteen minutes it was all over. The bombers regrouped in their original formation and flew away undisturbed by any sign of defence. Our column resumed its slow march to the dining hall amid the din of a hundred anxious voices. A sweating NKVD officer ran over and with a trembling voice started berating our guards. "Why are you late?! There's no need to stop just because our air force is having bombing exercises!" Then he turned to us. "There is no war! Can't you understand it?! You idiots! There is NO WAR!"

At noon we heard Molotov's speech to the nation denouncing the dastardly attack by their erstwhile "friends." We had to wait about twelve days until we heard Stalin's special address to the nation. In his raspy voice with its heavy Georgian accent he spoke about the Germans' treachery and exhorted all citizens to fight the Fascists with all available means. He ended with, "Our cause is right. Victory will be ours." But he sounded tired and dispirited. When he finished, the reaction of the listeners standing in front of one of the many loudspeakers varied. The enthusiastic juvenile thieves and bandits raised on Party slogans shouted, "We'll show those cannibals!" But those who remembered the First World War muttered, "God have mercy on us!"

Within hours of the German raid, the ack-ack (anti-aircraft) guns, the four-barrel Maxim guns, the searchlights and the barrage balloons went up all over the city, belying later Soviet claims that they were caught totally unprepared.

The rest of that Sunday and following night we spent locked up in the dormitory buildings, being let out only for meals. We passed the time gazing at the sky from the barred windows and listening to the wail of air-raid sirens, the whirr of low- and high-flying planes, bursts of machine-gun fire, and the clatter of ack-acks. That night we sat in total darkness looking at the searchlight beams. We were all scared. Our fear was heightened by the feeling of being walled up with no place to run or hide. Next morning was quiet. At work people were subdued. Curly-headed Polubenik had already gone back to his Air Force unit. Our boss, Boris Ivanovich, with an air of importance, clean shaven and smelling stronger than usual of "Moscow Lights" cologne, called an early staff meeting from which, as an unreliable foreigner, I was excluded. The confidentiality of the meeting lasted only an hour or so. After all, ours was a cramped drafting office. It appeared that instead of iron beds, our factory would now be producing metal components for hand grenades. Drawings were needed for the new layout of the factory, for new presses and dies as well as new casting forms. Luckily, I retained my place in the corner and was told to continue the detailing of the latest model of an iron bed.

On Tuesday, the beautiful Zhenya Titova, risking a face-to-face meeting with the former boss whose advances she had spurned, came to see us. She told us about the fallen roofs, twisted beams and other damage done by the air raid to the 43rd Aircraft Factory. Nikolayev had received call-up papers to an aerial photo reconnaissance unit and was leaving the next day. Zhenya embraced and kissed him with tears in her eyes. She took one step back, looked at him again and said, "Go and fight for Russia. Have no mercy for these animals who keep invading our land every twenty years. And come back in health." In the next few days, I was to witness many similar farewell scenes, and in all of them the note of sincere Russian patriotism rang loud and clear. The injustices of the Communist system, Stalin's terror, the dire living conditions and the constant fear of being denounced by your friends and imprisoned, if not shot, for uncommitted crimes did not kill in them their love for Holy Russia.

I was the last in the office to say goodbye to Nikolayev. I owed him so much. For his words of praise and encouragement. For taking great risks by mailing some of my letters outside prison. For telling me so much about his life. For discussing the works of forbidden authors, like Merezhkovsky and Leikin. For being a friend. We looked into each other's eyes, and we shook hands. We both wanted to say something but did not. There were too many people around. When he was leaving, the boss came out of his office to say goodbye, but Nikolayev, as if not noticing him, slipped by through the open door and into the corridor. We heard his steps as he ran quickly down the stairs and slammed the front door. That was the last time I saw him. I hope he survived the war. Thirty million Russians did not.

The following day they called me to the warden's office at the main gate. A parcel had arrived for me. It was from my parents who somehow had managed to scrounge a kilogram of bacon and some biscuits. They had sent it before the mail was disrupted by the war. It was a great gift, but I could not help thinking that my family probably needed it more than I did. My office friends told me to stash it away in our drafting office in a padlocked, heavy iron box where we kept office supplies. I took some bacon and biscuits to share with my cellmates. I ate a thin slice of it every day, trying to make it last longer, the way I had eked out the butter in Czortkow. Then somebody from our office who had access to the key to the iron box stole a big chunk of my bacon. I suspected Cybis, the janitor. Then the rest of it was stolen and gobbled by the *zhuliki*.

The war was going badly for the Soviets. They were retreating on all fronts. "The heroic defence by Red Army units," as reported by the Soviet press, was being carried on in a different place each day, and it was clear that the German Army was pushing forward faster than in any other blitzkrieg. The air raids continued around us but on distant targets, not on the centre of town. One day after an air-raid alert was sounded, we saw two Messerschmitt 110 planes (two-seater fighters) being intercepted by a squadron of the stubby I-16 Soviet fighters. One Messerschmitt flew away, but the other one hid in a large cumulus cloud. The Soviet fighter planes, flying in a nice tight formation, circled the cloud waiting for the German plane to come out. It did. But, in a most unexpected manoeuvre, it flew for a few seconds parallel to the Soviet fighters. A short burst of fire from the rear gunner of the Messerschmitt sent one of the I-16s down in a wild spiral. The Messerschmitt hid in the cloud again only to emerge and repeat the trick. Another Soviet plane went down in smoke. The rest of the squadron got the message. They dived sharply and scuttled over the rooftops like a flock of scared starlings.

Nobody discussed the war in our office or anywhere else. Stories in the newspapers about some Ivan Ivanovich from some unnamed regiment hitting a low-flying fascist plane with a hand grenade or about an SS shock troop platoon being taken prisoner by a woman tractor driver from an anonymous kolkhoz did little to improve the sagging morale of the public. We had little doubt the correspondents who were concocting these inane stories never left their editorial offices.

One day at noon at the beginning of July, I was waiting with a group of prisoners for a guard to take us to the dining hall. It was at the same gate where we saw the first air raid less than two weeks before. The gate turnkey and our guard had some stories to tell to each other, so we were standing there in the hot sunshine, some sitting on the ground, some leaning against the shed wall. When we heard the droning of a German aircraft, we looked up trying to find it in the clear sky. And there it was, flying very high and coming very slowly in our direction.

"Don't panic," shouted the guard. "It's one of ours. If it is a Kraut, why would it fly so slow?"

"Maybe it's carrying a heavy load," I said loudly.

The guard looked at me with contempt and opened his mouth to say something but at that very moment I thought I saw the glint of bombs and then I heard the whine of them coming straight at us. I hit the ground as the flash of fire and the deafening noise of the explosions tore through the yard. I flattened my body and pressed my face into the dirt. After a few seconds of silence I heard the hail of grit and pebbles falling on the tin roof of the shed behind me. Some of it fell on me. I did not move, expecting any second the sharp pain of a wound. Nothing happened. I opened my eyes, realized that I was unhurt and dived in the open door of the nearby paint workshop. By now people were running in every direction, except for a few whose bodies remained on the ground. The twisted leg of one of them kept twitching. A small boy, rigid against an upright bed frame, was hooting like an owl, his eyes rolled back in their sockets, his whole body jerking with giant tics. I saw that a large gap had been blasted in the wall between the two courtyards. And through the gap I could see that the one-story office building had been ripped apart. In an exposed office room was the body of a person slumped at a table. The building was on fire. All around was uproar and confusion. A highly disorganized gang of firefighters appeared. I saw Doctor Epstein of the prison hospital crouching on the ground beside a stretcher on which a pregnant woman was lying. A puddle of blood was forming under her. Doctor Epstein was holding her wrist and kept repeating, "Fascists, fascists."

Some prisoners who were waiting in front of the gate had been killed by the blast and shrapnel. Their crumpled bodies lay on the ground motionless. Nothing happened to the gate or to the turnkey. He stood there near the closed gate, jingling the keys on a ring which dangled from his belt and looking bewildered and dismayed at the sight of people crossing from one courtyard to another through the gap in the wall instead of his gate. People were coming to see what had happened. Others were running away, fearing another air attack.

Soon after the bombing, the prison guard commander appeared with more guards followed by the political commissars and the smiling Shishkin, head of the whole prison complex. They had "an important message" for us. In view of the worsening situation, it had been decided to release all prisoners immediately. The prison staff would be working all night preparing release and identification papers for everyone as well as clothing, food and railway passes. Those who wished to volunteer for the Red Army were to contact recruiting centres in Kiev the next day. Supper was to be served early. After that we were to go to our cells and, in the morning, to part as free men.

Very early the next morning somebody went for a pee and looked outside through the window. What he saw made him run back to the cell and wake everybody up. "I'll be fucked! You should see the nice surprise Shishkin has prepared for you, you free fellows. See for yourselves the breathtaking decorations they have prepared for our release! They are better than the ones we had for the First of May!"

That sounded ominous. We rushed to the windows. Where the brick wall near the gate had been blown down and also along Degtiarevskaya Street, a new triple fence of barbed wire with an additional wooden watchtower had been built overnight. The number of armed guards had been doubled. And when the dormitory door was opened to let us out for breakfast we faced, instead of the easygoing guard we called Diadia (Uncle) Misha, a couple of new armed and angry-looking guards who escorted us to the dining hall. The new guards took us through the routine that we had almost forgotten. "Form in pairs! Silence! No talking! No looking around! Look at the nape of the neck of the man in front of you! March!" A few hits with rifle butts and kicks with boots forestalled any questions about the promised release and freedom. There were extra armed guards in the workshops, and every time an air-raid alarm sounded we were quickly ordered back to our cells, locked up and kept there until the all-clear.

On the 5th of July (I think it was), we were told that an order had been issued to evacuate Kiev. The situation of the Soviet forces on the Ukrainian front was precarious, to say the least, and the official communiqués were already mentioning Germans attacking in the direction of Korosten and Belaya Tserkov, and coming closer to Kiev. Because all inmates of Soviet prisons and labour camps were regarded by the Party and NKVD as real or potential "enemies of the people," the evacuation of prisons was always given top priority, even over bringing supplies to the front. Prisoners who could not be evacuated were killed. In Brygidki Prison in Lwow, for example, all the exits were blocked, the building soaked with gasoline and set on fire with the inmates inside. Similar mass killings had been reported from other prisons threatened by rapid German advances. Other tens of thousands of prisoners were forced to march eastwards. Those unable to keep up were shot on the spot by the guards.

The speed of the German onslaught shattered any hope for an orderly relocation of factories to beyond the Ural Mountains. At our prison factory we were told to destroy anything that might be of some use to the Germans. Only the electric motors, ripped from their concrete bases, were to be saved. Gangs of prisoners immediately started breaking machinery and tools, swinging sledgehammers with glee and looking with satisfaction at the broken lathes, precision machine tools and the entire equipment of the printing shop. Windows were smashed and doors ripped from their frames. There was a bit of confusion about the fate of the ubiquitous portraits of Stalin and other communist icons. "Who would be brave or stupid enough to swing a hammer against the image of our Beloved Leader, the Sun of Mankind? But if you leave the portraits intact they might be desecrated by the hands of fascist hyenas." Tough choice. The educators and political commissars, when asked to make a decision, would bristle and answer in a menacing manner. "Watch out, you scum. You may get an additional ten years just for asking such a Trotskyite question." And then they'd turn and scurry away.

In these times of stress, the age-old Russian xenophobia came to the fore. The Russian prisoners became more abusive and aggressive towards foreigners. They taunted and menaced us with threats such as, "It's time to finish you off, you fascist cannibals." A delegation of young criminals went to our Chief of Security, Comrade Zarya, for permission to kill all foreign prisoners. Apparently Comrade Zarya demurred but left some hope for the disappointed patriots by saying that, should there be a change in the Party policy, their voluntary services might yet be used.

Some people were released. At our office, the old scribe Bashko was summoned to the personnel office and came back shaking all over. He kept mumbling to himself, something about being set free by the Antichrists and about going to his village. Only when he started wrapping up his meagre possessions—a pen, an inkwell, a couple of pencils and a chipped tea mug—did we figure out that he had indeed been freed. The boss Boris Ivanovich came in and told me *sotto voce*, "You'll be going to a camp in the north but not as far as the land of white bears. In fact much closer. Consider yourself lucky." The designer/draftsman Popov and others were trying to wheedle more details from him, but he put on his favourite enigmatic expression and retreated to his office. In the prison and in the factory yards rumour was rampant.

The front line was getting closer and closer to Kiev. Malin, the librarian, shook his head at how fast the Germans were closing in on us: "They're almost at Belaya Tserkov! It's only seventy kilometres from here." Now at night we could hear the distant rumble of artillery fire. For a while I was thinking of lifting a manhole cover, lowering myself into the sewers and hiding there until the Soviets left town, which I reckoned should happen within a couple of days. Thank God I did not do it. The front stabilized, and it would take the Germans two months to enter Kiev.

On the morning of the 8th of July, the prisoners were divided into groups of about 200 men each. We were given our usual daily ration of bread and a small piece—perhaps six ounces—of raw, nearly transparent pork fat dipped in salt. The fat came from the pigs raised on the prison kitchen slops and slaughtered the night before. Brand new padded winter jackets from the prison stores were also handed out to us. After a lengthy roll call we formed a long column guarded by escorts who were carrying rifles with fixed bayonets. The guards droned the familiar warning: "One step to the right, one step to the left is considered to be an escape. The escort will use firearms without warning." Then the prison main gate was flung wide open, and we were off.

It was a scorcher. From the cloudless blue sky the sun was pouring down molten heat. In vain the convoy escort tried to mould our group of trudging cons into some semblance of a unit marching in a quasi-military formation. Prisoners never march well. They stumble. They limp. They adjust their togs. But always within the perimeter drawn by the lines of bayonets.

We marched through the streets of Kiev. People seeing columns of prisoners would quickly turn away, stepping into the nearest courtyard or vanishing around the corner. Onlookers could be accused by the ever-suspicious escort of giving the prisoners some secret signs, of counting them or of trying to identify them. Any of these imaginary crimes could lead to their immediate arrest.

The guards drove us at a fast pace. To our pleas for a rest and a drink of water, they would bark back *"Davai! Davai!"* (Get going!)

The heat was becoming unbearable. Besides the padded winter jackets issued to us that morning, we carried little makeshift sacks with our personal belongings, but after an hour of marching even these seemed too much to bear. Some cons started throwing away things they carried. Some stripped to their underpants. The guard near me picked up a new winter jacket discarded by somebody but after carrying it for only ten minutes, he too dropped it in the dust. We kept marching on without a rest, without a stop. When we reached the outskirts of town the streets changed into dirt lanes lined on both sides by one-story houses with weathered picket fences and rows of blooming pink mallows.

Then an unexpected thing happened. We saw women, many women, most of them old, rushing out from their houses with jugs and buckets full of water and wading bravely into the columns of marching prisoners. They ignored the threats and shouts of our escort. They yelled back at the guards, giving as good as they got. "Stay away from the poor souls, you unbaptized red Satans! Let them drink! They look like they'd die right now. You Trotskyite tormentors of these innocent laddies! God will punish you for your heartlessness!"

The guards were taken aback by the sudden onslaught of the furious babushkas, and it took them a few minutes to pull them out from the knots of prisoners who were fighting among themselves over the jugs and buckets. But about one in ten of the prisoners got at least a few gulps of water. When more babushkas appeared with water, they were fended off by the guards' bayonets, but some of them still managed to splash the heads of marching cons by throwing the water up and over the heads of our escort. I was not among the lucky ones.

We found out from one of the guards that they were taking us to Darnitsa, a railway junction on the other side of the Dnieper River, the left bank. It was not very far from our prison, but they took a tortuous route to avoid streets clogged with evacuees and army units. After many turns and detours, we found ourselves on the main approach to the bridge. The street leading to the bridge and the bridge itself were choked with thousands of people carrying trunks and suitcases made of wood, and pushing carts, prams and wheel-barrows. Detachments of soldiers trying to move forward were lifting their feet on the spot while their leaders grew hoarse from yelling at people to make way. A number of trucks and a bus, stalled from overheated engines, added to the confusion. People panicked at any sound of a plane, but this or any other sudden movement would clog the bridge even tighter. Into this bedlam of madding throngs, the leader of our convoy eased his charges. Time seemed to stand still as we shuffled ahead step by step. We finally worked our way across the bridge only to be directed by bristling bayonets to run down the escarpment to an assembly area on the shore of the river.

We sat down on the grassy, moist ground. The semicircle of guards and the chord of sand at the river's edge marked the boundary of our temporary camp. The river was shallow there. We were allowed to wade in ankle deep and drink until we could drink no more. As we had no mugs or cups, we drank by crouching on all fours and lowering our heads until our lips touched the surface of the murky water. We looked like a herd of ungainly sheep being watered. While drinking, I tried to ignore the flotsam, including a drowned, blind kitten. A little below the drinking area, the river's edge served as an open-air latrine.

With my hands, I dug a hole in the wet sand and buried in it all the treasures that I could no longer carry: the letters from my family, most of the photographs, my sketches of the prison yard and the highly idealized drawing of Maria Ivanovna, the slim, demure prison nurse. I left my sweater, my threadbare blanket and the new padded jacket lying on the grass. However, Romcio Szymanski, a quiet, club-footed fellow who had been my cellmate in the labour colony, picked up my padded jacket, adding it to his already sizeable burden. I never dreamed that that jacket was yet to save my life.

And so we kept plodding on in the merciless heat of the early afternoon. The sandy road led through a pine forest redolent of melting resin. The sky was full of silver-grey barrage balloons. Here and there groups of soldiers stripped to the waist were digging long ditches. A guard asked one of the men what they were digging. With typical Russian indifference the soldier shrugged his shoulders, wiped the sweat from his brow and said, "The devil knows. They tell you to dig, so you dig. If they tell you to fill them in, you fill them in. Those on top know what they are doing, or so they say."

Before we reached Darnitsa junction, a railway official stopped us. He spoke to the convoy commandant, looked at his pocket watch and pointed to a line of about twenty mustard-yellow freight cars and a few flat cars standing on a faraway railway track. When we drew nearer we saw the electric motors and kitchen cauldrons from our prison already on one of the flat cars. They started loading us almost immediately.

After a routine but thorough personal search, we were sent into the car one by one until there was no more room. We got no food and no water. The sliding doors were banged shut and the two handles of the lock outside tied up with a piece of twisted barbed wire. Our escort probably did not get any food either. They were in a foul mood and without any provocation fired a few rounds at the roof of our car just to bully us and keep us quiet. Then the ack-ack batteries started firing every fifteen minutes at some invisible German raiders. The train pulled out in the middle of the night when most of us weary prisoners were fast asleep.

For those who dared to think, it was difficult to fathom. All around us there was a desperate need for transport and the supplies it brought. Fronts were collapsing for want of ammunition. Reserve troops had to march hundreds of kilometres for want of trucks and trains. Tens of thousands of wounded were dying for want of medical care and supplies. Yet trains were available to evacuate prisoners guilty of such crimes as stealing a few corncobs from a kolkhoz field or for falling asleep during a lengthy political meeting.

It was no longer a secret. Our destination was some corrective labour camp in an area known as Vyat-Lag, a group of labour camps sprawling between the town of Kirov (later changed back to its tsarist name of Vyatka) and the autonomous Komi Republic in the basin of the Vyatka River. Not the Arctic Far North but roughly on the same latitude as Churchill on Hudson Bay. The area was west of the Urals and still a part of Europe but conditions there were similar to those in Siberia, which lay beyond the mountains.

As soon as they learned where we were going, all the trusties shed the "loyal activist" skin, which had curried favour in the Kiev prison, and reverted to their true colours as hardened criminals. There was no room and no favours for grovelling toadies in the taiga camps. For informers and stool pigeons, yes, but they lived in constant fear of being lynched by fellow prisoners. The camps were run by clans of ruthless cons who, with the tacit approval of the official camp administration, terrorized all other prisoners, forcing them to work in the most atrocious conditions. These criminals distributed the food only after they had eaten their fill. They never worked themselves. They were the ruling class known as *blat*, a kind of mafia. They would get the best and the warmest clothing from the administration or take it by force from other prisoners. Their boast was, "*Blat* is above the ministry."

Once we entered the cavernous railway car, a gang of young criminals lost no time in asserting the privileges that they said were due to them as members of *blat*. They occupied the best places—on the mezzanine close to the sliding doors—and squeezed out everyone else from the space they felt they needed to be comfortable. They viciously beat up the few who questioned their usurped rights. There were no more than a dozen of them in our railway car, which held about seventy prisoners. But they were strong, loyal to each other and absolutely ruthless. They recruited younger boys, *urki*, as their spies and informers.

The night did not bring any relief from the oppressive, steamy heat for the tight mosaic of intertwined bodies covering the floor. We slept feverishly. The early midsummer dawn brought some hopes for water and the morning meal. But no signs of relief came. We passed a big town, Poltava, without stopping. The train did stop frequently, but between stations, in the middle of nowhere. The rest of the time it went slowly, and occasionally backwards, for long stretches. We shouted in unison: "Water! Water!" but there was no reaction from anybody. It seemed as if there were no guards on this train. With the sun climbing higher, air in the boxcar became hotter and hotter and our throats drier and drier. Those who were lucky enough to sit close to the high little corner windows sometimes saw railway workers and yelled for help and water but their pleas fell on deaf ears. The fear of the NKVD was so widespread that nobody wanted even to notice prisoners. Slowly we were becoming resigned to our fate. But the *urki* burst out hysterically at times, screaming at the top of their voices while hurling themselves against the closed sliding doors. Then they would fall on the floor, beating their breasts and sobbing uncontrollably, like cruel, spoiled children.

Another night lowered the black curtain on the human drama. Fights erupted in the darkness over the few places where slightly cooler night air seeped in through the chinks between the boards of the car walls. Some individuals who had managed to keep their mug, cup, or jar drank their own urine but it did not bring much relief.

I was lucky to have a place in the corner on the lower deck and two good friends of mine as immediate neighbours: Henryk Charytonowicz, a lanky enigmatic fellow from the Pripet Marshes, and a fifteen-year-old Jewish boy whom we called Klein. It was his surname but it also became his nickname. Klein in Yiddish means "a little one" and, as he was frail and short, it seemed appropriate to call him just Klein, which he did not mind. We talked Polish in whispers. *Urki* hated it when they could not understand what others were saying—they immediately sniffed some plot against them.

"Do you pray?" Klein asked me quietly.

"Yes, I do," I answered. "Why do you ask?"

"You are lucky," he said. "I cannot do that. My father told me always to pray aloud, so that God knows that you are not ashamed of praying. And He likes to be praised in full voice, not by low mumbling. But I am too scared to pray aloud. The *urki* would mock me first and then beat me up. Especially if they heard my Jewish prayers."

I rattled off another dozen Hail Marys in my mind. Some of them for little Klein.

We passed another infernal day in stupor and resignation without water or food. Occasionally, when the train came to a halt, the heads of prisoners would go up with desperate hope only to fall back with silent sighs and the stillness of death masks.

It was already late evening when the train stopped again. We heard voices. First far away. Then louder and clearer. The sound of boots grinding the cinders along the railway track came closer. It stopped for a while, and then we heard the noise of car doors rolling back in the wagon next to ours. Prisoners cried for water and guards swore. That revived our car. We were next. Never in my life had I expected to see prisoners greeting their guards so. We heard the familiar voice of Diadia Misha cursing the barbed wire twisted around our door lock as he tried to undo it. The door opened. Diadia Misha and two other guards climbed inside. One of them ordered two strong and servile Polish prisoners, Jelecki and Grablewski, and two *urki* to follow him to the station's water tower and start fetching pails of water for our car. The other two guards, after announcing that we would get bread and soup later on, ignored all questions and complaints and started the routine roll call in a matter of fact way.

The roll call went smoothly. Nobody was missing but one lad was found dead lying between an unperturbed con and the railway car wall. The *urki* found it amusing and teased the fellow "who liked to cuddle up to a corpse."

"Nothing wrong with that," said the corpse's bedfellow. "He did not stir up for over a day and his cold body was a godsend in this devilish heat."

The cons who went to the water tower returned with four pails of water and started serving it in an orderly manner. One mug per head, starting with the ones who were whining most. Some drank it at one gulp. Others were trying to sip it, much to the annoyance of the waiting crowd. The guards removed the corpse, hopped down and rolled the sliding door shut. At this very instant the *urki* grabbed two nearly full pails of water and hoisted them up to the upper level for themselves. No one protested. What was left for the rest of us was less than half a mug each.

In the evening the guards brought more water and millet gruel served in shallow aluminum bowls. No spoons. There were not enough bowls for everybody so whoever gulped his ladleful of gruel first and licked his bowl clean had to pass it on to the next one. It went fast. The guards collected the empty bowls and left two pails of water and bread rations for everybody, which the *urki* volunteered to distribute, and moved to the next car. To no one's surprise the *urki* drank most of the water and gorged themselves on our bread rations leaving for the rest of us only whatever they could not eat. They knew the power of ruthless terror and did not expect any opposition.

That night Klein, Charytonowicz, another Pole named Matulajtis and I talked in whispers about what could be done to stop the *urki* from stealing water and food. Charytonowicz was for a reckless attack on the *urka* gang, but the rest of us persuaded him that he could not count on help from the other cons who, though thirsty, starved and desperate, were too cowed. We could complain to the guards. After all, we were not yet in the northern camps where the criminal gangs were all powerful. But who would be brave enough to do it? In the end we found a way to inform the convoy commander that seemed feasible. Charytonowicz had a few scraps of writing paper on which I (at night, under cover of darkness) would write, in Russian, a plea for help. Little Klein volunteered to play the dangerous part of the ploy. During the morning roll call he would tell the guard that he had been sick for quite a time and that he had been under treatment in Kiev. "I am in pain now," he was to explain to the guard. "I have no more pills but I do have the prescription which Doctor Epstein gave me a few days ago. Would the guard take it to the convoy paramedic who may have the pills or some other drug that may relieve my pain?"

Klein played his role perfectly. With the morning roll call over, and the guards ready to jump down from the railway car, he pushed himself forward, pressed the folded piece of paper into a guard's palm and recited his lines with a voice full of pain. The guard looked a bit puzzled but shoved the paper into his pocket, jumped down and rolled back the door.

In the afternoon during a lengthy stop between stations, five or six guards appeared in our car. Everybody stood up. The guards did not say anything for a while, just kept looking around. Then one of them turned to the *urki* and said, "Some fine goings-on in this car. We would like to hear a bit more about it." The guards were peeved at their former "loyal activists." They felt betrayed by turncoats who, after years of preferential treatment, reverted without hesitation to the lifestyle of common criminals and foes of the penitentiary administration. There was a deathly silence in the car. The *urki* looked a bit uneasy and smiled at the guards, hoping that there was another reason for their visit. Then one of the guards roared, "Come on, sons of bitches, fucking cocksuckers! Who steals water and bread, their blood rations, from fellow prisoners?! Speak up!"

The cons kept silent. The *urki* kept smiling. Suddenly there was a bit of commotion, and little Klein pushed himself forward through the circle of men surrounding the guards. His face was pale. He bit his lip, made half a step forward, and thrust out his arm nearly touching the chest of the chief *urka*. "Him!" he said in a loud clear voice. And then, pointing his finger at others, repeated, "And him. And him. And the one that's hiding behind the Romanian!"

The whole car thought that Klein had gone out of his mind. It was like signing his own death warrant. But before the *urki* had any chance to deny anything the knot of guards went into action. They went after the *urki* with a fury. They were hitting hard, kneeing them, hammering their bleeding faces and pounding their necks when they doubled up with pain. The *urki* yelled as if they were being flayed alive. They screamed for mercy. "That's enough, my dear guard. Have pity. I'll never do it again. Oh! Stop hitting so hard, I beseech you, my little guardian." But the beating went on and on.

Suddenly Diadia Misha looked at his revolver holster and saw it was empty. He went berserk. His bloodied fists were flailing with increasing speed and a stream of loud obscenities gushed non-stop from his twisted mouth. The other guards were slowing down. One of them, realizing the reason behind Diadia Misha's madness, grabbed his arm and told him that he had left his revolver in the guards' car, that he did not take it with him. That stopped Diadia Misha. He seemed relieved. He wiped his sweaty brow and spent the remnants of his waning energy on two hefty kicks aimed at the nearest grovelling *urka*.

The guards told Jelecki and Grablewski to take over and then left, taking with them the hard core of the wailing *urka* gang. They were to spend the rest of the journey in a punishment cell—a barbed-wire cage set up in one of the boxcars.

In our car, the din was slowly subsiding. The *urka* underlings were not stupid. They quickly put two and two together and were wondering aloud about the strength of the "doctor's prescription." One of them, shaking his head, said to Klein, "They will kill you when we get to the camps."

"Let them try," answered little Klein. "And if they do, so what?"

The terror was gone but the conditions in our car were still far from satisfactory. However, most of us had experienced similar conditions before and a tragedy seems less tragic when encountered for the second time. We passed the Ukrainian city of Kharkhov and then the train turned north towards Russia herself.

On the fourth or fifth day of our journey we passed Kursk. Then the train came to a halt, not at any station but in a place where the railway track ran parallel to a river. It was late afternoon. We saw our guards standing along the edge of the river. In addition to the usual pistols and rifles, two of them carried machine guns, which they positioned at each end of the train aiming them in the direction of the river. Seeing that, I was overtaken by a growing fear. "That's it," I thought. "They've got an order to finish us off." Other prisoners must have had the same feeling. We looked at each other without saying a word and when the doors rolled aside, and we heard the order, "Get undressed and get out! All of you. And make it fast!" some of us turned to shake hands with friends while trying to look composed and brave.

The convoy commander approached our naked crowd and smiled broadly. "You stink so badly that even the railwaymen at the stations we pass are spitting at the smell. Behave yourself and keep order. I let you bathe in the river for a quarter of an hour. The river is shallow. No diving. No tricks. No swimming. And if anybody strays too far he'll get three kopeks' worth of lead in the arse! Get going!"

The water was warm. But as my feet sank slowly into the cool ooze of the river bottom it was total bliss.

Another surprise awaited us in Tula, the last large town before Moscow. As our train was rolling in on one of the many tracks of the station we realized that we had arrived there during a heavy air raid. A series of deafening bomb explosions swayed our train and bullets from an escort plane tore open a railway car standing on the next track. The German planes were flying low, barely above the ridges of the station roofs. The train was still in motion when our guards jumped off and set their machine guns on the platform with the barrels trained at the doors of our cars. The bombs kept falling, some frighteningly close. Nearby buildings were on fire and clouds of acrid smoke drifted along the tracks. The air raid was still on when our train pulled out. Luckily, we had no casualties, which made some Russian prisoners remark, "Clever guy, that Hitler! He tries to have the prisoners on his side."

Late the next morning the train stopped at some suburban station. The guards then opened the doors, pointed out to us the outlines of low buildings on a hazy horizon and with great reverence kept repeating "Moskva. Moskva." So it was Moscow, their Shangri-La, their Xanadu, the Red Rome. The place where the omnipotent, pipe-puffing Stalin lived and ruled over his 150 million freedom-scared subjects.

It was a hot day and the guards let us keep the doors open. Of course, any attempt by a prisoner to step down on the platform would invite a rifle shot from a guard. But the guards were in a good mood that day because the tuck shop at the station was well supplied—by Soviet standards—with such delicacies as white bread rolls, cookies, and kvass (a cold drink made from fermented bread and malt). What else could one want! They even bought cigarettes and biscuits for those few cons who had money.

A train arrived and stopped on the other side of the platform just across from ours. In an instant, a squall of women's voices, loud shrieks and whistles filled the sunny corridor between the trains. The *urki* leapt to the doors and windows like a pride of snoozing lions awakened by the whiff of passing gazelles. Shouts from the guards and the clicking of rifle bolts froze them at the lip of the doorway. By now everybody's eyes were glued to the train across the platform. The unfolding sight was more than an eighteen-year-old like me could have even dared to fantasize about.

That train was full of women prisoners, the majority of them young, mostly teenagers. Underage female criminals like that were known in underworld parlance as *shalman*. They were the female *urki* and just as crafty, tough and ruthless.

The guards, knowing what would happen, let prurience get the upper hand over their common sense and soldiers' duty. They left the car doors open and assumed an air of studied indifference.

On both sides of the platform, sex frenzy drove the young players to an exhibitionistic, voyeuristic grand spectacle. Discarding every bit of clothing, they responded enthusiastically to calls from the other side to give them some *tsyants*, prison slang which could be modestly translated as "visual inspiration." The open doors became prosceniums for the *urki* and *shalman*, each crowding forward to upstage the others. Those who found no room near the doors clung to the barred windows.

Glassy-eyed *urki* rhythmically stroked their turgid wands while the open-mouthed *shalman* maenads thrust forward and caressed their mossy pelvises. The pleading shouts of "Look! Look!" flew back and forth. And each trajectory of falling sperm was greeted by squeals of delight from the distaff side of the platform.

I thought the women across the platform good-looking, maybe even beautiful. But that was my impression of them after they were gone and it still lingers. What they were truly like in reality, I don't know.

The rest of us were just as excited and aroused by the naked *shalman* as were the *urki* but, inhibited by our "putrid Western morals," we remained mere onlookers. Our morals, religion, upbringing and dignity would not let us display our emotions the way they did, just as we would not grovel to get an extra ladle of soup or beg for forgiveness when not guilty. We felt superior to them.

We started wondering how long this display of sexual prowess would go on because neither the *urki* nor the *shalman* betrayed any signs of losing interest in their amorous frolics. But the sudden appearance of the convoy commander stopped the bacchanal in mid-stroke. The doors were slammed shut and the clinging nymphs and satyrs shooed away from the windows. The abrupt end of the exhibitionistic trysts sent the *shalman* into paroxysms of rage. They swore at the guards with such conviction and such uncouth originality that even the hardened criminals kept making tsk-tsk sounds while shaking their heads.

Chapter 14

VYAT-LAG

After Moscow we had another two or three days of heat with little water or food. We passed Gorky and on the eighth or ninth day of our journey we reached Kirov. Our train did not stop there but continued for another twenty kilometres or so to Slobodskoi, our destination and the end of the railway line, which we reached at midday. From there we marched to our camp. It was not far. The "road" was little more than a wide dirt track. It was hot. And as we trudged along the wide sandy trail, we stumbled on the varicose veins of half-buried pine roots. There had been nothing to eat or drink since our frugal morning meal and my tongue felt wooden, closing my parched throat. The guards urged us on with the constant *"Davai! Davai!"* and promises of buckets of water when we got to our camp. They believed that drinking water would weaken the marchers and that unquenched thirst and the vision of plentiful water at the end of the march would urge cons to push themselves to the limit.

On one flat stretch of the trail, rain had left patches of wet soil covered with a fine film of water. Maybe it was deep enough for a cat to lick up but not for prisoners who, ignoring the guards' threats, fell down on their faces trying to sip the brackish liquid, undeterred by horse droppings at the other end of the wet spot. I joined them, but first I scooped with my hands a small hole which promptly filled with muddy water. I dipped my mouth into it. But all I got was a mouthful of foul-smelling mud. It was hard to spit it out because of the lack of saliva. The fine grit stayed in my mouth until we reached the camp.

The Slobodskoi camp was in a large clearing in the midst of a pine forest. The ground was littered with the signs of construction —fresh chips, sawdust and pieces of wood. The pale, rough planks were oozing beads of sticky sap. The hot air smelled of pine resin.

About a dozen long, one-story sheds served as prisoner dormitories. One of the sheds was designated as an administration building and beside it was the usual array of smaller structures, such as a kitchen (known in camp jargon as *koptyorka*, literally a sooter, because of the soot belching from the wood-stove pipe), a shack where bread was weighed and cut into portions, a shed for tools, and another one for storing clothes. The outdoor eating area in front of the kitchen had crude benches and tables made of heavy, rough planks nailed to the butts of logs driven into the ground. The entire camp was surrounded by a wooden fence over four metres high, topped with barbed wire and enclosing a square of about 150 metres on each side. In each corner was a watchtower with a platform reached by ladder from the outside of the fence. The area enclosed by the fence was known as the "zone." Outside the fence were the guards' quarters, in a building near the main gate. Next to it was an *izolyator*, the dreaded "hole." In this case it actually was a hole dug deep in the ground. It had a hinged cover made of a wooden frame criss-crossed by a grid of stretched barbed wire. This *izolyator* was frequently used for "disciplinary measures." A prisoner found guilty of some misdemeanour would be pushed—naked in summer or clad in trousers and a padded jacket in winter—into this hole for a period of time ranging from one to five days depending on the severity of his offence. Surviving five days in the *izolyator* was unheard of because of the clouds of mosquitoes and *moshka* (a voracious kind of no-see-um) in summer and the freezing cold in winter. Even one day of it in winter would bring pneumonia.

In no time we were put into work brigades of about thirty men under a *brigadir*. A brigade was split into three groups of ten, each with their own mini-boss, a *desyatnik*. But all better paid, cushy jobs were quickly grabbed by *blat* and their henchmen. Administrative jobs, even those of the lowest kind, such as shack orderlies, latrine cleaners and water carriers, were highly coveted because they meant survival. They had no work norms to be fulfilled, and so always got a steady supply of food. On the other hand, these workers were excluded from the Socialist Competition and Stakhanovite Movement because it was well nigh impossible to compute the performance percentage of cleaning an open-air latrine.

Almost all *brigadiry* were professional criminals with long sentences. They had connections through *blat* with cooks, store minders, paramedics, accountants, guards, in fact, practically everybody who would take or offer a bribe. Without such a *brigadir*, a brigade would soon be put to work on the lowliest and hardest tasks and its members would starve to death. A *brigadir* knew everything about work, but he did not work himself. He was a fixer. His closest friends did not work either. But, helped by his *desyatniki*, he would see that other prisoners worked. The work norms were set by the Head Management of the Camps—the Gulag. These were totally unrealistic and impossible to meet by honest work. Only by cheating could a prisoner fulfill 100 percent of the prescribed norm. And only by achieving 100 percent could he get his full daily ration of food.

There were hundreds of ways of cheating, from the ingenious to crude cheating or stealing. The camp jargon for such underhand methods of beating the system was *tufta*. All *tufta* called for the cooperation or at least the tacit approval of the camp officials. It was the only way to square up to the camp accounting system and balance the books, because the productivity targets were so unrealistic. And yet they had to be met, at least on paper—when there was paper. In prison, officials wrote on wallpaper. Here it was lumber. Pieces of fresh, wooden boards were used for vouchers, receipts and so on. Woodsheds became the filing cabinets and sometimes teams of cons would be sent to shift stacks of boards to find an old invoice urgently needed by the chief accountant. Even during the evening roll call, the *komandir* would tick off our names from a list written on a long plank.

As soon as we entered the shack assigned to us, Malin (the prison librarian from Kiev) looked around with a knowing eye. He had always claimed to be a first-timer without any criminal past, an office worker imprisoned for some trifling offence. But with the air of experience, he surveyed the long rows of double-deck sleeping platforms and declared this had not been built as a prison dormitory but more likely as a military field hospital. He could tell because the building's construction was of much higher calibre than that of a labour camp. He quickly checked the condition of the iron wood stove in the middle of the dorm and selected a place for himself on the upper platform, not too far from it but where he would be screened by the opened front door from the sight of a person entering the shack and from the blast of cold air that came in with him. I also staked my place on the upper deck but near a window. Above it I found pencilled in Russian, "Estonians built it" and underneath the window the first line from the German marching song, "*Wenn wir fahren gegen* England." (As we drive against England.) Estonians always had pro-German leanings.

Soon after we came to Slobodskoi camp, I asked to be transferred from the juvenile to an adult brigade. I was now eighteen, so it was done. I preferred the company of grown men, and although there were plenty of hardened criminals among them, they were not as wild and noisy as the "glorious youth who have the privilege of growing up under communism untainted by the miasmatic decay of pre-revolutionary ideas." It might have seemed to be an advantage to stay with the underage cons, and so have a lower work norm, but in practice it made no difference to my food rations because the only way anyone, young or old, met their norms was by *tufta*. And the older cons were better at it.

Next morning I found myself marching with thirty or so other adult convicts to the workplace, about one hour's walk from our camp. Our way led along a swath cut through the pine forest and already cleared of tree trunks and brush. Our job was to continue the earthworks started by other brigades. The camp officials never told us, but rumour had it that we were building a new railway line to link Slobodskoi with Syktyvkar, the capital of the autonomous Komi Republic, home of the Komis and Samoyeds.

It was a dull and steamy day. A slight drizzle set in even before we got to our destination. As we came closer, we saw groups of other prisoners already at work. Our job was to cut a roadbed through a hillock and then dump the earth in a swamp so that the railway line could cross it. That sounded simple enough, although it was not. Our tools were not only primitive and clumsy, they were also heavy and blunt. The wheelbarrows were made of thick boards and their wooden wheels were solid, rimless and wobbly. Even when empty it took a lot of strength to push them. Where we were digging, the cut through the hillock was five metres deep in places. It was too high to throw the dirt over the top and so the cut had to be widened to make room for an intermediate, wide step on which the dirt from the bottom of the trench was shovelled first. From there it was thrown up over the edge of the cut and loaded into wheelbarrows to be carted away to the nearby swamp. It was back-breaking work to throw wet earth over your head or to push even a half-full wheelbarrow along the narrow boards laid atop the quivering bog. Often a wheelbarrow would slide off a board and stick in the mud. Then two or three people were needed to wrestle it out.

Because I was so small and thin, I had to use a lot of force to push the blunt and notched edge of my spade into the ground. Stomping on it with my thin rubber galoshes, which were falling to pieces anyway, did not help much. The soil at the bottom of the ditch was clayish and stuck to the spade's blade. I had to scrape it off every couple of minutes. My back ached and my hands were covered with raw blisters. I could only fill my wheelbarrow half way. If I heaped it up, it became too heavy for me to keep steady while pushing it along a narrow plank over the marshy ground.

Around noon all eyes were scanning the horizon for the sight of an emaciated pony pulling a small cart with a barrel and two men on it. At the first cry of, "Here they are!" all cons threw their spades and pickaxes on the ground, let the wheelbarrow handles slide from their hands as if an electric current had run through them, and formed a line where the cart usually stopped. One by one, with their grimy hands, they would take the banged-up bowls and wooden spoons from the equally dirty hands of the kitchen helper and turn to Stiopa, the cook. Stiopa, clad in a filthy apron, stood on the cart wielding a ladle made of a half-litre can attached to a long wooden handle. With it, he vigorously stirred the soup inside the barrel while being urged by the hungry gang. "Give it another stir, Stiopa. Use your muscles!" They knew that if the soup was not stirred well, the grains of barley or millet would settle on the bottom of the barrel and let Stiopa play favourites by dishing out thick soup from the bottom of the barrel to his friends and the watery stuff from the top to others. Sometimes a few fish heads and scales or rubbery dumplings were to be found in the hot liquid. In addition to the half-litre of soup, there was a second course: one or two heaping spoonfuls of a thick kasha (a porridge of millet, buckwheat or whatever grains the cook had) scraped off the flat, wooden stirrer into the rim of each man's bowl. This was the highlight of the daily menu.

The noon meal break was the only official time off during the working day. But there were additional unofficial breaks, albeit short ones, called at the discretion of the *desyatnik*. These were known as "smokers," even for those who had no tobacco or did not smoke, and "breathers," when even a heartless *desyatnik* would notice that the workers were about to collapse from exhaustion and order a ten-minute break.

The working day was long. By the time we were marched back to the camp it was already dark. Once there we would immediately form a line to the sooter for our evening bowl of soup, which was even thinner than at midday. Afterwards, the wicker baskets loaded with our bread rations would be brought to the dorms for distribution. The portions were supposed to be 550 grams (just over a pound) but they looked suspiciously small because the bread had the texture and consistency of a wet rubber sponge. To raise the weight, extra water had been added to the dough, making the bread soggy and sticky. But it smelled delicious. The usual prison ration of a teaspoon of sugar a day had already been cancelled. "You must understand that there is a war going on," the camp commander told us. "We cannot provide you with luxuries."

The Bukovinians from Romania, who craved even the illusion of a full stomach, would soak their bread ration in a large quantity of very salty hot water to make a runny mush. This would, at least for a while, quell their pangs of hunger. However, eating so much salt made their legs swell, and they suffered badly when they had to stand and walk all day. Brought up in the poverty-stricken Carpathian foothills, they had been underfed all their lives. With the worsening deprivation of the camps, their health soon went downhill. Their spirits also sank quickly into despair and hopelessness. With the starvation diet in Soviet prisons and labour camps, they were the first to die.

For a few days we were regaled with a rare delicacy at midday meals. Barrels of heavily salted fish going bad were found in some food depot and sent to the prison camps. The chunks of fish were glazed with salt used as preservative, but it was not stopping them from rotting in the summer heat. Amazingly, nobody got sick.

One day at noon a group of men happened to be passing near our work site. They were tall and blond and did not look Russian. As they were passing by, some of the cons shouted in German (which was the second lingua franca after Russian in the Soviet empire), *"Wer bist du?"* (Who are you?) They stopped and glanced at our guard. He had already started his afternoon nap, sitting on the ground with his back against a pile of dirt, his rifle between his legs and the visor of his cap pulled down over his eyes. Reassured, they came closer to talk to us. They were Finns banished from their land in 1940 after the Soviets invaded their country and forced them to live in a village not far from our camp. They worked as lumberjacks. Seeing some of our fellows gobbling that noon meal of rotten fish, they said that they seldom if ever ate as well as we did.

It may seem odd that our guard slept. But his only job was to make sure that we did not escape or contact people from outside. He was not concerned about whether we worked or not. This was up to our *brigadiry* and *desyatniki*. As for escaping, there was no place to escape to.

In the afternoon of our first day of rest, the sun shone and the air was warm. I sat with some of my Polish friends on ground covered with wood shavings in the far corner of the camp zone. We were all roughly the same age, between sixteen and nineteen, and we had been together at Kiev and then in the railway car. There was the club-footed Romcio Szymanski, the taciturn Dionizy Koczan, the ebullient Sinko, the soft-spoken Bastomski, the intriguing Henryk Charytonowicz, myself and brave little Klein, the only one of us younger than me. We talked about our past and our future but not about the present. There were other young Polish prisoners in the camp, but they were latecomers. Most of them arrived early in 1941, when we were still in Kiev, but they were not part of our fraternity as they were in prison for criminal offences such as stealing, hooliganism, rape and murder. In Soviet eyes these were forgivable offences that carried shorter sentences than ours and no stigma would be attached to them after release from prison. As political prisoners we were beyond redemption from the Soviet point of view, but secretly we were proud of it.

Anybody eavesdropping on our small talk would think we were leading carefree lives in normal conditions, planning studies, vacations or travels. We joked about our living conditions and the cruel but stupid prison staff. All our discussions betrayed an incredible optimism based on the groundless belief that our tribulations were of a passing nature and that it was only a matter of time before our lives would return to normal. That attitude may have been totally unrealistic, but we needed to talk such nonsense to keep our spirits up.

Henryk Charytonowicz kept us spellbound with his stories about the Pripet Marshes, about stalking the tooting black grouse at sunrise, about catfish bigger than the fishing boat and about his amorous conquests of invariably beautiful and willing maidens. When it came to women, we followed the rule someone said came from Kipling's *Jungle Book*: "Boast and believe the boasts of others." (Kipling—in Polish of course—was a childhood favourite of mine.) Henryk's reminiscences smacked of the upper-class life, which belied his claim to be a member of a poverty-stricken Belarussian family. But he swore like a true *muzhik* (peasant), and that talent pre-empted many a question about his roots. While he was talking, he would knead a lump of pitch mixed with fine dust, making a kind of Plasticine, which soon started taking the shape of a human body. By the time we finished our afternoon get-together, Henryk was adding the finishing touches to an exquisite miniature of Myron's *Discobolos*. He was a talented artist at drawing and painting too, but he himself thought little of his "doodles."

When we were returning to our shack for evening roll call, Henryk suddenly stopped, letting the others pass, then put his hand on my shoulder and said in a quiet voice, "Listen, I trust you. Listen carefully. If you get out from here before me, or if you survive me, try to get in touch with my family who live near Pinsk. Everybody knows them in that area. Tell them about me. My name is not Charytonowicz. My name is Skirmuntt. Before the war my father was the Polish ambassador in London."

The subarctic summer was nearly over. The nights were becoming colder, and sleeping squeezed between two snoring cons was no longer uncomfortable. Even feeling somebody's hot breath down my neck was no longer annoying. In the dorms we slept on bare boards. No mattresses, no blankets. Yet it was not cold enough to warrant an all night wood-stove attendant, and so the fire would go out soon after we fell asleep. The best way to fight cold at night was to find a companion to sleep back to back with you, one man's padded jacket spread on the boards underneath and the other jacket on top as a cover. With our hands crossed on our chests and our knees pressing against our bellies we slept fitfully until the shrill whistle of reveille. Urged by the curses of *brigadiry*, our half-asleep, colourless mass of prisoners would start spilling outside towards the kitchen. Once there, we would greet the yawning cook Stiopa with an imitation of a smile and a fawning "Good morning," hoping for a miracle of thick soup. No such luck. Instead it was the usual thin, grey, lukewarm liquid usurping the name of soup, which Stiopa impassively ladled out. But even that revived us, and we appreciated it more than we had the creamy coffee with hot rolls that we took for granted at breakfasts before the war.

The orange morning sun shone on our hunched mob of soup slurpers standing at the tables, but its rays were only about as warm as the smile of a hostess at patrons finally leaving her night club at dawn. Through the open gate I could see the nearby ferns and tree stumps sprinkled with white hoarfrost and in the distance a forest floating on a cushion of mist.

Slowly we shuffled our feet in the direction of the roll-call area, trying to stop the chilly morning air from seeping underneath our shirts. Then the red-faced guards, cradling their bayoneted rifles, formed a human corridor outside the main gate. And as each brigade left for work, one of the guards would tag along with it.

A new prisoner arrived at our camp. He had left Lwow to escape from the fast advancing Germans only to be arrested by the NKVD at one of the railway stations in the Ukraine and put on a train loaded with prisoners that just happened to be there. When the train reached Kirov he, with a few others, was taken off and shipped to our Slobodskoi camp. He had not yet been charged with anything and so was unable to answer the first question asked of new arrivals, "Under which paragraph are you here?" As they used to say in prison, "He had no paragraph." At least, not yet. The NKVD would soon find one to pin on him. State prosecutors in the Soviet Union liked to repeat Lavrenti Beria's boast, "Give me a detainee and I will find a paragraph."

The newcomer's name was Wioncek. He was Polish, close to twenty-five years old, and in excellent shape despite his two-week ordeal on the prison train. Before the war in Poland he was a well-known young boxer who was about to be promoted to the national boxing team, and even now his biceps were nearly splitting the short sleeves of his sport shirt. Just slightly scuffed brown shoes and trousers with a crease still visible completed the picture of bourgeois elegance. He thought his journey as a prisoner an aberration that might happen once in a lifetime. He was glad to meet some compatriots, but when we told him about the horrors of camp life and the dangerous *urki*, he listened to us with a kind of you-must-be-kidding expression on his cheerful face. He did not have to wait long to see for himself.

Next morning he went to work on the earthwork with our brigade. He took his shirt off, swung his spade and pushed the wheelbarrow with the enthusiasm befitting an innocent newcomer. During the first smoke break, while he stood leaning on his spade, two of the toughest *urki* approached him. Astonished, Wioncek watched one of them pick up his shirt from the ground and start putting it on, while the other *urka* undid the shoelaces of Wioncek's shoes and tried to take them off his feet. Sixty men watched in silence wondering what he was going to do.

Round one ended as soon as it began. Wioncek flung his spade aside and flicked his arms, slamming the two *urki* into the dirt. They got up very slowly, their lips cut and bleeding. They were probing at their chests gingerly as if touching an exposed nerve. Then they melted away to rejoin the other gloomy *urki*. The rest of us kept looking at each other without saying a word. Our guard feigned total disinterest, but he could not take his eyes off Wioncek, who finished folding his shirt and resumed digging.

After that nobody touched Wioncek until Ola, the nurse, one day pronounced him very sick and ordered him to be taken to the sick bay in an old log cabin outside the zone, but close to the guards' quarters.

Nothing was heard of Wioncek for a few days. Then Trukhanov, the battered *urka* whose pride was hurting more than his ribs, decided to broach the subject delicately with the omniscient cook Stiopa, who told the astonished *urka* that Wioncek removed a small window at the back of the cabin and ran for the woods. Nobody noticed anything. The guards had not had any extra men to mount a special guard for him. The man on duty in the guard room could see the front of the cabin but not the back. However, Ola the nurse had assured them that Wioncek was so weak that he could not even make it to the outhouse. Trukhanov said he asked the cook what happened to Ola over it. "That whore!?" was Stiopa's reply. "She escaped with him."

It must have been one of the rare successful escapes from the camps. The fact that Ola was a local girl surely helped them. She would have known that once they reached Kirov the rest would be relatively easy. All they had to do was to jump on one of the hundreds of trains packed with evacuees from near the front. We knew that the authorities failed to catch them because if either of them had been caught, they would have been brought back to our camp. The guards would drag them in, beat them mercilessly until they were half-dead and then keep them in the hole for a few days so that all prisoners could see that attempts to escape were futile. After that, the unlucky escapees would be sent to prison for another trial and an additional sentence.

Quite unexpectedly, we were moved to another camp—all of us, including the administration and the guards. It was not far, about half a day's march. The camp was called Cheptsy. It was an old camp with the usual array of dorms and huts built of squared logs. The silvery grey walls, shake roofs, high wood fence and watchtowers betrayed their age by the patches of moss and lichen growing in the sun-starved areas. For years this camp had been used as a base for logging on the nearby Cheptsa River, a tributary of the Vyatka River and hence the Volga, which flows south to the Caspian Sea. We shared the camp with other prisoners who were there when we came. All of them were tough criminals with cunning and ruthlessness written on their wizened faces. They gave us just a glance and seeing our tattered clothes and empty sacks ignored us for the time being. New work brigades were formed and next morning we were shepherded to the river's edge to start our new job.

The river Cheptsa, though small by Siberian standards, was as wide as the Seine in Paris. The trunks of huge pine trees, felled hundreds of kilometres away, floated leisurely downstream. These giant trunks with the treetops and branches lopped off were of varying thickness and roughly twenty metres long. Standing at the water's edge, we snagged them with anchor-shaped hooks attached to a long rope and then towed them ashore. In groups of twenty, we would haul them up a sloping ramp that was made of tree trunks stripped of bark, and then stack them on the flat ground well above the high-water mark. Some of the largest logs were a metre across at the butt end and it would take forty of us to pull them out of the water. A back-breaking job in more ways than one. The sight of a chain of men bent down so low that our noses were nearly touching the ground, our toes digging into the wet soil of the slope as we pulled the rope cutting into our shoulders, reminded me of an Egyptian temple relief showing the construction of the Great Pyramid. All this was accompanied by the loud urgings of the *brigadir* and the throaty voices of us prisoners chanting in unison: "Get it! Again, get it!"

We had to keep the log's upward momentum going. Once that was lost there was no way to stop the log from rolling back and breaking the bones of those who did not jump out of its way in time. The cold weather made that work even more risky. Men harpooning the floating trunks and those who were attaching the pull-out ropes invariably got wet up to their knees. In the early morning a narrow band of ice would form along the shore. It was not thick enough to step on, but it made the approach to the landed trunks more difficult.

A bonfire on the shore was burning all day for the benefit of those soaked by the icy water, but it was not enough to dry out our wet clothes and shoes. Night and day most of us had wet feet.

Stacking logs was the one job I did not mind. It was hard work for the tall men in the line. Their shoulders bore the brunt of a log's weight but, being probably the shortest in the gang, I had to stretch myself and walk on tiptoes just to touch my shoulder to the underside of the log we carried. But I panted and swore convincingly like the rest of them.

At the far corner of our dorm, *blat* and *urki* established their domain. They did not go to work. They slept a lot or listened time after time to the story of *The Count of Monte Cristo* told faultlessly by their protégé storyteller. He knew several books by heart, but so did they and woe to him if he accidentally omitted the smallest detail. They sent their underlings to fetch their thicker soup and bread from the kitchen. But most of their time they spent gambling.

One evening we all witnessed the punishment meted out by the *urki* to one of their own gang for cheating at cards. They grabbed him and held him down on a bunk. He was screaming like a pig being slaughtered. It took them a long time to find a hammer and a long rusty nail and then an even longer time to hammer it into the top of his skull. His eyes popped out. He gurgled blood. The convulsions of his body were stifled by the weight of those sitting on top of him. He died fast.

Only then did they start looking at each other as if to say, "Hey, maybe we did go too far." The chief *urka* ran outside and within minutes returned with the camp's paramedic who was so frightened that he could hardly utter a word. He listened to the *urki's* story of how the poor man had been hit on the head by a grappling hook at work by the river shore but, being a proud worker, he had refused any medical attention and kept working all afternoon only to keel over just after he finished his supper. The terrified paramedic kept nodding and repeating, "Yes, yes. Of course."

The hunger was getting worse. Our bread rations were reduced by a hundred grams to one pound per day—not enough to sustain a sedentary man let alone manual workers. For two weeks the noon meal and supper consisted of a bowlful of hot water with a few wisps of shredded cabbage in it and no salt. The bread was also salt-less. That was really a calamity. After a few days, not only my stomach but my whole body was crying out for salt. We craved it. Usually addicted smokers would sometimes exchange their daily ration of bread for one cigarette but during the salt famine they would offer their last cigarette for a pinch of salt.

Lack of vitamins also started taking its toll. Night blindness, from lack of vitamin A, became quite common and after sunset there were prisoners in every brigade who had to be led by the hand. That condition and scurvy, from lack of vitamin C, could have been alleviated by drinking a brew made of pine needles, but the kitchen staff were too lazy to prepare it. Scurvy, that blight of sailing ships and prison camps, was widespread. Prisoners succumbed to it in varying degrees. Loose teeth and deep ulcers on the body were the most common symptoms, followed by the swelling of arms and legs, which prompted the camp wits to exclaim, "Ivan! My dear, you're looking better. You're putting on weight. In no time we'll have you outside the zone!" They were right. Usually the swelling appeared a few days before death. Some people were more resistant to scurvy than others. They would develop only some of the symptoms. I did not escape it. My gums were bleeding, my teeth started getting loose and my back and legs were covered with ugly, festering ulcers, but I did not suffer from the night blindness, perhaps because of better pre-war nutrition and the butter my family had sent me when I was in prison in Gorodnya. Also as a result of starvation, muscle tissue withered away and wrinkles began to show up, even on the faces of young people. I began to look much older than my eighteen years.

We had no place to wash our clothes, no bath and no haircut for months. We were an ugly-looking lot. Hunger was consuming us and we thought of nothing but food, talked nothing but food and dreamt only about food. It was so bad that some Jewish prisoners were even daydreaming about being liberated by the German army. When *urki* (who always managed to procure an extra bowl of soup or a potato) complained to the political commissar about the hunger, he would reply: "Remember what Comrade Lenin said about hunger. When one man chases one rat, there is no hunger. When ten men chase one rat, then there is hunger."

Then the *urki* would shout: "But there are no rats around here for us to chase."

"Well, no rats, no hunger. Are you disputing the correctness of Comrade Lenin's statement?"

Nobody would. Besides, it was pointless. The entire Soviet Union suffered from the lack of food. The soldiers on the front lines were often without food for days. So why would they bother about prisoners in camps where even the guards and the administration staff were half-starved.

One thing which did happen during that time, although nobody noticed it, was the total disappearance of sex from our lives. Physical and mental. It just vanished as if it had never existed. Not only sexual desire (which for some had already died a long time ago), but also any notion of sex was obliterated from our thoughts, our dreams and from our memory so thoroughly and to such an extent that we did not even remark on its absence. Only our language remained full of lewd obscenities. But these became mere nouns, adjectives and verbs, totally bereft of their former sexual meaning. At that time a naked woman walking through our camp would have been seen by the inmates simply as an unclothed human of female gender. Maybe pitied for being cold. Nothing more.

Hungry days and cold nights passed by. We kept moving from one job to another without any apparent reason. It looked as if the camp administration had no work plan at all. After a few weeks of logging we were shunted to tree felling. But for us it was mostly cutting up the trunks of the trees felled two or three years ago. We had to cut the long trees into shorter, more manageable pieces about four metres long. The saws, made of poor quality steel, were blunt and could not be sharpened by the equally shoddy files. We worked hard, but the results of our work were negligible.

The area where trees had been felled was close to a kolkhoz potato field. For our brigade it was a gold mine. Our guard would turn a blind eye to a couple of cons sneaking into the potato field.

Once there they would crawl on their bellies, so as not to be seen by the peasants from the tiny kolkhoz, and dig with their frozen fingers for potatoes missed during the harvest. With a bit of luck they would return wearing their jackets on their shoulders like capes with the sleeves dangling down heavy with booty.

The guard would have the first pick of the trove. The rest was shared by the gang, one or two potatoes apiece. We would bake them in the ashes of the ever-burning bonfire. We ate them in total silence, but everybody's eyes would rest on a small cube of pork fat skewered on a twig with which our guard turned his potatoes into a feast.

Sometimes women from the kolkhoz would bring milk or pickled cucumbers in glazed, hand-painted jugs and try to sell these to the few prisoners who still had some money or to exchange them on the sly for pieces of prisoners' clothing or tools. Alas, I had no money nor anything to barter. Grablewski, one of our Polish trusties, thought himself a great wit. One day he said to one of the women:

"Auntie, would you swap your jug of milk for syphilis?"

"I don't know if my man needs one," she replied. "Is it government property? Are you sure there is no stamp on it? I don't want to get in any trouble."

One night shortly after roll call, brave little Klein, myself and another young Polish fellow whose name I cannot remember, huddled together trying to find the best possible arrangement for our bodies, our three padded jackets and half a thin, torn blanket. We were on the upper bunk that I usually shared with Klein, but the third fellow joined us that night because a young Bukovinian who shared the lower bunk with him was about to die. He was moaning constantly and stank of urine and putrid scurvy ulcers. We yelled at him to be quiet but that did not stop him from moaning and jabbering in Romanian. Anyway, we were just about to fall asleep when I heard a loud voice repeatedly asking, "Where is Topolski?" I recognized the voice of Malin, the big Kiev librarian, and shouted "Here!" In the dim light of the solitary kerosene lamp I recognized his burly figure as he followed the direction of my voice in the semi-darkness. He found my bunk and with his face close to mine, he said in his usual quiet but clear voice, "Listen. Today I saw in *Kirovskaya Pravda* [the local newspaper] a short article that said that as the result of the agreement between the Polish government in London and the Soviet government, a Polish army is being created in the Soviet Union and a general amnesty has been proclaimed for all ex-Polish citizens. I don't have it because Sashka tore it out to show it to other Poles, and then he lost it or used it to roll his cigarette. No doubt you are going to hear more about it tomorrow from our political commissar."

I jumped down from my bunk and ran to share the story with my compatriots. Some of them were stunned by the news. Some were overjoyed. But a lot of them were skeptical and thought it just another hoax. I believed Malin, but somehow I too had some lingering doubts. The news was so unexpected and so good as to be almost unreal.

In the morning outside the kitchen as we waited for our soup, everybody was talking about the amnesty for Poles. All my Polish friends were beside themselves with joy. Some of the Russians thought that it was a neat way to dispose of the anti-revolutionary foreign element, "Send them to the front and let the Germans kill them." The *urki* thought we should have been killed a long time ago anyway without any fuss.

The whole day passed without any official announcement. Nobody from the administration would admit that they had seen the paper with the news about the amnesty for Poles. Decades of living in fear of saying something that could be construed as a political statement taught them to keep mum. And the word *amnesty* smelled strongly of politics. Malin, put off by the lack of official confirmation, grew silent.

At the morning roll call we tackled our camp commander about the news. He would not even take his eyes off the list he was reading when he answered, "I know nothing."

And so nothing changed. The same thin soup, the same hard work. Only the nights were getting colder. The Romanian youngster kicked the bucket and the *urki* drowned a helpless, mentally deranged con in the latrine ditch. Just for fun, they said.

But after a few days, some prisoners who were working as lumberjacks in an area about ten kilometres north of our camp brought news that tallied with what Malin had read in the Kirov newspaper. On one of the forest roads they met three Poles who had been released a week before from the labour camp near Syktyvkar and were on their way to Kirov. On their release they were given new documents, food rations for one week, new clothes, 300 rubles and a railway ticket to Kuibyshev, a city on the Volga River where the Polish Army HQ was said to be.

This was good news, but our camp administration kept denying any knowledge of the amnesty. In the evening, I joined other Poles to talk over our situation and why the news about the amnesty was being kept secret. We came up with many plausible reasons but none of them seemed convincing. Then a weepy, whiny fellow none of us thought much of was allowed to voice his pennyworth of common-sense village philosophy. He spoke in a squeaky voice, blinking his eyes faster than usual.

"Well, Tovarish Nachal'nik's gotta meet his numbers, you see, and he needs people for that. Even bad workers are better than none. Besides, if he lets us go, the camp's food'll be cut and there'll be less stuff to steal. There's no use bitching to anybody around here. They don't give a shit about us. And there's no way to talk to anybody on the outside. So we just gotta sit tight and wait. Something will turn up one way or another."

When he finished talking he looked pleased with himself and with being able to have his say for once without us yelling, "Oh, shut up!" in the middle of his first sentence. What he said made sense but we were not in the mood for waiting. Then I said, "Let's go on strike."

There was a long silence. The word *strike* was taboo among the Soviets. Somebody said, "You know what they will do? They will shoot you."

"But within a month we'll be dead anyway."

"Some may die, some may survive. Amnesty is no good if you are dead."

After kicking it around for a while, I understood that we had all agreed to go on strike, but in the morning only six or seven of us refused to go to work. The *politruk* threatened strikers with severe consequences and tried to explain to us the idiocy of our behaviour. "In capitalistic countries workers go on strike against the owners who exploit them, but in the Soviet Union everything belongs to the working classes. You are the owners. So how can you strike against yourself?"

In the end, as a punishment, we did not get any food, which was more effective than the threat of death. Next day I was the only one on strike and only for half a day. However, we learned something from that short-lived strike. We did not get the usual harsh treatment meted out to "counterrevolutionary mutineers." Nobody was thrown into the dreaded hole. We sensed that we were no longer ordinary prisoners but were something special. And that buoyed our spirits at a time when we needed it most.

There were further changes in our life. Now all thirty or forty Poles were in one work brigade. Work and food were still the same, but the escort was lax. Smoke breaks became more frequent. We talked a lot about our future as soldiers. Most of us had some basic military training in Poland, so we would straighten up at the roll call and march in step to and from work singing pre-war Polish marching songs, much to the delight of our guard, who threw out his chest and marched in step with us like a proud officer.

We were expecting an official announcement about our release but when it came it was still a surprise. One day the pony with the cart arrived much earlier than usual. Instead of the barrel with soup, it brought a scribe from the camp office trying to keep his balance by performing quite creditable rhumba steps. Even before the cart came to a stop he shouted at our guard. "Get your Polish army back to the camp at the double! Some fat pine cone [big shot] wearing leather riding boots has arrived and wants to see the Polish lords."

The "Pine Cone," a high-ranking NKVD officer, had on not only leather boots but also a shiny leather belt with a holster for his Nagant seven-shooter and a bulging leather briefcase. He wore his cap at a jaunty angle and well back on his head to show off the curls of his black hair. When we filed in, he stopped talking to our camp commander, butted out his cigarette, turned to us and said with a grin,

"Greetings." Without further ado he began a carefully orchestrated speech.

We listened in silence to his lengthy overture about the cowardly attack by the fascist hyenas on the peace-loving Soviet Union and about the heroic defence of the workers' paradise. It took him a long time to go through all the platitudes without which a speech in Russia was not a speech but just a worthless talk. He modulated his voice from the barely audible beginning of a sentence through the crescendo of the convoluted subclauses leading to the final fortissimo of "Stalin!" The holy name of the beloved leader, used in every possible form of grammatical declension, was followed by a dramatic pause that the listeners were supposed to fill with thunderous applause. But he looked shaken and dismayed when instead of cheering, he heard the virtuoso solo cadenza of clapping by the camp commander. Something was terribly wrong. Something was happening that was beyond his comprehension. This gang of smelly starvelings, their arms folded, responded with silence to his inspired exhortations. They were exchanging side glances among themselves as if to confirm their scorn and to stop those few hesitant ones, who were sitting with half-clasped hands, from making any noise.

The speaker went on and on. Finally he said what we wanted to hear. The Soviet Government had signed a treaty with the Polish government-in-exile in London. A general amnesty had been declared by the Soviets for all Polish citizens held in prisons and labour camps and also those who had been forcibly resettled. Those who wished could join the Polish Army for which recruitment had already begun. Soon the Polish Army, he said, would fight the fascists alongside the unconquerable Red Army.

At this moment, the fellow standing on my right turned his face to me and pointing his finger at his forehead said in German (so as not to be understood by the officials), *"Ohne Sterne."* Without the star. It was clear to me what he meant. He would not join any army where he would have to wear a cap with the Communist star on it.

I remember his defiant jaw covered with a teenager's scraggly beard. His green eyes challenged me to agree with him. Through my mind raced the stories of him and his friends fighting with rifles and hand grenades against the Bolshevik tanks entering his beloved town of Grodno in 1939, and of his later exploits in the Polish underground organization. And I thought, "What kind of man is he who, after years of prison and being on the verge of death by starvation, sets the conditions under which he will accept freedom offered to him by his jailer? Is he mad? Is he an incurable romantic? Or is it just because he is Polish?" Looking straight into his burning eyes, I nodded in agreement.

The fat Pine Cone wound up his speech talking about the difficulties in which the Soviet Union found itself because of the war. He talked about the shortages of food and supplies in general, about the overworked administration and the strained transport.

"You will understand, citizens, that we will release all of you, but not at the same time. You'll be released in batches, gradually." And then he turned to our camp commander with a broad smile: "Tovarish Nachal'nik, and who in your opinion deserves to be released first?"

The commander, scratching his chin, looked all around the room. Suddenly he noticed me. He flung his arm out in my direction and then, with an imperious gesture, swept it towards the open door saying, "That son of a bitch. He doesn't give a shit about working and organizes strikes to boot. Scum!"

Despite the announcement and my being pointed out as the first to go, nothing changed in our dreary routine life for another two weeks. For some people the details of the amnesty came as a rude shock. The official wording specified that only those who were Polish citizens in 1939 would be released. Jelecki, Grablewski and a few others suddenly realized the mistake they had made at the time of their arrest. Hoping for better treatment, they had declared themselves Belarussians or Ukrainians. But the sorriest sight was the bewildered faces of the Romanians, Czechoslovaks and Ukrainians who had been lured by Communist propaganda to run away from their homes to go to the Soviet Union. Were they to stay here and rot, while the "enemies" of the Soviets were set free?

Chapter 15

COLD COMFORT

At the beginning of October 1941, the first batch of about ten Poles was told to be ready for immediate release. I was one of them. Some of those who got out with me were my good friends, others I hardly knew because they were the latecomers who had arrived at the Kiev labour camp shortly before the outbreak of the German-Soviet war.

In our group was little Klein (the *urki* never carried out their threats after being denounced on the train); the delicate Bastomski from Wilno, whose behaviour betrayed his upper-class Jewish origins; Romcio Szymanski, that club-footed epitome of goodness; a laconic fellow named Dionizy Koczan; and a chipper youngster whom we called Magda—he was soon to become one of the parachute heroes of the Battle of Arnhem in Holland.

We were issued with new padded jackets and trousers but didn't have them for long. The camp officials fancied them for themselves and within hours we had to exchange them for their old and tattered clothing.

Diadia Misha escorted us the twenty kilometres to the transit prison north of Kirov where the actual release was to take place. But it didn't. The transit prison officials found some irregularities in the transfer documents and refused to admit us. So we spent half that night marching back again to the tune of Diadia Misha's most inventive swearing. The next day we got no food because our names had already been struck off the camp register. In the late afternoon we again trekked to the transit prison and after hours of arguing and shouting were finally let in. It was an insane scenario. A gang of convicts with their guard begging to be let into prison.

We stayed in that prison for two days. Then without any ceremony Dionizy and I were called to the prison office. The lieutenant on duty handed us our certificates of release. There were no photographs on them, just a stamp, an illegible signature and a few lines of print. Very little to show for two years of prisons and labour camps. He told us we were to stay around Kirov and report to the NKVD every six weeks. Then a bread cutter brought scales and two long loaves of bread. He checked the weight and cut off a slice from each loaf because they weighed a bit over the two kilograms due to each of us. I asked them if there was by chance a pair of some old shoes as mine had fallen to pieces. No, there weren't any.

"In the army they'll give you a fine pair of boots," said the lieutenant. And then, as an afterthought, he added, "Wait a moment." He untied a burlap bag standing in the corner, looked inside it, fished out a small pouch with my name on it and tossed it to me. I caught it in mid-air and looked inside. I stared in disbelief at things taken from me after my arrest two years before—an old pocket comb, a photo of my older sister Henia, my father's pocket watch and my grandmother's long watch chain. It looked dull, but I knew it was pure gold. I pocketed the whole lot. A guard came and took us to the main gate. The turnkey opened it and, without bothering to check our certificates of release, said, "Get going!" As we passed through the gate he told us, "Kirov is about six kilometres from here. Don't take the road. Go through the fields. It's shorter." He pointed with his hand to a nearby snow-covered open field. "Then cross the river by the bridge. You have to go to TES-2. Thermal Electricity Station Number Two. Ask people for directions but it's a long way on the other side of Kirov. When you get there, go to the workers' hostel and report there."

He went back inside. Then, as a free man for the first time in two years, I heard the bolts slide in and the key turn from outside a prison gate.

"You go first," I said to Dionizy. As we entered the snowy field, I tried to follow in his shoe prints with my bare feet. To walk barefooted on the snow is not pleasant, but after a few minutes when the temperature of the skin on your feet and that of the snow gets equal, it becomes bearable. Luckily for me it was not very cold that day. Flakes of snow were falling from the dark grey sky. In front of us the city of Kirov looked like a low island of haze and smoke. We ate our entire supply of bread in less than half an hour, and were still hungry. After years of starving, even a full stomach does not kill the pangs of hunger. In one place we found a garden patch. The cabbage had already been harvested but the stubby stems were still protruding from the snow. They were frozen hard, so we had to keep them in our mouths for a long time before they thawed and became chewable. Still, it was a pleasant addition to our diet.

In Kirov, despite our appearance, nobody paid much attention to us. We got lost. The passersby we asked for directions would not stop but would start walking faster and spreading their arms with a shrug, saying only, "I don't know. I don't know."

We found a militiaman, and when we asked him how to get to TES-2, he checked our documents and then took us to the nearest NKVD office. There the duty officer checked our papers again and after making several phone calls ordered one of his underlings to show us the way to where a truck was to pick up men working on the night shift at TES-2. The underling obviously did not relish the idea of being seen in our company, and as we walked he said to me, "Aren't you ashamed to walk barefoot through the city?"

The truck for TES-2 dropped us off at the plant-workers' hostel where we were greeted with yells of, "Go away! We have enough lice of our own. We don't need yours!" The hostel was indeed packed solid. People crowded the triple bunks and even the corridor was full of workers sleeping on the floor.

The political officer to whom we reported was sitting at a desk in a tiny office. He looked at us with sympathy, checked our papers rather perfunctorily and pushed back his cap on his head. Then he leaned back on his chair and sighed. With his head tilted back, he gazed at the grimy ceiling as if expecting a revelation or miracle from the God he was not supposed to believe in. He stayed like that for a while. Then he scratched his ribs on both sides of his body at once, got up with another sigh and said, "Let's go!"

When we were crossing the courtyard, he looked at my bare feet and told Dionizy to wait. Beckoning at me to follow him, he turned back towards the hostel. He opened the door of the dormitory and called for the janitor. An elderly cripple hobbled towards us and looked relieved when he learned that we were seeking not a place to sleep but any pair of old shoes for me. He retreated to the far end of the room, went down on his knees and elbows, and then vanished under the long, continuous sleeping bunk. While we stood in the open door waiting for him, the foul but pleasantly warm air carrying the stench of unwashed bodies wafted around us, reminding me of the time-honoured prison dictum: "Nobody died from stink but the entire Napoleonic army perished from the cold."

The old cripple returned triumphantly waving a pair of worn-out *lapti*, a peculiar footwear once common to all Russian lands. It could be best described as a kind of moccasin woven from strips of willow bark with plaited bark thongs attached. They look like shallow baskets. To wear them you first wrap your feet in old rags or paper plus straw or hay in winter. Remarkably light and warm, they are more comfortable than Guccis but wearable only in dry weather. During very cold weather, the natives splash water all over them. This freezes before it soaks in, making them windproof and so even warmer despite subarctic temperatures. They don't last long for walking, but peasants could weave another pair as they went along the road. In the old days villagers used to measure distance by the number of pairs of *lapti* it took: "My aunt lives in a village about two pairs of *lapti* from here." However, wearing them was always associated with poverty and the village girls would look with disdain on the cavalier who "climbs a willow tree barefooted and comes down well shod."

I was grateful for this unexpected gift though it did not make my frozen feet feel any warmer because I had nothing to wrap my feet in. On the way out we stopped at the local bread store. There was no bread there but we were issued ration books. "Mind the first two pages," said the man as he handed over the ration books. "These are for your bread. With the rest of it—where it says fats, meat, kasha and sugar—you can wipe your ass."

As we walked along, the *politruk* told us that we would be working at the TES-2 power station as sawyers and to be there at seven next morning at the main gate. We crossed some railway tracks and a small orchard, and found ourselves on a small market square where the *kolkhozniki* were selling a few carrots and beets from their tiny private gardens. The city folk would come there to barter their used clothing and other junk. But the *politruk* had not come here to shop. He looked around and marched briskly to a cart with a poor imitation of a horse harnessed to it. The horse was covered with frost, and its head hung down inside its empty feed bag. The wisps of vapour escaping from the bag were the only sign that the horse was alive. On the cart stood two barrels of pickled cucumbers and wedged between them sat a *muzhik*. He was muffled up to his ears and his fur hat came down so low that all you could see of him were two peering eyes. He recognized our *politruk*, slid down off his cart and, holding his whip at "Order arms," listened without moving. After talking to him in a low voice, the *politruk* took him by the elbow and steered him towards a tea shop while making signs to us to follow them.

The tea shop was full of people, but a hush came over them at the sight of the blue crown of our *politruk's* NKVD hat. Without a word being spoken, the corner of the room emptied, leaving a table free for us. A woman server brought glasses of muddy beer for the *politruk* and the *muzhik*, and glasses of *kipyatok* (boiling water) for Dionizy and me. Beer was unobtainable for ordinary citizens and the sight of it stirred the whole room. Some of the customers rose to their tiptoes to see if it was true. The *politruk* kept talking in a confidential but persuasive manner about some lodgings, occasionally pointing at us. The *muzhik's* name was the same as that of our former prison guard, Diadia (Uncle) Misha, and I thought to myself that there must be a million Uncle Mishas in the Soviet Union. He was short, and he never lifted up his beetle-browed, wizened face. With his head down, he kept counting the protruding knots on the dirty pinewood floor and repeating, "*Da, da.*" Yes, yes. His head sank lower and lower with every *da*. Only the second glass of beer brought a smile to his face as he lifted it to his cracked lips. He emptied it in one prolonged quaff, and let out an equally long, loud belch. The *politruk* took it as a sign of agreement and rose quickly, paid the cashier for the drinks and within seconds was gone, leaving the three of us looking at each other in silence. Then it was the new Uncle Misha's turn to say, "Let's go!"

Uncle Misha introduced himself as a Vyatsky *muzhik*, a peasant from the Vyatka region. We did not understand each other very well because he spoke the strong local dialect. He said he was taking us to Marievka, a nearby hamlet, where he had an *izba* (a peasant's cottage) in which we would stay with him, his wife and his daughter-in-law and her two kids.

On the drive to Marievka, Uncle Misha did not talk much but muttered oaths and curses directed at the *politruk* and his idea of farming out his charges to a poor *kolkhoznik*. But he had nothing against us and in fact was rather friendly. He stopped at the kolkhoz paddock to return the cart and the nag to the stable and from there we took a quarter-of-an-hour walk to his house in Marievka. The hamlet had only one street with about a half-dozen houses on each side. All were made of squared logs. The low peaked roofs were covered with mossy shingles. The tiny square windows had frames decorated with intricate hand-carved patterns. But everything had an air of neglect and decay. The wide dirt road went only as far as the last two houses. Beyond that a white, lacy curtain of birches screened the solid wall of tall pine trees that stretched as far beyond as one could see.

News, however, travelled fast in this area. Some *kolkhozniki* who had seen us in the tea shop returned to Marievka before us and spread the story about Uncle Misha and his new lodgers. As we approached the third house on our right, we saw a middle-aged woman standing in front of the gate. A black kerchief knotted under her chin underlined the oval of her handsome face, but her mouth was twisted by anger and frustration. She yelled in a wailing voice at us and at the unperturbed Uncle Misha.

"Are you out of your mind, you old fool!? Bringing those lousy criminals to our home!? So, the big commissar bought you and your house for a glass of beer. Can't you see there is no room for them? If you let these bag snatchers in, you'll be sleeping with Kozukha in the shed." (We learned later that Kozukha was the name of their cow.) Then she turned to Dionizy and me. "Go away, you thieves! There is nothing to steal in our little house anyway. We don't want you here. You stink! Take them back, Misha, to where you found them!" And in a desperate move she spread her arms as if barring the way through the gate. It was an empty gesture as the remnants of the rotten picket fence had fallen down a long time ago, and there was nothing to stop us from going around either side of the gate.

We listened quietly to her abuse, though being called a bag snatcher hurt. In prison circles, purse snatchers were considered the lowest of all thieves and were branded as individuals devoid of any skills or ingenuity.

"Oh, shut up, you black whore!" growled Uncle Misha. He brandished his whip at her, holding it by the thin end. Seeing it, she stepped aside and he led us inside.

The *izba* was a one-room house entered through a lean-to stable. Its main feature was a large adobe stove, a veritable mountain of yellowish clay which took about a quarter of the available space along the wall beside the door. It was as high as the room itself. The stove had a hip-high ledge for pots and at the back of the ledge was a scooped-out hearth for burning wood and for cooking. On either side of the stove was a kind of mezzanine floor for sleeping made of wooden beams topped with hardened clay and reached by a ladder. Strings of dried wild mushrooms and bunches of herbs dangled from the rafters. In one corner of the *izba* the barely burning wick of a tiny lamp cast glimmers of light on an icon of Saint Nicholas circled by paper roses. Beneath it, on a ten-year-old calendar, Lenin was dispensing his blessings on the multiracial proletariat masses.

A low partition wall split the room in two. The smaller area was the women's domain used for preparation of food. It had a small table, shelves for clay bowls and jugs, and in the corner sat a mini-boudoir with a small triangular table for a wash bowl with a mirror above it. On the other side of the partition was a large pinewood table and benches. Near the window stood a small wood stove, made of cheap iron, and a low clothes chest, which Uncle Misha used as his workbench. He was a kind of a cobbler, mainly repairing *valenki* (felt overboots) for the villagers. Whether working or not, he would spend hours sitting on his cobbler's stool daydreaming about the two passions of his life: tobacco and beer. Occasionally, with his warm breath he would blow a small round hole in the ice-covered windowpane and peep out through it onto the empty street, hoping to see something of interest.

We spent barely five minutes inside, just enough to look over the palatial (by our standards at that time) surroundings and to get acquainted with Uncle Misha's daughter-in-law, her pale three-year-old daughter, and her snotty four-year-old son, who greeted us with an impressive string of crude curses, much to the delight of his proud mother. His father had been drafted into the Red Army and shipped to the front. They had had no news of him since the outbreak of war.

Moments later the daughter-in-law told us that unless we went immediately to the bread store to pick up our ration of bread we would lose it, as one day's coupons were not good the next. We ran almost all the way there. What's a five-kilometre run when the prize is 650 grams of bread? We did not have any money, but a kind soul in the bread store paid for us. The rationed bread was very cheap, a nominal price of a few kopeks.

When we returned, the children were already sleeping. The rest of the family was still at the table, finishing their watery soup and scratching the bottoms of their bowls with their beautifully hand-carved wooden spoons. Their diet was not much better than that in prison. In fact their clayish bread, its flour stretched with potatoes and bran, looked worse than the bread rations we had just bought at the store. Being kolkhoz members, they had no right to such rations and so had to make their own bread with whatever was at hand on the kolkhoz. But they took these dire living conditions for granted, and if anybody started complaining someone would say: "Remember the famine of 1922? Or the one of 1930?" and everybody would go silent.

They asked us to join them at the table and gave each of us a glass of tea brewed from dried wild berries. I nibbled at my piece of bread crust which I was keeping for my breakfast. They did not ask many questions about our stay in the labour camps. They had heard it all before. After all, at that time some ten million people or more were held in prisons and labour camps in the Soviet Union. Our strange Russian baffled them at times, and the talk soon petered out. The young mother, who looked and sounded shrewish, yawned a few times and joined her sleeping children at the far side of the stove. Starukha, our landlady, washed the bowls and was raking the glowing coals in the oven before closing it off with a semicircular metal cover. Uncle Misha began scratching himself vigorously all over his body. It was the sign for bedtime. Our hosts were the first to climb the ladder. They settled down on balding wolf skins close to the wall of the stove where there was more head room near the peak of the roof. Dionizy and I climbed the ladder after them and crawled onto the far corner of the bunk, nearer the outside wall, keeping our heads low to clear the underside of the sloping rafters. The fire in the oven must have kept going for a long time and for a few hours it was unbearably hot up there. Until the fire died down, Uncle Misha and his wife slept naked. But as the temperature in the *izba* dropped, they would gradually pull on their clothes again and get up in the morning fully dressed.

The *izba* was a repository of smells. The background of sauerkraut, wood smoke and dried mushrooms was like a painter's canvas on which dabs of other colourful odours stood out here and there. Each scent had its own source and a well-defined area in which it ruled over the others. The smells served as a guide in the darkness of night. On a moonless night you could tell that you were close to the window and Uncle Misha's workbench by the smell of pine pitch in which he dipped his cobbler threads. A scent of sage warned that you were too close to the landlady's dressing table and to tippy shelves with pottery bowls and jugs. There was no fear of bumping against the sauerkraut barrel because, though empty, the smell of pickled cabbage would nip your nostrils when you came nearer. The stink of Kozukha led you to the exit door. Once there, sniffing out the family's primitive latrine (a hole dug out in the clay floor of the stable) was a cinch.

The family alarm clock woke us early. The stars were still shining when Dionizy and I reported for work at the TES-2 power plant. We joined the group of newcomers who were huddling together near the main gate of the plant and stamping their feet in the predawn chill. About ten of them were our friends from the camp who, like us, had been released the day before in batches of two or three.

Some of them had been squeezed into the workers' hostel. There they slept on the bunks of those who were working the night shift. Bastomski, Klein and Magda had been lucky to get an empty cubicle in a house for old women, but a couple of others were just let loose and told to fend for themselves. Besides us there were a dozen Russian women and men, all of them civilian refugees from areas near the war front. They were town people dressed in overcoats, shoes with galoshes, scarves and mitts, and they looked out of place.

The foreman arrived clad in a strawberry-roan rawhide coat and matching high boots. At a distance he looked like a cow walking on its hind legs. He said *"Davai!"* and herded us into a wide open field lit by naked light bulbs dangling from overhead wires. There the night shift of sawyers was waiting for us to take over their wobbly sawhorses and blunt saws.

Our job was to saw metre-long logs into three for fuel for the boiler room of the electricity plant. The logs came to us floating in a system of elevated troughs, a kind of conveyor belt. The troughs were lined with ice, and from time to time we had to fish out the floating logs with our freezing hands. We gave up trying to flip out the logs with a stake or a spade because that usually ended in splashing ourselves with icy water, which was worse.

The foreman told us that we were on piecework paid at the end of the shift. Then he gave each of us a pair of large mitts made of jute. We put the mitts on and lifted our first log onto our sawhorse. As we were standing facing each other, ready to make the first notch, Dionizy said, "There is a canteen for the workers somewhere around the plant. Let's work hard and make enough rubles to buy lots of soup with kasha this evening." I nodded in agreement and added, "Fine with me. Right hand first."

We were not novices at this work. Weeks of practice in Cheptsy camp had taught us to go lightly with the saw and use slow, long strokes. We knew how to keep going without a break by changing over to use our left hands when the right got tired. But we soon realized that it was going to be a tough job. The saw was really blunt and was biting into the green wood very slowly. It would often seize, and to take the saw blade out we had to turn the log upside down on the sawhorse or across another log and climb on top of it in order to spread the cut and free the saw.

Our pile of sawn wood looked like a lilliputian pyramid and the prospects of big pay at the end of the day seemed more and more remote. For once, Dionizy was unusually talkative. In spite of his empty stomach he was elated by the feeling of being free. Yet once in a while he would look around as if to check that there was no armed soldier to guard us.

The rosy sun started peeking out above the forest line on the horizon, changing the black blocks of the power plant into a fairy castle enveloped in pink clouds of steam. Dionizy's face, already red from frost and toil, became even redder. Two men to the right of us stopped sawing and left in search of some screened place to relieve themselves. The moment they turned their backs on us, Dionizy dived on the ground near their trestle and picked up a cigarette butt. It was still glowing but so small that he could hardly hold it between two fingers. He pressed it to his lips and inhaled deeply, just once but enough to bring bliss to his face.

On our left two women wearing townie overcoats were still trying to saw through their first log. One of them sat down to sob silently while her partner tried to push the long saw to and fro on her own.

At noon break those who had money went to the canteen for cabbage soup and *vinegret* (boiled chopped beets drenched with vinegar). These two items were the standard menu. The cabbage soup sometimes had traces of fat floating on top like little eyes but usually it was listed as *shchi postnye*, "fasting cabbage soup," meaning that not a gram of fat was used in making it. There was not much shredded cabbage in it either, only a lot of vinegar and salt. Sugarless wild berry tea was the dessert. But that day we did not have any money for the midday meal. Instead we kept sawing logs, hoping for a windfall pay at the end of our working day.

From the moment of our release, I could not stop thinking about the gold chain and the watch. I kept them on me and could feel them whenever I moved—the chain tight around my waist and the watch in my pocket cold against my thigh, for I had no underwear. Nobody knew about my treasure, not even Dionizy. I decided it was safer to keep it secret. I knew that both of them were valuable, but who could I sell them to and for how much?

The irony struck me. How silly, I thought. Here I am nearly dying from starvation and cold, and these things are worth more than a long line of bowls of hot soup. And surely I could get something better than bark *lapti* for my frozen feet. Tomorrow, I told myself, I am going to do something about it.

By late afternoon both of us were exhausted. Our arms ached and the saw was jamming more often. The red sky at sunset announced a clear night and heavy frost. It was getting dark fast, and the lights came up before the foreman arrived. With a wooden yardstick he quickly measured our pile of wood and scribbled something on a piece of brown paper for us.

"Here. Take this to the office. They'll pay you there. Also, you can take some firewood—one log each."

We joined the lineup at the office cradling our fire logs. When I gave the foreman's chit to the cashier, he just glanced at it and pushed across the wicket ledge six rubles and some change. I was stunned. But before I could ask for an explanation, he saw the look on my face and reached for the chit. "Here it is. Read it for yourself. Four and a half cubic metres at a ruble and a half per cubic. Okay? Next!"

So that was it. For our hard day of honest work we had earned enough to pay for three bowls of soup between the two of us at the canteen plus a few kopeks over for our daily bread ration at the nearby bread store.

We walked home in silence through the moonlit snowy fields. The logs we carried were not heavy, but because we were trying to balance them on our shoulders, our hands were numb with cold. The burlap mitts made little difference. The black wall of the forest on the horizon seemed much higher than in the daylight. More than once while making that nightly trek we heard wolves howling far away. The glimmer of the yellow lights of Marievka offered some hope of warmth inside Uncle Misha's *izba*.

The next day Dionizy and I made more money, at least three times what we earned the first day. Not by working harder (which was impossible) but by the honest *tufta* learned in the camps. Now our piles of sawn wood were empty inside, held up by triangular frames which we rigged from uncut logs. Then we "appropriated" the logs cut the day before by the two townie women, who did not show up for work. Our wobbly piles passed the foreman's quick once-over.

Noon break I spent inquiring wherever I could about the name and whereabouts of the plant manager. One of the places I chanced on when looking for information was the local militia office. Militia units acted as the local police force, separate from but subservient to the NKVD organization and dealing mainly with problems of public order, petty crime and the enforcement of administrative laws. At the office I met a sympathetic young militia commander. He told me the name of the plant manager and the place where I could find him. He was away, I was told, but in a day or two he'd be back at TES-2.

In the evening as our group of Cheptsy ex-cons waited in line in front of the cashier's office, we saw someone hobbling in towards us out of the darkness. It was the lame Romcio Szymanski, whom we had not seen since our release from prison. When he came closer we heard him panting and saw beads of sweat on his forehead despite the cold wind. In a hoarse voice, he told us that he had come to say goodbye. Earlier he had been taken to the first-aid clinic where the doctor found him very sick with pneumonia and probably tuberculosis. He said that he was sorry to leave us but he was being sent to a hospital in Kirov and pointed to a truck standing nearby. Then he slowly undid the buttons of his almost new padded jacket, took it off and handed it over to me saying, "Take it. It's really yours."

It was the same padded jacket that I had flung on the bank of the Dnieper River when I found it too heavy to carry in the scorching heat as we were herded from the Kiev prison to the Darnitsa railway station. I looked at him as he stood in front of me, feverish and oblivious to the cold, clad in the thin padded vest that he usually wore underneath the jacket.

"What about you?"

"I'm fine," he whispered. "I won't need it in hospital." And, turning to the others, he waved a feeble goodbye. Then he shuffled off to the waiting truck. There he had to be helped into the driver's cab, which had no glass in the side windows.

As the truck left, Dionizy said to me, "Don't feel guilty about it. It's better that you have it than some son of a bitch who'll tear it off him in a hospital morgue." By a quirk of fate, Romcio giving me his jacket saved his life as well as mine. But I had to wait nearly half a century to find that out.

Early in 1988, Henryk "Charytonowicz" Skirmuntt, the diplomat's son raised in the Pripet Marshes, happened to mention in one of his letters to me that soon after the war he had run into one of our Cheptsy gang of ex-cons on a train in northern Poland. It was Romcio, very much alive and working for the regional forestry department in the Baltic port of Szczecin. I decided to trace him. After months of inquiries and cutting through the bureaucratic jungle of Communist Poland, I received a letter from the Forestry Department of Szczecin Region stating that, "Romuald [his proper first name] Szymanski was employed by this Department from 1949 until his resignation in 1952. His present whereabouts are unknown."

In June 1988, on the last day of my vacation in Poland, I found myself waiting in the Warsaw Central Telephone Office for my turn to place a long distance call home to Canada and spotted a copy of the Szczecin telephone directory. In it I found six R. Szymanskis and their addresses. Within a week, six identical letters went from Canada to six Szymanskis in Szczecin. I received a reply from a Roman Szymanski, a young man in his twenties, who wrote that he was most intrigued by my letter and its references to camps and prisons in Siberia. He said that he had never heard of Poles being held prisoner there and had decided to locate the real Szymanski for me. Indeed he did. A week or two later a fat letter came from Romcio in Szczecin.

He somehow got through the pneumonia. Then he was pronounced fit and discharged, but while walking along the corridor to the exit, he bumped into his doctor who took one look at him and said, "You can't go out without a coat in winter after pneumonia! You'll have to stay here until we find some clothes for you." And the good doctor harboured him and kept him on the hospital diet for three months longer until enough patients had died to outfit him with their clothes.

Romcio said in his letter that when he left the hospital he had long hair and a scraggly beard. Clad in oversize bright yellow trousers and a black fedora, he sent passersby into fits of laughter. He was arrested again on some frivolous charge and spent nearly a year in the Nizhny Tagil labour camps. Released in 1943, he managed to trek south to Alma Ata. He could not find any work, but did find an abandoned wooden warehouse. He survived by dismantling it bit by bit and selling the pieces as firewood. After a few days the locals got used to the sight of him and reckoned that he was doing some legitimate work. Every day he carried his booty to the local market for sale. But when he sold the last planks he had no income and no place to live. Soon he found himself in prison again, charged this time—despite his clubfoot—with being a draft-dodger. All in all he spent five years in slave labour camps all over the Soviet Union, including a spell in the coal mines on the Chinese border.

In 1947 he was repatriated. In 2000, I went to Poland and met him again. He was waiting for me outside his house in Szczecin. We embraced, then took a step back to look at each other.

"Long time."

"Long time." He nodded. "What would you like to drink?"

With the extra money Dionizy and I earned by *tufta* on that second day at TES-2, Dionizy bought a small matchbox full of homegrown tobacco from some enterprising man. That evening Dionizy proffered to Uncle Misha the tiny matchbox of shredded tobacco leaves with a gesture worthy of a squire offering a Havana cigar to his club mate, and invited Misha to roll himself a cigarette.

"A fine lad you are, Denis," beamed Uncle Misha, who russified Dionizy's name. They became good friends on the spot.

I still picture them as they sat in front of the glowing iron stove: Uncle Misha on his stool and the newly christened Denis on the workbench. With their eyes closed, both of them inhaled gently and then, with the lower lip pushed out and curled up, blew the smoke out in one long breath that ended with a blissful, near-silent "aah."

Chapter 16

DEPUTY CHIEF ENGINEER

Although I was working or walking around all day, my health was not good. I had persistent diarrhea, discharging blood and mucus. My scurvy ulcers kept breaking out and oozing, and the recent frostbite made my life even more miserable. Whenever I entered a heated room or even when I stayed outside during a thaw, my toes, heels and the sides of my feet would swell, turn a bluish purple and itch terribly. Nothing seemed to stop that hellish itching. Only soaking in sauerkraut brine, as suggested by Uncle Misha's wife, would bring temporary relief. On top of that, the skin covering the Achilles tendon just above the heel of my right foot broke open, probably as the result of an ulcer on top of the frostbite. A deep fissure formed there, where it had no chance to heal. Sometimes the wound would close overnight only to split again during the morning walk to work. After a few weeks of this, new skin began to grow out and up from the edges of the break like puckered lips. The two lips eventually met with enough play in the skin to stop it from opening up when I walked.

But before that, one morning I told the foreman that I had to go to the infirmary and I used the visit as an excuse to give me time to see the plant manager. At the doctor's office a buxom nurse disinfected and bandaged my raw tendon and gave me bismuth powder for my guts.

The plant manager's office was in the same building as the infirmary. My quiet knock on the door was answered by a loud, "Yeah! Crawl in!" The thunderous voice of the office's occupant belied his looks. Behind the large desk sat a middle-aged, bespectacled creature. His grey suit and matching grey moustache over a half-opened mouth were in complete contrast to the fear-inspiring roar I had just heard. He lowered his head so that he could look at me over his spectacles. "What do you want? And be brief. I have very little time."

I came closer to his desk to hide my willow bark moccasins and told him in a few sentences that I was working in his plant as a sawyer but that my real profession was a designer/draftsman with a lot of experience and that I had worked a long time in Kiev. Though he kept listening, he showed no noticeable interest in what I was saying. He removed his glasses and holding them in one hand conducted an invisible and mute orchestra playing some piece of music I couldn't hear. He was looking out through a half-frosted window and from time to time would say "*Da-ss.*"

During my stay in Russia I heard many times this extended hissing version of the usual *da* (yes), but I could not figure out the meaning or the reason for it until an old-timer from tsarist days explained it to me. Back then, when listening to somebody (usually of higher rank), it was considered polite to nod your head from time to time and say "*Da, sudarin.*" (Yes, my benefactor.) With changing times and customs the word *sudarin* was dropped as inappropriate for a free, post-revolutionary society. However, some people would still start to pronounce it after *da* out of habit or politeness. In a way it betrayed one's age and perhaps one's social origins.

I told the plant manager that I would be more useful to the Soviet Union if I worked in my own profession. I finished my spiel, but before he could make a wry face I added, "By the way, I would like to sell a valuable pocket watch. It's a silver Omega with a gold jacket. I could have sold it many times, but I was waiting for some-body who could really appreciate the quality and the beauty of it. It is not working properly now. It will go for a few minutes then stop. All it needs is a good cleaning, but I am sure that there are watch-makers in Kirov who could repair it in no time." I pulled out the watch from my trouser pocket and laid it on the desk in front of him. Without saying a word he looked at it for a long time, especially at my family crest engraved on the back of the watch case. He wound it with a couple of twists of his fingers and, seeing the second hand moving, put it inside his mouth and closed his lips. With closed mouth and closed eyes, he listened to the ticking made louder by its vibration against the roof of his mouth. He took it out and wiped off the saliva with his sleeve.

Then, hefting the watch in the palm of his hand, he licked his lips, leaned forward, and looked straight in my eyes. "How much?" I returned his gaze and, tilting my head slightly to one side, replied slowly, "Five rubles."

This was a ridiculously low price. Something like five dollars nowadays. But he understood. There was a moment of silence followed by a long *"Dass."* From a leather wallet he produced a new five-ruble bill, folded it in two and pressed it in my hand. Then he pulled an empty chair close to his desk and for the first time he was polite. He said, "Please. Be seated. I'll be back in a moment."

He returned with a tall man dressed in a black double-breasted suit, white shirt and flashy tie. The newcomer smelled of cheap eau de cologne and his dark hair glistened with brilliantine. The plant manager steered him in my direction and, smiling affably, pointed at me and said, "Sergei Sergeyevich, I have found a man who will be of inestimable value to you. His name is, uh—"

"Topolski, Boguslaw Aleksandrovich," I prompted.

"Dass, Boguslaw Aleksandrovich, who will fill the position of your deputy. We will set him up in the small room at the end of the corridor near your office. Please make all necessary arrangements for a table, chair and drafting equipment. Whatever they can find. His starting salary is set at 400 rubles per month. Show him his new place. I'll talk to you later."

Leaving the plant manager's office I bowed to him in the same way we high-school students had bowed to our high-school principal in Horodenka.

Sergei Sergeyevich introduced himself as the chief engineer of the plant and took me to the room that would become my office. It was small and dingy with garish wallpaper on the walls. On a table was a primitive drafting board supported by a couple of bricks. The racks on one wall were stacked with tightly rolled old blueprints, all of them covered with a thick layer of dust.

My new chief looked a bit uneasy. He did not know what to do with this ragged ex-con foisted on him by his boss. He talked in general terms about the heavy workload, deadlines to be met and the extra effort needed to ensure a quick victory over the Hitlerite cannibals. But as he spoke he could not take his eyes off the disintegrating *lapti* on my feet. Still staring at my feet, he mumbled to himself a line from Griboyedov's comedy *The Mischief of Being Clever:* "Poverty is not shameful but a swinish misfortune." And yet the thought of having his status lowered by harbouring a deputy shod in willow bark moccasins bothered him more than wearing them bothered me. He took me outside to a shed on the side of the plant to see the man in charge of stores. There he pleaded for a pair of rubber boots for me.

"Nothing doing," said the store manager, but he eventually took pity on me and produced a pair of new *lapti* and two squares of a thin, very coarse felt to wrap my feet in before putting them on. As we walked away Sergei Sergeyevich kept casting furtive glances around, ready to bolt into the nearest doorway rather than be seen in my company by any of his friends. He told me he'd see me in my new office the next day and then vanished.

Pangs of hunger and the cold wind swept me off my cloud nine and back to the reality of the snow-covered courtyard. So far so good, I thought, now is the time to do something about my gold chain.

First I asked the kind, young local militia chief to sell my chain. He took it to the State Gold Purchasing Agency, but the price they were offering seemed too low to me. So I told Sergei Sergeyevich that I needed time off to go to Kirov to get glasses—my pair from Kiev had been smashed in Cheptsy during a fight. Two days later I got a lift in one of the trucks that circulated between TES-2 and Kirov.

In Kirov, I went from one open-air market to another, offering my gold chain for sale. First covertly, then more and more openly, and finally brazenly. I was astonished at the lack of interest shown by everyone I accosted. They would look at it, check its marking, then shake their heads and give it back to me. Most said the same thing.

"Sonny, it's very nice but what am I going to do with it? I cannot eat it. Now if you had some clothing or shoes for sale, some hooch or maybe some tobacco, then we could strike a bargain. Try to find some Jews. They'll likely give you good money for your gold."

I tried. Around the railway station I found Jewish refugees who would look knowingly at the hallmarks on my gold chain and nod their heads approvingly. But they too would hand it back to me with a sigh and the recurring refrain: "Now if you had some other stuff for sale . . ."

I was sure there must be some people in Kirov who would buy gold, but I had no way of finding them in a strange city. I was in a hurry and impatient as only a hungry and cold human wreck could be. By noon I had given up any hope of finding a buyer. The people of Kirov were starving on their thin food rations. I continued to walk through the streets of Kirov with a fistful of gold being hungry, hungry, hungry.

Finally, I went to the Gold Purchasing Agency where they recognized the gold chain as the one which they had seen the day before. Once again they put it through all the tests. After signing the agreement of sale, I received seven hundred and fifty rubles in cash. But they cheated me. I should have received a voucher, allowing me to buy goods at a well-stocked store with low prices that was otherwise reserved for Party members.

At the free-enterprise, open-air market I bought a few dried pears, which I ate immediately. My next acquisition was a pair of old trousers, which looked somewhat like riding breeches, and a red-and-black checkered shirt made of a coarse material. And I was very lucky to find a *kolkhoznik* who sold me two kilograms of a kind of flour and five kilograms of potatoes encrusted in mud. The flour was packed in an old shirt sleeve and the potatoes in a burlap bag, which was a godsend as I had nothing to carry these things in. My next stop was the optometrist where I managed to buy a pair of glasses—much too strong for my eyes but the only ones available. What a difference they made! I put them on and suddenly the blurry impressionistic Kirov was sliced into wedges of razor-sharp perspectives, each with myriad details. Doorways sprouted cornices; houses, numbers; corners, street names. The ghosts of matted gold Cyrillic letters emerged from rusty red rectangles above store windows.

People acquired faces. Their clothes had buttons; their shoes, shoe-laces.

A disquieting thought ran through my head. If I can see them so clearly, then surely they can see me just as well—my torn trousers, my willow bark moccasins festooned with bloody bandages. My poverty was offensively visible. When passing me, people looked the other way. I was not just another poor person; I was something that should not be seen in public. I pretended that I didn't see them, and I tried to carry myself in what I imagined to be a dignified way.

I walked in the direction of the city centre. There, I was told, was the Univermag, the universal store. People talked about it rather disparagingly. "Some store!" they sneered. "On the first and third floor—tooth powder. On the second and fourth—toys. And on the fifth—offices." But for me it seemed like Ali Baba's cave. Five storys it was, spacious and well lit. It was a pleasant surprise for me because apart from tooth powder, toys and unlimited quantities of gypsum busts of Lenin, Stalin, Marx and Engels, there were other things for sale. I spent a long time walking around the store.

When I was going down the wide steps leading from the third to the second floor, two men in leather coats joined me, one on each side. They squeezed me tight and for a while we were walking in step three abreast. When I made a move to free myself from them, they tightened the squeeze and one of them said in a low voice, "Don't try anything stupid. Just walk quietly with us."

I kept thinking, Am I being robbed or arrested? On the second floor they walked me to the end of a long corridor. People scurried away as soon as they saw us coming. One of the men flashed a small identity card and said, "Your documents."

My first feeling was relief that I was not being robbed. The second thought was more scary, Am I going to prison again?

I fished out my Certificate of Release from the pocket of my torn trousers. They scrutinized it in silence, then held it against the light to check for any signs of alterations. There was no photograph on it, only a faint purple stamp and a florid signature. They kept silent and ignored my questions. One of the plainclothes NKVD agents (for that's what I assumed they were) took my certificate and vanished with it into one of the office rooms. He returned with it in about a quarter of an hour, handed it back to me without a word, and then dismissed me with a couple of flicks of his hand.

I resumed my shopping and left Univermag with a pair of rubber-soled, leather-like black shoes on my feet (about four sizes too big for me) and a grey *kubanka* hat on my head. This deep, pillbox hat had a flat, blue crown of thick, matted wool rimmed with grey lamb's wool flaps. These could be turned down in cruel weather to warm my neck and ears and to make a visor over my forehead and eyes. I also had a fleecy sheepskin that one of the cashiers had been using as a floor rug under her desk. It took me a long time to persuade her to sell it. Later on I cut a kind of a vest out of it and stitched it into my padded jacket as a lining. On my way to where the trucks for TES-2 left from, I saw an English language primer in a bookstore window. The saleswoman looked puzzled when I asked for it but sold it to me without questions.

Together with other people, I waited a long time in a narrow alleyway for the TES-2 truck. It was a bitterly cold night. The truck came late. On the outskirts of town the truck stopped and the driver and his helper climbed onto the back of the truck to collect the illegal but time-honoured "fares" from us. Ignoring my shiny new shoes and the new *kubanka* hat, they refused to take any money from me.

After my return from the shopping expedition, I was surprised to find that two women had installed themselves together with a small desk in my office. They were mother and daughter, both of them evacuees from besieged Leningrad, given some fictitious job at TES-2. They were among the lucky ones who managed to get out from their beleaguered city through the ever-tightening ring of German armies. At the time they were escaping from Leningrad, the daily food ration for non-manual workers was down to 125 grams (four ounces) of bread. During the nearly three years of siege, over one and a half million people starved to death.

The mother was around forty, her daughter half her age. By Soviet standards they were well dressed, but they looked worn out and their faces were grey. They were reluctant and, more likely, forbidden to speak about their experiences in that city of courage and hunger.

They were Jewish and spoke beautiful Russian with the soft Leningrad accent that set its inhabitants apart from the rest of "unwashed Russia"—to use Pushkin's phrase. It was the accent that harked back to Leningrad's glory days as St. Petersburg, the tsarist and intellectual capital of Russia. The pair talked to each other in a barely audible murmur full of pauses and glances comprehensible only to themselves. In the canteen, they used knives and forks to eat the chopped beets and cut their bread ration into dainty thin slices, washing them down with sips of hot water. In the office, the mother would leaf idly through the pages of old ledgers, occasionally circling some words and figures with a red pencil. The daughter would sit motionless at the corner of the desk, gazing through the half-frozen window at the bleak walls of the plant buildings. Her elbows rested on the desktop, her clasped slim fingers propping up her chin. Her face was expressionless except for the sharp vertical furrow that would sometimes appear on her white forehead.

We talked a little. One day upon reading in the *Kirovskaya Pravda* about the new "Lend-Lease" agreement between the United States and England, I said that now with America giving full support to England, Germany's defeat was only a question of time. Hearing this, the mother lifted her face from the ledger and admonished me. "It is neither England nor America but the heroic socialist Soviet Union led by its Leader who is to smash the Hitlerite hordes and win the war." One had to have an unshakeable faith in the Communist system to utter such words in those days.

A few days passed, and I was still waiting for an assignment to reassure myself that I did indeed have a job there. One afternoon Sergei Sergeyevich—my boss about whose existence I was beginning to have serious doubts—floated into my office on a cloud of cheap perfume. Such perfumes were much sought after by some drinkers who preferred them to the prosaic vodka. As one of them once confided to me, "Brother, when you belch after washing down a bowl of cabbage *pirozhki* with a swig of the Flames of Moscow, you have paradise in your mouth!"

But Sergei Sergeyevich seemed more interested in the allure of the perfume than its taste. As he bowed to the ladies, his chin swung clockwise to describe a perfect circle and then stopped at its highest point. He dilated his nostrils, half closed his eyes, and put a Mona-Lisa-like smile on his lips. This dramatic entrance was all but ignored by the mother and daughter who, after a moment of hesitation, deigned to acknowledge this display of Kirovian gallantry with a quick nod. For me, he reserved the routine greeting, "How are you, Boguslaw Aleksandrovich?" and, not waiting for my reply, quickly sat down on the chair from which I had got up to greet him. But he gave a sigh of relief when he glanced down at the new, oversized shoes that had replaced my willow bark *lapti*. He carefully unrolled a drawing that he had brought with him. It was drawn on old, brittle paper, yellowing from age and with dark brown frayed edges. At first glance, it looked like a diagram of some enormous radio receiver with a maze of lines and hundreds of unintelligible technical symbols. Sergei Sergeyevich struggled to keep the paper from rolling up again by spreading it with his hands, then by weighing it down with the brick that I used to sharpen my pencil leads and finally with a heavy inkwell. During these manoeuvres he spoke with a voice so authoritative that it cast doubt on the validity of what he said.

He droned on with the usual preamble about the necessity of doing more with less for the benefit of the patrimony. That word was coming into vogue in those days, patriotism replacing internationalism. Stalin understood that re-awakening the old patriotism would spur on the Russians more than the slogans of international proletarian solidarity, which never took deep root in their souls. As Sergei Sergeyevich preached on, he kept glancing over his shoulder at the two Leningradders and barely looked at the drawing. Suddenly I heard him saying, "We are in need of a diagram for the secondary commutation for the city of Kirov. That is your task."

My heart sank. But an instinct for self-preservation stopped me from flinching or making any sign of surprise or dismay. I did not have the foggiest idea what a secondary commutation was. I was hoping to glean some clues about the nature of my task from the torrent of Party line platitudes gushing from the lips of this Kirovian fashion model. I punctuated his soliloquy with an occasional nod, and I kept looking back and forth between him and the drawing, at the same time smoothing out the creases on it with my hand. Occasionally my nose would all but touch the paper as I pretended to scrutinize the areas covered so densely with lines that they looked as if they had been drawn by a comb dipped in ink. I decided to follow the example of the last tsar, Nicholas II, who, so the story goes, had no idea what his ministers were talking about during cabinet meetings and so kept mum, while exuding the air of an expert. When my boss finished, I asked him how much time I had to complete the job. It seemed to me that he did not know what to answer. He thought for a while, straightened his tie and then said, "The sooner the better." Still facing the ladies, he glided sideways to the door and completed his exit with a spectacular gambado.

I took a long look at the drawing in front of me. One thing soon became clear. The dark rectangle in the centre of the sheet represented TES-2 and the heavily lined circles inside it probably were the generators one, two and three. But the rest of the drawing was totally incomprehensible. The thin lines, thicker lines, triangles and squares, zigzags and abbreviations in both Cyrillic and Latin script made no sense at all to me. I took the drawing and went to the building where the generators were. The generator room had a floor of yellowish square tiles flecked with tiny black grains. With their colour and waffle-like texture, they looked almost edible. The walls and ledges of the room were covered with a thick layer of dust and the glass in the windows was grey with dirt and garlanded with cobwebs. The whole room was filled with the hum of the generators and the clapping of the transmission belts.

I stood in the middle of the room enjoying the warmth and the view of the black behemoths tethered to their concrete bases. The generators were German-made and very old. The men who operated them needed all their ingenuity to keep them going. Replacement parts were not obtainable and when something broke down they had to fashion their own. The foreman, who was tinkering with the pressure gauges, saw me. He wiped his hands with an oily cloth and came closer to shake hands.

"What's new?" he said, lifting his chin up and pointing at my rolled drawing.

"Not much. They want to go ahead with a secondary commutation."

"What kind of shit is that? They better get new ball bearings or the whole caboodle will grind to a halt one day. Those shitheads will always think of some stupidity just to get away from the real stuff they can't cope with."

He spat on the floor. I asked what he thought about the secondary commutation.

"Nothing. I don't even know what it means. And I bet that not one of them knows either. Office nitwits. That's what they are. Wasting good Soviet paper and pencils. The parasites."

I spent half of the following day going through the dusty rolls of technical drawings stacked on shelves in my office. Among them was one blueprint from pre-revolutionary times. It somewhat resembled the drawing brought by Sergei Sergeyevich. The title on it had something to do with "Directional Reversing," which was just as puzzling for me as "Secondary Commutation." But it was a beautiful print with white lines and letters, contrasting with the cobalt blue of the print's surface. The draftsmanship and the lettering were exquisite. A work of art. I have never seen anything like it before or since in my many years as an architect.

But what was I going to do? "*Tufta!*" shot through my mind and within seconds I knew. I would divide each drawing into several parts, shuffle them around, and combine the tsarist and current drawings into one, using my imagination about how to link the lines to form an integral design. Symbols and rectangles filled with fictitious notes would cover the jarring juxtapositions. That work could take a few days, maybe weeks, before anybody would discover my total ignorance of the subject.

I also knew that sooner or later I was going to leave TES-2 and Kirov to seek the Polish Army that was being formed in a yet undisclosed place. So if they fired me, it would simply speed up my departure. I decided to take the risk.

Sergei Sergeyevich was impressed with my makeshift tracing paper, which I made from the only available white paper. It was of poor quality—something like the white wrapping paper that is used nowadays in deli shops. This I soaked with linseed oil to make it transparent and then rubbed it dry with old newspapers. A very laborious process it was. It took hours and hours of rubbing until the paper was dry enough to take India ink. He nodded approvingly when he saw me using the slide rule, drafting instruments and especially the small rotating compass which Russians aptly call *ballerinka*. But as my drawing became more and more intricate, his visits became less frequent and soon he stopped coming at all.

I was pleased with my work. The drawing looked very professional and, for me, finding a new connection in the labyrinth-like design for an unfinished line that stopped in the middle of nowhere was a challenging and entertaining pastime. The abstruse design went ahead faster than I expected and, as I could not take the increasing anxiety any more, I decided on a showdown. I called on Sergei Sergeyevich and told him that the diagram was ready for his approval and signature. He did not show up for two days, claiming other important engagements. On the third day, I cornered him in his office. He would not even unroll my *chef-d'oeuvre* but said, "Let's go see Tovarish Nachal'nik."

When Sergei Sergeyevich spread the "Diagram of the Secondary Commutation of the City of Kirov" on the boss's desk, the moment of truth had arrived. My heart was racing like that of a captured sparrow. Both of them bent down over my drawing. Sergei Sergeyevich was sliding his bejewelled index finger from one place to another saying, "That's correct. Just as I suggested." Tovarish Nachal'nik was hmming and *dass*-ing like a steam locomotive.

Suddenly my tension disappeared. It was clear to me that neither of them knew anything about the "Secondary Commutation." They could not even read a technical drawing. The foreman from the generator room was right.

The meeting was soon over. I was told that some adjustments would have to be made in the diagram, but on the whole that the job was well done and that it might well reflect on my salary revision scheduled for the coming year. Although it was nice to hear that I might get a raise, it wouldn't help much. Apart from our bread rations, there was almost no food for sale.

Unexpectedly, the brother of Uncle Misha's daughter-in-law arrived home on leave from his unit at the central front. A day or two later, when Dionizy and I returned late from work, we found a welcome party for the soldier in full swing. There were only a few men there, among them the village *bayanist* (accordion player).

There was a bevy of village girls all dolled up for the occasion. Dancing was in full swing. With the dearth of male partners, girls were dancing with girls. As soon as we entered the *izba*, we were both offered a glass of *samogon* (moonshine vodka) and a couple of *pirozhki* (small dumplings) stuffed with mashed potatoes and onions. We toasted the hero on leave, gobbled the *pirozhki* and, knowing that we were outsiders, made ourselves scarce by climbing the short ladder to our sleeping deck above the stove. From there we could watch the party without being seen.

The older generation sat at the long bench near the window where Uncle Misha held sway. From time to time he would leave this sedate group and sneak between dancers to make his way to the buffet table for a furtive nip of muddy hooch. As the soirée progressed, the dances changed from the Siberian variation of a foxtrot and old-fashioned waltzes to the more traditional and local folk dances. Between the dances the young men and women would sing *chastushki*—witty and somewhat risqué quatrains.

The boys' quatrains were more earthy and the girls would close their ears with their fingers, pretending that they didn't hear them. As the level of the *samogon* in the bottles on the table went down, so did the level of propriety of the girls' *chastushki*. But, with a bow to modesty, they sang them with their eyes closed. The tired *bayanist* and the men started making moves to end the party, but the girls would have none of it. They kept on dancing and singing with more vigour than when they began the evening. The *izba* was full of laughter and songs, the air heavy with vodka fumes, tobacco smoke, perfume and sweat.

That was the only time I saw Russians enjoying themselves to the hilt—carefree, happy and oblivious to the dark tragedy surrounding their lives.

The party broke up in the early hours of the morning. A drunkard tried to play "Kamarinskaya," a favourite from tsarist times, on the *bayan* and its owner pleaded with him to leave his precious instrument alone. Another man noisily sucked an empty vodka bottle hoping for a miraculous last drop, which failed to materialize. The girls sighed with relief as they eased their feet out of their tight shoes and began searching for their own rubber boots in a pile by the door. Uncle Misha successfully negotiated all six rungs of the ladder and rolled over on his wolf skin. Soon he was asleep—belching, snoring and farting in turn—while his wife blew the flickering embers in the oven back to life to heat up some water, rolled up her sleeves, hitched up her skirt, and started the general cleanup of the *izba*.

Uncle Misha nursed a hangover for two days, and then proposed a samovar party—he'd lucked into some wild berry tea. Hearing him, Starukha said that she'd found lice in our clothes and suggested that the tea-drinking party be followed by a sauna. While we were all in their little sauna shed beside the *izba*, our clothes were roasting in the hot oven to kill the lice and pop the nits. Uncle Misha had the last word. "Such an evening cleans us both inside and out. It used to clean our souls too, when we had one—before the revolution."

A few days later Uncle Misha asked Dionizy and me if we could go with him to Kirov. He had heard that kerosene would be on sale in one of the shops there. The winter had barely started, and he had only one litre of kerosene left for the lamp.

Yes, we could. Nobody would miss me in my office and for a pinch of tobacco the foreman could fix Dionizy's absence from work. Uncle Misha wangled himself permission from the kolkhoz manager to take a primitive-looking sleigh with a skeletal nag, and the following day at dawn we were off to Kirov.

The road to Kirov, like most Russian so-called highways, was never ploughed, so the snow was hard packed and the ruts were so deep in places that the sleigh slid along on its floorboards instead of the runners—hard work for the poor horse who could not count on an adequate meal for his labours. In fact, the horse's large feed bag looked almost empty except for our bottles for the kerosene. Our own supplies, too, were limited: a stoneware gallon jar full of pickled cucumbers and our bread coupons with which we hoped to get some bread in the city. Uncle Misha held the jar of pickled cucumbers between his legs to keep it from freezing. It was a sunny but cold day. Luckily for us there was a bed of straw in the sleigh, covered with a thick tarpaulin and wolf skins in which we buried ourselves.

Everybody in Kirov knew where the kerosene was being sold, which was a bad sign. But when we sighted the lineup it was worse than all our fears. It meandered for many blocks, twisting and turning around the corners and buildings. It was depressing. We left the sleigh and the nag tied to a lamppost in one of the side streets and joined the queue. A man came up and, with an indelible aniline pencil, wrote inside our wrists a number denoting our place in the lineup. It was two thousand, seven hundred and something. Thus numbered, we did not all have to stay in line. One was enough to keep our place, so we took turns.

Nothing much happened during two days and one night of waiting except more and more cold. The bread shops refused to honour our coupons. They thought ours were counterfeit as their colour differed a little from the ones issued in Kirov. All we had to eat were the ice-cold pickled cucumbers and even these lasted only till the evening of the first day. There was no restaurant or canteen nearby, nor any other place where one could get even a glass of hot water, let alone a place to get in out of the cold to warm up. We had a miserable time trying to sleep back to back on the sleigh. Our feet were half-frozen.

The queue was inching forward at a snail's pace but by noon of the second day we could see from our place in the line the door of the store and people leaving it with bottles filled with yellow liquid. Some of them would hand over their booty to friends or family to take home and then return to the end of the line behind us.

We were about fifty metres from the front door when a man wearing a filthy white coat came out of the store, grabbed the upper door bolt with one hand and, pushing back people with the other, tried to close the door. Hearing the yells and curses of the crowd, he raised his hands up in a gesture of surrender and shouted, "Citizens! There is no more kerosene!"

There was more shouting and swearing but in the end the resigned crowd drifted away one by one without further signs of protest. Uncle Misha mouthed frightful oaths as we were marching back to our sleigh. He was furious. On the way back to Marievka he talked to himself and swung his whip over the poor horse but did not hit him—somebody might see and denounce him for abusing a kolkhoz horse.

It was November, 1941. The Soviet Union was undergoing its deepest crisis in the war against Germany. Its future was being decided on the forefields of Moscow. And it was touch and go. All foreign embassies were evacuated from Moscow to Kuibyshev (the former Samara) southeast of Moscow. In Kirov, there were signs that the administration and authorities were weakening. Party people were seen packing their belongings and leaving the city. The NKVD and militia became less cocky and turned a blind eye on people who were breaking the law. There was no anarchy, but people were abandoning their jobs and because of that the administration and public services were crippled. Robberies of bakeries and food stores were not uncommon. The food supply dwindled even further.

The dreary days continued. Each morning I got up in the dark in the cold *izba* and after perfunctory ablutions—"Even a mangy cat does a better job of washing himself," remarked Starukha—I said my morning prayers standing before the icon in the corner. Uncle Misha obviously approved of that, though it bothered him that I crossed myself only once, instead of the three times required by the Russian Orthodox church. Yet he would remain quiet with his head lowered, and if he heard Starukha chattering in the kitchen, he would scold her with a bellow.

"Keep your fucking maw shut, you black whore! Can't you see he's praying to God!?"

After the second hoot sounded from the plant's boiler-room chimney stack, Dionizy and I would go out through the sleeping village. A few milky white wisps of smoke from the chimneys drifted up to the underside of the black umbrella of the sky. Here and there a yellow light flickered in a window. We walked through the creaking snow with our heads low to dodge the piercing cold gusts of wind, bending forward and dropping our shoulders so that our skin would have the least contact with our cold clothes. Led across the fields by the star-studded belt of the mighty Orion, who reigned over the western horizon, we would head for a small spruce copse and from there turn and find our way through the drifting snow of the open fields to a track leading to the distant glow of TES-2.

At the plant's gate a sheepskin cone with a man inside would peer into our faces, recognize us and nod, and then show us in by bending his giant mitt in the direction of the main door. Here, without exchanging one word, I would part with Dionizy. The wood-drying kiln where he now worked was at the far end of the sprawling plant.

My office was warm. In semidarkness I would take my glass and saucer and go to the end of the corridor where, on the top of an iron wood stove, the janitor's teakettle lid went up and down releasing puffs of steam. I would take my glass of boiling water back to the office and, if I had not gobbled my whole ration of bread the night before, I would take out from my breast pocket the square inch of bread crust I'd saved and nibble at it while sipping the hot water. At noon there might be a plate of chopped cold beets for lunch. Afterwards there was nothing to eat until the bread delivery to the store between seven and nine in the evening. Even that became unreliable and twice we did not get any bread. No explanation either. The news about non-delivery of bread reached Marievka before we did. As I was falling asleep in my lair, I heard the quiet voice of Starukha's brother saying: "Poor devils! They got up and go to bed on an empty stomach." These words did not lessen the feeling of hunger, but it was nice to hear that somebody cared.

Many times, going to work or coming back to Marievka, I would be stopped at the level railway crossing just outside TES-2 by long trains carrying the famous Far East Siberian divisions to the Moscow front. These hardy soldiers were travelling on open flatbed cars in 40°C below zero. They were warmly clad in new, well-padded winter uniforms and as often as not they wore long, sheepskin coats. They had with them rifles, Pepesha submachine guns, Degtiarev light machine guns and heavy Maxim machine guns of the old but reliable 1910 design, quadruple anti-aircraft machine guns and heavy mortars. With the exception of the mortars, they were the same weapons I saw when the Red Army entered my hometown, Horodenka, two years before. Undetected by Hitler's intelligence network, new Soviet divisions like these surprised the Germans at the gates of Moscow as much as the unusually hard and early winter did. The German army froze to a halt.

By the end of November, Starukha's brother had become a more or less regular visitor. One evening he came in looking agitated. "Boguslaw, I saw a Polish officer today. At the railway station. He was in a Polish uniform with a four-cornered hat with an eagle on it. It's true. God help me. I saw him just as I see you. A long cavalry coat on him with, I am not lying, epaulettes! There was a crowd of men around him all jabbering in Polish. A railwayman told me that this officer organizes transport for volunteers to the Polish Army. So help me God!"

Now, that was great news for me. A bombshell. And in spite of the conditions imposed on me at the time of my release forbidding me to leave the Kirov area, I decided then and there to go to the railway station the following day and leave with the first batch of would-be soldiers in search of the Polish Army.

Having made the decision to find the Polish Army, I put all systems on go. When I said aloud that I would be leaving, nobody seemed to be surprised.

"You doing right thing, Boguslaw. There's nothing to keep you here. Your place is among your own," said Uncle Misha. Starukha nodded but said nothing. Neither did Dionizy, and when I asked him to go with me he shrugged, saying that he would like first to check how true Starukha's brother's story was. I was a bit peeved by his lack of enthusiasm and decided to go alone anyway. In the morning we parted on good terms.

I had no problems with packing and getting ready for the long journey ahead. I was wearing all my clothes. A burlap sack and a *chemodanchik*, a small plywood box with a handle, contained all my worldly possessions. In the burlap sack, there were about thirty potatoes and some flour bought in Kirov. In the *chemodanchik*, I kept a photo of my sister Henia, a map of the Soviet Union which I had torn out from a school book, a bottle of India ink, a mapping pen and my English primer. In my pocket, I had my Release Certificate, and about twenty rubles. And that was it.

In the morning as I got ready to leave, Dionizy was already gone and so was the daughter-in-law with her children. Only Uncle Misha and Starukha were watching me as I stood in front of the icon under the stern gaze of Saint Nicholas and prayed for God's help in my venture. Then I turned to them.

"Forgive me, if I did something wrong or offended you in any way. It's time for me to go. Goodbye."

Starukha kept looking straight at me but seemed unable to say anything. Only her shoulders quivered as if she felt a sudden gust of cold wind. Uncle Misha took a step forward, gave me a mighty hug and his voice broke as he said, "You've done nothing wrong, Boguslaw. God be with you."

When I left the house I did not look back. It was December the first, 1941, when I left Marievka. I marched at a brisk pace. I had to. There were at least five thousand kilometres to go.

Chapter 17
BEYOND THE URALS

The Kirov railway station rested not on the ground but on the shoulders of the human mass that surrounded the building. Or so it seemed. Tight throngs of people filled every square inch of space around and inside the cavernous building. Men and women of every age. Small children and grandparents. Civilians and military. Every one of them carrying bags, sacks, boxes, suitcases and the small kettles without which no Russian would embark on a journey. It looked to me as if thousands of people, milling around, were searching and looking for a place to sit down, for friends and families who were not where they were supposed to be, for officials who could answer questions or listen to complaints, for lost children, for bread lines and water, for a place to relieve themselves and for trains that would take them out of that bedlam. The main waiting hall, corridors and platforms were coated with people lying on the floor or sitting propped up by their baggage. Those who had already spent days waiting for their train had a vacant look on their grey faces and waved aside people asking questions or bringing the latest rumours. There were no loudspeakers, no information office, no timetables. Crowds besieged ticket offices, which were closed most of the time, and tried to enter the superintendent's and station master's offices but were thrown out before they could even ask a question.

Kirov station was a big one and busy even in peacetime. It was an important railway repair centre on the European part of the Trans-Siberian Railway, the main line connecting Moscow with Vladivostok on the Pacific. Swamped during the war by the waves of refugees and military transports, it could barely cope with the demands on it. The thirty or forty tracks beside the station always seemed to be occupied by trains. If my memory serves me well, only the first two railway tracks had passenger platforms. If a train arrived on the twenty-ninth track, then its passengers had to cross twenty-eight tracks by walking on all fours under the standing trains. Because the makeshift toilets in both trains and station were few, primitive and usually blocked, these tracks were covered with fresh or frozen excrement. Some trains would leave without any warning and would maim or kill the people under them. Empty tracks were just as dangerous. On those lines people got killed by trains passing through the station at full speed. I was yet to learn that these conditions were common to most stations at that time. Travelling was not for the faint-hearted in those days. People often waited three or four days for their train. Some waited two weeks. Getting off the train in order to get some water or food or to verify a rumour about another train due to leave earlier was risky. It could mean crawling under scores of trains there and back. And it could lead to a fruitless search and missing the train you'd been on.

I pushed through the crowd looking for the Polish officer, and there he was—at the far end of the main platform near the Traffic Control Office, surrounded by a group of men who hung on his lips as he repeated for the thousandth time the instructions to each new-comer. He conformed to Starukha's brother's description of him in every detail—a slim, tall man with bushy eyebrows and a drooping moustache. On his head sat a four-cornered officer's hat with the burnished Polish eagle of our Legionnaires. He was a *rotmistrz*, a cavalry captain, and below the hem of the long overcoat I could see his shiny riding boots and spurs with jingling rowels.

He replied with a textbook salute to the awkward attempt I made at a military greeting with the hand holding tight to my sack with thirty potatoes. Then in a slow and clear voice he said once again, just for my benefit, that the Polish Army recruiting centres in central Russia were being closed but new ones would be opened in Central Asia. Depending on the availability of transport, former Polish soldiers eligible for enlistment would be sent there in groups. Those in transport were to receive bread rations in the evacuation centres at the larger railway stations. The bread rations would be issued against the group ticket, which would also serve as the enlistment document along with our personal identification papers.

"Make a list of your names now," the captain said, handing out a small piece of brown wrapping paper. "State also your rank and branch of service. That will have to be approved by the liaison NKVD officer and by the superintendent of traffic, who will find room for you on the trains."

Some of those who surrounded him had heard that story twenty times already but wanted to hear it again and again. It was a motley crowd made up of ex-cons like me released recently from prisons and forced labour camps; prisoners of war; men who had spent the last two years working in dire conditions in so-called free resettlements; evacuees; and deserters from the Soviet army.

As soon as the captain had vanished beyond the matte glass door of the Traffic Control Office, a middle-aged man from our bunch said to the fellow who held the piece of brown paper given to him by the captain, "Give me that!" in a voice that defied any opposition. A moment later he had converted somebody's trunk into a desk, spread the sheet of paper on top of it, sat down on an upright suitcase and, prodding the man nearest to him with a pencil, said, "Your name, age and rank."

He had an air of authority about him and nobody from our group of about forty men asked, "Who appointed you?" Soon it was my turn to answer questions. I felt I had to lie. Strictly speaking, I was not a reserve soldier. I was called up at the beginning of the war because of my paramilitary training at our high school, but I did not complete the two years of military service in Poland that was obligatory for all able-bodied men by the age of twenty. But just to be on the safe side, I said that I *was* a reserve soldier, having completed my national service at the 49th infantry regiment. I gave my rank as a private and my age as twenty-two instead of eighteen. At that time, after months of virtual starvation, my cheeks were hollow and the skin on my face was grey. I could have said that I was thirty-eight and people would have believed me.

Our self-appointed chief, who introduced himself to us as Sergeant Zolotnicki, appeared to be a resourceful man. He immediately claimed a part of the platform as the area allocated to his "unit" and chased away outsiders. And he told us not to go anywhere without first informing him. The following day he went to see the cavalry captain and returned with a group railway ticket for all of us. Then he sent two men with the ticket and our individual documents to the bread store to collect our rations. Apart from his peremptory voice and clean-shaven jowls, he had only a well-cut though old and shiny overcoat and two gold front teeth to bolster his authority.

After two days of waiting on the platform, the train arrived. It was not easy to find it because it was shunted to a distant track away from the station. The train was a mixture of passenger and boxcars. By the time we had gone under and around trains to reach it, Sergeant Zolotnicki was already there standing on the steps of a passenger car, urging us to get in and occupy it before anybody else did. He made a good show of reading aloud our names and letting us in one by one while shooing away other travellers.

Our car was what they call in Russia a hard car. Pairs of hardwood double seats facing each other lined both sides of the central aisle. On one side of the aisle the four seats in the middle of the car had been removed to make room for a cast-iron coal stove. There were no toilets or water. A couple of light bulbs kept the car in a pleasant dimness at night. During the day we could view the icy outside through the narrow and dirty windows. All of them were jammed and could not be opened. The walls were of simple hardwood panelling. Everything in this vintage second-class car from tsarist times was solidly constructed.

I managed to get myself an aisle seat opposite the iron stove and put my sack with potatoes under the bench. After two days of squatting on the freezing platform, the hardwood seat felt like a royal throne. But I never suspected that I was going to spend an entire month sitting on it.

Sergeant Zolotnicki supervised our settling in. To fill the vacant seats he selected and brought in a few outsiders, but with a warning.

"That's it. Don't try to bring in anybody else. Not even your grandmother if you see her freezing outside. And if any stranger tries to climb in, kick him in the face."

The man sitting across from me was different from the others. He was fat with ruddy cheeks and a permanent, benevolent smile. The space between our seats was narrow and every time his fat legs touched mine he would apologize profusely, even when it was not his fault. In the middle of conversation, he would grab the edge of the bench with both hands and lift himself up a bit to break wind, but he never forgot to say, "Excuse me." It was unusual in those days to find someone so polite.

His name was Redzik and before the war he had been a policeman in a small Polish town. Arrested by the Russians as a "lackey of the bourgeois regime," he made the usual round of prisons and camps, but by a stroke of luck got released almost immediately after the amnesty for Poles was announced. Upon his release in Kirov he was given a job as a cleaner in—of all places—a meat-processing plant. The staff at the plant were curious about his past as a policeman—to them a living symbol of the capitalist oppression of the working proletariat—and seemed proud of having "one of those" working among them. The work at the meat-processing plant was a godsend for him. There was a general rule that you could eat as much meat as you wanted to on the job but could not take any out. For Redzik this was no problem. He volunteered to stay on as a guard after hours and slept there at night.

"I would wake up at night and go to the stock room for a midnight snack of sausages and ham. Sometimes the foreman would treat me to a glass of hooch on the sly. Very good these Russkie people were to me. God bless them. But my faith saved me too. Had I been a Jew I'd have starved to death. Nothing was kosher there."

All this was a bit too much for Sergeant Zolotnicki. He was annoyed by Redzik's equanimity. "Mister Redzik. And your Russkie NKVD interrogator in prison, was he kind and polite too?"

"Heavens, no! He beat me up with a leg from a broken chair. No mercy from him. But you see, Mister Sergeant, he had to. That was his duty. If he didn't, he'd lose his job. Me too, if I interrogated him in Poland, I'd clobber him well and square. That's my psychology." I think Redzik meant philosophy. He looked around with a broad grin on his magenta face, very pleased with himself and his dictum.

We were flabbergasted by Redzik's exposé and remained silent. Later on when Redzik went outside onto the little platform at one end of our moving car for a difficult pee into the icy wind, Sergeant Zolotnicki pointed to the door closed behind Redzik and said in a confidential tone, "Watch out for that character. He looks and sounds to me like a Bolshie agent planted here to undermine our morale."

I don't remember leaving Kirov. It must have been during the night because when I woke up we had already passed Molotov and were heading east towards the Ural Mountains. Sleeping sitting up is never comfortable, especially when you cannot stretch your legs. For a while I was considering sleeping on the floor under the bench, but the dirt and dust there were so bad that I gave up the idea. Nonetheless, a few men, whose standards of cleanliness and hygiene were even lower than mine at that time, went ahead and slept there anyway. A witty newcomer promptly dubbed their sleeping area "Wagon-lits Orient Express." He was one of the two brothers chosen by Sergeant Zolotnicki to complete our unit.

The Pikesfeld brothers stood out from the rest of us because of their quality clothes and their voluminous and elegant luggage. They were in their twenties and in excellent physical shape. They were from Cracow, which they had left in a hurry to flee from the advancing German army, and landed in the Soviet-occupied half of Poland in 1939. From there they were exiled by the Communist regime to a small northern village near Syktyvkar in the autonomous Komi Republic, land of tundra and reindeer. They lived there not so much by toil and sweat as by bartering their valuables, clothes and trinkets with the natives for food. They still had their pre-war Polish passports and also valid immigration visas for Australia. It was obvious that they treated joining the Polish Army as a stage in their journey from the land of Northern Lights to terra firma under the Southern Cross. Both of them were well educated and intelligent. The younger brother was musical and whistled all day long the tunes and melodies from his vast repertoire of classical music. Money seemed no problem for them and they often bought extra food at exorbitant prices. Outgoing and with a good sense of humour, they mixed well with most passengers.

Sergeant Zolotnicki was addressed by most of us as *Szef* (Chief) —although that title in the Polish Army was rightly reserved for company sergeant majors. The sergeant brought some semblance of military routine to our car. There was reveille at seven in the morning, then half an hour for a pretence of washing ourselves with a cup of water from a bucket prudently purloined from a firemen's equipment room in the Kirov railway station. Those who had a razor, the will and the need—I still had no beard worth mentioning—would also shave. Then everybody stood up and Chief intoned the "Our Father" and "Hail Mary" prayers followed by us all singing the traditional morning hymn, "At dawn all lands and seas sing praises for Thee, God Almighty." The Pikesfelds, although Jewish, sang it along with us but as praise for Yahweh. In these turbulent times atheists were few and far between. Chief, who had a deep and sonorous baritone, could turn an indifferent crooner into a real songster just by staring at him and by singing crescendo until he got the right response. He also led our singsong sessions far into the night. We sang the songs we learned as children at home or at school; Boy Scout songs; popular folk songs; dozens of army marching songs, some of them going back to the seventeenth century; wistful bivouac songs; bawdy songs and tavern songs; well-known waltzes; and mushy tangos. The sessions ended with everybody standing up for a solemn rendition of the patriotic hymn, "We'll not forsake the land of our roots"—the hymn the onlookers and prisoners sang at the Tarnopol station when we were loaded onto a Soviet train taking us out of Poland.

After morning roll call, Chief would name the men responsible that day for clearing frozen feces from the brake platform at the end of our car, bringing fresh water, or delivering coal for the stove. Everybody knew that "delivering" meant stealing, either from a heap of coal at a railway station or—which was more common—from the locomotive tender. Bringing the coal was tricky. It took two men to find the coal, to negotiate with the guard or to divert his attention, to load the sacks and to bring it home. The driver and the firemen of a locomotive would usually turned a blind eye on a man climbing the tender and throwing down large chunks of coal to his mate below. But the guards, militia or soldiers sometimes took their duties seriously and raised Cain, forcing a "deliverer" to flee. Moreover, any nosy railway official who had a bad day or suffered from indigestion could spoil a well-planned "delivery."

We hardly noticed that our train was passing through the Urals. Instead of awe-inspiringly high mountains dividing Europe from Asia, all we saw were some snowy hillocks crowned by anemic-looking spruce trees. The next station was Pervouralsk and soon we were in Asia. The crossover was quite a letdown, best summarized by a Corporal Zuk. After a short visit to the station's latrine, he declared, "Gentlemen! I just had my first crap in Asia and it was no different from Europe. Take it from me."

Our train was carrying us toward the former Yekaterinberg, renamed Sverdlovsk by the Soviets for the Bolshevik commissar who executed Russia's last tsar there in 1918. I seldom ventured out of the train. The 1941–42 winter was unusually cold. When we reached Sverdlovsk the thermometer fell to 50° C below zero.

Chief took pity on me, the youngest and the smallest, and excused me from any outdoor duties during that arctic spell. Our stop in Sverdlovsk lasted two days. On the first day of our stay there, a political commissar who stood on the railway platform overheard some of our men talking Polish and shouted, "Poles?" When we nodded, he jumped up the steps, opened the door of our car and waited until the din of forty yapping men stopped. Having caught everybody's attention, he made a three-word announcement: "Sikorski's in Moscow." General Sikorski was at that time the leader of the Polish government-in-exile in London. Saint Peter opening the gate of the kingdom of heaven and announcing the visit of a redeemed Lucifer would not have had more impact on the angels than the commissar's news had on us and on the average Soviet citizen. In order to avoid any questions, which could have led him into a political minefield, the commissar saluted and vanished as quickly as he came. The following day we read on the front page of *Izvestia* a communiqué about the Sikorski-Stalin meeting in Moscow. Apart from the usual platitudes, it mentioned the Polish Army in the USSR. It gave no details about its whereabouts but, even so, it boosted our morale. The goal of our journey now seemed less hazy and less remote.

At Sverdlovsk, the Trans-Siberian line turned south as far as Chelyabinsk before turning east again. But there our train would turn off the Trans-Siberian line to continue hugging the eastern foothills of the Ural Mountains, carrying us southward to where the Polish Army was being regrouped, or so we hoped. On the second day in Sverdlovsk, we lost two of our companions. One was seen with all his belongings boarding a northbound train standing on the neighbouring track. We never knew why. Another one failed to answer the morning roll call. He was found dead under the bench, his usual sleeping place. He was a quiet man in his fifties. Nobody would have missed him if it hadn't been for our daily roll call.

The body was carried out by a second pair of brothers in our group, the Dombrowskis, who volunteered for the job. When they returned from that impromptu funeral, they told us that there was a large pile of frozen corpses behind a railway shed and the stiffs were to remain there until spring thaw, awaiting burial. The dead man's bundle and the contents of his pockets, as well as his documents, which had a high black-market value, were considered to be a fair honorarium due to the brothers for performing the last rites.

News about the death of that man spread to the other cars. In our train there were two or three heated boxcars carrying families of farm people who were also hoping to meet up with the Polish Army. They had been deported in 1940 from their homes in Poland to the miserable Siberian kolkhozes. They were victims of the so-called free-resettlement scheme, a Soviet plan to disperse and weaken what they called "unreliable and socially dangerous elements." These "dangerous elements" in the car next to ours were mainly women with their children and aged men heading south in quest of the Polish Army, which, they believed, would take care of them. We had little contact with them. There was no direct passage between the passenger car in which we travelled and their boxcars, which were entered by sliding doors on the sides and so were accessible to us only when the train stopped. As far as I know, nobody from our car ever went to see and talk to these "civilians." In cold that froze our spit before it hit the ground, nobody wanted to stay out even a minute longer than was absolutely necessary. Besides, every one of us was too much of a coward to confront those starving and wailing creatures without being able to offer them some help.

But during a stop, two of the boxcar passengers paid us an unexpected visit. Both were men. One introduced himself as Father Krol, a thirtyish Catholic priest who had somehow managed to conceal his true identity from the Soviets for two years while working as a farmhand on some faraway kolkhoz. The second man, Franek, who was much younger, was his acolyte. Father Krol regretted that nobody told him about the man who had died under the bench and that he had been unable to say the requiem for him. Then he talked about the stark conditions of the people in the boxcars and their expectations of miracles that would save them. In the end, Chief Zolotnicki wound up offering the priest and his acolyte the two free places in our car. They accepted readily and within minutes they brought their few belongings and settled in, looking very happy.

The Dombrowskis were poles apart from the Pikesfelds in every way. They were professional thieves and looked alike. Both Dombrowskis were in their late twenties, short and squat with dark hair starting about one inch above their eyebrows. When they talked to somebody they would constantly shift their eyes, watching the space first beyond one ear and then beyond the other of the person they were facing. Nothing seemed to escape their surveillance. They spoke the overblown language of trashy novels, but occasionally a word from thieves' cant would slip in. They parried questions about their past with a grin and sayings like, "Wouldn't you like to know?" or, "Who can remember that?" All we learned from them was that they came from central Poland and spent a year or so in the tough Ukhta-Pechora labour camps in northern Russia.

There was a third man called Adam, who had joined our group with the Dombrowskis. They sort of adopted him, if one can adopt a six-foot hulk. He was a kind and slow-thinking fellow, impressed by his suave and artful new pals. It took him a long time to find out that they were thieves, though they kept using him as a decoy. They would make Adam keep a place for them in a bread line while they themselves queued well behind him and carried on a nonsensical conversation with him by shouting. This attracted the attention of the people in the line who were particularly bemused at the look on Adam's face, for he was genuinely perplexed by the absurd questions thrown at him. At the same time the brothers "worked" the pockets and bags of people around them. After that, they would slip the stolen rubles, penknives and cigarettes into Adam's coat pockets. He carried these to the railway car without knowing it, leaving the Dombrowskis "clean" in case they were arrested and searched by militia. He also carried their coal, which they "bought" from the train driver. Adam was strong, trusting and naive.

At one station, the brothers brought in some heavy planks with which they built themselves a mezzanine sleeping platform which was supported by the baggage racks. Now they could sleep comfortably above us with their legs stretched out. On the whole, they were friendly and helpful to us, but one day the Pikesfelds' passports with their precious Australian visas went missing. The Pikesfelds paid a gold coin to the Dombrowskis as a reward for "finding" the passports.

At the next long stop, Chelyabinsk, the Dombrowskis hopped off the train even before it came to a full stop. They came back in high spirits, cradling a bottle of vodka and carrying—almost in mid-air—Galya, an apple-cheeked, buxom hoyden.

Nobody knew what to say about this new addition to our car full of men, so we said nothing. The Dombrowskis installed her on their deck, which was above our eye level. She spent all her time there between the two brothers, climbing down only when she had to go out and that was mainly at night. Every time she crossed the car, forty pairs of eyes escorted her to the door and back to the upper deck. Even when our thoughts started drifting to other things, a muffled giggle from the platform above would shortcut them back to the Siberian Circe. If anybody among us was really bothered by her presence, it was our newly acquired spiritual leader, Father Krol.

Pikesfelds' largesse for the return of the missing passports had changed the lifestyle of the Dombrowskis. On every station they would buy moonshine, bread and onions at black-market prices and stow these luxuries on their upper deck in front of their protégée. Both brothers drank heavily and, following the Russian custom, would strip naked during their binges. Their feeble attempts at singing usually ended in bouts of retching. At times they would become belligerent and spoil for a fight.

At one of the small stations, the Dombrowskis returned from their prowl full of excitement. "We need a few men to help us right now. We've found a real treasure. We promise you a feast tonight!"

The entire car crowded around them eager to hear the details. It appeared that on one of the cars of a train with military supplies they had spied a whole load of cases of canned food. The train was on one of the tracks not far from ours, but it was protected by a sentry. However, as it was nighttime there was less risk of being caught.

"How do you know there is canned food in these cases?" asked the older Pikesfeld, the skeptic.

"I can tell a case of soldiers' grub when I see one. They are a special shape, and the colour is different. Don't go if you don't want to. Besides we need a man with brawn not brains. Come on, Adam! We need one or two more." They took Adam and two more guys. Galya went with them as a decoy to distract the soldier on guard.

They came back triumphant. Adam, the mule, was bent double carrying the loot on his back. Drops of sweat were dripping from his brow. When the wooden case was pried open our circle of onlookers gasped in unison.

Inside, neatly arranged and protected by wood frames, were artillery shells. We were not disappointed: we were terrified. For stealing army food you could get five years, but for stealing ammunition the penalty was death. The dozen or so shells had to be taken away one by one behind the station and thrown down the latrine hole. A dozen risky trips. When the danger of being caught had passed, the Dombrowskis took a lot of ribbing about the feast they promised. But they didn't think it was funny. They were grumpy and vented their bad humour on Galya, giving her a black eye for carrying out her task of distracting the sentry with far greater zealousness and enthusiasm than was necessary.

Father Krol had taken over from our Chief at leading morning prayers. He lengthened them considerably and usually ended with a short sermon. The Dombrowskis' frolics got under his skin and in one of these little morning lectures he threw a few jabs at those who "practise an unhealthy familiarity that poisons the atmosphere of the entire car."

The elder brother was lying on their deck with his head propped up by his elbow and listening to the homily. He was stung by the priest's allusions to his conduct. "Father, it's easy to preach a clean life for someone like you who tied a knot on his peter and carries his nuts around for display only. But for us, mere normal mortals, living clean is well nigh impossible. Somebody's got to sin, if only to keep your job going."

Father Krol pretended he didn't hear it. So did the rest of us. The last round had gone to Dombrowski, but we weren't sure who was right. The veil of ambivalence hung heavily over the whole car.

A few days passed. All of a sudden the Dombrowskis lost their aplomb. They became gruff and even between themselves talked in monosyllables only. Then they took Chief into their confidence and had a long chat with him, embellished by a lot of nods on both sides. They quit drinking vodka and developed a distaste for liquids as if suffering from hydrophobia. For them urinating had become an ordeal.

At the next station Galya was kicked out by the Dombrowskis without so much as a goodbye peck on the cheek, and the brothers were told by a nurse at the First Aid Post that Orsk was the closest place to get treatment for clap.

Over the next few days the pair turned into male vestals, poking and staring sadly at the fire in the coal stove. A few seats away Father Krol sat with his eyes raised to the dirty ceiling. With his hands clasped on his belly, he rotated his thumbs around each other, changing often from forward to reverse gear. He looked totally engrossed in pious contemplation except for an almost imperceptible smile on his lips.

The news about the Japanese attack on Pearl Harbor on December 7, 1941, was greeted with jubilation by us and the Russians alike. With the Yanks now on our side, we had no doubt that we could beat Hitler. But when we read that Roosevelt said America would produce 50,000 military planes in 1943, we thought it mere propaganda. Nobody could do that. Well, they did. And more.

But from day to day our lives were less affected by the big news and world-shattering events than by news of a bread store being shut; a railway line closed for three days to all non-military trains; or a friend left behind because a train left early without warning. I remember Chelyabinsk not for the glow of the iron smelters and steelworks, nor because it manufactured more than 50 percent of all Soviet tanks during the war, but because of the thin soup with a couple of slices of liverwurst floating on top of it that was being sold in the station buffet. I remember buying eight bowls of that soup, throwing out the liquid and then eating the slices of grey sausage. A princely feast.

It was the daily ration of bread that kept us alive during our train journey south. At almost every railway station (or close by) was a bread store. Some of them, at so-called *evakopunkty* (evacuation centres), distributed bread for civilians being cleared from the war zones; others were for military personnel. Strictly speaking, we did not belong to either category. Our communal railway ticket was issued for "Polish Citizens repairing to the Polish Army," so we tried to wheedle out bread rations from both. Even with plenty of chutzpah we were not always successful. Corporal Zuk was our best trump card when dealing with a reluctant or suspicious bread-store manager. Although of short stature, he had an air of self-confidence and a gift of the gab that confused his adversaries, who would give way to the torrent of his ingenious arguments. While speaking he would thrust his foxy face into the face of the man he was talking to, forcing him to step back. This physical retreat was the first step in demolishing his opponent's ego. The rest was easy. Zuk not only looked and sounded aggressive, he was aggressive. Even the muscular Dombrowskis would give him a wide berth.

In Troitsk, after we had collected our bread rations at the *evakopunkt*, Corporal Zuk rushed back to our car panting and yelling, "Out! Out! All of you. On the double."

We could sense the urgency in his voice and in an instant we were on the platform wondering what had come over him. He stood on the top step of the car, two empty burlap sacks (one of them mine) folded over his arm saying, "There's no time for explanations. Just do what I tell you." Then he began yelling like a professional drill instructor.

"Form in twos! Right turn! Forward march!"

Running to the head of the column and passing our chief, Zuk gave him a reassuring pat on the shoulder as if saying, "Don't worry. I am not after your job."

"One, two! One, two! Left, right! Left, right!" He marched us to the back of the station and with a booming "Halt!" stopped us in front of a military store. The door of the store was wide open, and we could see inside it lots of boxes and sacks stacked on shelves. Near the entrance was a counter with scales and ledgers. A young lieutenant perching on the counter looked with curiosity at our unit and at its commander, who approached him, saluted and reported.

"Citizen Lieutenant! Commander of the platoon reports his unit on the way to the Headquarters of the Polish Army, ready to collect provisions."

Again Zuk saluted smartly, beckoned at Chief asking him to produce the railway ticket and ordered two men from our group to come closer. He handed over to them the empty sacks, yelled at the rest of us "At ease!" and, assuming a waiting stance, started picking his yellow teeth with a thin splinter of wood that he had pried from the counter.

The young lieutenant, looking confused, stammered, "Yes, yes. But let me check first at the office upstairs."

Fool! When he returned a few minutes later it was Corporal Zuk who was standing behind the counter counting the loaves of bread and weighing sugar on the scales. Zuk even found a packet of fish-fat margarine. At the same time, with a stub of a pencil he was entering the quantities in the open ledger.

While the lieutenant stood speechless, Zuk shoved the loot in the sacks held open by his temporary subordinates. He signed the ledger with a flourish. With a broad smile he saluted the lieutenant who stood open mouthed, watching Zuk and his platoon marching away.

"One, two. Left, right." The troop marched faster and faster and, once it turned the corner of the station building, broke into a wild, unmilitary run.

Another bread bonanza came a few days later. One of the Dombrowskis saw me sketching a snowy landscape with my pen and ink. He watched me for a while, then shook his head. "How can anybody draw a line like that without a ruler?" He pointed to the telephone poles and wires on my drawing. I tried to explain to him that the lines were not as straight as they seemed to be and with a bit of practice anybody could do it. But he wasn't listening. His mind was already clicking over as he stared and scratched his chin.

Our train stopped next at a small station. We were shunted away from the main tracks. Then with the clanking of chains and bumpers our engine freed itself with a shudder that rattled through its retinue of passenger and boxcars. It lurched forward and, gathering speed, shrank itself into a smoky exclamation mark on the horizon. Within minutes it whooshed past us heading the other way on a parallel track, greeting our stares with two scornful hoots. This was going to be a long stop.

The thieving brothers came back from scouting and winked at me to come outside. On the platform we three went into a huddle. They had a bread talon for two persons, a chit issued by the store clerk who verified identity cards. The talon was a cigarette-box-sized piece of stiff brown paper with a large black numeral printed on one side for the number of portions and a date stamp on the other side. With that you went to another wicket where the bread cutter would cut, weigh and hand over the bread. That was the usual procedure at many bread stores.

"Take a good look at this talon, artist," said one of them. "Could you with your pen and ink change 2 to 202 portions?"

Yes, I could. But I told them that 202 portions would never work. That was far too much. Twelve, maybe. That would be plausible.

"Penalty's the same for 12 and 202," they argued. Finally we agreed on 22. I would change the talon, but I would have nothing to do with getting the bread from the store. My share of booty would be five portions. "Agreed?"

"Agreed."

That evening I ate two kilograms of bread at one go. Only a man who has starved for two years would believe it. The remaining portion I exchanged for a piece of yellowish fat of unknown origin.

One of our fellow travellers was a former public prosecutor named Godlewski. He was a retiring, shy and frail-looking individual. At times I saw him talking quite animatedly to a colleague, a court martial judge named Wojciechowski, but with the rest of us he would just exchange polite greetings and a few words for basic questions and answers. It was not surprising that the Dombrowskis were not too well disposed to their natural adversary. They were quick to notice that the public prosecutor would volunteer to bring water, to wait in a bread line to collect our rations or to clean the car, but somehow he avoided ever "delivering" coal for our stove. The brothers made frequent loud allusions to "His Honour" who shirked his communal duties. At one of the larger stations the needling became unbearable for Godlewski. He grabbed the burlap bag, hopped down the steps onto the platform and strode toward the coal shed.

Within minutes somebody in our car spotted him on the platform, this time being marched between two militiamen. Slung over his narrow shoulder was a sack with a few lumps of coal. I ran outside along with the judge, the Pikesfeld brothers and another fellow. We saw Godlewski and his escort go into the station building. The elder Dombrowski joined us. He now had unwonted pangs of conscience and ran in front of us, barring our way with stretched arms.

"Gentlemen, allow me! I put that judiciary arsehole—who with all his education and intelligence cannot filch a couple of coal lumps —in this shit and I am going to get him out of it."

We found a small room with a glazed door which the militia used as their office. Inside we saw the two militiamen questioning our prosecutor. They checked his documents and took a few notes. Then they pointed at a chair and at the wall clock as if saying, "Sit here. We'll be back in one hour." And they went out leaving the office door half open.

We rushed in. "Quick! Quick! Take your coat off. Here, put on mine so they won't know you. Hurry up! Give me your hat and put on his cap. C'mon! Let's go!"

Public Prosecutor Godlewski looked at us but didn't move. He jerked his arm free from Pikesfeld who was trying to pull him out of the office. He dug his heels in and clutched the edge of the table he was sitting beside.

"Gentlemen! Please go and leave me alone. Can't you understand? I, a public prosecutor, was caught stealing coal. I was arrested and formally charged with theft. I am not going to break the law again by escaping. If you want to help me, please bring my bag from the car and leave me here."

We all thought that he had gone out of his mind. Judge Wojciechowski pleaded with him to leave. He mentioned something about extenuating circumstances and duty to one's country but to no avail. The Pikesfelds were also trying to persuade him to get out. "Nobody will ever forgive us if we leave you here."

In vain. He looked at us coolly, almost with contempt. He wiped his fogged-up glasses with the remnant of a handkerchief and waved us off with an authoritarian gesture as if dismissing a gang of unruly spectators from his court. He stared down Dombrowski who seemed ready to drag him out of there by force. Then the younger Dombrowski rushed in. "Come on! The train is about to leave."

So we left him there. While we were trotting along the platform back to our train, the elder Dombrowski explained it for his brother.

"You see? His brains got fucked up from fear."

Not far from me on the opposite side of the car sat a thickset man, completely bald. He was about fifty years old, always clean shaven and, as much as his well-worn clothes would allow, neat in appearance. He wore steel-rimmed glasses. Clips from a fountain pen and a pencil protruded from his breast pocket. I cannot recall his surname but it was one of those surnames in which substituting one vowel would change it from a Polish name to a Ukrainian name. But his overly correct pronunciation of the Polish nasal vowels "a" and "e," combined with a strong differentiation between the "h" and "kh" sounds, betrayed his Ukrainian origin. All these nuances of speech would be lost on most Poles from central and western Poland (including my mother), who could not hear any difference between these sounds.

He was well educated and under his bald dome there was a concise encyclopedia of important facts and dates. In the middle of somebody's story he would interrupt to set the record straight. "Permit me to make a small correction, gentlemen. It was not one of the Karageorgevic but General Potiorek who said it in 1914."

He gave the impression of being a lawyer, or more likely, a high-school teacher, for he insisted on helping me with the English alphabet in my primer. But he always saw to it that the bucket was full of water and would sweep the car floor or remove the ashes from the stove even when it was not his turn. He must have been aware of the animosity that has smouldered between Poles and Ukrainians for centuries and he was doing his best not to let it flare up in our micro-society.

Then an unexpected thing happened. One afternoon the elder Dombrowski turned to my teacher and said loudly so that everybody could hear: "Listen, Baldy! I've been watching you for a long time. You detest all of us because we are Polish. Every time we sing, 'We shall not forsake the land of our roots' you cringe and you clench your teeth and your face goes red like a beetroot. Get out of here at the next stop, *hrytiu* [a derogatory nickname for a Ukrainian peasant]. We don't want to see your snout again."

Nobody said a word, not Chief Zolotnicki, not me, not even our priest. The Ukrainian packed his small plywood suitcase and tied it up with a string. At the next stop he slipped out of our car. We heard a short whistle and the train started moving. The incident was never discussed or mentioned again.

Our car could be entered from one end only. The glazed door at the other end was locked solid and the little platform leading to it faced the blank wall of the boxcar in front of it. It was on this little platform where we saw one day at dawn the outline of people standing there. The glass door was covered with a thick layer of ice, and we could not see clearly how many or who they were. Standing with their backs to our car door and lashed by the freezing wind rushing by our speeding train, they could not hear us banging at the door and tapping the windowpane. We knew they must have got on at the last stop, which was around midnight. "Are they still alive?" we wondered. Or were these now frozen corpses with their hands welded onto the handrail?

The train stopped and we ran outside prepared to see the worst. Well, there were three of them. Not quite dead but not far from it. They were like ice statues dusted with snow which smoothed the folds of their clothes giving them the look of formalized sculptures. Icicles hung from their beards, moustaches and eyelashes. They could not speak and they had to be helped into our car. We sat them around our blazing stove. When their lips started thawing they told us that they had missed their train and got separated from a Polish group like ours heading for Buzuluk, a town near Kuibyshev (Kuibyshev has now reverted to its pre-revolutionary name of Samara). According to them, Buzuluk was the new headquarters of the Polish Army in the USSR. When they saw our train leaving the station, they hopped on the platform of our car. They kicked the locked door and banged on the ice-covered window, but we did not hear them over the rumble and din of the moving train. They stayed with us only to the next stop, which was Orsk.

At Orsk, men from our group who went to reconnoitre the station found a representative of the Polish Army. His main task was to stop any Poles from going west to Buzuluk. The recruiting centre there was being wound up, he said, and all Polish units there were being moved south. Several new recruiting places were to be opened soon in Uzbekistan and all new transports were being directed there. No specific locations were given. In fact we saw on one train a unit from the 5th Polish Infantry Division on their way to Dzhalalabad somewhere near the Chinese border. Everything was in flux.

The three frozen men decided to ignore the recommendations of the Polish Army representative and boarded the first train going west in the direction of Buzuluk. So did about half a dozen other men from our car. As we eventually found out, their choice was right. It saved them weeks, if not months, of hungry wanderings through Soviet Central Asia.

One more man died in our car as did one in the neighbouring boxcar during our stay in Orsk. The Dombrowskis, who took the corpses to the outdoor morgue, came back cursing and swearing. They had to carry them a long way, yet somebody else had emptied the pockets of the stiffs before the brothers got hold of them. "Don't ask us to do it again! You can do it yourself. We are not running a charitable funeral business," they fumed.

That day we heard about another pile of frozen corpses. Wheeler-dealer Corporal Zuk and his pals told us that, when they went to steal some coal, they saw a train passing slowly on a far track away from the station. It was a long train made up mainly of open flatcars but with a few boxcars with searchlights on their roofs. On the flatcars were German prisoners of war, standing, sitting or lying. Most of them were huddling together in small groups. Some of them wore army coats, a few of them just jackets and trousers. As the train moved off, some of the prisoners pointed at their bellies and mouths showing that they had nothing to eat. It was one of those December days which was 40°C below and windy. On every second or third car was a Soviet guard toting a machine gun. On the last flat car, there was a pile of dead Germans encased in ice. The guards poured water on the corpses so they would not roll off the car. At the end of the journey the bodies would be proof that nobody had escaped. Zuk and his friends asked a railwayman where they were taking them.

"Devil knows. To some faraway place," he said. "Far enough to make sure that all the Fritzes will be dead before they get there. Serves them right. We didn't ask them to come here."

Corporal Zuk and his friends had been hardened by their time in labour camps, but I could tell from their faces and voices that even they were appalled by the enormity of what they had seen—cold, planned murder by exposure.

Chapter 18

THE COMMISSAR FROM FARAB

I wish I could remember what happened to the Dombrowskis, but after Orsk they were no longer with us, and we had more room for ourselves in the car. Without the Dombrowskis around, there was also less tension. After Orsk our train made better progress, too. The stations and the stops were less frequent, and we noticed that the climate kept changing every day. It was becoming warmer, and by the time we reached Chelkar the snow had almost disappeared.

At one of the small stations a conductress came in, not so much to check the validity of our ticket but, I suspect, out of sheer boredom and curiosity about these foreign travellers. She was dumpy and carried a large leather conductor's bag, which dangled low and bumped her ample rump. On request she recited from memory all the stations we would pass though on our way to Tashkent. But Farab, the destination listed on our ticket, was not one of them. It was not on my simple map either, so we asked her about it. She told us that Farab was a small town beyond Tashkent on the Amu Darya River. She had passed through there, she said, but hadn't seen any army camps and anyway she would rather not talk about anything to do with military matters. The place where the railway line crossed the Amu Darya looked pretty far away on my map. We had already been travelling for more than two weeks and were not even halfway there.

I remember the stop at Aralsk on the shores of the Aral Sea because Judge Wojciechowski bought a large fresh fish from a fisherman. Nowadays he would not be able to do that. The Aral Sea has shrunk and is dying as a result of the Soviet policy of taking the waters of the Syr Darya and Amu Darya rivers and diverting them into the newly created cotton-growing areas of the Kizil Kum and Kara Kum deserts. Because of this crazy water resources management, Aralsk is no longer a port but an inland town about thirty kilometres from the shrunken shoreline. The Aral Sea is silting up, fish have died and the fish-processing plants have been kept going only by bringing fish from the Arctic. To top it all, the salt mixed with sand from the dried-up bed of the Aral sea is now being carried along by the winds and killing the new cotton fields, thus completing the full circle of the Soviet "planned economy."

We were passing through one thousand kilometres of the semiarid vastness of the Kizil Kum desert. The infrequent stations had exotic-sounding names like Dzhusaly, Kzyl-Orda and Turkestan.

The lingering uncertainty about our future became even more pronounced after we met a Polish liaison officer at Arys station. For the first time we saw a Polish soldier, an officer, who wore the battledress of the British Army, so different from the tailored formality of all other army uniforms we knew. He said that the new Polish Army recruiting centres were about to open in Soviet Central Asia and we all were to proceed south to where the already existing divisions were being relocated from Russia. But he was unable to give us any specific dates or places. This did not sound too encouraging, but we remained optimistic that something would turn up sooner or later.

For me, going south was bringing another glimmer of hope. The idea of escaping from the Soviet Union to Afghanistan, which I had conceived when I was still in the Kiev prison, had never left my mind and every day we were getting closer to the Afghanistan border.

We all had great hopes for Tashkent which, though officially just the capital of Uzbekistan, was also recognized as the leading centre for the whole of Soviet Central Asia. History repeats itself, they say, and I often thought about the similarities between our journey, and the description of the mass migration by train of starving Russians in 1919. Fleeing from the famine that followed the Communist revolution, they surged southwards to Tashkent because of its reputation as the breadbasket "city of plenty."

Tashkent, however, was a disappointment. Our train stopped under the huge bilingual sign "Tashkent-Toshkent." The first name was Russian, the second Uzbek. But as soon as we began to scatter all over the station in search of food, we heard the shouts of the rail-waymen urging us to get back on board fast as the train was about to leave. So much for the bread bonanza at Tashkent.

If Tashkent was a disappointment then the next stop, Kizyl Tepe (Red Hill), was a bigger one and the one after that a calamity—at least for me. Kizyl Tepe was a tiny station where the train stopped for several hours. A hundred or so metres from the station building was an open-air market—a few stalls with rickety tables bearing small bowls of *katik* (thick yoghurt), flat pancakes of millet flour, huge sweet onions, small black raisins and dried apricots. But the prices were steep, and practically nobody from our train could afford to buy these delicacies. The native farmers selling their produce regarded our motley crowd of beggars with suspicion. One of the starved travellers from our train, who stole a boiled beetroot from a stall, barely saved his life by running faster than the half-dozen Uzbeks who pursued him with their curved knives drawn. There is no doubt in my mind that they would have killed him if he had not managed to lose himself in the innards of our train. The angry Uzbeks kept walking around the train for a long time waiting for him to emerge. It now seems unreal that anybody would kill a man for stealing a boiled beetroot, but at that time we thought the Uzbeks' reaction normal and even justified.

There was no bread store at this station and so most of us did not eat that day.

Somehow I didn't notice when our train rolled by Samarkand—perhaps at night. The next station, Kermine (later renamed Navoi) was seven kilometres from the town itself, but there were a few buildings near the station and a small open-air market. The market was very busy that day because a second train full of Russians arrived shortly after we did. Hungry travellers were milling around looking for affordable food. There were always some who had plenty of money, so the locals were unwilling to bargain with those of us who had little to spend. I only had five rubles left and so was checking the prices at every stall. Then I spotted a group of petty thieves, *zhu-liki*, who were prowling the market. Two of them tried to sell me a leather belt, which they had probably stolen minutes before. I felt flattered at being taken for a prospective customer. They even put the belt around my waist. "Just see how it fits you. Beautiful! Buy it. It's cheap, a real bargain." When I said that I had no money, they seemed to believe me and left me alone.

An old Uzbek woman was selling flat, pancake-like bread made of some kind of coarse flour. It was still warm and smelled delicious. I asked how much and she answered in Uzbek, "Two rubles, one." I asked her if she would sell three for five rubles, but either she did not want to or did not understand Russian because she turned away from me. I was not going to give up and decided to show her my five-ruble bill and three fingers. Surely she would get that.

I reached in my breast pocket for money. The five-ruble banknote was not there. The photo of my sister Henia was gone too, and so was my Certificate of Release. I was without money and without documents.

It was clear to me that the two *zhuliki* stole them when they were putting the belt around me. I soon found them. They listened to me, then said with mocking sympathy, "It's terrible what this war is doing to people. Thievery everywhere." Leaning toward me, one of them added in a confidential tone, "Now scram, you stupid arsehole, before we knock your block off!" They felt safe as they had probably already passed my paltry treasures along to another of their gang members.

I found a militiaman. He was not a bit interested in my predicament.

"What do you want me to do?" he grumbled. "I can't write you another certificate. That's not my job. Don't bother me. Go away!" When I insisted that he do something, he got annoyed.

"Fuck one out for yourself, and if anybody asks you where you got it say you found it." I pleaded with him to write at least a chit saying that I had reported the theft of my release document. He would not even listen to my pleas and waved me away.

My situation was serious. More than that, hopeless. Without my Certificate of Release I could not get coupons for bread, and as it was my only document of identity, I could be arrested at any time by the militia or NKVD and thrown in prison on any pretext. To verify my claim that I had been released from the labour camp, I would have to plead with them to get in touch with NKVD authorities in Kirov, which I had left illegally.

I have a hazy recollection of what happened during the three or four days that followed. Some of the men in our car showed themselves to be real friends in need. We had to use all our ingenuity and try every trick to get the bread ration for me. We pleaded with the officials, cajoled and cheated them. I was forging the bread coupons with mixed results. Sergeant Zolotnicki, our Chief, once got the bread for me on the strength of his commanding stature and imperious voice. "You have to issue another ration for this soldier of mine whose name was inadvertently omitted from the platoon's list." But the most successful was Corporal Zuk, who could bamboozle any clerk with his fast talk and pushy manner. "What's the matter with you, man? It says twenty-eight rations and you give me twenty-seven," Zuk would yell, pushing into the face of an astonished clerk an invoice with twenty-seven clearly written on it. "What kind of an idiot gave you this job of store clerk if you can't count up to twenty-eight?! Go back to your kolkhoz where you belong and start your apprenticeship by counting the cow patties around the barn! Look at him, people! How can we win this war when an imbecile like him works in the bread store? Don't handle the bread with your filthy hands, you uncultured oaf! You never heard of hygiene?" It worked almost every time.

When we reached Farab, the point of destination shown on our ticket, the local NKVD official told us to board the large barges tied up behind the station on the nearby Amu Darya River. They were to take us about a thousand kilometres to the autonomous Kara-Kalpak Republic on the southern shores of the Aral Sea. Once there we would work in kolkhozes and "await further instructions." Those who had previous experience of travelling by barges on Siberian rivers warned the rest of us that that kind of travel was worse than hell. Usually the food ran out after a few days and the barges didn't come even close to the shores until the end of the trip. Besides, we were heading to join the army and not to pick cotton or hoe the baked soil. In our car there was a unanimous "No!" to his demand. We decided to stay put.

The local commissar, a swarthy and shifty-looking man, a Turkman or Uzbek, had already had more than enough of refugees, tramps and deserters in his small town and was trying to spread those blessings over other preferably distant areas. He was very persuasive, and if he lacked the right Russian word to describe something, his consummate mime artistry filled the gap. He kept his audience spellbound. "Go and see for yourself the wonders of Turtkul and Nukus in the very fertile and rich delta," he said, "and fill your stomachs with ripe melons and golden apricots. The people are kind there and generous. Menfolk departed from there a long time ago to fight on distant fronts for our fatherland and for our beloved leader Stalin. Women are lonely there." When he said that, he closed one eye. "They will greet you with bowls of millet and yoghurt, fish from the Aral Sea." The starving listeners' Adam's apples were moving up and down as they swallowed saliva and his story. Some of our fellow passengers, weary of trains after nearly a month in a railway car, were willing to give it a try. But most men from our group decided not to go.

We remained adamant about staying on the train and told the miming commissar that we wanted to see a representative of the Polish Army or some high-ranking NKVD official. The local commissar was annoyed at us for not swallowing his spiel and for our strange request. "Now, where do I get a Polish officer for you? From a store? You cannot find even salt or matches there. Be reasonable!"

We didn't want to be reasonable and we would not leave our car until our request was met. The commissar was angry and puzzled at the same time. Refusing a demand from a NKVD officer? He had not seen that before. People from the other cars of our train were already getting on the barges. What was so special about this batch of ragged ex-cons?

He surveyed the situation. There was nobody around to prop up his authority, and we looked a determined and nasty lot.

"Well, if you don't, then to hell with you. For all I care you can stay in this car until you rot. All I know is that tonight this car's going back where it came from. With you or without you." And off he went.

Several men from our car chickened out at the last moment and joined the "civilians" on the barges. The rest of us stayed on. The next two days and two nights we spent retracing our route back towards Tashkent, but we did not get that far. During the second night we were awakened by the sounds of our train being shunted and our car being coupled and uncoupled.

When I woke up it was still dark. I went out, and in the black sky I saw a garland of multicoloured light suspended high above the horizon. It was a formidable and awe-inspiring sight. It took me some time to realize that the garland of light was made up of the snowy peaks of high mountains lit by the rays of the rising sun, which was still hidden from us in the valley. The colours of the snowy crown kept changing from amaranth to orange, to yellow and then to a dazzling white. The belt of light was getting wider, descending to the lower regions and changing its luminosity into the pastel shades of the exposed rocks. But the bottom of the bowl was still filled with darkness.

"Hi! Pretty, isn't it?"

I turned around, and at the top of our car's steps I saw the silhouette of the younger Pikesfeld. He had gotten up well before me and had already been at the lilliputian station where we stopped. It was the end of the line, he told me, and the place was called Vanovskiy. "We are in the Fergana Valley," he said with a detectable tinge of pride in knowing. "This is Tien Shan." And he swept half of the horizon with his hand. "And that"—completing the circle with a theatrical gesture—"is Pamir, The Roof of the World."

Our stop in minuscule Vanovskiy was not as accidental as it first seemed. One of those ubiquitous political commissars appeared in the morning, smiles and benevolence spread like bitter marmalade over his flat face. He must have heard about our confrontation with the officials at Farab because, when he rounded up our recalcitrant group, he began to speak in a most endearing and convincing way about the necessity of sending us to work in a kolkhoz. It was to be only a temporary arrangement, just time to recuperate and "fatten yourselves up" before facing a medical examination at the recruiting centre.

"And when would that be?" asked some doubting Thomas.

"Any day or even earlier," was the pat answer, which we had heard thousands of times before. "Let's go, citizens, right now," he pleaded. "The transport is waiting for you."

"I don't fancy this artillery," said Zuk, pointing at the line of two-wheeled carts pulled by grotesquely small donkeys that stood behind the station. Everybody laughed, including the commissar. Still, he wouldn't give up.

"Think it over, citizens They will wait for you till the evening."

Still adamant, we returned to our car but we were at a loss as to what to do. We knew that we had to find some food, but in Vanovskiy there was neither an *evakopunkt* nor military provision office where we could try to get our bread ration. The cart drivers talked about an open market a few kilometres from the village. Maybe it was a ruse just to get us out of the station, but our rumbling stomachs told us to go and investigate.

While we sat in our car planning the sortie, we enjoyed the balmy breeze coming in through the open doors and windows. White lambkin clouds grazed in the deep blue sky. A flock of chattering starlings settled on a nearby almond tree and coffee-coloured water rustled in the ditches along the railway tracks. How strange, I thought. March weather in December.

The younger Pikesfeld stood on the platform and gazed at the truly magnificent view of the mountains. He was whistling Ravel's *Bolero*, which had become his favourite tune for the last few days. To this day when I hear it being played it does not evoke in me the images of an Andalusian courtyard filled with the clacking of castanets and the swish of flounced skirts. Instead it brings back the picture of curved adobe walls, mulberry and almond trees lining irrigation canals, and mustachioed natives sitting astride their tiny donkeys.

The mantra of *Bolero* was interrupted by the voice of our priest, Father Krol. "Brethren! Occupied as we may be with our endeavours to obtain our daily bread, let us not forget that today is *Wigilia* [Christmas Eve] and that it would be fitting for us to spend the evening together thanking God that we are still alive and still harbour our hopes. Let us celebrate by exchanging wishes for a better future and singing a few carols for the sake of His glory and our Polish tradition."

Well, that spurred us on. Our entire group spent the day combing the vicinity for food. By the evening we had some local nan (flat bread), sheep milk yoghurt and local ersatz halva which was made of pressed millet soaked with beet syrup—and which tasted terrible. There was very little of anything: a small pancake of flat bread and a couple of spoonfuls of yoghurt per person but a lot of the almost inedible halva. Corporal Zuk as usual rose to the occasion and distinguished himself by bringing a large jug of illicit arak (local alcohol) and a couple of bottles of the sickly sweet Sovetskoe Shampanskoe (Soviet champagne). With no coal around we resorted to burning planks from the Dombrowskis' love nest in order to boil water for our *kipyatok* and to stave off the night's chill.

Frequent swigs of the booze soon changed the solemnity of our vigil supper into merry revelry. The gooey halva, washed down with a combination of arak and champagne, proved to be more than most of the imbibers could handle. Only the Reverend tried to preserve the decorum of our vigil. His lips barely touched the edges of the mugs of hooch proffered to him by his drunken flock. His unctuous remarks annoyed even his faithful acolyte Franek, who tried to force him to drink by pushing the neck of the champagne bottle into his mouth saying, "Take a good gulp of it, Father. You can't refuse this toast. The health of Virgin Mary! Down the hatch!"

The morning after is never pleasant. Ours was even less so, for it was that Christmas Day when our group began to disintegrate. Sergeant Zolotnicki was told by the railway officials that our car would be taken to Kokand, which was the nearest junction. Once there, everybody would have to get out of it voluntarily or be evicted by militia. It would be up to us to decide our next step. The option of working in kolkhozes was still open to us.

Almost everybody in our group (which by that time was reduced to about twenty men out of the original forty plus) had a different idea about what to do next. Some decided to accept work at the kolkhozes, some to go back to Farab (the ticket was probably still valid), board the barges and try their luck in the Kara-Kalpaki area of the Amu Darya delta. Others wanted to go back north in the belief that the HQ of the Polish Army would still be there. The brothers Pikesfeld opted for Tashkent. Some men said nothing. I would be looking for the elusive Polish Army, but I planned to go south, trying to get as close as possible to the Afghanistan border. The border town of Termez and Afghanistan's capital Kabul, where the British Consulate was supposed to be, had never left my mind. However, my immediate goal was the fabled and romantic "Golden Samarkand." This ancient city on the silk route to China was the city of Alexander the Great, of Genghis Khan and Tamerlane. I, too, wanted to see its splendours.

It may seem strange, but when we reached Kokand and spilled out from our car onto a crowded station platform, there were no sentimental farewells, no talk about meeting again or even keeping in touch. How could you keep in touch? Who knew where they would wind up? You just shook hands with a guy you shared your life with in a crowded railway car for nearly a month, all the while looking over his shoulder to see whether a train was coming in.

A train came. It was packed. We stormed the doors, pushing and kicking those inside who were barring the entrance. The people behind us were trying to get on by pulling us back down the car steps. We had to claw our way in, cursing and swearing. The loud obscenities and blasphemies we had learned in the labour camps and prisons stunned most of the travellers standing in the gangways and corridors. Hearing such profanities, they would recoil in disgust and fear, making it easier for us to wedge forward. A railwayman closed the door from the outside, squeezing us even more. As I stood at the open window in the door, I saw the two Pikesfelds still standing on the platform. They were holding their big leather suitcases and some smaller pieces of luggage. They looked desperate, their eyes darting from one end of the train to the other as if looking for a miraculous opening. I heard the younger yelling at his brother, "With these damned suitcases we'll never get on any train!"

The train started moving. It would have been cruel to wave to them. They looked hopelessly lost. Ready to burst into tears. That's how I saw them for the last time.

In my car, I saw Father Krol and his inseparable helper Franek. I inched my way along the crowded corridor towards them. When I reached them, the friendly and usually talkative Franek became rather tongue-tied and Father Krol seemed to be engrossed in silent prayers. I found it puzzling. Something, somewhere, had gone amiss. No other men from our group were to be seen, at least in that section of the car, so I stayed with them, and we continued for at least a couple of hours until we stopped at Ursatiyevskaya, a junction station where the Fergana Valley spur and the main Tashkent-Krasnovodsk lines meet. Through the window we saw some of our gang leaving the train. These were the ones wanting to go north to Buzuluk or Tashkent. Franek and Father Krol stayed put. I turned to the priest.

"I guess we are all going together to Samarkand." There was a moment of silence before the priest replied. "Well, not exactly. We are going to Dzhizak." Then he rather reluctantly added that during a stop at one of the stations he had met up with some Polish deportees who asked him to go with them to Dzhizak because not far from there in a prosperous kolkhoz was a sizeable Polish community in need of a spiritual leader. They would welcome him there with open arms. He and Franek, the priest explained, "took it upon ourselves to respond to the spiritual hunger of the shepherdless flock, much as I, myself, and Franek would prefer to continue our quest for the Polish Army." This was news, and I said that I too wouldn't mind spending some time in a "prosperous kolkhoz." But this was the last thing they wanted to hear. In a syrupy voice, Father Krol started talking about the "inadvisability of imposing on a community a burden probably heavier than they could sustain." He kept mumbling generalities in a similar vein, occasionally asking, "Am I not right, Franek?" to which Franek would answer back, "Uhm, hmm."

My pride would not let me pursue the subject. At Dzhizak, Father Krol and his sidekick got off the train. We parted with a tepid handshake. Through the open window, I watched them crossing the tracks, and when they were about to disappear into the main door of the station the priest turned around, saw me in the carriage window, and semaphored a benediction in my direction.

Nearly all the passengers got out too, which I thought rather strange. We were then shunted to another track. Some new people came in, but there was still plenty of room. I settled into a window seat on a bench in one of the compartments. Once again I was alone, hungry, without a slice of bread or a ruble in my pocket and no ticket or documents. The train started moving. I curled up in my corner, pulled my fur hat over my eyes and fell asleep.

Chapter 19

THE ROSE TATTOO

Shouts and noises in the next train compartment woke me up. The door to the corridor slowly opened and in came two individuals. They were young men of the most crude and mean countenance. They looked around with their eyelids half-closed and a sneer on their fox-like faces. They wore rumpled trousers that were too long and too wide (the height of elegance and conspicuous consumption in the Soviet Union at that time) and once-white turtleneck sweaters.

Without the slightest hesitation one of them took down a suitcase from the baggage rack, opened it and began checking its contents. An elderly Russian, the owner of the suitcase, yelled at him, "Leave that alone, young man. It's not yours!" The man rummaging through the bag took no notice of that outburst, but his friend, with the palm of his hand, pushed up the nose of the owner and at the same time with the other hand slammed the top of his head. "You talk too much, my dear friend!" Blood started trickling from the old man's nostril.

There were six or seven people in the compartment, but we all remained quiet, as if not seeing what was going on. Only a middle-aged woman said loudly in a voice full of indignation, "What scandalous behaviour!" The amused rummager looked at her.

"And you, grannie, when you are not being fucked don't wiggle your tootsies."

By then both thugs were going through the pockets, bags and suitcases of the other travellers and another bandit came in from the corridor. He held an open jackknife in his hand and he looked even meaner than the first two. They pocketed the money they found but did not touch the documents. They also took some trinkets and pieces of clothing but only brightly coloured ones. My turn came.

"Let's see what's in your little *chemodanchik*." I opened it, and when they saw my mapping pen and the bottle of India ink they looked puzzled. "Who are you anyway?"

"I am an artist, and I just came out of the labour camps." I rolled up the leg of my soiled padded trousers to show them the oozing scurvy ulcers on my calves and ankles. They looked at them, nodded their heads, and were just about to leave when the one with the knife turned to me.

"You're an ex-con. Can you make tattoos?"

"Of course I can."

"Then come along with us. We need an artist."

There were more of them—three more men and two women. They had a whole compartment for themselves. But they also sat and slept wherever they felt like it. They made the rules and were the masters of the entire train. Conductors pretended not to see them and were deaf to the furtive complaints of the terrorized passengers.

They ate well by robbing the travellers. Most of the day they spent playing cards, gambling among themselves for the spoils of their forays on the train and through the station platforms and stores at each stop. At every opportunity they would also try selling their swag—sometimes back to its rightful owners. But they were leery of the militiamen and NKVD officials, and they would make themselves scarce whenever they saw one at a station. If pickings were slim or the situation became too hot, they would just leave the train and hop on another one.

The two women in their early twenties who were with them were also thieves, or rather pickpockets. They were quite plain but not ugly, and they were lazy. They would spend all day talking to each other and combing their hair. They would eat whatever the *zhuliki* brought them but never complained, even when food was in short supply.

At night they would turn into languid houris, keeping the boys happy by apportioning their charms equally to all of them. They undertook their task cheerfully, occasionally cracking jokes that only they could understand. The older girl—at least she looked a bit older—was very good at nipping any jealousies in the bud and keeping peace in the gang. "Don't start any trouble, Kosoi (Squinty). None of this stupid rivalry. There's enough for all of you and a bit to spare. Besides, in half an hour you'll all be fast asleep!"

At the beginning, the tall, jackknife *zhulik* who had told me to join them was the only one who would speak to me and give me some bread and other scraps of food left over from their irregular feasts. Still, it was more and better than what I used to get on my own. The rest of the gang treated me like a non-person, a kind of being you can see through, even though I was spending most of my time in their compartment.

My first tattoo project was for my tall captor—changing the anemic butterfly on his forearm into a rose. He was tattooed all over and there was little space left on his body for a new design. Only then did their attitude towards me change.

"Look at that! A rose he said he was going to draw. And it starts to look like a rose!"

It was gratifying to have such an appreciative audience.

Usually, I first drew the design on a piece of cloth from an old shirt with an aniline pencil, or "chemical" pencil, as the Russians called it. Its mark could not be erased with a rubber eraser. The lines drawn with it would turn deep purple when moistened. This moistened cloth template I would then spread and press on the tattoo site. Afterwards, I carefully peeled it off, leaving the purple image on the skin. Now it was ready for needling and inking. This was done with two needles held parallel, close to one another but not touching. The narrow gap between the two contained a drop or two of ink, just like the double nib of a drafting pen. The sharp end of the needle on top projected a bit more than the end of the lower needle. With the top needle held at a shallow angle I would prick the skin and then, using the bottom needle as a fulcrum, rip the flesh, creating a small wound into which the ink would flow. To rip and fill a straight line took an unflinching client and an artist with a steady hand. Usually my clients were stoical and unwavering—anything for the sake of these symbols of bravery, status, affiliation and fashion.

After needling, the tattoo area was rubbed vigorously with a wad of cloth dipped in ink to make sure that the blackness penetrated every perforation in the skin. Within a day the tattooed area (and sometimes the whole arm) would swell, probably as a result of infection. But the swelling was considered a good omen. "The design takes in," as we used to say. The most painful part of the operation was still to come. This was on the third day when the broken lines and other imperfections revealed by a thorough washing of the tender tattoo site would have to be corrected by needling and inking once again.

In prison we prepared the tint for tattooing with the soot from a burning candle mixed with sugar and water. On the train I decided to use my India ink.

My client, the jackknife *zhulik*, displayed a lot of patience and bravery. He was being encouraged by the spectators, who grimaced and closed their eyes tight every time I plunged the needle a bit deeper and drew a few drops of blood. It was as if they were the sufferers.

"Don't worry, my little brother. It's nearly over. And what a beautiful rose you'll have on your forearm! You can almost smell the scent of it. May I turn into an old whore if I am lying! A real artist this scurvy-ridden Pole is. My turn next!"

The two girls also liked it. "Ya can't deny nothin'. A rose it is." But they were not too enthusiastic about having additional tattoos on their bodies in spite of urgings by the men in the carriage, who proposed some inventive if not startling designs for diverse parts of their anatomies. Being professional female thieves, they already had the traditional fish tattooed on their left breast.

Quite frankly, I did not think much of my efforts. To make a good rose out of an insipid butterfly would have been a challenge to a top craftsman, let alone a mere part-time skin pricker like me. My rose-cum-butterfly looked more like an octopus suffering from stomach cramps than the queen of flowers. But who was I to criticize the taste of my audience?

From that time on, our compartment became a tattoo atelier and pictures of hearts aflame, anchors and crosses were covering more and more square inches of the gang's swollen and painful skin.

When I asked my Maecenas, the jackknife *zhulik*, where we were going, he shrugged his shoulder, "Who the shit cares? Does it matter to you? Where the train goes, we go. The train stops, we stop." I had a strong feeling that we were heading not for Samarkand but going back to where I'd come from.

By morning we were indeed back in Ursatiyevskaya, the junction station where the last of my Polish recruit comrades had gotten off. The train, or rather a dozen or so of the carriages without the engine (I was slowly getting used to the locomotives' disappearing tricks), stopped at the station's sidings for two days. These two days in Ursat-iyevskaya I spent inside our compartment tattooing and tattooing. The gang was in a foul mood. Their business on the station and dining hall was a failure. They were overconfident and their blatant thieving angered people there so much that they called the militia and raised a hue and cry against my patrons. Not wanting to betray the location of their lair, the gang scattered and did not return to the car until dark. There was nothing to eat, and they started squabbling and fighting amongst themselves. The prospects of a successful robbery seemed rather remote. I realized that any liaison with them was dangerous, and I decided to leave the gang at the earliest opportunity.

I left the gang much earlier than I expected and in totally unforeseen circumstances. Our train left Ursatiyevskaya during the night when we were fast asleep. At the break of day, somebody shook my shoulder. It was one of the robbers. He leaned over me, touched his lips with index finger and whispered "*Suki.*" Bitches—a contemptuous name for militiamen. Everybody in our compartment was wide awake, silent and scared. On one side in the grey light of pre-dawn we could see a militiaman standing on the platform opposite the exit steps from the car. He held his rifle at the ready. Another one stood on the other side of our car. One of the gang scuttled quickly on all fours along the entire corridor to check the other end of the car. He soon came back with the bad news. We were surrounded by the militia, and they were after us. There was nothing we could do but wait. Even if we had found a window that would open, it was too risky trying to escape. We knew they would shoot on sight without any warning. So we sat and waited for them to make the first move. It was getting lighter, and I noticed another group of militiamen standing on the track alongside. Behind them on a brightly lit signboard I could see the name of the station. I was back in Kokand, the place where we remaining recruits had finally been forced to abandon our own railway car, and where I'd last seen the Pikesfeld brothers and their suitcases.

The militia moved in swiftly. They started at the far end of the car checking the tickets and the documents of passengers and herding in front of them all those who did not pass muster. By the time they reached our end, they had already netted over twenty suspects. This time there were none of the threats and shouts we expected from militiamen. They were cool and efficient. We were herded off the train with the others arrested. As we stepped onto the platform, they lined us up in threes flanked by militiamen armed with rifles with fixed bayonets. My heart twitched when I heard the convoy *komandir* reciting the formula so well known to me: "One step to the right, one step to the left is considered an attempt to escape. The convoy will use arms without any warning. March!"

We started going. Thoughts like flashes of lightning zigzagged through my head. "No! No! It cannot be. I cannot go back to prison. Not to a dank cell with a judas in the door and stinking slop buckets. God help me!" But my mind was working so hard on trying to find a way out of my desperate situation that I could not concentrate on praying.

As our convoy was passing out of the station through the main entrance, I saw a large square in front of it crowded with Uzbek recruits. There were hundreds of them, all dressed in their colourful *khalaty* (a kind of coat that looks like a knee-length dressing gown) and black and silver embroidered skullcaps. Each carried a small kettle in one hand and steadied a rolled quilt on his shoulder with the other. The recruits were trying to enter the station building at the same time as we were leaving it. They were squeezing our column from both sides. The guards swore but could not do much as the Uzbeks who pressed against us were being pushed by the mass of recruits behind them.

I saw my chance. In a split of a second I dived under the rifle of the guard at my side and lunged head on at the human wall in front of me. The crowd was so tight that the guard could not turn his rifle with its long bayonet in my direction. Those recruits who had seen what happened made an effort to let me through. Nobody tried to stop me. After a while the crowd grew thinner and the going was easier. Finally there was an open space, and I broke into a run that felt as if it shattered the world record. I could still hear the alarm whistles of the guards. I ran through some market stalls, then I turned into one street, then another, jumped over a couple of fences, and for the first time I looked back. Nobody was chasing me. Through the back gardens and the orchards, I made a huge circle and returned to the station. There were no militiamen in sight. I ran through the door leading onto the platform, pushed aside a ticket collector and hopped on the car steps of a train which was just leaving the station.

I had to ride standing on the car steps for a long time. Maybe one hour, maybe more. The corridor of the car was packed with people, and it was only at the next stop, when new passengers storming the car compressed those standing inside even tighter, that they squeezed me in.

Once again I found myself in the junction station of Ursatiyevskaya. The train I was on was going north, so I got off and spent the rest of the day dodging militia and roaming the crowded station in search of food. Late in the evening a long train consisting only of passenger cars arrived at the station. It looked like one of the official evacuation trains for important people. Militia and the railway staff barred any would-be passengers from boarding it. But I saw that it was going in the right direction—to Samarkand—and I was determined to get on it at any cost. The guards kept the crowd away from the train. One of the doors was held half-open by a woman conductor. She was standing with her back to me with one leg on the ground and the other on the car step ready to heave herself up. She held on to the handrail and kept casting glances left and right checking if all the doors were closed. Then, as she looked in the direction of the locomotive, she blew her whistle and waved a stick with a small white circle on its end. The locomotive responded with a toot and a mighty snort. With a couple of long leaps I covered the no man's land between the crowd held back by the guards and the train. Using the gap between her back and the door frame, I jumped inside the car. She saw me jumping in but could not stop me. With both of her hands busy and the whistle in her mouth she could not even shout as the train started drawing away from the station. By the time she lifted herself in and closed the door, I was already in the next carriage.

The passengers in this car looked like a well-to-do crowd. They were probably the entire staff of some important establishment being evacuated to a safe location. All eyes turned on me, this ragged beggar/intruder whose entrance was less than welcome. The expressions on the faces of passengers ranged from curiosity to open hostility.

I pleaded with them to let me stay. "Please let me hide under the benches. I have no ticket and no documents and the officials will be here any minute searching for me. I am Polish, going south to join the Polish Army. Please save me."

Long silence was the answer. Then a bearded man said, "Don't be taken in by this sob story. I don't believe one word of what he says. You let him crawl under the bench, and at night he will slice open your bags with a razor blade and rifle your luggage. Call the guards or throw him out right now."

A few men grunted to support him. Only one woman said, "Maybe he is telling the truth?" The whole carriage went silent again. As I stood without uttering one word but pleading for com-passion with my eyes, an elderly man sitting on the bench closest to me shifted his knees to one side, looked under his seat, then at my face and grumbled, "Crawl in."

Minutes later I heard the agitated voice of the conductor asking if anybody had seen a wretched creature who sneaked on the train at the last stop. Nobody said yes, and nobody said no. She trotted through the aisle to the next carriage and slammed the door behind her.

They say that dogs enjoy the smell of food just as much as eat-ing it. I did not. Dozing under the bench I heard the sound of food being unwrapped from its paper. Then the heavenly scent of stale sour bread and garlic sausage, accented by the crackling skins of onions being peeled, whetted my pangs of hunger. Only heavy sleep quieted my stomach.

The old man who had offered me shelter woke me up in the morning. Peering under the seat and kicking my shoulder gently with his galoshed heel he asked, "Where are you going, youngster? This is Samarkand."

"Thank you,"' I said, loud enough to be heard by the others as I slipped out of the car onto the platform lit by the lukewarm rays of the rising sun.

Chapter 20
GOLDEN SAMARKAND

"For lust of knowing what should not be known,
We take the Golden Road to Samarkand."
                        – James Elroy Fletcher (1884-1915)

The white and green Samarkand railway station was almost deserted at this early hour. A most unusual sight it was, after all those stations packed with hordes of people. Here, just a few people left or got on the train, and half a dozen railway officials and militiamen milled about the platform. The lack of crowds made me conspicuous, which was bad for somebody scruffy like me without ticket and documents. So instead of going to the exit, I walked quickly in the direction of the nearest shed, and turning the corner, I promptly squatted with my trousers pulled down as if struck by a sudden bout of diarrhea—a common sight in those days. I reckoned that if any of the guards saw me in that undignified pose, he would perhaps call me an uncultured animal and tell me to beat it but would not attempt to come closer to check my papers. Nobody did. The train gone, all the officials went inside the station building, and I walked away unhindered from the platform through the side gate.

In the centre of a square at the back of the station stood a solitary, round kiosk, the kind where they sell cigarettes and newspapers. There was a lineup of about fifteen men in front of it. A wide avenue lined with dust-covered hedges led from the station to some grey, three-story buildings surrounded by bare trees. But nothing in the least resembled the image of the exotic Samarkand I had expected.

As I stood there pondering my next step, I heard a clear and loud, "My respects to you!" in Polish. Rather startled, I turned around and saw a man of an indeterminate age dressed in a shabby suit, scuffed canvas tennis shoes and a cloth cap who, without waiting for my reply, continued to address me.

"The honourable gentleman looks like he wouldn't know which way to turn. Straight from the Moscow express I venture to guess? Welcome to Samarkand, land of opportunity for those who have brains and use them."

I was taken aback not so much by his correct guessing of my nationality (for some reason we Poles could spot our kin in a crowd of people dressed alike) as by the unmistakable accent of a Warsaw con man giving his spiel.

"It's a long way from here to town and you, sir, may have some difficulty pedalling there in those two gondolas," he said pointing at my oversized shoes. "I am sure you must have put them on by mistake. I suggest that you exchange these exquisite shoes of yours crafted by Hiszpanski [a renowned high-class shoemaker in Warsaw] for my lightweight Pepegi [popular Polish pre-war gym shoes made by the PPG factory] which are a tiny wee bit tight for me and hurt my delicate, tiny toes. You will be a clear winner in this exchange, and we'll celebrate the deal with a snort of peppermint vodka. On me."

The deal went through, and we were both pleased with the exchange. I enjoyed the lightness of the gym shoes on my ulcerated feet. He looked a bit doubtful after he put on my Kirov Univermag shoes with the toes pointing up like Charlie Chaplin's, but he steered me in the direction of the round kiosk that, it now appeared, was selling not newspapers but *pertsovka* (peppermint vodka). We joined the queue and in no time we faced a cheerful babushka at the wicket who was both the barmaid and the cashier. The transactions went fast. The peppermint vodka was all she sold. A tin noggin was chained to the shelf of the wicket. For a ruble she would fill the noggin with vodka from a large bottle. The customer would gulp it at one go and hand over the empty noggin to the guy behind him. The sweet peppermint vodka was just the thing for that chilly morning. It warmed my innards and cheered me up.

My new acquaintance never introduced himself, and we continued to address each other as "sir." He said that he had a profitable venture in Samarkand and was looking for a partner. But he was evasive about the nature of his business.

"Just come along with me and you'll see. I am sure you're going to like it."

"Okay," I said, and off we went to Samarkand.

My new companion was witty and an inexhaustible source of filthy jokes, which kept me amused as we marched along the dusty road.

I learned that there was a new Samarkand built by the Russians not far from the railway station. The old town, the true historic Samarkand, was a few kilometres further down the road. The new and the old Samarkand were separated by a wide valley with a few meandering rivulets. As we approached a stone bridge spanning the first of these, the man from Warsaw looked at me knowingly.

"We begin here," he said with a grin on his face. "I'll be standing on the bridge waiting for the first customer and you hide yourself behind that fence." He pointed at a crumbling stone wall overgrown with bushes. "You do nothing. Just observe what I do and come out only when I call you. With a bit of training you may still become a railway porter." He winked at me, and I knew that he was up to no good.

I did what he told me to. He sat down on the parapet of the bridge, scanning the valley and the road and from time to time casting a glance over his shoulder at the place where I was hiding, as if to make sure that I was still there.

A man coming from old Samarkand was approaching the bridge. When he came closer I could see that he was old, maybe sixty or more, and was carrying two suitcases. He was halfway across the bridge when my shady acquaintance blocked his way by planting himself in front of him. The white-haired oldie tried to bypass him but every time he made a step to the right or left his challenger would stop him with a puffed-up chest.

The old man looked perplexed standing there, holding his suitcases and saying something that I could not hear. Then my mentor grabbed the handles of the suitcases and tried to jerk them out of the oldie's hands. When that didn't work, he tried it again using more force, but the old man just stared him down and hung on. It seemed that only then did the old man realize what was happening. He put both suitcases down, grabbed his attacker around the waist and lifted him up. My boss's feet were pedalling in the air. The angry old man threw him on the dusty deck of the bridge, then lifted him up and threw him down once again. He was literally wiping the dirt with him. The man from Warsaw was yelling "Help! Help!" in my direction but to no avail. I was already running away as fast as I could from the wrath of the enraged oldie and the likely vengeance of my betrayed "business partner."

I went back to the new Samarkand where I was hoping to find any kind of work. I still had a few rubles left but not enough to buy even a small chunk of bread on the black market. I tried every possible place: communal living quarters where I offered to work as a cleaner for just one meal a day, workshops and stores, offices and factories, only to be told in every place, "Get out of here—fast!" Samarkand was overrun with refugees and the chance of getting any job was nil. Passing the entrance to a large hospital, I suddenly remembered that my sister Maria, who was studying medicine in Cracow before the war, used to say how difficult it was to find people who would wash and shave corpses in the hospital's morgue. In a trice I barged into the administration office and told the astonished office workers that I had considerable experience in washing and shaving corpses, and I would like to work in the hospital's morgue. A woman sitting at a nearby desk was terrified by my unkempt look and even more so by my announcement. With her mouth wide open she was poised on the edge of her chair ready to bolt from the room. Then a man, also shaken by my intrusion, spoke up in a feeble voice.

"I regret but we don't shave corpses in this establishment."

So that was that. Glancing back as I went out, I saw the man looking around at his co-workers. With one hand he pointed at the door I was closing and with the index finger of the other hand he drew a circle on his forehead.

The old town was not any better. The long street leading to the cluster of disused *madrassahs* (Muslim religious seminaries) was flanked by dilapidated adobe buildings with small shops run by co-operatives of craftsmen and merchants. The shops were little more than narrow, dim niches and they held little for sale—some clay and iron pots, parts of harnesses and glazed tiles. Some of these niches had beautifully carved old wooden doors frayed at the bottom by age and wear. When I asked for work the men working in them would dismiss my pleas with a shrug of shoulders or ignore me altogether. Most of them could not or would not speak Russian.

The square that formed the centre of old Samarkand was called Registan (as I found out years later). All the historic buildings around it were in a state of total neglect, even Tamerlane's famous fourteenth-century Bibi Khanum mausoleum which had been badly damaged by Soviet Marshal Budenny's artillery during the civil fighting in 1924. Looking for a place to sleep, I went inside it through a hole in the wall. The floor was littered with pieces of broken masonry and greenish blue tiles that had fallen from the dome. The place stank of urine and excrement. In the shadows, I saw the prone silhouette of a man gasping his last. His death rattle chased me to seek some other place to spend the night in "Golden Samarkand."

Not far from there I found an open market that, in spite of the late hour, seemed to be still busy. But I gave it a wide berth when I saw that the people there were not the usual buyers and sellers but two fighting gangs of *zhuliki*, one Russian and one Uzbek.

Walking through the winding streets of the old town, I suddenly spied a teenager wearing a high-school uniform, the kind we used to wear in Poland before the war: navy blue with light blue piping down the trouser seams and around the jacket cuffs. When I called to him in Polish, he stopped, eyed me with suspicion, but then came closer. He told me that he and his parents came to Samarkand voluntarily from Soviet-occupied Poland because they had heard about the large, prosperous Jewish communities of Samarkand and nearby Bokhara. They were large but not that prosperous. "We help each other and we make a reasonable living," he explained. He seemed a bit uneasy about being seen with a scruffy scarecrow like me, but before we parted he told me about a bakery in the old town that sold a limited amount of "commercial" bread at a nominal price, without coupons. It opened at midnight, he said, and there were long lineups in front of it.

The bakery was easy to find. There was indeed a lineup in front of it but not as bad as I had feared, certainly nothing like the two-day kerosene queue in Kirov. After two or three hours of queueing I bought the maximum allowable (700 grams) of white bread—a rare treat. With great reluctance, I sold about one third of it to a man who was still waiting to get in. I did not want to sell my bread, being starved myself, but the man offered me far more than the usual black-market price, and I needed money. I gobbled my bread and then started to look for a place to spend the night. I walked the dark streets until I stumbled upon what looked like a pile of planks covered with canvas. I crawled under it, curled up on the ground and within seconds, I was fast asleep.

I woke up with a start to a loud Boom! Boom! Ta-ra-ra-ra. Boom! Ta-ra-ra. I peeked around and saw that I was sleeping in a kind of a crawl space full of coiled ropes. Close above me was a rough ceiling of wooden planks and an unseen orchestra playing "The Entry of the Gladiators" just above my head. Low walls made of pieces of canvas blocked my view to the outside. I pushed myself to a spot where two pieces of canvas overlapped and pulled them aside. Seeing the end of a whip and a pair of legs in riding boots just in front of my nose, I scrambled backwards like a frightened ground-hog seeing a dog waiting at the mouth of its burrow. I really didn't know what to make of it. Once again I tried to get out and this time I succeeded. Only then I realized that I had spent the night under a stage on which a circus band was now holding its morning rehearsal. A few men handling long poles and ropes were raising the circus tent above us. The riding-boots-with-whip had inside them a mustachioed gentleman crowned with a bowler hat. One of the workers noticed me and was trying to catch the attention of the bowler-hatted master by pointing at me. But before this whip-holder figured out what was wanted from him, I took to my heels and vanished among the morning crowd of shoppers on the market square.

That day I met yet another fellow countryman. He was older than me, and in just as bad shape as I was. He too was Jewish, and when I asked him why he didn't seek help from the Jewish community there, he waved my question aside. Later he explained,

"Don't kid yourself about Jewish solidarity. They hate me here because when they refuse to help me it bothers them twice as much as when they refuse to help a goy. Come with me. I heard that somewhere around here there's a Red Army volunteer recruiting centre. Let's go and sign up. Maybe even before we sign up they'll give us some bread and a bowl of soup."

That sounded tempting, but I had misgivings. "You know," I said, "after my five-thousand-kilometre-long ordeal of searching for the Polish Army it doesn't seem right to volunteer for the Bolshie troops."

He looked at me. "Let's eat a bowl of soup first and then worry about allegiance. Come on."

We did not have to make any heart-breaking decisions. We never found that recruiting centre. In fact, when we asked people about it, they just shook their heads and looked at us in disbelief as if we were total idiots. Sometimes I wonder what would have happened to me if we had found that recruiting centre.

Dispirited and dejected, we returned to the open market outside Registan Square. It was a warm and sunny day. We sat on the stone threshold of an abandoned house. The sand-coloured walls of the surrounding buildings looked old and mellow framed with black shadows cast by the cornices and lintels. Above us the cupola of the brilliant blue sky looked like half of a huge soap bubble reflecting the lustrous blue dome of the Bibi Khanum shrine. The Uzbeks were milling around the market, some riding donkeys so tiny that the rider's feet touched the ground. With throaty grunts, they urged their long-eared steeds on and prodded them by jabbing their haunches with sharpened short sticks. On rickety wood stalls and hemp mats spread on the dusty ground, the fierce-looking merchants displayed their wares—sun-dried pieces of cantaloupe, peaches and black raisins. The merchants and their customers gabbed and smoked and kept drinking straw-coloured tea from little bowls brought from the *chaikhany* (Uzbek tea houses) by small boys. All these luxuries were beyond our means.

Even now, the haunting melodies from the lands of Ali Baba and Scheherazade bring into my mind the exotic images of those days—beautiful but forever marred by my memories of the constant hunger I suffered there.

In the evening I parted from my companion. We shook hands and wished each other better times. He had decided to stay in "Golden Samarkand." I walked back to the railway station to continue my trek southward.

The 300-kilometre journey from Samarkand to Kagan must have been uneventful because I do not remember much about it. What I do remember is that I travelled all night on a train of boxcars full of Russian refugees who were going to Ashkhabad. That was not where I wanted to go, and so I had to get off at Kagan to catch a train on the branch line to Dushanbe (then called Stalinabad), the capital of Tajikistan. For on that branch was Termez, a town on the Soviet-Afghanistan border, the town I had long dreamed about as my gateway to freedom from the Red Paradise.

The next two days I spent at or rather around the Kagan railway station. Behind the station building there was an *evakopunkt* in a large, old, two-story house. There were several supposed travellers in the house, all Russians, some waiting for a train, some content just to stay there with no intention of leaving. There was a middle-aged couple, three or four men in their early thirties, and myself. The once-stylish, old house was in miserable shape. Most of the windows were broken. Shards of glass littered the dirt on the beautiful parquet floors. Unhinged doors with legs made of bricks pried from the walls served as makeshift cots. The delicate trellis work of the veranda was being used as kindling for small cooking fires in the front garden. We huddled together in the main room on the ground floor. All the other rooms had been used as toilets by the passing hordes of refugees. This pre-revolution building must have belonged to some rich notable and his family. How they would have wept if they could have seen what had become of their lovely home.

The local *kolkhozniki* were doing a brisk trade selling food and tobacco to the passengers of trains stopping at the station. I bought a bottle of well-watered milk from an Uzbek. After sipping two-thirds of it, I refilled the bottle with water from a ditch. The concoction now looked light blue, but I still managed to sell it for five rubles to a

Russian who beckoned me from an open window of a crowded train standing at the station. He took just one gulp and then threw the bottle at me. He missed. The bottle hit the cinder walkway but did not break. The bluish liquid started gurgling out, but I grabbed it and drank the rest of it while the Russian at the window was cursing me and my ancestors. It tasted good.

In Uzbekistan, we also ate *makukh*—pressed cakes of the cottonseed pulp left over from the oil mill. The inch-thick slabs were yellow, speckled with black, and hard as wooden planks—too tough to gnaw. Farmers would crush the slabs and add the pulp to cattle fodder. We heated it over an open fire to soften it enough to break into small, chewable pieces. It was the next to last resort for starving people, one notch above grass and tree bark. It also caused diarrhea. The locals would laugh when they saw us chewing it and spitting out yellow saliva. I ate it many times, even in the army—on the sly though, because eating it there was forbidden for health reasons.

After two days of waiting at Kagan, a train going to Stalinabad stopped at the station. That train was a mixture of passenger cars, boxcars and open freight cars. The boxcars were carrying people evacuated from the war zones to work on the kolkhozes in Tajikistan—Russians, Ukrainians and Poles. The gondola cars were heaped with coal.

The crowd from the train spilled out all over the station in search of water and food. The local farmers were selling the usual wares—boiled beets, *kish-mish* (raisins), large flat, purple onions that were very sweet and as big as tea saucers, and the watery milk which the women from the train were trying to buy for their crying babies. A young Polish fellow named Dziekonski found a place for me in a passenger car.

Inside the car, I found everything that I was afraid of finding, a throng of people embodying human misery on the move—grey-faced men, women and children sitting on the benches or on the floor between the benches. Any space not occupied by people was filled with bundles, bags and suitcases. There was a pervading stench of cheap tobacco, unwashed human bodies, excrement and the vomit of wailing babies.

Dziekonski, a former prisoner like me, sat on the bench nearest to the door. With his hip he pushed and pushed the man sitting next to him, squeezing him into the corner at the window, thus making enough room for one of my haunches. The train had just pulled out, and we had barely begun the ritual of the opening questions and answers—When released? Which camp or prison? From what town in Poland?—when we saw half a dozen characters entering our car through the door at the far end. They wore half-sneers, half-scowls on their rat-like faces. Each with one hand in a pocket and the other scratching the chin, they moved slowly along the aisle scrutinizing the passengers. Three of their companions were girls, who kept glancing at the bundles and bags piled on the racks. I recognized the familiar scenario of a train robbery. So did Dziekonski. We knew that when they found we had nothing worth stealing they might beat us up instead. In the same breath we said, "Run!" and bolted from the car.

But the gang noticed us giving them the slip. They followed us. For a moment we faced the blank wall of a boxcar but then climbed the ladder to the roof. We ran to the far end of it and when we looked back, we saw above the edge of the roof the head of one of them. He yelled to his mates, "Here they are!" We had to run.

Standing on the edge of the roof and eyeing the gap separating it from the next car, I saw in my mind a flashback from an old Western movie—a sheriff and his posse chasing bandits along the roofs of a speeding Santa Fe train. How I had envied them then! What fun they must have had jumping from one roof to the next, I used to think. But here it was no fun.

The gap between the huge Russian cars was wider than between the smaller American boxcars. We didn't have to crane our necks to see the railway ties blurring past below. Still, the distance between the two roofs was no more than two big steps, maybe just over one metre. Anybody could jump that on the ground. But here on top of the speeding and swaying boxcars it looked scary. The gang was closing on us. I jumped and landed safely on the next roof. Then Dziekonski made it with a metre to spare. The gap did not stop our pursuers. The chase went on from car to car until we reached the last boxcar. After that there was only an open car full of lumps of coal. With our backs to the ladder at the end of the last boxcar, we climbed halfway down and lunged forward across the gap and into the open coal car. This was the end of the retreat and there we had to make our last stand. We picked up heavy chunks of coal and were ready to throw them at the first *zhulik* who dared to come down the ladder. Seeing that, the *zhuliki* stopped and talked for a while among themselves. Then one of them shouted, "What do you have in those?" pointing at my little suitcase and Dziekonski's bundle.

"Nothing that would be of any interest to you."

"If you have nothing interesting then you have nothing to lose and nothing to fear. So why escape?"

Before we could answer, the youngest of them slid halfway down the ladder and, ignoring our fighting stance, jumped down right in front of us. He was fast and fearless.

"Let's see what you have in there!"

He reached for my suitcase, jerked it out of my hand and, upon opening it, saw the writing paraphernalia. That did not interest him. He turned to Dziekonski and undid the knot on his bundle. A torn shirt and an aluminum spoon spilled out.

Turning to his friends who were overseeing the operation from the rooftop, he yelled, "The shitty weaklings have nothing. They weren't lying!" And like a trained gymnast, he jumped from the edge of the open coal car, caught the ladder with his hands and pulled himself up to rejoin his gang. It looked as if they hadn't found anything worth stealing in the car with refugees either. Instead of going back, they settled down on the roof, rolled up a cigarette, took turns at puffing at it and enjoyed the sunshine.

Their girls rejoined them after a while. Two of them sat on the edge of the car roof facing us. One of them was wearing my *kubanka* fur hat, which I had left on the carriage bench. I signed to her that this was my hat, and she nonchalantly tossed it back to me. Both girls were young and healthy looking. Dangling their legs and chattering, they looked happy. The wind was blowing their hair and was lifting the hems of their rumpled skirts. They wore no underwear.

Watching them I realized that, happily, the complete indifference to females that had overcome me while in the camps was only a passing stage. I was no longer immune to glimpses of feminine charms.

The train was slow. We were crossing the bleak, almost uninhabited grey desert. It took four hours of uninterrupted going to cover the distance between Karshi and Kerki, the stretch chosen by the gang to rob trains. At Kerki they all got off and, while waiting on the platform for a return train to rob, they chatted amiably with the railway guards and militiamen.

Dziekonski and I moved back to the stinky passenger car. It was getting dark, and in the evening chill it was too cold to travel in the open. We snoozed sitting back to back on the aisle floor. I heard somebody saying that we should be in Termez by early morning.

Chapter 21

KOLKHOZ KIZIL SHARK

Termez. A town on the Amu Darya River, the border between the USSR and Afghanistan. A small circle on the map where my eye, wandering southwards from the grey-green areas of subarctic Russia, would stop. The end station of my five-week-long train journey. Gateway to freedom.

As soon as the train stopped, the shabby crowd of passengers scattered along the platform. Some started an orderly line in front of the door of the yet-unopened bread store. Some ran to the loco-motive to fill their kettles and pots with boiling water from the engine. Others relieved themselves beside the railway track, observing an unwritten rule—women to the left, men to the right. All this went on under the watchful eye of the ten-foot-high con-crete statue of the Great Leader of the Nation.

Having no ticket and no documents, I climbed over the fence behind the coal shed and started to reconnoitre. In half an hour I reached the town's centre but there was no sign of any river. I kept walking south. It was safer not to ask for directions. The streets lead-ing to the river were patrolled by militiamen and border guards. I noticed that my badly torn, cotton padded trousers were attracting the attention of passersby. I walked and walked—maybe one hour, maybe two—until, at last, between some grimy shanties, I spotted the river. There were more guards standing around the well-fenced jetty. The Amu Darya seen at a distance looked stony and shallow. The few bushes on the shores in which one could hide were leafless. The conditions for stealing across the border were not propitious, at least not there and not at that time.

Of course, there were many other problems in trying to reach freedom through Afghanistan: the possibility of being handed back to the Russians by the Afghan authorities; walking the 500 kilometres alone through the arid lands to get to Kabul where the British consulate was; and having no maps, no money, no documents, and no food or water. But I was hoping that some of the Afghans might have retained the time-honoured custom of giving away scraps of food to a passing beggar. While I was mulling over all these things my spirits started to flag, and I decided to postpone the escape for the time being and find a companion for the great adventure.

Feeling rather downcast, I returned to the station. The train was still there, but I didn't see Dziekonski. I pushed my way along into a crowded cattle car. People inside told me that the bread store never opened and the boiling water from the locomotive reeked of kerosene. That cheered me up a bit. At least I had not lost anything by going off on my own.

The cattle car I was in had a pretty good cross-section of the wartime travelling public in Russia: families evacuated from the western regions, Jews fleeing the German tide, soldiers on leave, officials on unofficial trips, and riff-raff who considered trains their permanent abode.

In this train there was a large contingent of Poles: those released from prisons and forced labour camps, and a good number of the so-called free-resettlement deportees. These were mainly women and children kicked out of their homes in Russian-occupied eastern Poland and shipped to the forests of Siberia, the steppes of Kazakhstan and the deserts of Kirghizya to work on collective farms.

That day I had nothing to eat and was trying to sleep off the hunger. After a few hours the train stopped at the small station of Sary Assiyan in the Surkhan Darya region at the foothills of the Baysun Tau mountain range.

All refugees, evacuees and those who could not give a good account of themselves for being on the train were ordered off by NKVD officials. It was a dark night and the air was cold. A few trucks took our group of about 150 people to the centre of town and deposited us in front of the local *klub*.

Inside, the *klub* was dank and smelly, lit by a dozen naked light bulbs dangling from an invisible ceiling. The families and individuals began staking out floor space, marking their claims with their bundles and pots.

I did not belong to any group. I was alone and entirely on my own. But I had joined the evacuees who were being taken to Sary Assiyan as there was a chance that a meal would be prepared in town for them and, in the absence of any list, I might get something to eat. Nearly everybody had the same thing in mind.

Alas! There was no food anywhere in sight. Hours passed and we were getting hungrier and hungrier. Then a smartly dressed *politruk* appeared. He hopped on the stage and standing arms akimbo (the beloved posture of the Soviet military) announced that his colleague from the cultural/educational unit would now deliver a lecture on the present international situation. The announcement was greeted by hoots, groans and derisive laughter. A lean, red-headed man let out a prolonged fart for which he received a round of applause.

After the lecture was over, the *politruk* removed the map of the world from the wall, rolled it up tightly and, wielding it like a spear, cleared the way to the exit for himself and the lecturer.

I went outside, and not too far from the *klub* I heard a group of young men speaking Polish. They were standing in front of some kind of a canteen or restaurant where a watery millet soup was being sold for one ruble a serving. There were four of them, and one was carrying a shiny large teakettle. They had only two rubles between them. I butted in and told them I could help.

In Soviet restaurants the system was the same as in the bread stores. At one counter you buy the coupons and then you go to the next counter to collect what you bought. I wasn't as bold at kiting as the thieving and swindling Dombrowski brothers, who had talked me into changing a two to twenty-two and gotten away with it, but the scheme was the same. One of them bought a talon for one portion of soup. I copied the numeral, changing the one into eleven. The scheme worked nicely. A couple of minutes later the proud owner of the iron teakettle emerged from the canteen with the steaming results of our ploy. We passed the kettle around, drinking from the spout the hot, gluey ambrosia.

We could hear a commotion inside the restaurant. Two self-appointed cleaners were fighting with some men who were trying to take over their job. The johnny-come-latelies coveted not the job but the perks that came with it: licking out the chipped enamel bowls before returning them to the kitchen. When our kettle was empty, the eldest of the four gave me an approving wink and a playful kick in the ass. I was now one of them.

Another meeting was called in the *klub*. This time we were told that all refugees would be split into small groups and sent to the kolkhozes in the region, where they would get lodgings and food for their work. Indeed, next morning representatives of neighbouring kolkhozes started arriving to select their new workers. It had the air of a slave market. They were looking for strong men and women, shunning the elderly and the children. My newly acquired friends and I were quickly claimed by a tall Tajik dressed in a brightly striped *khalat* held together by a wide sash with a curved knife in an ornamented sheath stuck into it, a black skullcap embroidered with silver thread in a yin-yang pattern and baggy pants tucked into high-heeled riding boots. This was typical dress for the local men, although some of them, instead of a skullcap, would wear a cerulean turban. The Tajik spoke no Russian but, gesticulating vigorously, made it clear that we should go with him to his village where there would be work and food waiting for us, lucky fellows!

The five of us followed him to his heavy, two-wheeled cart, pulled by a mangy Bactrian camel. The cart was making slow but steady progress. The camel dictated the pace, oblivious to the urgings and what sounded like strong threats and curses from his master. The road was little more than a dirt track. Sometimes it was difficult to tell if it was a road at all. We were fording fast-flowing mountain streams, bumping over acres of stony fields and passing through patches of cultivated land with occasional clusters of almond and peach trees. But it was still winter. The trees were bare and the landscape was bleak.

The track was getting steeper and steeper as we started climbing the foothills of the snow-capped Baysun Tau range. Then on the slope of a mountain we saw a hamlet, just two dozen or so small houses with barns and stone fences. Our new boss pointed it out to us with his whip and said, "Kizil Shark!" (Red East), the name of the little village where we would live and work. We were billeted in the village school building, an adobe structure about thirty feet long. It had two rooms. The larger one for the five of us had a tamped dirt floor and an adobe stove in the corner. The second room, which was very small, would soon be occupied by a later addition to the village's population, an emaciated Polish farmer with his dazed wife and a very sick baby a few months old.

Our boss brought in a smooth-cheeked man of an indeterminate age who spoke with a shrill, high-pitched voice that sounded like a crowing cock. He was the farm's stock keeper. It appeared he was a eunuch who lived and slept in the women's quarters. He counted us on his fingers, vanished and reappeared ten minutes later with our supper, a large bowl of runny, dark gruel and five flat, round breads. That was it. By exaggerated miming, he made it clear that we would be served the same repast tomorrow night and every night.

Later on our boss, who in fact was the collective farm manager, the eunuch stock keeper and a young man paid us another visit. The young man was a teacher from another village and knew a few words of Russian. Acting as an interpreter, he told us that our main task was to dig new irrigation ditches and repair the old ones.

The kolkhoz Kizil Shark used to be a private farm but was taken over by the Soviet government in the 1920s after the Basmachi uprising was finally crushed by the Russians. The Basmachi were farmers of Central Asia who had opposed the nationalization of land. Nowadays they would be called mujahedeens. The kolkhoz had retained many of its original characteristics. The current farm manager, the man who chose us, had four wives and a number of serfs, including the eunuch. All of them were listed now as independent members of the collective farm. The manager himself was related to the former owner who had escaped to Afghanistan. All were covert Muslims and their loyalty to the atheistic Soviet regime was questionable. They blamed the Communists for their many troubles. Almost all able men in the area had been drafted into the armed forces. Most of the work in the fields was being done by women, who always worked in groups away from men. Food was scarce.

The stores in towns were empty. Work norms were being increased every few months. And to top it all, the manager's pride, his black horse, had been requisitioned by the army. I was amazed to learn that even in these remote areas the German propaganda was working all too well. The locals whispered among themselves that Hitler was a good Muslim and the German Army would free them from the Soviet yoke.

Soon it became clear that the arrival of the blue-eyed beggars, as the natives called us, would not improve the stagnant economy of Kizil Shark. It appeared that two of our group, the Szachlewicz brothers, were professional thieves—and petty thieves at that. Talking to each other, they used thieves' cant and were obviously proud of their métier. They had grown up in the small town of Dawidgrodek in the Pripet Marshes of eastern Poland. They claimed that for a while they worked as acrobats in a circus and to prove it to us they would walk on their hands with great ease and agility. However, their main vocation was stealing. One day, somebody from their village had denounced them to the local militia. A lenient judge sentenced them to three years of correctional labour. They wound up in the coal mines of Vorkuta near the Arctic Ocean. But they bragged that they never overworked themselves there. Their camp girlfriend was sharing with them her extra earnings made from selling her charms to the camp staff. Her standard honorarium was one onion. In arctic regions an onion was a rare treat.

In fact, the Szachlewicz brothers abhorred even the idea of any regular work. They offered to build a sauna for the kolkhoz but the locals considered such ablutions a foreign concept. The brothers then offered to organize a performing arts ensemble using local talent. While not rejected outright by the wily kolkhoz manager, who was afraid of being accused of an anti-cultural attitude, it was "postponed" by him until after harvest time. Meanwhile, the brothers were stealing whatever they could and selling it at night in the neighbouring village. In fact there was very little to steal, and their loot was indeed pitiful. Occasionally, in order to keep in practice, they would steal from each other.

* * *

Like most colonial powers, the Soviets had set their regional boundaries in Central Asia without bothering about ethnic differences—or if they did, it was a case of divide and rule. Not knowing the local languages, I seldom could tell whether the locals were speaking Uzbek (a Turkic language) or Tajik (a form of Persian). However, the farm manager and the stock keeper were delighted when they found that I could read and write Russian. In 1940, the Cyrillic alphabet was introduced in the Soviet republics of Central Asia, the third alphabet in less than twenty years after Arabic and modified Roman. Being the only literate person in the kolkhoz, I was made the production accountant, a promotion that pulled me out of the lowest caste of manual workers. The main part of my job was to measure the linear or square metres of land hoed, cleaned, dug or ploughed by each worker and then calculate its percentage of the daily output based on the production norms set by the state. As a rule, I doubled or tripled the results. Everybody was happy because such high productivity levels had never before been reached in Kizil Shark kolkhoz. However my remuneration remained the same as before: one round flat barley bread and a bowl of gruel per day.

We were starving. Even the thieving Szachlewicz brothers could not lay their hands on any extra food. But we had two unexpected meals. One day the stock keeper shot a starling and gave it to us. We cooked it on the adobe stove over a fire of dry cotton stalks and shared it among the five of us.

The second unscheduled meal was more substantial. It was the farm manager's dog. At night we choked it with our bare hands. Then we skinned it and chopped it up with a shard of windowpane. The grisly execution took a long time. In the middle of the night, we buried the bones and the skin in a shallow grave under the dirt floor. The chopped meat boiled in the teakettle was not very tasty because we had no salt. Next morning when the farm manager called and whistled for his dog, the older Szachlewicz said to his brother, "Tell him to stop whistling. This fucking mutt is jumping in my stomach."

One of the women working on the land, preparing it for cotton seeding, was good looking. There was always a nice if somewhat impudent smile on her uncovered face. The *paranja*, a horsehair veil, was not worn by the women when working in the fields. A couple of times she gave me a ball of a rock-hard goat cheese the size of a chestnut, which I would put in my mouth and suck. It was delicious and lasted a long time. Her name was Khaticha Djarakul, one of the two names that stick in my memory from my days in Kizil Shark. The other name is that of Kara Tursyn, the quiet ploughman whom I followed as he furrowed the rusty-red and stony soil with a primitive plough fashioned from the forked branch of a tree and drawn by a pair of oxen.

Kara Tursyn's Russian was limited to ten words, matching the extent of my newly acquired Uzbek. But as his innate talent for mime would do credit to Marcel Marceau, our conversations were both extensive and exhausting. Every so often he would touch my chest with his grubby finger and praise me. "Speak Uzbek good."

In the evenings, after we bolted our gruel and bread, there was plenty of time to lie down, to pray quietly and to daydream. The prayers were important. They kept our flagging spirits up. It felt good to believe that there was Somebody listening to our silent blubberings and perhaps miraculously offering a way out of that nadir of despair. Even the thieving brothers would mumble their Hail Marys and cross themselves before falling asleep. At these times we reminisced about the more pleasant episodes of our past, idealizing the pre-war years or daydreaming about the future—anything that would lift our thoughts beyond our grim reality. I would dream about rearranging my collection of colourful stamps from the French colonies with their miniature pictures of sailing ships, butterflies and tropical plants. Or I would fantasize about myself as the janitor of a small apartment house. My chores finished, I would be sitting in the freshly swept courtyard on a wheelbarrow turned upside down, eating endless sausage rolls and buns.

At one time or other we have all pondered the hypothetical question: "If a fairy godmother granted you only one wish, what would you ask for?" Had I been asked such a question during my prison days and even after, almost to the last days of my stay in the Soviet Union, I would have answered without hesitation, "A chunk of bread that would last forever." Bread was life. All other things were mere embellishment.

The Polish farmer, the latecomer to the kolkhoz, was faring badly. He was working hard, digging the irrigation ditch with a cast-iron mattock. The poor fellow had to share his bread and gruel with his wife and her baby as neither of them was entitled to any food from the kolkhoz. The farm authorities were indifferent to the family's plight. The baby died a few weeks later of sheer starvation. What happened to the farmer and his wife I don't know because suddenly I came down with typhus.

It was the last day of January, 1942. My recollections of the days that followed are not, as one might suspect, blurred. In fact, what followed was a total blackout with a few flashes of consciousness that vividly engraved themselves on my memory. The familiar camel and cart, driven by a stranger, were taking me off to a hospital in Sary Assiyan. Whenever the wheels of the cart bumped on a large stone, a thunder of pain would hit my head and reverberate mercilessly. Next, I remember sitting naked in a shallow wooden tub half-filled with cold water. Then, two babushkas snipping my lice-ridden, shaggy hair and a glimpse of a long hospital corridor with unpainted walls and with part of its roof missing.

One night I remember seeing for a few seconds the faces and hands of a doctor and a nurse in the yellow light of a solitary candle against the black background. The sharp point of a syringe was hovering over the vein clearly visible under the transparent skin of my wrist. The scene was like a painting by Zurbarán. Day after day my entire body was enveloped in a layer of heat.

I woke up in the greyness of pre-dawn. My head was clear, the fever gone. In the anemic light sifting from the bluish square of a window, I could see six or seven beds, each occupied by someone. They were talking. I listened to them for a while and then started to listen more intently. Whatever they were saying, it made no sense at all. I could not see their faces. They spoke in Polish and Russian.

One kept repeating in a hoarse voice, "The Uzbek locked me up in a pigsty and then beat me up for eating their swill." The other soothingly replied, "Take this comb, Zoya. It is a good comb. Mother gave it to me." And in the corner another moaned constantly, "My God, my God. No more permits. No more."

As I was listening to this jabbering I thought, "Holy Mother, either they are mad or I am. In either case I am in a loony bin!"

A nurse appeared at my bed. She was wearing a white smock over her everyday dress. She carried a tray with a couple of bottles and a thermometer on it. Her hand went to my brow, then to my wrist to check my pulse. She looked at me and smiled. When she turned around to leave, I whispered in Polish, "Sister." Polish chivalry requires addressing all female hospital workers, be it a nurse, a cleaner or kitchen help, as sister.

"Sister," I repeated, "what's the date today?"

She looked at me over her shoulder, smiled again and said, also in Polish, "Eighth of February."

Then she added, "We had a lot of trouble with you, sir. You were trying to run away from the hospital. You had typhus just like these." She pointed at the other beds, on which the patients were continuing their typhous mumblings. "But now you are all right. You know, from those who came here when you did, you are the only one who survived."

"Sister, I am hungry."

"I know," she replied. "They'll be bringing soup, soon."

I had been hungry for the last two years. There were times when I had seriously contemplated eating the bark of a tree or licking the grease from a railway car axle. But this hunger was like nothing before. My entire body was crying for food.

They brought the soup. A small bowl of warm liquid. I licked the bowl clean, and then it dawned on me that eight days were almost entirely erased from my memory. How was that possible?

The doctor came. Like doctors the world over, with a quick glance he scanned my face and body, tilted his head to one side and said, "And how are we today?"

"Doctor, I am hungry."

"Hungry," he repeated. "Hungry means healthy." He turned to his assistant. "Sign him out today, will you?" And they left the ward.

An old man brought me my torn pants, my shirt well starched with sweat and grime, and my fur hat. But my PPG sneakers were nowhere to be found. He went once again to check the storage shed. Meanwhile, I sat on my bed and surveyed the room. The primitive beds were covered with coarse blankets. No sheets or pillowcases. The pillows were filthy—stiff and shiny from dried saliva and bloodstains. A shallow spittoon with its multicoloured contents sat in the centre of the room. There was nothing worth stealing.

The old man returned with a pair of so-called *che-te-zeds*, an abbreviation of the Chelyabinsk Tractor Works and the name given to the crude footwear fashioned by cutting off a segment of a discarded tire, turning up both ends and tying the whole contraption with a piece of wire. I am not sure that it was better than nothing.

For the first time in my life I realized what it means to be an old man. I could stand up, but I was too weak to walk. I could not lift my feet off the floor. All I could do was shuffle my feet along the ground. But I left the hospital.

The street leading to town was separated from the hospital grounds by an irrigation ditch filled with muddy water, which had to be jumped over. It wasn't wide, maybe three or four feet. But how could I jump over it? I could not even lift my feet so I waded into the cold, thigh-high water and crossed my Rubicon.

I was shuffling my way to the town. Slowly, very slowly. A loud "Hey, you!" stopped me. I looked around and there was Dziekonski, the lanky Polish fellow with whom I faced bandits on the train to Sary Assiyan. He was now thinner and his beard longer. He had recognized not me but my trousers. He told me that today in town in the school building, a Soviet medical commission was selecting volunteers for the Polish Army. I dragged myself there and joined the line of would-be heroes. One by one they would enter the building and when they left, the commission's verdict would be written all over their faces.

My turn came and, when I opened the door of the room where the commission was, there in the midst of a group of uniformed officials sat the doctor who had released me from the hospital just a couple of hours ago.

"Are you joking?" said the doctor, looking at me. "Go back to the kolkhoz, eat well, recover and try again. Some soldier!" The others nodded, and one of them shouted, "Next!"

I hung around the school until the evening hoping for something to happen. I had had nothing to eat since my plate of soup in the morning. At sunset a military truck arrived with two soldiers to take all the men selected by the medical commission to the railway station. As they read each name aloud, a man would answer "Present!" and climb onto the truck. A few men failed to show up. When the name Trompka came, nobody answered. The soldier shouted again. "Trompka!"

I saw my chance and yelled back. "Present!"

He looked at me with disbelief. "Your age?"

"Twenty-two," I lied.

He scowled. "Go away! Trompka's forty-six."

The driver of the truck stepped on the running board, stretched his neck to look backwards and check if the tailgate was closed, slid inside the driver's cabin, pulled the visor of his army cap down over his eyes and started the engine. The truck spun its balding tires, spurting plumes of grit and pebbles, and jerked forwards. Soon it became just a dusty blur, the vanishing point of the perspective of the road lit by the orange light of the sunset.

I was not going to be left behind. I had to go to the station. Again I started my slow shuffle. Darkness fell as I passed the last houses of the town. The distance between the town and the railway station was eight kilometres. If only I could find a piece of wood or a stick to use as a cane! But there was none. I was getting more and more tired. It was a moonless night, and in the darkness I could barely make out the dirt track leading to the station. Then I heard children crying. It was quite loud. Rather wailing than crying. I thought that there must be some houses very close, but I could not make them out because it was too dark. Probably some Uzbeks beating their children. But the heart-rending wailing didn't stop.

Now the sound seemed to be coming from the other side of the road. I turned around and with a start I saw half a dozen devils about fifty feet behind me. They had pointed ears and their eyes were shining in the darkness. That's bad, I thought, I must be hallucinating from hunger and exhaustion. I resumed my shuffle. After a while I looked back. The devils were following me. I stopped, and they stopped too. One of them gave a long, mournful howl, just like a child being beaten. Suddenly I understood. This was no hallucination; this was a frightening reality. I was being followed by a pack of jackals waiting for me to fall down.

That gave me a surge of strength. God only knows where it came from. Hours passed. I shuffled on and on. My knees were getting weaker and weaker and my breath shallower and shallower. Each time I stopped and looked round to see if the jackals were still following me, they would stop too, ready to rush in at what seemed my imminent collapse. My eyes strained to find some sign of the station. At last the black silhouette of a building broke the desert horizon. And beside it, the red and green beacon of the railway semaphore. I knew now I could make it.

The Polish recruits from the army truck were still there waiting for the train. It arrived just before dawn. I was too weak to scale the three steep steps into the railway car. Mercifully, a strong man lifted and heaved me inside. I crawled under the nearest seats, burning my elbow against the steam pipe, and fell asleep.

Chapter 22
MAKING OF A SOLDIER

The next two days I spent in semihibernation under the wooden seats. The compartment was occupied by some of the Polish draftees from Sary Assiyan including their leader, a certain Sergeant Major Zajaczkowski. He held the railway ticket and the food rations issued by the Soviet Army office for the entire group, which also included food for all those who failed to show up. I was hoping that perhaps I would get some of that extra grub. No such luck. Indeed, every time I crawled out from under the bench, I was confronted by the indifferent if not hostile stares of the men who were jealously guarding their unexpected bonanza. And so I spent my time lying on the filthy floor sleeping or staring at the underside of the bench. The grime on it had settled into amorphous patches that defied my persistent efforts to find in them some images conducive to day-dreaming. My view on one side was blocked by a rust-eaten metal partition panel to which a hissing steam pipe was clamped. The other side was more entertaining—a dozen feet shod in a variety of bizarre footwear: rubber boots with wooden soles, jodhpur leggings with canvas shoes, sandals and slippers woven from straw or from hemp cord or from willow bark. The occasional protruding toe with an ingrown, dark blue toenail or a calloused heel peeking from a split shoe seam added a whiff of interest to this low-level show.

We were going to Kermine where my irreplaceable identity card had been stolen. Now Kermine was the garrison town and the recruiting centre of the Seventh Polish Infantry Division.

Another day and night passed without food. Now and again I would make my way to the toilet with its smashed bowl and basin to quench my thirst with rusty water from the one tap that still worked. Next day, when the train stopped at Karshi, I managed to barter my fur hat for a bottle of well-watered, bluish milk. And that was all I had until the train reached Kermine the following day.

A few months later, by chance, I ran into "Sergeant Major" Zajaczkowski, who by then had prudently demoted himself to the rank of a mere corporal. Our eyes met. He recognized me and, after a moment of silence, said with a disarming smile, "You know why we did not give you anything to eat? We thought you were a kike."

In front of the station, Polish soldiers in British army battledress greeted, sorted out, grouped and yelled at the incoming stream of Polish-speaking men, women and children. We men were directed to a nearby holding unit to await the Polish Army medical examination. If we passed, we would go on to the formal induction procedure and allocation to a unit. Nobody was asking for identity cards or documents. On a small table set on the ground in front of a one-story building, two soldiers were struggling to make a list of the new arrivals, writing their names, age and rank with a pencil in a lined exercise book.

The newcomers were divided into groups of ten and each group was assigned to a tent. With my new companions I entered ours. There was nothing inside the tent. Just stony and gritty ground with scattered small clumps of some dry, prickly, greyish-green desert weed.

The occupants of my tent were a motley bunch, ranging in age from teenagers to grizzlies. All had drawn faces, beards at least a month old and tattered togs. And all were thin and starved. After a few introductory grunts, we curled up on the ground awaiting the announcement of our first mealtime. It came none too soon. The line-up to the kitchen where the soup was to be served and bread issued was long but orderly and patient. Those at the front, who peeked through the chinks between the boards of the wooden kitchen door, relayed the comforting or disturbing news to the rest of the queue:

"The soup looks thick."

"There may not be enough bread to give everybody their 450 grams."

"A staff sergeant is yelling at the kitchen hands, probably for stealing food."

"What d'ya mean probably? Sure they did! Bastards!"

A man in front of me was restless. He kept looking ahead as if to check the number of people in front of him, then cast glances at the people behind him, sometimes making half-steps to the side. I thought he was suffering from diarrhea and had to go, but was afraid of losing his place in the line. Another few minutes passed. Then he said, "I don't have a *kotelok*."

This was serious in those days. A *kotelok* (the Russian diminutive for kettle) was indispensable for survival. It was a generic name for any pot, or can or bowl with a wire handle, or a jar with a string handle or anything to pour your water, soup, or kasha into. It was as important as one's hand. Nobody would lend or part with his *kotelok* even for a moment.

The lineup started moving forward. The man was getting desperate. He didn't even have a cap or a hat to use as a bowl. I saw this being done in the camps many times. After a while the hat becomes coated inside with sticky food and does not leak any more.

We were moving closer to the kitchen door. The man was in a panic, pleading in vain for help from everybody around him. Finally facing the solemn figure of the white-hatted chef who was holding the ladle like a wand of office, he lifted the hem of his greatcoat and fashioned from his coattails a creditable imitation of a tureen. Without blinking an eye the chef poured the prescribed two ladles of millet soup into it and turned to the next in line. He had seen it all before.

The hot soup plus 450 grams of hard tack lifted my spirit and injected some energy into me. In the next few days I reverted to my calling as an organizer and fixer. With so many people around and a skimpy but steady supply of calories, small-scale enterprises began to flourish. A large *chaikhana* (an Uzbek tea house) at the edge of the holding unit area was a busy place. Soldiers, natives and newcomers would spend hours sitting cross-legged on their haunches on low platforms made of rough wooden planks and drinking weak but hot straw-coloured ersatz tea from small bowls. Here the walls made of woven matting gave some protection to the tea drinkers against the cold wind and here one could exchange the latest gossip, meet new people and from time to time strike a profitable deal.

The *chaikhana* was a man's domain. No woman would dare to cross its threshold. Never mind the Revolution and the equality of the sexes. That was all right, even highly commendable, but for somewhere else. Here women still wore the *paranja* over their faces and kept their heads down when walking in public. It was Central Asia and nobody would dream of changing customs two thousand years old. But near the railway station some of the female refugees from the snowy north were offering "a fleeting illusion of love" for half of the daily bread ration. There were few takers.

One of the fellows with whom I shared the tent had a lot of wooden matches, maybe a hundred boxes. The value of matches changed from town to town, depending on the local supply. And there was a shortage of matches in Kermine. I helped him to sell these at a handsome profit. I found another way of making a couple of rubles. I had a straight razor—I wish I could remember how it came into my possession. It was handmade by a prisoner in a Siberian camp who crafted it out of a steel file and two handles of aluminum spoons. It was very sharp, and occasionally I would augment my earnings by offering my services as a barber. This was better than another way we had learned to shave ourselves—with a piece of glass from a broken bottle.

Those March nights in Kermine were cold. A tiny wood "stove," fashioned from a small tin can with holes pierced around the top and bottom, kept our tent warm in the evenings, but the unattended fire would go out in the middle of night. As often as not I would wake up in the morning with my hair welded to the tent wall by frost. For fuel we used the wood of the saxaul tree, which grows in the sand desert of Kara Kum. The wood, which is extremely hard, burns slowly, giving an intense hot flame. Native blacksmiths used it in their forges instead of coke.

All of these things were happening against the background of hunger and diseases that were rife in the Seventh Polish Infantry Division in Kermine. Typhus, typhoid fever, malaria, dysentery, and a pernicious indigenous disease known as *papatachi* were rampant in the area. Gravediggers, as well as men to carry the corpses in reusable coffins to the cemetery, were much sought after. For this hard work they were given an additional bowl of soup—not enough to replace the energy it took.

One day near the railway station I ran into the art historian Zynio, the younger of the Lempicki brothers who had been captured with me at the Romanian border. We were delighted to see each other alive but, because it was near time for evening roll call, we had only a few minutes to tell our stories. Zynio looked gaunt, but his eyes sparkled as he told me that he was among the few hundred lucky recruits who were about to be sent to England for training and service with the Polish Air Force squadrons there. The fact that the newly appointed Polish ambassador to the USSR, Professor Stanislaw Kot, was a family friend before the war in Lwow probably played some role in his becoming one of the lucky few. Before his release he spent over a year working as a lumberjack in labour camps near Kandalaksha, close to the border of Finland and south of the Kola peninsula. His brother Roman, the conforming, timid Latin lecturer, survived by working as an orderly in a prison hospital. Zynio also brought news of my mentor Tadzio Siuta, the brilliant historian with the encyclopedic mind. Tadzio, too, got out of the camps and was now working in the editorial office of our army newspaper *Bialy Orzel* (White Eagle). But the most dramatic news Zynio shared was about his sister Irka. He had seen her recently in Kuibyshev and told me her story.

Irka underwent harrowing times in the Karaganda labour camps of Kazakhstan. One winter, the camp she was in was cut off from the rest of the world by a week-long *purga*, a blinding snowstorm. With no food left in the camp, all lines of communications down and all roads buried and hidden by the blizzard, the camp *komandir* asked for a volunteer to go to the district capital by horse-drawn sleigh to summon help. Irka was the only one who offered to go, and the camp *komandir* took up her offer, even though she was a prisoner. She drove the horses over a hundred and fifty kilometres through the total whiteout in subzero temperatures and made it. She was returned under escort to her camp to continue serving her sentence there. I trust the food the camp needed went there with them.

I wish I could say that Tadzio and Irka found each other again and lived happily ever after, but that was not way it turned out. Zynio told me that his sister had barely got out of the camps when she met and married one Tabaczynski, an elderly counsellor with the newly established Polish Embassy in Kuibyshev. As we spoke, Irka and her fifty-ish groom were just about to move to Teheran.

Despite his new assignment Zynio still wore the quilted trousers he was issued in the labour camp and *che-te-zed* rubber shoes crudely fashioned from sections of an old truck tire. It struck me that in those days it was easier for an ambassador to procure a ticket to England for his friend than a pair of shoes.

The Soviet authorities were providing the Polish Army with rations for 44,000 soldiers a day. But by the end of February the number of our soldiers in the USSR was double that. What's more, there were thousands of Polish women and children hanging around the army camps. We fed them by sharing our already halved rations.

Although the criteria of the medical selection board were lenient so as to allow as many as possible to join the army, I was constantly worried that I would be rejected on account of my weak post-typhus condition and my short-sightedness. One evening I managed to sneak into the medical commission room and copy down the eye examination chart. I learned the first five lines by heart so that I could appear before the doctors without my glasses.

Polish Jews had a hard time at the recruiting centre. The Soviet constitution recognized Jews as a nation, not as a religious denomination. The Polish Army was allowed to recruit men of Polish nationality only, thereby excluding Jews who, according to Soviet law, belonged to the Jewish nation. Soviet liaison officers were attached to the Polish recruiting centres to see that this rule was observed. Also, many Poles were resentful of the alacrity with which the majority of the Jewish population in Eastern Poland greeted the invading Soviet troops in 1939 and embraced the Communist system.

Despite this, thousands of Polish Jews who claimed to be both Polish and Roman Catholic were enlisted. This provided an extra income to some enterprising individuals. First they started spreading rumours about ad hoc tests on the knowledge of prayers and catechism being given to recruits who said they were Catholics but whose facial features or accent might cast some doubt on their claim. Then these Polish entrepreneurs organized courses on the basic prayers and tenets of the Roman Catholic religion for those who thought they needed it. The fees charged were linked to the time needed by the catechumens to learn the subject. The Jews, being used to schooling, were quick to learn not to cross themselves with the left hand and in no time were reciting faultlessly, though without much conviction, "Our Father" and "Hail Mary." The instructors, disappointed with small profits, were quick to add more material like the Seven Deadly Sins, Seven Christian Virtues or Five Church Commandments, things that even the most devout nun would stumble over.

February the 20th was my birthday and, by chance, the day I had to appear before the medical commission. With three score other recruits I was ushered into a long corridor. We were told to undress and wait. They took us into the doctors' room four at a time. Most men in my group looked as if they had just returned from a three-month vacation in the Nazi Dachau concentration camp. They were skeletons wrapped in parchment skin. Their legs and arms were covered with oozing ulcers, a sign of advanced scurvy. They had yellowish cheeks and feet glazed with dirt. All of them were puffing up their chests and were holding their chins high as befits men about to be pronounced the fearless descendants of Mars.

With three others, I entered the doctors' room. Two doctors, their helpers and two scribes were working fast in a no-nonsense atmosphere.

"Your name? Age? Born? [To this last question I was always tempted to answer "Yes!"] Religion? Profession? Relationship to the military service?"

"Get under that height measure! Step on the scales!"

While this is being done, the scribes write furiously. The doctor glances at my back for any signs of a curved spine and follows my feet with his eyes to check for flat feet as I cross the room.

"Turn around!"

Then follows a procedure that has not changed for generations. He pulls down both of my lower eyelids simultaneously using his right index and middle fingers while holding my testicles in his left hand and says, "Cough!" He indicates the eye chart on the wall and says, "Read!" I recite from memory, "B, O, M, G, R, D . . ."

At the third line he says, "Enough" and turns to the sergeant.

"Fit. Category A."

The sergeant nods. The scribe enters the verdict in the ledger-like book, then, peering at me over his steel-rimmed spectacles, says, "Signals. Seventh Company of Signals." Then he lifts his head and with his nose points to the exit door.

I walked out of the building with slow measured steps, legs wide apart and slightly swaying shoulders. A sailor's walk, a walk I assumed to project an image of self-confidence and strength. I was in a state of euphoria which soon cooled by a few degrees after I learned that the Seventh Signals Company was stationed in Keni-mekh, a small village forty kilometres away. To get there before night-fall, I started the long pilgrimage at noon with several other fellows detailed to the same unit. One of the men was attracting every-body's attention; he was wearing only one shoe, the other foot was bare. The shoe was of excellent quality, even elegant. He introduced himself as Lance Sergeant Raymund Kucharski and explained that a couple of days ago somebody stole his other shoe. He was still hopeful that the stolen shoe would turn up one way or another and in any case he would not throw away the beautiful brown shoe he was wearing. He kept marching on, humming a little tune and stop-ping now and then to balance on his bare foot in order to polish his shoe by rubbing it against his trouser leg.

We were anxious to get to Kenimekh before sunset. The thought of a hot meal kept pumping adrenaline into our veins. Still it was an arduous march. It took us nine hours to reach our unit. When we finally straggled into the Company's compound, a noncommis-sioned officer (NCO) on duty told us that it was too late for any meal or for issuing uniforms, and herded us into a barn to spend the night.

This was too much for me. Within minutes I was knocking at the door of the commanding officer's billet. I heard a clear, "Come in." I entered and saw a fatherly looking man dressed in pyjamas getting ready for bed. Before I could finish my reporting formula and per-mission-to-speak routine, he said, "Sit down, please, and continue."

He listened attentively to my complaint and started asking many questions. He introduced himself as Captain Florian Kotowicz, a reserve officer, a teacher by profession, from the town of Jaroslaw, in central Poland. I told him that my paternal aunt, Helena Zabierzewska, lived in Jaroslaw and it appeared that he knew her. He seemed to be genuinely interested in my story. When he finished puffing away at his pipe he knocked the ashes out of it, opened the door and called for the duty NCO, then told him in a quiet but firm voice, "Wake up the cooks and the corporal in charge of stores, and tell them I want the newcomers to be fed and issued uniforms and blankets immediately. You understand what I have said? Good. Dismissed." He shook my hand and said, "Good night." Then added, "Starting tomorrow we'll be playing soldiers."

The tents of my unit were set on the outskirts of the little town or, I should say, a large village, Kenimekh, on the edge of the Kizyl Kum desert. It was the starting point for the camel caravans leaving for otherwise inaccessible areas southeast of the Aral Sea. Apart from the long rows of tents, there were several mud huts occupied by the administration, stores and kitchen. An irrigation canal, with arthritic, stubby willows clinging desperately to its yellowish clay banks, ran across the flat area of our camp.

We marvelled at the quality of our new uniforms, blankets, underwear, mess kits and other soldier paraphernalia being issued to us. All this equipment was shipped from England via Murmansk on the Arctic Ocean. The uniforms were made of the best wool, the cartridge pouches and webbing of beautiful light tan leather. The shaving, mess and sewing kits were luxurious, at least by our standards then. Our sewing kits consisted of canvas envelopes with all kinds of treasures inside. There were twelve needles of different sizes, made of fine quality Sheffield steel, three spools of thread and a skein of darning wool, also spare brass buttons and a thimble. A fine needle had a high value on the local barter market. But what if during kit inspection they found a needle missing? The army dealt harshly with thieves.

Every soldier was issued with an iron ration. It was hermetically sealed in a golden box. We were forbidden to open it unless ordered to do so. Legends were created about its contents. Some suggested that it was solidified bull's blood and milk. Others talked of Swiss chocolate spiked with rum and cod liver oil. Eventually legends turned into the dark brown reality of a substance that in taste and texture resembled caked Ovaltine.

For a time some soldiers would put away some of their new treasures. They would wrap old rags around their feet instead of putting on new socks, or eat from old tin cans and bowls, trying to preserve the pristine state of their new mess tins.

The food was scarce, and we were still hungry all the time. There was tea for breakfast, slightly sweetened but without milk. At midday, the Polish time for dinner, there was soup and some cereal gruel with traces of mutton or camel meat in it. I found the camel meat quite tasty—in those days anything edible was tasty. In the evening, our supper was tea or a watery soup and the daily ration of 650 grams of bread. In their free time soldiers trying to add to these thin rations would cruise the village houses, greeting the inhabitants with, "Any bread? Any milk?" The locals were reluctant to sell these staples for rubles but would gladly accept a pinch of tea as payment. Real tea in those times was almost unobtainable and could only have been stolen from army stores.

We had uniforms but no weapons and no equipment. Our training was limited to "square bashing"—basic drill, guard duties, rudimentary outlines of army organization and learning Morse code from an instructor whose teaching equipment was limited to one tin whistle.

But we sang everywhere we went. In fact, we could not escape from singing, "Loud and clear!" as our instructors demanded. "If you are tone deaf, it doesn't matter. Learn the words and shout them out loudly." Starting from singing the morning prayer, we sang when going for our fifteen minutes of morning physical training, when going to the kitchen, returning from the kitchen, going to the drill area, during the drill and after the drill. We sang during our rest time, before and after meals, and ended with singing the evening prayer. "It's good for you. It expands your lungs," explained one instructor.

The nights in Kenimekh were still cold. Two blankets were not enough to keep us warm at night. But we slept well on the tent's dirt floor only to be awakened by the shrill whistle of reveille or perhaps by the tinkling of camel bells from a caravan setting out at dawn for the long trip to Khiva.

One day, quite unexpectedly, I received an order to report as a student cadet to the Infantry Officers School in Kermine. There was a shortage of officers in the Polish Army now being formed in the USSR. All but a few of the 12,000 officers taken prisoner in 1939 by the Soviets were murdered by them eight months later, more than 5,000 of them in the notorious Katyn Forest massacre. In normal times you had to have at least a high-school diploma to become an officer, yet I had left school a year and a half before getting mine. However, the minimum qualifications for candidates for the Officers School were lowered, allowing those who had not quite completed high school to apply.

An army truck took me together with several other would-be officers to Kermine and deposited us in the middle of a square enclosed by mud walls and buildings. It was an old farmyard the size of a football field. Some of the lean-tos around it still had carts, drays, troughs and ploughs inside them. A large barn had become a lecture room. Smaller farm buildings were changed to offices, stores and kitchens. The rows of tents on two sides of the square were our new living quarters. A roofless latrine was tucked away in one corner, its ditch and long log seat screened by coarse jute sacking cloth tacked onto wooden posts.

We were greeted by a small group of instructors who, without losing a second, started barking orders.

"Take all your packs to the northwest corner of the square! On the double!"

"Form in two lines and number!"

"Odd numbers to the lecture room. Run! Even numbers stay put!"

"Anybody here who can play a musical instrument?"

Experienced soldiers kept mum; some of the greenhorns piped up.

"I can play piano."

"Guitar."

"Violin."

"I used to play clarinet in a band."

"Very good!" said an NCO. "We need people with talent. Now, you, the violinist, and you, Paderewski, take two brooms and a shovel from the storage shed. Shovel the shit from that barn and sweep the floor. Report when finished. On the double!"

As the two musicians started walking slowly to the shed, the NCO called them back.

"Why are you dragging your feet? Are you sick? Maybe you shat your pants? You look very gloomy. Has your Auntie Kunegunda died? A Polish soldier is always cheerful! Now, don't overdo it. Take that smile off your kisser. People will think you're queer. Repeat the order! Hmm. About turn! Go!"

This kind of shouting often contradictory orders, ridiculing soldiers' attempts to obey these orders, giving meaningless tasks, stretching soldiers' endurance to the breaking point, and asking for impossible things would go on and on for about six weeks. The older fellows, who were instructors themselves before they came here as students, explained to us this weird madness.

"When you have come here," they said, "with your high-school diploma, you think that you have swallowed and digested all the wisdom of the world. And you look down on the army as an idiotic institution that can teach you nothing. The officers you look at as puffed-up peacocks, the NCOs as nitwits. You want to know the reason behind each order. You wonder each time if it makes sense to do what you're told to do. We have to change you. And we do. In a short time we will prove to you that you don't know how to talk, how to walk, how to eat, how to sleep. You, yourself, will notice that you don't know how to wash yourself, how to polish your shoes, how to address your superior. In four weeks when I give you the order, in front of the entire company to make four steps forward, you will probably make three or five steps.

"And then one day, after being shouted at and corrected ten times for doing the same thing wrong ten times, you will return to your tent from the drill square exhausted, mad and probably sobbing, fall down on your cot, close your eyes and think, 'My God, am I really so stupid and clumsy?'

"And the same day we will notice that the hard clay of which you were made has become soft again and we can start moulding from it a new living creature, a soldier."

The Officers School consisted of two companies of student cadets each 120 strong, one administrative platoon and about a dozen officer instructors. In addition, each squad of ten cadets had one professional NCO leader who was not a student but lived the life of a cadet, sharing the same tent and food, doing the same exercises and being subject to the same timetable and discipline as his subordinates.

The commandant of the Officers School was a Major Merka. Following the pre-war army custom, he was seldom seen by his underlings. Once in a while he would deign to descend from his office onto the drill square, and there, speaking with a nasal twang, announce his displeasure at whatever was being done at that time and rudely criticize whoever happened to be around. Then, with an expression of utter disgust on his face and with his hands clasped behind his back, he would stalk off to his quarters, ignoring the faces of the saluting instructors and students frozen with fear.

My company commander was Lieutenant Edmund Nesterowicz, a lean man of medium height with ginger hair, his face almost totally covered by freckles. We heard that before the war he was known for his physical prowess and stamina, had completed the parachute training course and was being groomed as a possible candidate for Poland's modern pentathlon Olympic team.

Having passed two years of captivity as a prisoner of war in relatively bearable conditions, he seemed unable to comprehend the physical condition of those who had barely managed to survive the ordeal of prisons and labour camps. Our daily food ration gave us only half of the calories needed by a soldier in training, and yet the physical demands imposed on us were the same as in the pre-war officers schools when food and living conditions were excellent and all cadets were in top shape.

Apart from that, Lieutenant Nesterowicz was subject to frequent fits of anger. The sight of an undone button on a soldier's uniform or some minute speck of dirt on a soldier's boot or webbing would send him into a outburst of rage. One day during morning parade, while he was reading some new directives, he noticed a soldier rubbing an itching eye. All hell broke loose. First he screamed at the Company Sergeant Major, an old, grey-haired, professional soldier, for not noticing such a "disease infection" beforehand, then at us for being a disgrace to the Polish Army and for looking like a bunch of retired members of some Saint Barnabas Society. Then he threw the Daily Orders book on the ground, stomped his feet on it and disappeared into his office for at least twenty minutes while the Company, still standing to attention, was waiting for his return. I had two or three encounters with him over such trifles as leafing through my notebook during his lecture or being a few seconds late for the afternoon drill. Each time he threatened to throw me out of the school unless I mended my ways. His lectures on infantry tactics were a model of simplicity, not so much of the subject, as of his mind. Some of his didactic gems still stick in my mind.

"Night was created for night bayonet attacks."

"A soldier needs only two books in his life: Army Regulations and Pay Book."

Whether lecturing about a frontal attack on enemy trenches or crossing an artillery barrage, he would always finish his lecture with this: "And when you find yourself face to face with your enemy, it's hurrah, kick his balls and bayonet in the belly. That's all you have to memorize. Class dismissed."

However, it was my squad leader, Corporal Kuklewski, who made my life miserable on drill square and exercise fields. He, like the other instructors, was a professional NCO. Before the war he served with the Frontier Defence Corps, the elite troops of the Polish Army, which instilled in him a superiority complex vis-à-vis soldiers below his rank and all civilians regardless of their social status and wealth. It blended well with his innate, peasant simplicity and full confidence. Blond, short and squat, he knew everything that an infantry corporal was expected to know. Kuklewski looked down on his squaddies, sometimes with pity because of our clumsiness, sometimes with amazement at our inability to learn the procedure and the drill of the changing of the guard or how to fold our overcoats into a perfect cube. Once I heard him yelling at Private Schwarzbort, a graduate in philosophy from Lwow University, who at the command "About turn!" pivoted to his right instead of the left.

"This is not a university, Schwarzbort! You've got to use your brains here!"

On Sundays we would go to church. The masses were held in the Kermine community centre, which had been turned over to the Polish troops. The red stars, hammers and sickles, bald Lenins and mustachioed Stalins were giving way to crosses and religious prints.

Surprisingly, our garrison had acquired its own orchestra complete with violins, bass, clarinet, saxophone, accordion and a set of jazz drums. Its members were all Jewish, including the trumpet player who became our bugler. Before the war they were known as the Gold and Petersburski ensemble, one of the top (if not the top) jazz bands in Warsaw. In 1939, they fled from the Nazis to the Soviet Union. There they earned their bread travelling from town to town and playing hits of the twenties and thirties. The versatile dance band of Gold and Petersburski, though lacking in military demeanour, was much in demand. They not only banged out the national hymns and rousing military marches during parades but they also played incidental music at shows and theatrical performances, as well as background music for formal dinners in the officers' mess.

When the Gold and Petersburski ensemble was asked to provide church music during the Sunday masses, they carried it off with aplomb. The accordion sounded like the upper registers of the organ, and the saxophone's mellow rendition of the newly composed hymn, "God, may it come to pass that we return to a free Poland," was moving indeed.

Around Easter, the customary yearly confession and Communion services were arranged for the soldiers. My turn came. I had not confessed my sins since the morning of the day I was captured. Among the sins I confessed to was stealing food.

"And why did you steal food?"

"To eat. Because I was hungry."

"Stealing food because you are hungry is not a sin, my son."

Then I added that while in prison camps in my darkest hours I had vowed to make a pilgrimage to Jerusalem if I was spared.

"My son," the priest sighed, "if all of you fulfill your vows of pilgrimage, there's going to be a chain of people stretching around the globe and walking non-stop."

Polish priests in Russia were in short supply and very busy—even at night. Under cover of darkness the Russians and Ukrainians from the neighbouring villages would bring their babies to be baptized. Later a Polish chaplain was sent from England. He was amazed at the religious fervour he found amongst the soldiers, most of us survivors of prisons and labour camps and near starvation.

My physical condition was still poor. I had had no time and no adequate nourishment to recover from two years of prison rations and the recent bout of typhus. I could have asked to be transferred back to my unit where the training was less rigorous, but my ambition and pride would not let me quit the officers school. Often the veteran Corporal Kuklewski would shake his head and repeat, "Private Topolski, I have seen a lot of soldiers without a uniform but looking at you I see a uniform without a soldier inside."

One rainy day Lieutenant Nesterowicz arranged an impromptu exam. He started by asking questions about army organization. This subject was considered secret and taking down notes on it was strictly forbidden. Everything had to be memorized. The first dozen or so students failed miserably in their attempts to recite the organization of an infantry battalion. Lieutenant Nesterowicz was getting angry. His face grew pale, his freckles more pronounced. Scanning the room, seeking out the next victim, he spotted me leaning against a post. With a barely audible sigh and resignation on his face, he looked me in the eye and said, "You!" I knew the subject. With his head bent down, looking at the tips of his boots, he listened to my recitation, occasionally nodding at the end of a sentence. When I finished, he stared at me in disbelief, and then told me to come to the podium where a variety of weapons was displayed. He pointed at the 81 mm mortar.

"Imagine yourself an instructor in front of a bunch of ignorant recruits. Well, you don't have to imagine. They are right here. Tell them everything you know about the 81 millimetre mortar and explain its use."

The mortar was of a recent Soviet design, and it was quite new to all of us. But when you are really interested in something, as I was in such weapons, remembering details comes easily. While I was describing the weapon, first in general terms, then quoting data and figures, Nesterowicz kept nodding. When I finished he said, "Good!" and dismissed us.

A few minutes later as we were preparing for our noon meal, our squad leader, Corporal Kuklewski, stopped in front of me, plucked an imaginary piece of lint from my sleeve as if to stop me from getting too cocky, and drawled: "You Topolski, you are not so stupid as you look. A bit more of an effort there. Straighten up your back. Click your heels louder, and we will make a cadet officer out of you yet."

"To the glory of our fatherland," I replied, the prescribed answer to any praise uttered by one's superior. (In the cavalry officers schools it was more complicated. There the full answer was "To the greater glory of our fatherland, of the Polish cavalry, and of the horse and the mistress of our gentleman instructor.")

One morning as we were marching to our exercise field, the platoon commander, Lieutenant Katnik, ordered a feeble-looking fellow named Piontek to carry the base of the Maxim machine gun on his shoulders. The base had two small wheels attached for rolling it along the ground, but we knew better than to question the order to carry it. Its weight was substantial, 34 kilograms and 600 grams (you memorize its weight after you carry it for a while). That's 77 pounds, about what I weighed at that time myself. It was not only heavy but awkward to carry. Two shafts rested on the shoulders of the carrier with the two small metal wheels bouncing against his shoulder blades. After marching for a quarter of an hour, Piontek asked to be relieved. The second carrier did not last much longer and also asked to be relieved. My turn was next. I saw the smirk on the instructor's face as he watched me heave the base up onto my shoulders. But the bastard was not going to hear me pleading for relief. Somehow I carried it all the rest of the way to the exercise field. Nothing was said about it until the next day. Two fellows bigger than me, who felt the machine gun base was too heavy to carry alone and asked for help, found themselves expelled from the Officers School and ordered back to their units.

It did not seem to occur to the military mindset of those in charge that men near starvation should not be expected to do all the things in boot camp that well-fed cadets in peacetime had been able to do. Several times I saw cadets throwing out their unfinished dinner so that they would have time to clean their mess tins for afternoon inspection. The instructors had no pity. They drove us by the book. Some they drove to death.

I recall one of the extra-strenuous field exercises when a ten-minute smoke break—for the few lucky ones who had cigarettes— was called. The rest of us just fell flat on the ground, trying to get some rest. When the "fall in" order sounded, the company commander noticed one soldier who kept lying on the ground. It was Chlebowicz, a frail-looking man.

"Why isn't Chlebowicz getting up?! What's the matter with him? Sergeant! Go and see what is the matter!"

The sergeant went to Chlebowicz, knelt down, looked at his face and then checked his pulse. "Beg to report, Sir! He's dead."

At that time the whole USSR was in turmoil. The administrative system was showing signs of breaking down and in some areas lawlessness prevailed as millions of people travelled aimlessly in search of food to fill their bellies and a roof to shelter their bodies. The Polish Forces in the USSR had their own judicial system. Summary trials were introduced and the military penal code was severe. The death penalty was being meted out for things like black-market dealings, insubordination, stealing government property and theft of food for profit.

Several times when marching to our exercise area on the banks of the Zeravshan River, we heard the salvo of rifle fire. Coming closer, we could see the execution squad finishing their chores and loading the corpse and the blood-spattered wooden post onto the truck, while a young padre, already back in the driver's cabin, was mouthing the prayers.

There was never a lack of volunteers for the firing squads. Soldiers, some of them teenagers, were executed just for stealing fifty rubles, or a can of food, or for being AWOL for a few days. But we approved of the army's harshness and felt protected as much as threatened by it. I was scared enough, however, of being accused of stealing army property that I counted and recounted the needles in my sewing kit to make sure none was missing.

I don't recall ever discussing with my fellows an individual case that went to court martial. Most of us had been thrown together by chance and had no history of friendship or kinship with others in the camp. We had become used to having people die around us or drop out of sight without goodbyes. And now in the army, the chap who marched alongside you one day could be transferred to another unit the next day. Or to a hospital. We were too busy, too hungry and too exhausted to trouble ourselves about the fate of someone whom we didn't know and had never heard of. Besides, those who had spent two years under the Communist system had learned that asking what happened to a missing person was considered an offence in the Soviet Union. Still, the memory of the blood-spattered post and the pale priest praying for the executed soldier does not fade to this day.

Easter came. We celebrated it with a field mass and a dinner for the entire garrison together at tables in the open. It was a meal to remember—soup, rice, camel goulash and, to top it all, two small round loaves of white bread with a golden glazed crust. A Lucullan feast. There were the usual patriotic speeches and singing. Our orchestra played the familiar pre-war tunes that the Communist regime had forbidden us to play or even listen to for the last two and a half years, ever since Soviet troops marched into Poland.

During the dinner, garrison chaplain Krol asked all soldiers to donate a small part of their bread to a group of Polish children who were at that time on a train standing at Kermine station. They had been without food for two days and were still hundreds of kilometres from their destination. Nobody gave even a slice.

Then came the third of May, Polish Constitution Day. We celebrated it on the parade ground—one of the most moving occasions of my life. For the first time after two and half years of prisons and oppression, we saw our white and red flag rise slowly to the top of the flagpole. Our band played the "Dabrowski Mazurka," the Polish national anthem we all learned as school children. It begins, "Poland is not lost as long as we live." The familiar words held a new, deeper meaning for us in this foreign country, far away from the homeland where our families were living under German occupation. Now a well-drilled company, we snapped to attention to present arms in a picture-perfect salute but we could not hold back the tears of emotion which overflowed down our cheeks.

Our Divisional Commanding Officers kept changing, but one in particular was very important to us: General Tadeusz Bohusz-Szyszko. An experienced officer, he was sent from England to help organize our army in Russia. We looked up to him because of his success in the battle of Narvik during the German invasion of Norway. With the help of French Foreign Legion soldiers added to the Poles under his command, he held the Nazis at bay and even forced them to retreat, until the British ordered him to withdraw. It was exhilarating for us to see and serve under someone who had been able to stand up to the Germans and show them that Polish fighting men were every bit as good. But the Soviet liaison officers did not seem that impressed with his war record. What drew their admiration and their eyes was the superb quality of his light brown riding boots.

However, General Wladyslaw Anders, the Commanding Officer of the Polish Army in the Soviet Union, was the man who meant the most to us. Himself a former prisoner (in Lubianka Prison in Moscow), he was one of us, and we trusted him. The politicians who ran our Polish government-in-exile in London felt at times that Anders was getting too much power and becoming too independent. But Anders knew what he was doing. When Eastern Poland was still part of tsarist Russia, he had learned his soldiering in a school for Russian cavalry officers and was decorated for bravery while fighting with Russian troops against the Germans in the First World War. He spoke Russian well and knew the Russian character. He also understood the ruthless wiles of Stalin and his henchmen in the NKVD.

Despite his Russian schooling, Anders was Polish to the core. It became clear to us that he treated his command not as a perk or for self-aggrandizement but as a chance to do something for his country and his fellow Poles. His sense of mission on behalf of others, added to his bravery, intelligence and diplomacy, enabled him to stand before Stalin alongside General Sikorski on December 3, 1941, and play his part in getting most of what he needed for our born-again ragtag army. He talked face to face with the very dictator who had signed a decree ordering 25,000 captives shot—most of them from the educated elite of Polish society.

We soldiers didn't know then that it would be Anders who would manage to get us out of the Soviet Union. But we had faith that if anybody could, he would. From the army newspapers, we kept up on where General Anders was and what he was doing, but I never saw him until we were in the Middle East.

In mid-March we heard the first talk about moving the Polish Army to the Middle East. It looked as if our prayers to get out of the "workers' paradise" would be answered. However, our hopes were soon quashed by an official announcement. Some 30,000 people, both soldiers and civilians, were to be evacuated to Iran, but most Polish troops, including our Seventh Infantry Division, were to complete their training quickly and then be sent to fight alongside the Soviet Army against the Germans. Rumour had it that we might go to Stalingrad. One consolation came from our Company Sergeant Major Kotlar who told us, with all the authority of his forty-five years, "On the front line they'll feed you better." At least we had something to look forward to.

Nearly three months passed after that announcement, but the life did not change. If anything, it became harsher. Digging trenches, fencing with bayonets, mock attacks, mock retreats and long night marches were sapping our strength—the half-rations we lived on were not enough to replenish the energy it took.

Then, out of the blue, came an order to transfer all cadet officers from the signals units to the Signals Officers School at the First Signals Regiment in Katta Alekseyevskaya.

Chapter 23

OASIS IN THE HUNGRY STEPPE

Katta Alekseyevskaya in those days was a large village rather than a small town. It's on the Transcaspian Railway line between Samarkand and Tashkent. We marched the eight kilometres from the station to the Signals Officers School, which formed part of the First Signals Regiment. Together they took up about four acres of a large grassy flat square.

Beyond our tents was a small park with paths leading to a circle with benches and a large statue of Stalin in the middle of it. Somebody hung a rusty soup bowl on Stalin's outstretched hand. It looked as if he was begging for food. To the Soviet state security police this was a heinous crime, treason in fact. A special NKVD unit arrived and interrogated our soldiers about it for more than a week—a reminder of the long tentacles of the NKVD. I had heard of them snatching soldiers from Polish garrisons in broad daylight, and I knew I could never feel safe until we had left the USSR.

Inside the park was also a white stucco pavilion which we entered through a pseudo-classical style portico. It was now being used as the regimental headquarters with a radio centre and lecture rooms. The regimental kitchen and stores were in the former farm buildings which ringed a large paddock at the far side of the park. The land surrounding our camp was well irrigated and covered with the lush greenery of spring: mulberry and apricot as well as tall poplar, walnut and linden trees. There were acres of cotton, tobacco and maize. The well tended, little gardens around the peasants' houses were full of watermelon, cantaloupe and eggplant. Small vineyards abounded. But this rich and fertile area was an island in a sea of sand and rocks. Indeed, the arid land around it is called Golodnaya Step, the Hungry Steppe.

Outside the kitchen buildings were two huge boilers, stoked day and night to provide an unlimited supply of hot though unsweetened tea round the clock. Drinking unboiled water was forbidden.

We found more surprises in our camp, mostly pleasant ones. The number of soldiers living in each tent was reduced from ten to five. Each soldier had an iron bed with a mattress made of reeds. A small night table beside each bed, a rack for the rifles and a kerosene lamp provided unheard-of comfort. The meals, though still frugal, were well cooked and tasty. The cooks outdid themselves trying to make our dull diet more palatable. Granted that was not hard. We would eat anything.

The regimental clinic and a tiny hospital with six beds were run efficiently by Dr. Sadowski in spite of the dearth of medical supplies and the large number of people seeking help. Dr. Sadowski maintained that half of his patients went to his clinic just to see his two pretty nurses: Zosia, who could spot a malingerer the moment one crossed the threshold of the surgery, and Jadzia, whose figure was the inspiration of many soldierly compliments which she chose not to hear.

The commandant of our Signals Officers School was the avuncular Captain Florian Kotowicz, recently transferred in from Kenimekh garrison where I had met him that first night in his pyjamas. But the man truly responsible for the humane conditions existing in Katta Alekseyevskaya camp was the Commanding Officer of the whole garrison, Colonel Jan Rozanski. He took good care of his soldiers, bending army regulations if need be. In hot weather, he let his soldiers walk around in shirt sleeves. He would check if there was enough quicklime to disinfect the latrines. He ordered the duty NCO in the kitchen to see that every soldier swallowed the bitter anti-malaria pill, mepacrine—supplies of quinine having been cut off by the Japanese invasion of the Dutch East Indies. It was his idea to organize a weekly regimental "get-together" bonfire with singing, poetry reciting and humorous sketches. Lean and tall, always wearing riding breeches and highly polished boots, he looked every inch a professional soldier, which in fact he was not. He was a reserve officer, a successful businessman in civilian life. Often he would tell us, "I don't want to see any of you in the army when the war is over. Do you want to be a professional officer? A lieutenant maybe? That glittering pauper? Become a businessman like me and love and support your country by paying taxes." Evidently his views must have reached his superiors (or was it his reputation as a ladies' man?) because a year later he was replaced by a "real" professional.

A young lieutenant, Wieslaw Lewicki, was in command of our cadet company. The outbreak of war had prevented him from completing his veterinarian studies at Lwow University. He was intelligent, well mannered and quiet, almost shy. Well-dressed, but without a hint of flashiness, he wore riding boots a bit too big for him, and quickly became known as "Puss in Boots."

Lieutenant Lewicki was helped by two platoon commanders. Subaltern Ziemiak had a prominent, red nose that earned him the nickname "Noniu," which could be translated as "Schnozzlekin." Before the war, our other platoon leader, Subaltern Zaslona, had been the European champion of the 100- and 200-metre sprints. Later he gained more fame by reconnoitring no man's land during the Battle of Monte Cassino for which he received the Virtuti Militari (the highest Polish decoration for bravery) and a crippling wound in his arm. The last time I saw Zaslona he was working as an attendant at a swimming pool in Manchester.

Life at the new school was easier than at Kermine. Apart from morning physical training, we had only two hours of drill weekly. My health remained poor, but I didn't complain much—too many complaints could lead to dismissal from the school. I continued to be plagued by a kind of chronic bloody diarrhea. What is more, I still had the ulcers on my forearms, legs, and back caused by scurvy. This was most unpleasant. First a spot on my skin would become itchy, and then it would change into a painful swelling only to erupt like a small volcano, oozing pus and blood. Once it reached that stage it would no longer be sore and the skin around it would be pliable, like fresh dough. It wouldn't heal for weeks. An itchy scab would form and would break again from the pus forming underneath. These ulcers went so deep into my flesh that the penny-sized round scars are still visible on my calves more than half a century later. In May, fresh vegetables appeared, and with my ridiculously low pay I sometimes bought a cucumber or a small bunch of green onions. But they did not cure the scurvy as my guts were not functioning. Everything ran through me like water. I also had an attack of high fever with all the symptoms of malaria, but the doctor attributed it to *papatachi*, a local disease that luckily lasted only two days.

In the middle of June the weather turned hot. The temperature shot up to 40°C. Our woollen battledress and shirts were soaked with sweat. We enjoyed the daily evening swim in the lukewarm and muddy waters of the nearby irrigation canal. It was amusing to watch the gang of naked, grown men ducking, splashing and kicking water like little children and begging for "just five minutes more."

The local population, Uzbeks and Russians alike, being cowed by the Soviet regime, were afraid of fraternizing with us foreign soldiers. Our contacts with them were limited to bartering chunks of our bread rations for fruit, onions or tobacco leaves. They were reluctant to sell these products for rubles, which could buy little.

Unlike the locals, the passersby, outsiders and infrequent visitors were outspoken and would share gossip and exchange views with us. At the end of the school year, a few dozen Russian college students, mostly young women, arrived from Tashkent to work in the neighbouring kolkhozes. They were more blasé than the local Uzbeks and Russians about Soviet dos and don'ts and so quickly befriended some of our soldiers. The weekly evening dance on the terrace in front of the pavilion became a popular feature of our otherwise limited social life.

Lance Sergeant Kucharski (the dandy who walked 40 kilometres wearing only one shoe) had considered himself the handsomest bachelor in his native village. In no time he struck up a torrid romance with one of the Tashkent students. I never saw her, but after a while I had a pretty good idea what she looked like. He enjoyed commenting on her beauty and for him no detail of her charms was beyond description. He was sharing the tent with me and three other fellows, and we were impressed with his nightly escapades. A quarter of an hour after "lights out" was whistled, he would head towards the latrine clad only in his underwear, but carrying a tightly rolled battledress under his arm. From there he would wade across the canal, get dressed and jog to the village where his dark-haired Oxana lived. He would sneak back at the crack of dawn, often crawling between the tents, and with a sigh slide under the blankets just ten minutes before reveille. He would snore during the lectures, catnap when the company sergeant major was droning the daily orders and even fall asleep at times while marching.

One morning he came back without his newly issued summer underpants. Somehow he could not find them when he was beating the hasty morning retreat from Oxana's embraces. They were made of a fine, mesh-like cotton fabric. On the next rendezvous he found that Oxana had already transformed his intimate garment into two pairs of beautifully crafted panties for herself.

"Please understand," she said. "You will get another pair. They will not let you go around with your bare ass shining. But I could not find such elegance anywhere in the entire Soviet Union."

We found out before long that he had a wife back in Poland. But being unfaithful did not bother his conscience. Far from it. "If you have a fine watch," he explained, "you don't let it sit idle on a shelf without winding it up. Unless you use it, it might get rusty or stop working altogether."

In the spring of 1942, the Soviets pushed back the German Army on many vital sections of the front and regained the upper hand. Then the Communist Party started to reassert itself as the only and the ultimate power of the Soviet Union.

Stalin no longer felt beholden to the British, who had made the release and recruiting of Poles into our own army part of the price of getting the supplies the USSR needed to fight the Germans. From the Soviet point of view, the creation of the Polish Army in the USSR was a mistake—and a bad one at that. The presence of the Polish troops with their distinctive uniforms, national emblems and religious ceremonies had a disturbing influence on the local population. Polish Intelligence learned about Soviet intentions to disarm and intern our poorly equipped Polish Army, to accuse our leaders of pro-German leanings and to recreate it as a much smaller token force of compliant soldiery led by Soviet generals. Should this Soviet threat to our freedom become real and imminent, the following wild scheme of a possible escape was conceived by our chiefs. Most of the Polish garrisons were located close to the Transcaspian Railway line, certain sections of which ran parallel to the Soviet-Iranian border. For months it was the only rail line carrying oil supplies to the front from the Baku oil fields in the Caucasus. That single rail line carried two-way traffic, the trains passing each other at stations every twenty minutes or so. Most trains were composed of tanker cars, but there were also freight trains. On these trains hinged our entire escape scheme.

Among our troops we had two Railway Battalions made up of former railwaymen, and most of them were masters of their trade. At a specified time at night, our few armed units would storm the railway stations. The men from the Railway Battalions would stop and commandeer every passing train and start the mass evacuation of our soldiers south to Luftabad from where we would bolt on foot to Iran. It was a hare-brained scheme with minimal chances of success. I have no proof that it even existed. There is no record of it— at least I have never found any—but I heard about it around that time from several people. There was also a vague reference to it in the memoirs of General Klemens Rudnicki. Personally, I believe that the plan was concocted and deliberately leaked to the Soviets to make them understand that we would resist any attempt to intern us. The thought of having to fight an official ally and suffer bad publicity and the displeasure of the British and the Americans—whose material help at that time was still vital to the Soviet war effort—might have been what saved our necks and prompted Stalin to let us leave the Soviet Union and join the British forces in the Middle East.

Our company, the only armed company in the garrison, was now put on permanent alert. Live ammunition was issued. Each of our company's two platoons took turns at sleeping fully dressed. Trial alarms were frequent. After a couple of weeks of hectic training, the whole company could line up in full gear, blankets rolled, kit bags packed and ready for action eight minutes from the time the whistle woke us up in the middle of the night. We also practised what was euphemistically called "breaking contact with the enemy." What it meant, in fact, was escaping so fast that the enemy could not catch up with us, giving us time to form a new line of defence.

During one of these exercises, we had to run about twelve kilometres in full battle gear on a terribly hot day. Unlike some others, I finished the ordeal in relatively good shape, to the astonishment of the entire company. Our chief, Lieutenant Lewicki, kept looking at me and shaking his head. Several times he repeated, "How does he do it, this walking skeleton?"

In spite of my pitiful physical appearance, I felt more and more energetic and confident. The first time when, as a trainee NCO, I stood in front of the Cadet Company to give a command, my voice rang out strong and clear: "Atteeen-shn! Riiiigh-turn! Diiirection main lecture room, companyyy [here I made a three seconds pause] mash!" Giving commands is not as simple as one would think. You must have a loud voice and adhere strictly to the traditional pitch and intonation, elongating some vowels, deadening the others. I had a very low singing voice, a basso profundo in fact, which was rather incongruous with my slight stature. But it was ideal for giving orders.

They say that the earth should tremble when a company makes its first three steps. This time it apparently did because our Company Sergeant Major Szlamka, Sergeant Lukasik and the company scribe Sienkiewicz sprang from their office tent to see who shouted that command. Szlamka looked bemused, but the corners of his mouth curled up. Lukasik managed a half-hearted grin, which looked more like a snarl, displaying his two gold teeth. Sienkiewicz's face remained impassive, but he kept scratching his right jowl with his left hand. Then Szlamka said to nobody in particular but loud enough for me to hear, "Well, well. He has a chest like a married sparrow but he bawls out like a professional drill sergeant." I could tell that he was pleased. So was I.

The training of soldiers, not only in the officers school but also in the entire signals regiment, was now at a faster pace. New highly qualified instructors arrived. Some were sent from the Polish troops in Scotland and some had just been released from camps and prisons in Siberia.

The Russian girls from the town were the first ones to tell us that all Poles would soon leave the USSR for Iran. We knew better than to dismiss it as pure gossip. They may have learned about it from railwaymen who had been told to schedule extra trains or from bakers who knew that the supplies of flour were being cut back. We knew they had not made it up. Soon the rumours were supported by other signs. One day each soldier received four cans of food: corned beef, Irish stew, mixed vegetables and a tin of Carnation evaporated milk. With a needle I made the tiniest possible hole in my can of milk and let it trickle ever so slowly onto my tongue. I thought the taste of it exquisite, and I wondered if there were rich people somewhere who could afford to sip a can of this ambrosia every day.

The emergency food stores were being liquidated, and we were told that the stocks of canned food would have to be disposed of—not given away but offered for sale to the soldiers. This was good news for the well-paid officers and senior NCOs but bad news for us, lowly paid privates and corporals. We had no money to buy this fancy stuff.

As usual, the good old Colonel Rozanski found a solution, this one rooted in his entrepreneurial past. First the quartermaster was ordered by Rozanski to give each soldier enough credit to buy a gallon-sized tin of beautifully packaged and hermetically sealed English tea. This we could sell on the black market while the military police were kept out of the way. He ordered them to attend a special three-day refresher course in the pavilion. Money from the sale of the tea would give us soldiers a chance to buy more canned food and, of course, to pay back our loan.

The news about Polish soldiers selling golden tins of real English tea spread over the Uzbek countryside like dust in a sandstorm. Our camp was besieged by buyers willing to pay almost any price. Some men arrived on horseback from distant oases, often after riding for two days. I sold my tea to one of them for 600 rubles, the equivalent for me of eight months' pay. He had just reached the outskirts of our camp. The transaction took no more than one minute.

He immediately remounted his horse, still lathered with patches of foam, for the return ride.

A few days later we received Persian cigarettes. Two packs per soldier. They were handsomely packaged in neat, flat cardboard boxes with flip lids and embossed trade names. Inside, the cigarettes were wrapped in white tissue and patterned foil. Each cigarette had a silver crown printed on it. They were the height of elegance. Although not yet addicted to nicotine, I smoked them for fun. But hardened smokers used to the harsh Russian *makhorka* tobacco found them weak and bland.

One afternoon while we sat on a pile of firewood finishing our meal, a white apparition started gliding slowly through the kitchen courtyard. As it came closer to us it changed into a *starichok* (an old man) shuffling his bare feet in our direction. He was very frail. On the frame of his bones hung the sun-bleached remnants of trousers and a torn linen shirt that he wore in the Russian fashion, on the outside tied with a piece of hemp cord. Through the holes in his shirt we could see his ribs and a tin cross dangling on his hollow chest. Strands of white hair were escaping from under the rim of an old army cap. He carried an empty beggar's bag and a walking stick with its knobs and knots rounded and shiny from years of use. He stopped in front of us and peered at our mess tins filled with barley and pieces of meat. His light blue eyes, which looked as bleached as his garb, were darting from one mess tin to another. He looked fearful and apprehensive as he scanned our faces for signs of anger or displeasure at being interrupted while feasting. Finding none, he gave us a toothless smile and said, "God bless you, gentlemen. I hope you won't mind me watching you eat?" No, we did not mind at all. We filled his *kotelok* with barley and stew and also gave him a large chunk of bread. He was beside himself with joy, but he retained his beggar's dignity. Settling himself on the pile of wood at a respectful distance from his benefactors, he fished out a wooden spoon from the depths of his shirt pocket, spread his bag over his lap and, after crossing himself three times with his trembling hand, he started eating the way a landlord eats, not like a hired hand.

He was eating slowly but steadily like a machine. Every so

often, with his mouth full, he would stop chewing and savour the food with his eyes closed. It looked as if he was trying to memorize the taste of food the way a student tries to learn a difficult poem by heart. When his wooden spoon started scratching the bottom of his *kotelok*, the cook beckoned to him to come for a refill and he did.

The banquet over, he licked his spoon clean, clicked his tongue, crossed himself three times again, rose slowly to his feet and turned to us. "Esteemed gentlemen, I don't know who you are or where you come from, for I heard you speaking a strange language among yourselves. But when miracles happen it is imprudent to ask many questions. For all I know it is through you that the Almighty has answered my prayers to fill my stomach but once before I die." With his raised right hand in which he held his shiny stick, he sketched a benediction in the air for us and resumed his trek to nowhere. He declined our invitation to another meal the next day. "Never tempt your fortune too much. You'll regret it." Soon he vanished behind the bend of a narrow lane lined with young mulberry trees. We never saw him again.

Finally, in midsummer the evacuation of Polish troops from the USSR to Iran was announced officially. There were smiling faces all over the camp. Then the announcement of the date of our departure came, striking like the joyous thunder of the first spring storm. Sergeants and corporals were still yelling at their underlings but their dire threats were uttered without conviction. We were given just a few days to organize the evacuation of the regiment. Nobody wanted to leave any gifts for our former jailers. Food from the stores was distributed among the soldiers and the Polish civilians who were living in the garrison area and were to be evacuated to Iran with us. Each soldier had to take with him an additional battledress, blankets and a pair of army boots. We packed and repacked our kit bags and rucksacks dozens of times. We also took with us to Iran about twenty Russian women, several men and half a dozen orphans. The Soviets agreed to let them go in exchange for some of our Polish goods.

Finally, the long-awaited day had come. To celebrate our departure, nature sent forth the hottest August day she could. From the opal blue sky the sun poured fiery rays, which rebounded from the scorched hard ground. The building outlines shimmered in the rising waves of heat. Through it all, we worked feverishly. Tents were folded. With the tent poles sticking out from them they looked like huge bundles ready to be picked up by some giant tramps. At noon the last hot meal was being dished out by chief cook Marszalek and his two sweat-drenched helpers. In the middle of the drill square stood the rotund and officious Warrant Officer Jaskowiak. With ungainly pirouettes, he kept turning around like a weather vane. Scanning the garrison area with his all-seeing eyes, he barked orders in every direction.

"Corporal Lato's squad! Get some shovels from the farm manager and fill the latrine ditch!

"Private Mulak, fill the tent-post holes!

"Six men from the second platoon, go to the kitchen! Put out the fires under the tea boilers and help the kitchen staff to clean the cauldrons.

"You, you and you! Sweep the area!"

Late in the afternoon all garrison units lined up along the four sides of the drill square. The guard was dismissed. The daily orders were read, followed by the evening prayer. The bugle sounded, and the limp flag came slowly down.

Within minutes our companies regrouped into marching order. We carried all our equipment. Our rucksacks felt as if they were packed solid with bricks. The sun, though sinking closer to the horizon, was still baking us. Sweat darkened our woollen shirts and trickled down between our shoulder blades.

At last the pavilion door swung wide open and out came our CO, Colonel Rozanski, the good man who put men before regulations, accompanied by his adjutant, Lieutenant Materski, and the avuncular Captain Kotowicz. Like us, they were clad in full marching gear. The three marched briskly to the head of the waiting column, and we were off. On cue we broke into song. It was a Polish version of the French Foreign Legion marching song, to the tune of "J'ai deux amours": "To us, old vagrants, belongs the wide world and every tramp we meet is a brother to us."

When we were crossing the wooden bridge over the canal, I looked back. The camp area was marked by the rows of dirt squares trampled smooth where the tents used to be. The rays of the setting sun were piercing the dark brown lace of the silhouetted poplars, casting long diagonal shadows on the dirt road. A group of NKVD officers pretended to be busy checking for the umpteenth time the stacks of bedsteads, tables and tents we left behind. Beyond them on a low berm that separated their gardens and orchards from the camp, the families of Russian and Uzbek *kolkhozniki* were standing and watching us go. It was difficult to tell whether they were waving goodbye or just screening their eyes from the setting sun.

Chapter 24
FAREWELL UNWASHED RUSSIA

"Farewell unwashed Russia,
Land of masters, land of slaves."
— Aleksandr Pushkin (1799-1837)

It was getting dark by the time we reached the railway station. A long line of freight cars was waiting for us on the siding. The loading went fast. We dropped our rucksacks on the floor and then quickly sat on the doorway's lip to jump down again in order to escape the heat of the wagons. The smells of pitch from the railway ties and of coke cinders hung in the air. It was unusually quiet. Soldiers were sitting on the gravel or standing in small groups. Glowing cigarettes competed with the first stars in the fast darkening sky. Beyond the circle of light from the solitary hissing carbide lamp, a dozen or so women, their white dresses barely discernible against the dark hedge, were clinging motionless to their invisible lovers.

Just before midnight the engine arrived. Like a lumbering black rhino it charged past the station only to be stared down by the glowering red eyes of the point's signal. Shunted to our track, the beast retreated, then slowed and nudged the twin bumpers of the first car, sending shudders through the entire train.

Amid clanking of chains, railwaymen's whistles, muted sobs from the dark hedges, and orders to board shouted by dozens of self-appointed leaders, we scrambled into the still heat of the freight cars. The locomotive snorted and gave a short toot totally unworthy of this black behemoth, then slowly inched forward gathering speed. Then we saw a man running alongside, holding on to the iron bar of the wide-open sliding doors. His stride was getting longer and longer, until he seemed to be half-floating through the air. A few fellows grabbed his free arm and pulled him inside. He panted heavily for a few moments, grinned and said, "Shit! That was close." Whereupon he produced a small comb from his breast pocket and started combing his wind-blown hair. This last soldier to board the train was the Company's Lothario, Lance Sergeant Raymond Kucharski.

I doubt whether posh travellers on the Orient Express ever felt more comfortable and snug than I did lying on the cattle-car floor stretched out on a fluffy army blanket. Under my head, instead of a pillow, I had my haversack, bumpy with gifts from an out-of-season Santa—a tin of Argentinian corned beef, a wedge of processed cheese from Australia and a packet of crumbling, oily Indian Army biscuits. The sliding doors of the wagon were wide open, inviting in the warm breeze. Now and then the door opening would be slashed by streaks of lights from a passing train and buffeted by its wind and din. Then the somniferous clickety-clack of the wagon wheels would resume its duet with Corporal Rodzynski's snoring, which sounded like a catarrhal lion taking an afternoon nap.

Our train's destination was Krasnovodsk, a port on the Caspian Sea about two thousand kilometres away—it was going to be a long journey. The train passed through stations well known to me—Samarkand, Kermine, Kizil Tepe, Kagan—reminding me of my earlier poverty and hunger in these places. I marvelled at the speed with which fate had changed me within a few months from an ex-con on the run without ticket or documents into a confident young soldier. At the same time it seemed to me as if eons has passed since I left my home in Horodenka in December, 1939. So much had happened to me in three years. Being shot at and captured at the Romanian border. Growing up in five different prisons. Slogging away in labour camps in the snows of northern Russian. Wandering south via the Trans-Siberian railway in search of Anders's Army. I had left home to fight for Poland and return to my country with our army. Now at long last that goal was getting nearer.

We had a surprise at Mary—the town known to Victorian Brits as Merv, when it was the hub of border disputes between the Russian and British Empires. There we were told, "Get out of the train.

You're going to be fed a hot meal." And we were, courtesy of the all-powerful NKVD, who had been ordered by Stalin to make sure that the evacuation of the Polish troops from the Soviet Union went smoothly. It had been pleasant those last few days to nibble imported delicacies like corned beef, biscuits and cheese. But after a few days of cold food, it was a treat to sit down to a hot meal. And to have it served to us by women, even if they knew better than to fraternize with, or even speak to, these foreigners leaving the Soviet Union. After the meal, as we stripped to the waist and splashed ourselves quickly at the water taps in the yard in front, we saw the next shift of troops sitting down to be fed at the trestle tables in the long sheds.

After passing Chardzhou on the west bank of the Amu Darya (the river known to Alexander the Great and Herodotus as the Oxus), we had been travelling through the Kara Kum desert, which extends to the Caspian Sea. The name Kara Kum means Black Desert, literally "black sands," but all we saw was fine-grained, bright yellow sand. The U-shaped sand dunes got bigger and bigger as we proceeded westward from Mary. Here and there on the unwinding, endless, sandy scroll, gnarled, stunted saxaul trees would appear like oversized letters of some mysterious alphabet. From the train the desert looked devoid of life. The sudden sight of a ragged shepherd, squatting in a small ravine with two dozen sheep, started a half-hearted discussion about how anything could survive in this waterless inferno. No one came up with a plausible theory. Then Private Gajl voiced a maxim often quoted by Party propagandists: "Everything is possible in the Soviet Union." Nobody wanted to expend any more fast-waning energy to dispute this weighty argument, and our wagon reverted to its usual hebetude.

Another day, another station. This time it was Kizil-Arvat, a town enveloped in sands and oppressive heat. Our train stopped alongside a long line of cattle cars full of Soviet soldiers. They were being pulled back from the front line after a long spell of combat duties in the Caucasus. They had no clue where they were being sent. Many were wounded. Their summer uniforms were shabby, torn and filthy. Some of them were wearing rubber boots, some dirty sneakers. They had no weapons and no equipment of any kind.

They stared at us with amazement and apprehension. Uneasiness hung in the air. We looked at their emaciated bodies, their hollow eyes, their dirty and often bloodied bandages, with the sense of guilt common to soldiers in the rear when they encounter front-line troops. They asked us if we had any spare food, offering in exchange their sweaty smocks. They were all they could offer, but we would not take them. We shared our rations with them, but there was not enough to go round. Speaking in low voices, almost in whispers, they asked us a lot of questions, casting furtive glances left and right to see if any political commissars were around. But our answers muddled their minds even more. The idea that foreign soldiers could exist in the Soviet Union and that they were going free to some foreign country was beyond their comprehension. They saw our food, our equipment. They touched our belts and webbing to check if they were indeed made of real leather.

"How can that be? They told us, and we have read in the papers, that Poland does not exist, and yet here you are. A Polish Army dressed like staff officers, well fed. The devil take it! They always lie to us! The sons of bitches. But it's not for our brains to ponder these things. Besides it's dangerous. Without vodka you can't figure it out."

After some five long days, our train stopped among the hills a few kilometres before Krasnovodsk, the Caspian Sea port, in order to lower our risk from German bombers. A native woman appeared from nowhere carrying what we thought was a baby wrapped in her scarf. But when she came closer we saw it was a watermelon. She stood barefoot in front of us, dressed in a ragged *haik* (a hooded smock) and long pantalets tied at the ankles. Her face was covered with a horse-hair *paranja*. She kept repeating *kharpousi*, pointing her slim finger at us, and *nan* when she pointed it at herself. While speaking she never lifted her eyes off the ground. She wanted to exchange her watermelon for bread. Somebody offered her ten rubles for it—a very high price, but we knew that we couldn't take any rubles with us to Iran. She shook her head, saying "Yok." No. She wanted bread, not money. The offer was doubled to twenty rubles, then trebled. It attracted the attention of other soldiers, and the unbelievable auction went on and on while she kept shaking her head and repeating *yok*. What happened in the end I cannot remember. I know that Sergeant Glejf's almost jocular bid of 500 rubles was also ignored by that wisp of a woman in rags.

We waited overnight until our ship was ready. Next morning, while we stood in a long file waiting for hours under the sun for our turn to board, we were told for the last time to put all our rubles in the large plywood boxes scattered along the waterfront. I dropped my pitiful hoard into a box that was already filled to the brim with the sturdy, well-printed Soviet bills.

The ship that was taking us to Iran was a large oil tanker, the *Kaganovich*. It was empty and sitting high in the water. Soldiers and civilians, loaded with all their belongings, edged up and up the steep gangways. We had to balance between the ship's rusty hull and the long drop to the dock below, our steps carefully measured like those of mountain climbers. The flimsy rope handrail was of no use as we carried something in each hand and could not even wipe the sweat trickling into our eyes. There was no return from the ship. At the top of the gangway, the segments of the long, khaki caterpillar of soldiers fell into the black opening of the entrance only to reappear from the hatches above on the slightly convex deck. By the time our unit started embarking, the ship already looked so tightly packed with people that the proverbial sardines in a tin could be considered travelling executive class. But soon we found ourselves on the hot deck being followed by yet more units. Only the danger of squeezing someone overboard stopped the loading. All over the ship, people were scrambling to find a place to lie down, to sit down, to stand up. Any place.

Most of us had eaten the last bits of our rations in the morning. Now we learned that there would be no food and no water on this trip. This news was accepted with the equanimity befitting old lags of Soviet prisons and labour camps. We were so busy with nestling and rearranging the positions of our legs, arms and chattels that we had not even noticed the hawsers being cast off, nor did we feel the tanker giving the slip to Krasnovodsk to head for the open sea, leaving an oily, peacock-tail wake behind it. The blaze of the fierce sun directly overhead was slowly turning the iron deck into a giant frying pan.

A few mugs of water filled by the crew in their quarters were passed from hand to hand across and along the ship to the neediest souls. Some died, and their stiff bodies, held aloft by dozens of out-stretched hands, were passed overhead to the nearest opening in the ship's railing to be tossed overboard. There were no ceremonies and no formalities. Only the splash made by the falling body moved some people to cross themselves furtively.

Nobody shouted "Land ho!" some two days out when low-lying clouds on the hazy horizon solidified into mountains. Rather, a feeling of disappointment crept in at seeing landfall that far away. But a couple of jaunty tugboats were already approaching the tanker. They were to take us to the shore.

I was among the first of our bunch to stumble down the rickety gangway onto the rocking tugboat. Once there, about half of us were immediately sent below deck into the boiler room. We stood shoulder to shoulder, back to back, and belly to belly under a maze of hissing steam pipes while droplets of boiling water kept falling from worn-out pipe joints onto our shuddering necks. Each time the soot-covered fireman opened the door of the furnace, the soldiers standing nearest to it would frantically push back our squeezed knot of sufferers even more to avoid the fiery blast. I looked up at the face of Sergeant Major Solarski, at forty-four one of our oldest students. His eyes were glazed and his face chalk white. I thought he was going to die then and there standing up (but he didn't). We waited and waited for the others to board the tugboat. At last, a thud, a whistle and an awakened propeller shaft revived our sweltering swarm of soldiery. We were on our way.

We could feel the tugboat chugging ahead slowly for some time. Then a gentle bump told us that we had touched the jetty. The trap door at the top of the stair was flung wide open and the grinning face of Lieutenant Zaslona appeared against the background of the blue sky. "Get out!" he shouted. "And start breathing again." In seconds I was on the deck and clutching the handrail. In front of me sprawled the port of Pahlevi. My dream of faraway places had become reality. It looked exactly as I thought an exotic port should.

The hemisphere of the sky rested on the purplish grey massif of the Elburz range jutting from the horizon, which was screened by white buildings enmeshed in greenery. A long, tidy quay punctuated by palm trees and clumps of flaming bougainvillea underlined this picture of orderliness and freshness. At the end of the jetty a gate in the chain-link fence was open and an Iranian policeman wearing a light grey canvas helmet topped with a gleaming brass spike made a showy charade of directing traffic whenever a car or truck happened by. Two smiling young women in shorts, their arms resting on top of the fence and their faces shaded by the brims of New Zealand army hats, were shouting something to us but they were too far away for us to make it out. Behind them a long line of shiny, dark blue new Dodge trucks was waiting for us.

Our three-year odyssey through the land of Red Misery was coming to an end.

On the deck a sailor undid the rope guarding the top of the gangway, looked down to check if everything was in order, scanned the faces of the waiting crowd and, when his eyes met Company Sergeant Major Szlamka's, he nodded. Szlamka turned to us, pointed to the gangway with his chin and said, "Okay, boys. One at a time. Mind the nails on the plank."

Postscript

The "great adventure" continued for many years. I stayed with the Polish Army through Iraq, Palestine and Egypt. Then, as a part of the famous British Eight Army, it was on to liberating Italy—the best job I ever had. For most of that time I was with Signals at the HQ of the Second Polish Corps. After the battles of Cassino, Ancona and Bologna, just as the war in Europe ended, I was sent for further training in Kinross, Scotland. I was there when the Second World War ended in September 1945 with the official surrender of Japan.

Soldiering had become my profession. So what was I going to do with myself now? My goal had always been to return to Poland but that was no longer possible. Poland had become a Soviet puppet state and her Communist government stripped me of my Polish citizenship. I was deprived of the finest reward and emotion a soldier could get—a homecoming.

But the pangs of conscience, albeit rare among politicians, moved Prime Minister Winston Churchill to harbour the faithful Polish soldiers. He gave us a chance to rebuild our lives anew on British soil.

The following year in London I took stabs at studying teaching, art and then economics; had a girlfriend in the Sadler's Wells Ballet; acted in a Polish company and danced with a Ukrainian amateur ensemble; consorted with many Polish friends whose names—if not their parents'—would fill many pages of a Polish "Who *was* Who"; enjoyed life immensely; and failed every exam miserably (except English!).

Having lost my veteran's grant, I spent a couple of years in sundry short-term jobs: kitchen porter, cleaner, stevedore, house painter, beach photographer, machine operator, railway porter. I didn't mind being poor, as long as I had enough after lodgings to buy cigarettes and spaghetti. Sir Edgar Bonham-Carter, a casual acquaintance, helped restore my grant and so I studied architecture in Manchester for five years. During those dozen years I never applied for British citizenship, not being sure where I'd wind up. Citizenship is not something to be taken lightly. All that time I was stateless and carried the green passport of the United Nations Refugee Organization.

In 1957, I set off for Australia via sightseeing across Canada. Henry Slawek, a Polish friend living in Kirk's Ferry near Ottawa, asked me to drop by en route and that was it. I settled there on the fringes of the Gatineau Park wilderness among people who, like me, came from different corners of the world. They were friendly and helpful but minded their own business, never locked their houses and looked askance at newcomers who fenced their yards.

It was there I found good skies, tangled forests, clear tarns and Joan, who changed my life. After years of courting, I married her. It was within ten days of Canada getting its unique maple leaf flag. She's a journalist, frightfully independent, a staunch Canadian and—whether she knows it or not—a citizen of the world.

I became a Canadian citizen in 1962. Proudly. But not forgetting my old home and native land. By serendipity, Canada's national colours, like Poland's, are white and red. And the inscription on the crest of Canada—A MARI USQUE AD MARE—bears the very words of Poland's motto of bygone glory days when her borders stretched from the Baltic to the Black Sea.

It was Joan who cajoled and persuaded me to write my memoirs. Now she's after me to write the second volume.

Aleksander Topolski
Chelsea, Canada
Spring, 2000
www.withoutvodka.com